CW01270173

Korea 1950-1953 recounting REME Involvement

The Forgotten Punch in the Army's Fist

Written and compiled by John Dutton
and
Edited by Peter Gripton

First Published 2004 by kenandglen.com
Second Edition 2007 published by Las Atalayas Publishing
27 Rayner Drive
Arborfield
Berkshire
RG2 9FB.

Written and Compiled by John Dutton
Edited by Peter Gripton
Copyright © John Dutton 2004 - 2007

The moral rights of the author have been asserted. All rights reserved. No part of this publication may be reproduced, stored in a retrieval system or transmitted in any form or by any means, electronic, mechanical or otherwise without the written permission of the Publisher.

ISBN 978-0-9556753-0-0

Typesetting and Design by kenandglen.com
Avenida Rusia
12598 Pensicola
Castillon, Spain.

Printed in England

Acknowledgements

I wish to acknowledge my thanks to all ex-members of the Corps who took time out, to respond to my original quest in the form of a letter, which I had sent to as many Royal Electrical and Mechanical Engineer members of the British Korean Veterans Association as I could identify. Their replies in various forms have been included in the book in one shape or another. However there was so much that it would be nearly impossible to include it all in one book.

Sincerest thanks must also go to Brigadier C N Barclay CBE, DSO, the author of "First Commonwealth Division", which is in my mind, a bible on the Korean campaign; extensively researched and assisted by so many knowledgeable people. All those who contributed in their own way are listed in Appendix 'A'

Finally, I owe a debt of gratitude, to Mrs Doreen Bargery. Although being in the advanced stages of Multiple Sclerosis, she gave of her all to read, comment and correct, her memory will live with this book. Thank you Doreen, and one and all.

Preface

In due course an official history of the Korean war was produced, dealing with the campaign in general, and the British Commonwealth Forces in particular, covering every aspect of the fighting and political background.

By their very nature official histories take a long time to compile, and it is many years after hostilities end before they make their appearance. They are a record for posterity and for future generations of military students, rather than books from which the participants can refresh their memories, or derive satisfaction from reading an account of the exploits in which they took part.

This book has been compiled to fill that gap. Many books have been published on the Korean campaign but none to my knowledge mentioning the Corps of Royal Electrical and Mechanical Engineers, their Workshop Units, Light Aid Detachments and their personnel attached to the First line Units.

For the British Commonwealth this campaign is of special interest. It was the first war waged by the United Nations to curb aggression and uphold the free way of life. It was the first occasion in which an integrated Division – composed of units and individuals from many Commonwealth countries – served successfully together. It was perhaps unique in the variety of engineering problems that emerged as the campaign progressed. Therefore, this book will have an appeal throughout the British Commonwealth, and in particular to all members of the Corps of Royal Electrical and Mechanical Engineers (R.E.M.E), even if the units that they served with are not specifically mentioned. It has not been the intention to describe every battle and engagement in the detail that they merit.

Finally, I wish to record my sincere thanks at having had the opportunity to compile the story of those who kept the fighting edge sharp for the Commonwealth fighting men in Korea, their operations, projects, equipment modification and manufacture, in some cases from practically nothing, conducted by this unique, and famous Corps, within that Division, The Royal Electrical and Mechanical Engineers, henceforth the R.E.M.E.

Contents

Chapter 1	Background to the Campaign	
Chapter 2	The Invasion from the North	3
Chapter 3	27th Infantry Brigade 1950	5
Chapter 4	The move of 11 Infantry Workshop REME	11
Chapter 5	The activation of 10 Infantry Workshop REME	12
Chapter 6	Armour & Heavy Support Groups reinforcements	16
Chapter 7	10 Infantry Workshop REME 1950	31
Chapter 8	Advance to the North	34
Chapter 9	The advance of 11 Infantry Workshop REME to Sinanju	41
Chapter 10	29 Brigade Group & 10 Infantry Workshop	43
Chapter 11	45 Field Regiment Royal Artillery LAD REME	69
Chapter 12	The Chinese enemy - The second withdrawal southwards	96
Chapter 13	The first withdrawal of 11 Infantry Workshop	102
Chapter 14	The second advance north	106
Chapter 15	11 Infantry Workshop REME	112
Chapter 16	The Chinese spring offensive 1951	113
Chapter 17	10 Infantry and 5 Medium Workshops 1951	121
Chapter 18	11 Infantry Workshop REME forward to the Pukhan River	124
Chapter 19	The Commonwealth Force Gather Strength	126
Chapter 20	11 Infantry Workshop forward	129
Chapter 21	North again to join 10 Infantry Workshop	130
Chapter 22	The formation of 1st Commonwealth Division	137
Chapter 23	The Divisional Commonwealth Telecommunications Workshop	145
Chapter 24	Operation Commando	148
Chapter 25	29 Brigade & 10 Infantry Workshop	152
Chapter 26	29 Brigade HQ LAD REME	153
Chapter 27	1 Infantry Troops Recovery Unit	158
Chapter 28	16 Infantry Workshop	160
Chapter 29	Consolidation and counter-attack	169
Chapter 30	The winter of 27th November	174
Chapter 31	10 Infantry Workshop	179
Chapter 32	Late summer and winter	201
Chapter 33	The winter of November 1952 to March 1953	206
Chapter 34	The last phase during Spring and Summer 1953	211
Chapter 35	5 Medium Workshop in early 1951	215
Chapter 36	REME Inspections	221

Chapter 1

Background to the Campaign

Korea

The Korean peninsular protrudes from the Asiatic mainland to within 120 miles of the main Japanese island of Honshu. To the north is Manchuria, whose border with Korea for the most part runs along the Yalu River, which was to prove of considerable importance during the Korean campaign. Korea extends from north to south just over 500 miles and from east to west, at its widest point, about 135 miles.

Climate

The seasons of the year are similar to those in the United Kingdom (UK) but with much greater extremes of temperature; in winter (November to March) the climate is very severe, with frequent heavy snowfalls accompanied by bitterly cold winds. The temperature falls as low as minus 20 to 30 degrees below freezing point - or minus 52 to 62 degrees Fahrenheit. The months of July and August are probably the most unpleasant in the year, when torrential monsoon rains turn the whole countryside, including its roads, into a quagmire and movement becomes severely restricted. The rains are often accompanied by violent winds and, between periods of rain, there is an oppressive humid heat. In spring and autumn the climate is good, similar to the best conditions experienced in the UK, with temperatures in the high 90 to low 100+ degree Fahrenheit range.

Terrain

Except in a few coastal areas, Korea is almost entirely mountainous, although the peaks do not often exceed 3,000 feet. Valleys vary from being several miles wide to the narrowest of defiles with near vertical slopes on either side. The lower areas are often covered in dense scrub and trees. Rivers and streams, running mostly across (east/west) the peninsular, rise rapidly during the monsoon and the period of melting snow, but in the summer they drop just as rapidly and in places even the widest rivers become fordable. They are invariably frozen over in the winter and, at its coldest, the ice is sufficiently thick to carry the weight of a vehicle being driven across it.

Transportation

During the long Japanese occupation and then from its end to the beginning of the new hostilities, the civilian population as a whole did not use motor transport; consequently the roads were not metalled to any great extent. When the Korean Campaign started, good airfields existed at Pusan, Taegu, Seoul, Kimpo and Pyongyang and there were many airstrips. As the campaign developed, new ones were constructed and the existing ones improved. The main towns recounted in this historical account are: Pusan, the United Nations (UN) port of entry; Taegu, a major road and rail junction 60 miles north of Pusan; Seoul, the South Korean capital; on the 38th Parallel and the scene of the long 'cease-fire' talks; and finally, Pyongyang, the North Korean capital.

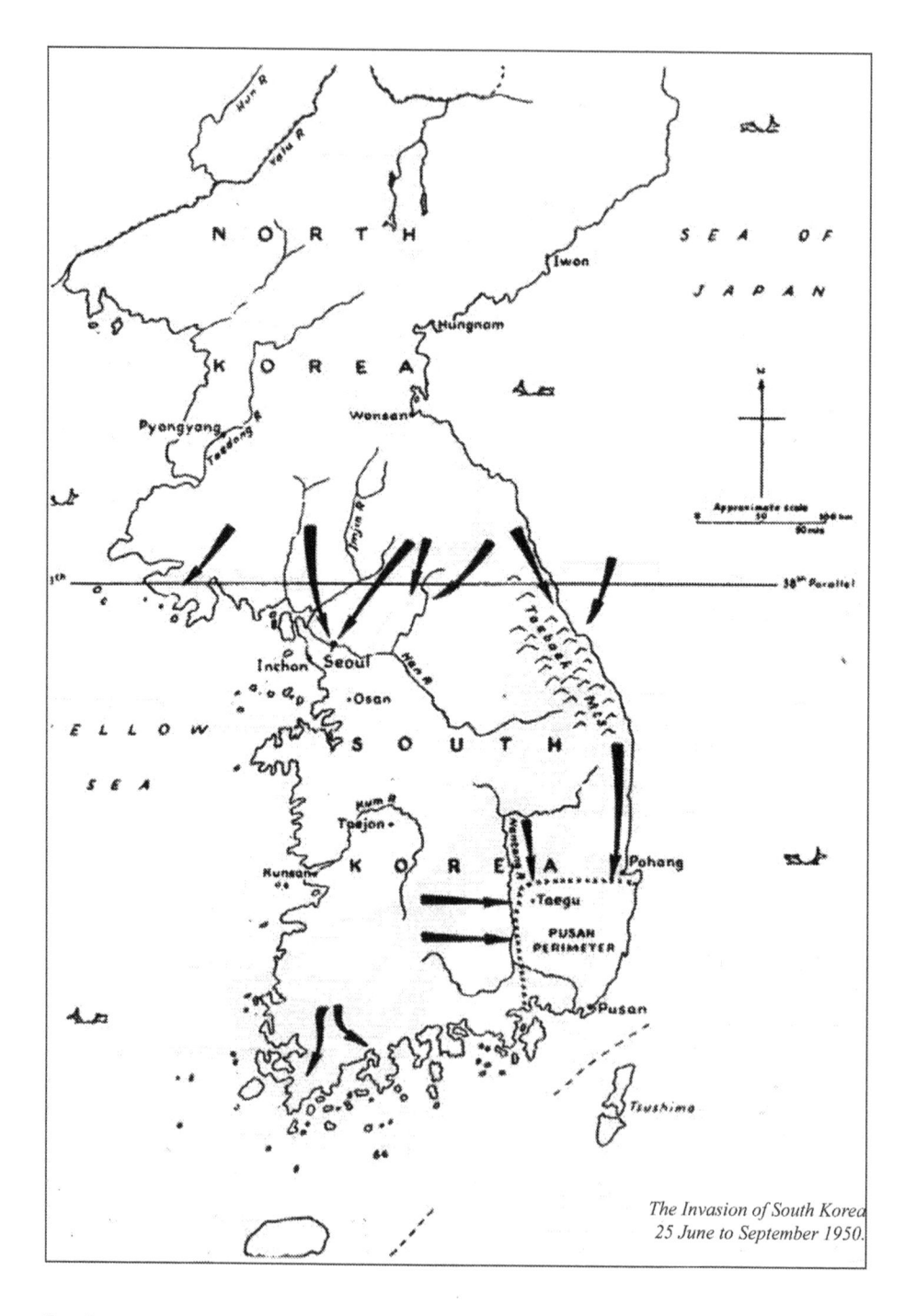

*The Invasion of South Korea
25 June to September 1950*

Chapter 2

The Invasion from the North

At the outbreak of hostilities, it is necessary to compare the strength and organisation of the opposing forces. The South Korean Army (SKA), of about 50,000 men, comprised some seventeen Regiments, organised into eight very weak Divisions. It had no armour and its 57mm anti-tank guns were incapable of dealing with the North Korean tanks. Its artillery consisted mainly of 105mm calibre weapons. The SKA had formed only in 1948, its troop training was mediocre and its staff work elementary, when measured against modern standards.

The initial assault from the north was by eight full-strength North Korean Divisions, well provided with Russian equipment and well trained since 1945 under Russian supervision. Their tank strength of Russian T34s was estimated at 250. These tanks were impervious to the SKA anti-tank weapons and a match for any of the American armour used in the early days of the campaign. Although the North Koreans were equipped with more aircraft than the South, these had little or no influence on the campaign. The North also had a few small naval craft, which were eventually destroyed by United States (US) and Commonwealth naval Forces.

Before hostilities began, it had not been appreciated that the South Koreans would be unable to withstand the onslaught unaided. The North Korean Army (NKA) overran South Korea in a matter of weeks, before American forces, or those of any other country, could intervene. On June 25th 1950, NKA forces crossed the 38th Parallel into South Korea at many points and also landed seaborne detachments on the eastern coast of its southern neighbour. The scale of that assault made it patently clear that this was indeed a full-scale invasion. World reaction to this, the first open act of aggression since the establishment of the United Nations Organisation (UNO), was swift and decisive. On the afternoon of June 25th, the Security Council met and called for an immediate cessation of hostilities, as well as demanding the North's withdrawal beyond the 38th Parallel.

By June 27th, it was evident that the North Koreans did not intend to comply with this demand, in fact their forces were still pressing on into the South. On this day, President Harry Truman ordered the US Navy and Air Force to support the SKA by every possible means. On the following day, British Prime Minister Mr Clement Atlee announced, in the House of Commons, that the UK naval forces in Japanese waters would be placed at the disposal of the American General (Gen) Douglas MacArthur. That was the first response from the UK. Next, the War Office was directed to study the global disposition of British Forces, with a view to providing assistance to the UNO, if possible without detriment to existing commitments. The very next day, both Australia and New Zealand also offered to make some naval units available. On June 30th, Gen MacArthur was authorised to use American ground forces (from Japan) in Korea and to bomb targets in North Korea. These decisions were eventually to cost the UNO approximately 350,000 killed and wounded. They also resulted in 1,500,000 enemy casualties as well as the near destruction of the Korean way of life.

On July 2nd, only eight days after the opening of hostilities, the first contingents of American ground troops arrived in Korea. The only formations close at hand that could be made available were four American Divisions from nearby Japan: First Cavalry Division (Div), Seventh Div, Twenty-fourth Div and Twenty-fifth Div, which were all infantry. These Divisions may have been admirably suited to their previous 'occupation' duties, but were neither trained, equipped nor up to the required strength to meet a well-trained and equipped enemy. However, the American Air Force was quickly reinforced and equipped to deal with the campaign to come.

Events moved fast, as follows:
    June 2nd: Seoul, capital of South Korea, fell to the North.
    July 5th: Suwon attacked and passed by enemy forces pressing further south.
    July 6th: Pyongtaek and Chonan, 24 and 36 miles south of Suwon, both fell.
In August 1950, Taegu, the last big town in the interior, also fell. A defensive arc, covering Pusan and using the Naktong River as part of its defence line, was established as the last line of UN defence. It was essential that this line, the Naktong Perimeter, be held, as Pusan was the only Port of Entry left in the UNO hands, through which subsequent reinforcements could disembark. Disruption of the enemy's lines of communication, by American air bombardment on a daily basis, enabled the UNO to gain time and muster its forces. This fighting force was to include the British 27th Infantry Brigade (27th Inf Bde).

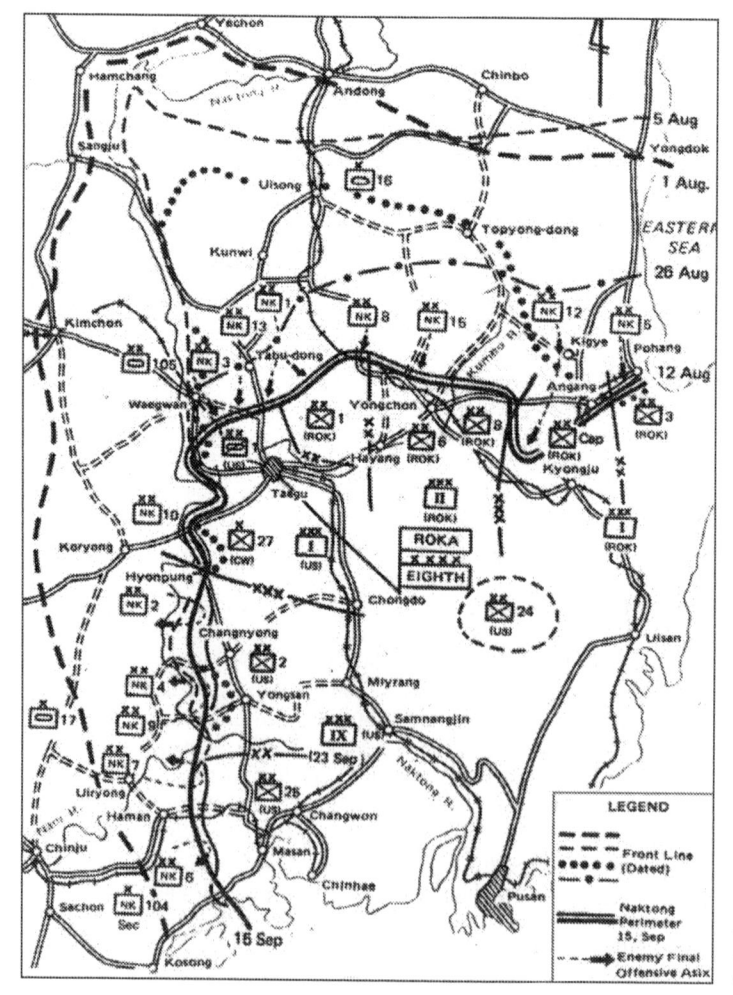

The Defence of the Naktong Perimeter 5th August to 15th September 1950

Chapter 3

27th Infantry Brigade August to November 1950

On the 28th August 1950, the outline Order of Battle for the 27th Inf Bde was:
  Headquarters (HQ) 27th Inf Bde and Brigade Signal Troop
  1st Battalion (Btn) The Middlesex Regiment
  1st Btn Argyll and Sutherland Highlanders (ASH)
  A troop of 17 Pounder (Pdr) Anti-Tank Guns, Royal Artillery (RA)
  Ordnance Field Park (OFP), Royal Army Ordnance Corps (RAOC)
  11 Infantry Workshop (Inf Wksp), Royal Electrical and Mechanical Engineers (REME)

On October 1st, 27th Inf Bde was increased to full strength by the addition of the reinforced 3rd Battalion Royal Australian Regiment (RAR) and also changed its title to the 27th British Commonwealth Infantry Brigade. One of the three Battalions, which was to see a considerable amount of the initial fighting, was The Middlesex Regiment. The experiences of Sergeant (Sgt) Peter Simmonds who served as their senior Armourer and other REME personnel (consisting of the following: 1 Armourer Lance Corporal, 1 Gun Fitter and 2 Vehicle Mechanics) have been included in this chapter.

The Middlesex had departed Hong Kong for Pusan on His Majesty's Ship (HMS) 'Unicorn', a fleet repair carrier whilst the ASH travelled on HMS 'Ceylon'. Both vessels were escorted by destroyers from the New Zealand naval forces. On board, the men had no set routine and were left to their own devices. On their arrival in Korea it took a while for the Middlesex's vehicles, spares, tools etc. to arrive on a cargo ship, so no repair took place for sometime. Not much of South Korea was left in Allied (or UN) hands; it was a miracle that any was left at all. The dividing line between the Northern and Southern armies was the Naktong River.

The Battalion had not been issued with Bren-gun Carriers in Hong Kong and only a few of the infantry soldiers could drive them. Thus for the REME personnel the first task was to travel to and from the station several times and drive the Carriers up to the Battalion from the station yard. They were then divided between the Machine Gun (MG) Platoon and the Mortar Platoon, whose members quickly learned to drive them. As an 'ex-boy' (ex-apprentice) soldier, Sgt Simmonds had done six weeks infantry training followed by a few weeks at Arborfield, where several subjects were taught, including driving. He did not learn to drive a Carrier there however, just basic driving skills. That was enough to get a licence but, on an up-grading course at Blackdown a year later, he covered the 'Wasp', a flame-thrower mounted on a Carrier. Driving them was an integral part of the course and proved to be very easy.

At this time, 27th Inf Bde was nominally part of the American First Cavalry Div, but was frequently moved from one Division to another, as trouble spots emerged in the push to cross the Naktong River. The arrival of the British Brigade somehow gave the Americans more resolve to be 'up and at them' again, after having been driven back so far from the 38th Parallel. Sgt Simmonds was at the time in the 'B' Echelon, but in close proximity to the Battalion. A few days before the Cavalry Div's push to cross the Naktong River, a US jet had detected signs that a sandbag road had been constructed overnight, just beneath the surface of the Naktong River.

As more troops were needed to fill the gap, on some high ground in the line about 400 yards behind the river, Sgt Simmonds was told to collect all the clerks, cooks, storemen and other non-combatant personnel to fill that frontal gap. It was dark and, during the time Peter was completing his reconnaissance of the 400 yard frontal gap, he remembers falling into something like a sand pit, whilst later placing his section of non-combatants. However they then had to go back and forth to collect boxes of extra ammunition and hand grenades. When, at dawn, what had appeared to be mere 'shrubs' became North Korean soldiers, climbing up to their positions, the Post Corporal fired his rifle at them without orders. This led to every gun in the Brigade opening up, a very costly mistake that cost the Corporal 28 days' stoppage of pay. The ragbag of a Platoon was able to relax, after Peter then went on another recce and discovered, no doubt with much relief, that the enemy had withdrawn.

Shortly after this, when the push northwards commenced, 'B' Echelon was left behind just south of the river. The advance was so fast that Peter Simmonds decided to leave his Lance Corporal (L/Cpl) behind with the 'boxes, Armourer' (which made up into a good little workbench), plus the majority of the spares. At the same time, he himself joined Tactical HQ with 'bags, Armourer' and a few other items he considered would be of use.

In the event, from all of the Battalion Infantrymen who were killed or wounded (which, throughout their tour of active service, sadly amounted to forty-two and ninety-four respectively), their weapons, when possible, were passed to Sgt Simmonds. He first inspected them and kept the good ones, then spent whatever was time was available on the remainder. Whenever he had too many, he sent the rest back to Company Stores, along with those for further repair by his L/Cpl at 'B' Echelon.

That L/Cpl was a lucky fellow. A few days after being left behind, he was working at the bench with its lid in the open position, when a shell landed just in front of the bench. Fortunately it did not explode, but the earth it had disturbed blew the lid down onto his arms and gave him one hell of a shock! It was rumoured that the particular gun that had fired the round had later been left behind, very well camouflaged. It was in fact a captured German 88mm from the Second World War (WWII), having then been passed from the Russians to the Chinese. 27th Inf Bde also found evidence of Russian and Chinese involvement, in the shape of artefacts in houses in the North and a few in the South.

The Allied advance on the front was also being determined by the terrain and was so fast that far too many of the enemy were left in the hills behind the front line. These enemy soldiers were still equipped with weapons and ammunition and became a menace to all the Allies advancing through the valleys, especially at night. They would throw hand grenades down from the hills, causing many casualties amongst the advancing UN troops.

The advance eventually passed through Seoul and over the 38th parallel without too much hostile action. The southern capital was again on fire, as it had been on the other two occasions when the Allies had passed through. The move of the Middlesex Btn and the remainder of the Brigade was now becoming a problem. With supply lines severely extended, it was difficult to maintain a steady supply of rations. Indeed, the Middlesex's Ration Corporal would sometimes arrive back from collecting the Battalion's rations so late that it was already time to set off on the next trip.

Sgt Simmonds volunteered to make a few trips to relieve the Corporal, until the situation could be improved. He found that the biggest problem was the state of the roads that had to be traversed. Peter was to do the ration detail several times in later months and in fact quite enjoyed it, as the rations were totally from American sources. The Battalion Ration Corporal would drive his truck to the nearest railhead and pull in alongside the supply train in the sidings. A Storeman in each carriage would ask for the name of the Regiment and how many men it had, then would collect whatever was required from what each carriage contained. If it was 'C' Rations, these would be packed in small individual boxes and all held in one wagon. The Americans did occasionally provide fresh food for the British Battalions and, on 'Thanksgiving' and the 'New Year' anniversary days, enormous turkeys were provided by the Americans for the whole Allied Army.

Peter Simmonds, who was the most experienced REME member with the Middlesex Btn, was asked to manufacture ovens from steel drums and corrugated steel boxes from corrugated steel sheeting, which had been taken from destroyed buildings in the nearest village. This was not the 'normal' Armourer routine, but it was now that his 'boys' service' training came into its own. The idea behind the request for the manufacture was that heat would be initially applied to the oven-drum outer container. Then the steel box, containing a frozen turkey, would be placed inside the heated drum overnight. Here, the bird would hopefully thaw, without burning.

Outside air temperatures were well below zero. The average soldier did not know what the actual temperature was, but Peter knew that a mug of freshly-brewed hot tea would freeze in only about five to ten minutes. A bottle of beer he had scrounged for Xmas Day froze and became just a piece of iced beer, in the shape of bottle, with glass all around it! Peter thought that they were just most unfortunate that particular year, as it was said that previous winters had not been nearly as cold.

The Middlesex Btn eventually reached Pyongyang, the North Korean capital, but 27th Inf Bde HQ was diverted to the western side of the city. The Battalion understood that this was probably to allow the Americans to enter Pyongyang first. Meanwhile, they themselves had been experiencing some problems with mines buried in the road. At this stage of the advance, some Battalion wags started leaving signs stating, *"The Middlesex can say with pride and joy that they were there before Kilroy".* By around this time. 27th Commonwealth Inf Bde now consisted of The 1st Btn ASH, the RAR, Princess Patricia's Own Canadian Light Infantry, a New Zealand Field Regiment of 25 Pdr howitzers, an Indian Ambulance Company (Coy) and the 1st Middlesex Btn.

It was during this period, the winter of 1950/51, that Peter Simmonds was unfortunate enough to slip on the ice and, as he fell, a piece of rice paddy stalk went right through his hand. In no time at all, his entire arm had swollen so much that the medical orderlies had to cut the sleeve of his combat jacket in order to remove it. He was despatched to a nearby Mobile Army Surgical Hospital (MASH) that was not a bit like the later 'Telly' version, except that the staff were drinking fruit juice laced with surgical spirit! Peter was there about a week and stuffed full of penicillin. The patients were housed in a large tent, heated by a petrol burner; so they were warm and well fed. One day, a visiting American General came to dish out 'Purple Hearts' (medals – not drugs!). He was putting one on each stretcher regardless of how the soldier had been wounded. He was about to put one on Peter's stretcher when the doctor told him, *"He's a Limey".* And so that was that – no medal for Peter! The weather was getting progressively colder and some of the American patients were actually sticking their bare feet outside the tent during the night, in order to get frostbite. This may appear to have been a little mad perhaps, but it was the 'recommended' way to get back Stateside or to Japan.

Peter returned to his Battalion to find himself detailed on yet another ration collection run, this time in a Bedford 15-cwt truck with an Irish driver, a very decent character. There were a number of Irish in the Battalion, probably one of the reasons why they also had an Irish Roman Catholic (RC) Chaplain. On the return journey, the driver got lost and it was getting dark. There was not a sign of life anywhere and the roads were barely wide enough for their vehicle. They came to a large gully with only a few not very strong looking boards spanning the gap as a bridge. Going back was out of the question but Peter did not know whether to get out and guide the driver across, volunteer to drive himself, or stay in the vehicle. The driver solved the problem by telling him to get out and guide him over. Peter Simmonds was very grateful to Paddy the driver, once they had made a successful crossing.

They were still in mountainous territory, with narrow valleys that restricted their movement but, eventually, before it was completely dark, they came down to a main road. Turning left by instinct, they passed through a village that housed a number of slant-eyed soldiers and a group of officers and non-commissioned officers (NCOs) who were studying a map. Not being totally certain of their bearings, they decided to go faster and clear that area. Merely a mile further down the road they came to their own location. The Commanding Officer (CO), Adjutant and a few other people were planning to attack the very village that Sgt Simmonds and Paddy his driver had just passed through. They then knew they must have had a guardian angel. They had assumed that the group of soldiers in the village had been friendly South Korean troops rather than the enemy!

It was not often that 'B' Echelon personnel had the opportunity, or even the desire, to go up to the positions in 'A' Echelon. They were nearly always located on mountaintops, at which the Americans had spent a few million dollars firing, without much success, before sending in the British to clear and hold. The old ration delivery problem inevitably came up again. As the mountains were a lot higher in the North than the South, it was more of a problem getting the rations up to the dugouts located near the summits. Someone had arranged for the local civilian population to help, but they were the enemy after all and probably half-starved. They had to be escorted up the mountainside by someone, so again it was Peter who stepped into the breech.

The weather had now become most severe and so had the problems that it was causing, with oil actually freezing. The men in the open trenches had to keep easing the bolts of rifles during the night and constantly moving the working parts of the Bren and Vickers guns, otherwise they froze solid. With the help of American transport to carry them, the British were advancing again, but at no great rate because, even with transport, forward movement was very slow. It got dark and their transport pulled in to a circle of American tanks, much like the old covered wagon days seen in 'The Westerns'. Peter Simmonds wandered around and was invited up to a tank by an American Technical Master Sergeant, who Peter then got to know quite well for a couple of weeks. Peter told him of his weapon-freezing problem and was told how to solve it, by using a certain brake-fluid that the American soldier had successfully used in Alaska. On return to his own unit, Peter issued this brake-fluid around the Battalion and it worked very well.

On one ration collection trip, Peter found the rations were stored on a wide but shallow river that had fully frozen down to its full depth. In the short time that they were there, the trucks' brake shoes froze onto their drums. Small fires were lit to thaw them out, a bit dangerous, but there was no alternative. At this same spot, a very large Afro-American soldier asked Peter if he would like some fruit juice. As it was in half-gallon tins, he said, *"Yes"*, but he had no means of opening it. The American must have been a member of a tank crew because he whipped out the largest automatic pistol Peter had ever seen and blew a hole through the top of the can, the bullet coming out through the side about a quarter of the way down. Peter remembered it as being good quality juice, despite it being full of flaked ice particles!

The Middlesex Btn now found itself in the Anju/Sinanju region, as far north as the British advance was allowed to progress before being stopped by the entry into the campaign of the Chinese Armies. The Battalion did a bit of withdrawing and advancing around the Pakchong region and were eventually in trouble, virtually surrounded. They had to withdraw fast, with the Australians charging up one hill and the 'Jocks' of the ASH up another, to give them covering fire, whilst they dashed through the middle. Sgt Simmonds was in the back of a Bedford 3-tonner and once again amongst the rations, but now poking a rifle out of the back of the vehicle. He was completely surrounded by boxes of tinned food and praying like mad that they would prevent any bullet from passing through!

One Platoon of 'B' Coy was attacked on a mountain and none of their Bren-guns would fire. The following morning, Peter was sent for and the guns and their operators were paraded behind the hill, while Peter tried to sort things out. He took a fully loaded magazine for each gun with him and fired each gun with no trouble at all. Peter then inspected each gun and found that most gas regulators required cleaning, but nobody had the tool for this operation except himself. This was very annoying to the Sergeant, because when he had joined the Regiment in Hong Kong, the CO had asked him to take all the Platoon commanders on weapon maintenance instruction, Saturday mornings, on the lawn in front of the Officers' Mess. He had thought the instructions had got through to them on *'The Importance of Cleanliness'*. However, on examining a magazine from one of the guns, Peter actually had to use a screwdriver to get a round out of the magazine.

As many readers will know, it is quite possible for a leading Company to meet no opposition when advancing and it seems that is what had happened to this Company, they must have led a charmed life in that they didn't have to use their guns for some time. However, their magazines had become wet in the rain, then dusty from the roads and finally frozen from the cold, but had never been emptied or cleaned. Peter later met a wounded REME soldier from this Company, on his way home to take an Artificer course in the UK. The soldier had glared at him and told him that their Bren-guns wouldn't fire. Peter imagined that nobody had ever bothered to tell him why!

On the advance north, the Middlesex Btn had to cross a river. It was extremely wide and, as they were to discover, tidal in nature. The plan was for the Battalion to go down to the riverbank in the dark, where US Engineers would supply boats and paddles, so that the crossing could be made at dawn. On arrival at the river however, someone had forgotten the paddles. It was broad daylight when the Battalion eventually arrived, with no sign of anyone on the other side of the river. It was not known at the time but the tide was fierce when it went out, and most of the Battalion went hurtling off towards the sea with it! Peter Simmonds found himself in the same boat as the Medical Officer (MO), the RC Chaplin, a Physical Training (PT) Sergeant and one or two others. Apparently they were the first of the few that managed to cross and a friendly crowd of North Korean civilian dignitaries met them. Like most wars, the civilians wanted little to do with it. As the Battalion made its way by boat again, as the tide turned, other boats appeared round the bend and they all landed up at the main bridge, which the Yanks were repairing. It had been quite an exciting day, with no shots fired at anyone.

The Battalion was then told to start packing up, as they were going back to Seoul to get a ship back to Hong Kong. There was to be no going back to UK after all, they was on a three-year tour and they still had about eighteen months to go. The Battalion was relieved by a South Korean Brigade and, on the second night as they were almost ready to depart, the Chinese made a heavy attack and the South Koreans disappeared, so the Battalion was ordered back into the war again. The Chinese must have been very close because, as they awoke in the morning, a battery of New Zealand 25 Pdr's was firing on the other side of the wall that they were lying against, the noise seemed to go right through their heads.

On another occasion, up in the mountainous terrain of the north and with snow everywhere, the Battalion was called out in the middle of the night. A very big withdrawal was now taking place, with over a million Chinese now said to be across the border. Although they had little support from aircraft and were also very short of transport, these Chinese troops were a formidable force. They made very effective use of mortars and were also prepared to travel across country. The Battalion had little enough transport itself; they relied upon the Americans if they had to move long distances.

At one stage, a very large convoy was heading south through a pass, which had steep cliffs on one side and a large drop on the other. One of the Middlesex's vehicles, a Bedford 3-Ton truck, had broken down and was holding up the whole column. Who could know what the position of the people at the end of the convoy was, with the Chinese catching up fast? It had snowed heavily during the night, it was still dark and the only vehicle available to assist was a Bren-gun Carrier just back from repair. So, being guided out of their site around the sleeping bodies on the ground,

The Forgotten Punch in the Army's Fist — Korea 1950-1953

the REME party made their way up to the pass. There was absolutely no alternative but to push the lorry off the road and down into the valley below. The Company Quarter Master Sergeant (CQMS) was quite 'cross' at this action, as he had all his goodies in that Bedford and was very reluctant to give them away!

Finally the Battalion was once again told it was leaving and to make its way to Inchon, which was also in danger of being surrounded at the time. An American ship was waiting for them, the USS 'Montrail'. It was one of those ships that one would later see in the war films, unloading soldiers down scramble nets onto small landing craft in the *'War in the Pacific'*. The waters at Inchon suffer from extreme tidal conditions, which had made Gen MacArthur's earlier invasion such a feat. Unfortunately, by the time that the Battalion got there the tide was going out fast, so they had to go out to the ship by small craft and then climb those scramble nets to get aboard. This was May 14th 1951, a day to remember. They had been only nine months in Korea, but with hardly any respite, just the odd couple of days here and there. They were delighted at the chance, at last, to have a hot shower and a really good breakfast.

Sgt Peter Simmonds and his team have probably forgotten much of what went on, but Peter thinks the following may give a flavour for what was to follow, in far more detail:

27th Inf Bde had been stationed in Hong Kong since the summer of 1949; their training in the local hilly country of the Kowloon territories was to prove invaluable during the Korean conflict. On August 19th, its Commander received orders to prepare to take his Brigade HQ and two Battalions to Korea in five days time. Initially it was not intended to send any supporting arms. As usual, emergency moves were accompanied by some confusion, instructions concerning establishments seemed to vary from day to day. Transport was handed in, with the intention that the Americans would provide the Brigade's requirements in Korea. This was altered only the day before sailing, when all the transport had to be redrawn, to follow later.

On August 24th, the main body of 27th Inf Bde left by sea on the aircraft carrier HMS 'Unicorn' and the cruiser HMS 'Ceylon'. It comprised HQ 27th Inf Bde and Brigade Signal Troop under Brigadier (Brig) BA Coad DSO; 1st Btn the Middlesex Regiment under Lieutenant–Colonel (Lt-Col) AM Mann OBE; 'A' Troop of 17 Pdrs and some Anti-tank guns. An OFP and an Inf Wksp were to follow later.

27th Inf Bde arrived in Pusan on August 28th. Disembarkation was reminiscent of other times in other countries. An American Negro band played on the quayside, a party of Korean girls sang *'God Save the King'* and Gen Walker, Eighth Army Commander, met the Brigadier. It was agreed that the Brigade would not go into action until its transport arrived, but this was soon changed, at Brig Coad's request, when the enemy attacked in strength a few days later, on September 1st.

By September 5th, the defence situation was now serious enough for the Brigade to wait no longer in taking up its defence position. It moved forward and took over a portion of the line on the Naktong River, south–west of Taegu. The front was immense, including a large bulge, some 18,000 yards long, with a gap of several thousand yards left and right of the Brigade. The line was being held by a combination of the 1st Btn ASH and the 1st Btn Middlesex Regiment, with support from American 155mm self-propelled Artillery and Sherman tanks. For the next two weeks, defence routines were rehearsed and carried out.

On the following day, September 6th, Captain (Capt) Buchanan led a patrol of ASH to Hill 228. Before leaving, he briefed his patrol that all wounded men must be brought back. He was wounded himself, but ordered his men to leave him. His body was found several months later. By September 7th, the NKA advance had 'shot its bolt' and UN Forces were about to undertake operations that, by the end of the month, were to bring about a dramatic change in the Korean scene.

Chapter 4

The move of 11 Infantry Workshop REME

On the 28th August 1950, whilst the Officer Commanding (OC) was taking his 'Orders', a telephone call was received from the Commander REME (CREME), Lt-Col RL Finlayson, with instructions that he was to take his 11 Inf Wksp REME to Korea, in support of 27th Inf Bde. Vehicles were to be loaded on August 31st and September 1st, with the unit ready to embark and sail on September 2nd.

One very useful member of the Workshop RAOC Stores section had just been awarded 14 days detention, but he was quickly marched back in front of the OC and the sentence amended to 14 days Confined to Barracks (CB). The next few days proved to be a hectic, though reasonably well controlled, chaos. A rapid assessment of outstanding work was made. That which could be completed was immediately tackled, while vehicles were checked and extra kit drawn up. The Quarter Master (QM) acquired useful items of field equipment, including about 50 two-man 'Pup' tents, which turned out to be invaluable. By the deadline, all the vehicles including the D8 and two Diamond 'T' recovery vehicles, were loaded. This also included the heavy vehicles and carriers of the Brigade. Their camp at Sek Kong was handed over to 16th Inf Wksp REME as caretakers, including some static equipment and a few men who were unfit to proceed to Korea.

The unit sailed on the afternoon of September 2nd 1950, being seen off by the General Officer Commanding (GOC), General Mansergh, CREME and the OC 16th Inf Wksp REME. Practically the whole complement of this 'replacement' Workshop had given a great deal of assistance with this move. 11 Inf's transport was an American 'Liberty' ship, the 'Cotton State', built during the 2nd World War at the Kaiser shipyard. All ranks were made as comfortable as conditions allowed and, after the rush of the preceding few days, they now had a short time to relax. During their preparations, they had been able to obtain the transfer of Company Sergeant Major (CSM) Robertson of the 1st ASH as the CSM to the Workshop. He was later to prove a tower of strength, once he became accustomed to the idea that tradesmen could be taken for guard duties!

A New Zealand frigate escorted the ship to Sasebo in Japan, from where they sailed on to Pusan in Korea as part of a small American-escorted convoy. They docked at Pusan on the morning of the September 7th, at which time, the enemy was within some twelve miles of the port, on the western flank.

CSM Robertson of the 1st Argyll and Sutherland Highlanders

Chapter 5

The activation of 10 Infantry Workshop REME

To establish the background to the activation of 10 Inf Wksp REME has been extremely difficult. But recently, whilst talking to a friend, Douglas Robertson, to my amazement he stated that he had been one of the first members of that unit. Doug is an ex-Chepstow boy and left his boys' service behind in February 1949, on posting to 18 Command Workshop (Cmd Wksp) REME at Bovington in Dorset. Whilst there, he attended one or two courses, was promoted to the 'dizzy heights' of L/Cpl and, like all 'good ex-boys', fell out with the civilians on the workshop floor, so set out to begin his travels!

Arriving at Thetford, Norfolk, in the summer of 1949, Doug was just in time to see 11 Inf Wksp REME leaving for Hong Kong. With his having been a late arrival, he was fed by unit staff and given a bell-tent to erect for himself. This exercise caused him a certain amount of trouble, but was good practice. The next morning he reported to the OC 10 Inf Wksp REME, a Capt Cook of the Royal Armoured Corps (RAC), who informed Doug that, after himself, he was the second person in the Workshop. This state of affairs did not last long but, until it changed, Doug was to be Chief Clerk, Motor Transport Office (MTO) and general 'dogsbody'. Doug is sure his memory is correct that, as a unit, the Workshop was to provide 'Field Training' for units and individuals, mainly of a regimental nature, rather than technical.

His story now blends with what was already known on the formation of 10 Inf Wksp. When Doug arrived in Korea, like the others he was informed that, although trained as an Armoured Recovery Vehicle (ARV) 'Churchill' commander, he would be re-mustered as an Armoured Fighting Vehicle (AFV) Mechanic and would join Capt Husband and his band of 'Happy Harriers'. His unit was 'a mobile force looking for work' - or that is how it seemed! With his limited ARV skill, Doug was now part of a team that carried out the first 'Centurion' engine change. For lifting the engine, they had a Scammell '6x4' that, even when stood on gun planks, was not high enough. A Coles Crane was then found and used successfully, even though the task eventually took around four days. This all took place just a few miles south of Pyongyang, while the American 1st Cavalry had been withdrawing. It was also around that time that a Centurion tank 'threw a track' and there was not sufficient time to cut it with the existing kit. Track blowing was soon to become a fact of life but, for want of an explosive charge, that particular Centurion had to be destroyed, becoming the first British tank casualty of that war.

Eventually the 'Harriers' joined up with the 8th Kings Royal Irish Hussars and their own Light Aid Detachment (LAD), thus making the first Heavy Aid Detachment (HAD). The 10 Inf Wksp elements stayed on, to join up with the 8th Hussars reliefs. Douglas himself had the honour to have been the first member of both 10 Inf. Wksp and the HAD.

In the spring of 1950, the Workshop was formed at East Wretham, Stanford Practice Training Area (PTA). It had a nucleus strength of only twenty-three all ranks, but with a full G1098 (a table of equipment that a unit would be issued with), as part of the Strategic Brigade 29th Bde Group. While the unit remained in the UK, it came under the direction of the War Office and under the control of Eastern Command. With its training direction from HQ REME Arborfield, local administration by East Anglia District and under the command of 29th Bde Group for exercises, life must have been most confusing, to say the least! Each month, trainees made up the unit to full strength all ranks, coming from Base Workshops for a three-week course. The camp at the PTA left a lot to be desired and, after some discussion, the District Commander insisted that the unit move to a better class of accommodation. It moved firstly to West Tofts PTA and then later to the ex-War Office Selection

The Activation Of 10 Infantry Workshop REME

Board (WOSB) site at Puckeridge, Ware. The original Stanford PTA was not totally neglected, as the road journey from Puckeridge to Stanford became a convoy practice drive.

So much for the unit's background. As 11 Inf Wksp REME moved from Hong Kong to Korea, 10 Inf Wksp REME was activated to a War Establishment, plus additional specialist sections, in keeping with the activation of the 29th Bde Group. 'Z' Reservists formed the majority of the Workshop strength, to the dismay of many, and resulted in about a 50% rejection rate by the Medical and Administration Officers, who had the task of vetting for suitability both in trade structure and in health. Many reservists had quite genuine domestic cases to be considered. The additional sections were an 'A' Vehicle increment and three 'Z' sections (Telecommunications), which made a vehicle fleet of 100. The Sergeants' Mess was 30 strong. During the work up, Major General (Maj Gen) Joslin, Director of Mechanical Engineering (DME), visited the unit.

On October 8th 1950, 10 Inf Wksp personnel embarked, along with the 1st Battalion Royal Ulster Rifles and a Field Ambulance unit, on the HMT 'Empire Pride' at Liverpool Docks. As previously mentioned, vehicles numbered 100, which meant separate sea transport to Korea and, whilst the vehicles remained on board ship, regular maintenance. At least one REME member accompanied the vehicles, primarily to look after the batteries. His name was Les Brotherhood, ex-regular, who had seen service in another 'forgotten army', the XIVth in Burma. Les had been on the 'B' reserve and was 'recalled to the colours' on August 9th. Re-kitted at the REME Depot, Arborfield, then sent to Colliers End Camp, Ware, Les volunteered for the trip with the transport. It meant civilian clothes and a civilian passport, but he slipped up because he lost out on the embarkation leave. His was cut short in order to report to the ship at Southampton, the SS 'Maplehill', a WWII American-built 'Liberty' ship.

Les's arrival was premature; the crew had not completed loading or the conversion of a large locker room on the open deck into a charging plant for the vehicle batteries. The ship's freezer and cold storage facilities were also out of action. It eventually sailed, about a week late, with the 'Refrigeration' fitters still on board, through Gibraltar, Suez and Aden. Les is not sure when they (the fitters) left the ship, nor what good they were supposed to have done! When crossing the Indian Ocean, whole sheep carcasses, cases of eggs etc, had to be dumped over the side! It was almost iron rations in the end! At Singapore, they were able at last to re-provision, but the freezer was still not repaired. The Chief Steward then reported that he had fallen and injured himself and needed treatment ashore. This was obviously a ploy so that he could leave the ship, in fact he already had his bags packed and he left his 'Bonded store' keys on the table!

A friendly but short welcome in Aden.

The Forgotten Punch in the Army's Fist — Korea 1950-1953

Hong Kong Harbour was a staging post for many on their way to Korea.

The 'Maplehill' arrived in Pusan about November 16th 1950. The transit camp had a lot of 'Odds & Sods' like them; they worked on the docks whilst they made up a vehicle convoy to move inland. When they did get going, their Coles' Crane would not go under a bridge just south of Taegu, so instead it was back to Pusan and then by sea to Inchon. The convoy carried on to Taejon for the night and, next day, they made it to 10 Inf Wksp location, north of Seoul. It was obvious that it had previously been a deep litter 'chicken farm', and one of the chicken houses was to be their accommodation after a much-needed bit of shovelling and brushing! Their total shelter at this time was one scrounged Yankee tent. There was a rumour going the rounds that the further north they went, the more blankets they would be issued with. North of Seoul it was meant to be twelve, but actually it turned out to be only four! This necessitated them forever sleeping in all their clothes, with a supplement of tarpaulins, camouflage netting, or whatever else they could lay their hands on.

It is thought to be 'general knowledge' that the Brigade was sent out to Korea with sub-standard equipment. A 1938 'Thorneycroft' engine powered the Generator Wagon for all the machinery. It struggled at its task but, with plenty of 'TLC', generally served its purpose until something better came along. The famous battle of the Gloucestershire Regiment at Imjin River involved the Workshop in making a strategic withdrawal to Yongdong-Po, ending in a location that had once been a cotton mill, but now very much derelict due to previous bombardments. At least they were luckier here and able to use some of the workers' accommodation. They had terraced single family-sized rooms with sliding doors and under-floor heating, which proved very efficient. Firstly, they used up the available wooden bobbins from the mill for the heating and then, when these ran short, made a cunning requisition on a telephone depot for telephone poles, which were also used for fuel. They remained in that site over the Christmas and New Year of 1950/51; some local Koreans came to the guardroom and sang *'Silent Night'*, which made them think longingly of home and family.

The activation of 10 Infantry Workshop REME

The situation was becoming grave. There was a vast exodus of transport moving south, day and night. Eventually it was their turn and orders were received to move – just move! It was snowing and, after a few miles they pulled into what appeared to be a school compound. They did not know whether it would be hours or days there, so they deployed to investigate the site and find themselves a good billet. It was while going through the corridors, looking into various rooms, that they failed to notice a hatch type trapdoor in the floor that had been removed. Les Brotherhood fell through it, breaking some of his ribs, which was very unfortunate. He was loaded onto a 15-cwt truck with his two packs, flat on his back, and finally found a British First Aid Post (FAP).

As there was a general withdrawal in progress, Les was transferred to an American clearing station, No.8 MASH and then put aboard a hospital train at Suwon. Thirty hours later he arrived at Pusan and a Swedish MASH, eventually getting to bed about 0300 hrs. After a few days, he was flown in a Yankee C54 aeroplane to Itakudie, Fukuoka, Kyushu in Japan, ending up again in American hands, at No.118 Station Hospital. Here he was issued with $5 in American 'scrip' that could be used to buy items in their 'PX' (the American version of our NAAFI). That was still not the end because, after a short flight to an Australian base at Iwakuni, Honshu, Japan, he was put aboard a large motor launch and taken across the inland sea to the 29th British Commonwealth Occupying Forces (BCOF) General Hospital at Kure. Les was just glad that he did not have to pay the fare! From there he was transferred to a convalescent centre on an island called Miyajima in the inland sea, where he made some good friends.

Les then went back for another spell of action, by train to Sasebo and then by boat to Pusan. Another journey by train for roughly forty hours followed, this time depositing him at Yongdong-Po at about 0530 hrs. Then it was on by truck to a transit camp just north of Seoul and a further thirty miles by road, northeast to 11 Inf Wksp - not back to 10 Inf Wksp, which was now at a place called Marsoguri, alongside a riverbed.

Ten more days and south they went again but, some four and a half weeks later, they moved back to Marsoguri. It was there that 11 Inf Wksp had salvaged the body of a '4x4' Gun-tractor that had been dumped. Amazingly, it was in far better condition than one that had come in for repair! It was also there that a Scammell Recovery rear hub nut came loose; maybe the locking tab had come off. However there was no chance of getting another axle. So, with some 'gentle chiselling' around the flattened thread, they tried to cut some sort of thread that would take the nut and lock nut, and eventually got it as tight as they could. It was then welded to the axle with a couple of lines of weld either side of the lock nut - and it worked! Work had carried on all night on this task, so they were kindly given the next day off. They never did hear what Base Workshops had to say. If the Scammell ever did go in for a brake-reline, it was never reported as having failed from that repair.

It was about this time that they moved again, thirty-seven miles to Uijongbu, via Seoul, and it was at this location that they caught up with 10 Inf Wksp. Les now hoped to finally get his kitbag back as it contained his civvies and some goodies, but no such luck! It was now May/June, with all the monsoon rain that ensued. It was no fun changing back-axles and so on, lying on their backs in the water that was running all over the site. In fact, to get over the immediate problem they moved their site about 400 yards to a drier spot. There was one more move, the last for some of the personnel, this time from Uijongbu to Tokchong. The unit had worked non-stop, but it was now time for some of them, mainly the 'Z' reservists, to go home. This was to be on board the MV 'Georgic', the ship that the author had originally arrived on.

Chapter 6

Armour & Heavy Support Groups reinforcements

29th Brigade Group

The outline Order of Battle for the 29 Independent Bde Group, from the 3rd to 18th November 1950, was as follows:

HQ 29 Independent Bde Group
1 Btn Royal Northumberland Fusiliers (RNF)
1 Btn Gloucestershire Regt
1 Btn RUR
55 Field Squadron (Fld Sqn) Royal Engineers (RE)
10 Inf Wksp REME

Arriving in Korea at the same time to augment the Order of Battle, were the following units, which in due course would become Divisional troops:

8 KRIH
'C' Sqn, 7th Royal Tank Regt (RTR)
45 Fld Regt RA
170 Independent Mortar Battery RA
11 (Sphinx) Independent Light Anti-Aircraft Battery

The Divisional troops were further increased in December 1950 with:

26 Fld Ambulance Royal Army Medical Corps (RAMC)
60 Indian Fld Ambulance

Capt Hesketh with a detachment from 5 Medium Workshop

Scanty press coverage

The North Koreans had invaded their southern countrymen on June 25th, but the media here in the UK had very little to report on the matter. Korea was located far away on the other side of the world, so who cared? Thus the War Office 'classified' its directives, in order to keep the lid on the fact that they were about to recall hundreds of 'Z' Reservists who would embark and sail, in due course, to Pusan in Korea (designated Port 'A') via Kure in Japan (designated Port 'B'), under a War situation.

There is a small village called Sutton Veney in Wiltshire, on the edge of the Salisbury Plain. It has had a long association with the Army; many Australians from the First World War are buried in the small village cemetery. Because of this association, on Anzac Day a service used to be broadcast from the Sutton Veney local church to Australia. Located on the outskirts of the village is an old hutted camp that used to be the accommodation to the local REME Workshop military personnel, known in those days as 27 Cmd Wksp REME. In late July 1950, a small group of officers came together in one of the wooden buildings, used as the Officers' Mess. The question on everyone's lips was *"Why are we here?"* At last, the answer came from the senior officer present, a Maj Gadsby. *"We are part of the 'Acanthus Force' and we are to go to Korea as part of the Commonwealth Forces contribution to the UN."* So nearly all was revealed, while the assembled officers would take up the following appointments:

Maj Gadsby – OC 5 Medium (Med) Wksp REME
Capt Gordon Ewing – OC 29 Independent Inf Bde Group, Support Troops LAD REME (the longest title in the Corps)
Capt Neil Prior – OC 23 Heavy Recovery Company REME
Capt Victor Moore – AO to 5 Med Wksp REME

The 'Z' Reservists started to arrive, with the officers first. Capt Jack Watson was an ex- WWII QM, with considerable experience and he took upon himself the task of arranging the allocation and collection of their vehicles and equipment. He had them marshalled at Warminster, before they were taken to South Wales for shipment to Korea. Jack Watson was soon on the telephone, commandeering what would be needed from wherever he could get it. 5 Med was a mobile workshop expected to carry out third echelon repairs in support of the Bde Workshops and LADs. As such, it was to prove to be an unwieldy affair and never really got down to its task in Korea. So much so that it left Korea after a short stay, to take up residence in an ex-submarine factory in Hiro, Kure, Japan.

On the personnel side, the timely early arrival of a small but vital number of regular REME men included a splendid CSM, Chief Clerk and a couple of NCOs. As each man arrived, he was placed on a nominal role and interviewed by either Maj Gadsby or Capt Moore as to trade suitability, medical fitness and present domestic situation. Those interviewee's not answering these three points satisfactorily (and I might add, to the individual's immense relief) were given a railway warrant and sent home.

A further influx of officers arrived to complete the build-up. Amongst these were Lt Ian Brandon, Capt Dennis and Capt Hesketh (Reserve). At this time, there were upwards of 200 men, being well looked after by their able CSM. On the first full muster, anyone with a full current driving license was requested to step forward. The reader may remember that in 1950, not everyone had a car and likewise a driving license. Fifty or more drivers with licenses were needed to go off and collect the vehicles from vehicle depots all over England. It was found that they had nothing like that number of drivers available. Within a short time, they had a list of people able to drive and, having issued the Army 'pink-slip', all fifty applications were taken to the Post Office in Warminster. Although taken aback by this large request for licenses, the Post Office staff undertook to issue them the next day. This they duly did and the lads were soon on their way. This was typical of the help received from people everywhere and it was very much appreciated.

The unit had no funds and no imprest account, nor the authority to open one to pay the men. Nevertheless, on approaching the local Westminster Bank, and giving an explanation of the situation quoting code word *'Acanthus'*, the bank manager immediately made a couple of telephone calls. It wasn't too long before there was an account and access to funds. Gradually at first and then at an increasing pace, the camp filled with a wide selection of vehicles, which the tradesmen inspected, together with all the specialist equipment they held. Most of the reservists had to have new uniforms and equipment, while weapons were requisitioned and issued. The CSM held the usual parades and inspections and in no time they were ready. Personal problems obviously cropped up, but 'higher authorities' were pleased to allow the local level of command to sort them out, without their interference.

The 'cold-weather kit' that was issued must have been designed for 'Noah's Ark', as it proved to be absolutely useless. General opinion was that it had originally made for the 'Finnish' or 'Russian' campaigns. The months of July and August slipped by and they were as ready as could be reasonably expected. A short leave was granted, from which everybody then seems to have returned. Loaded vehicles were sent to Barry, South Wales, having had all their doors shut and spot-welded, to reduce the risk from break-ins – but, inevitably, they were still broken into! They were then loaded onto freighters for the sea trip to Pusan, South Korea.

Embarkation orders were received but they still had very little information on Korea, with neither maps being issued nor briefings given. News from the national press was not good; reports indicated that the NKA had pushed well down into the south. So the last week in September eventually arrived and a special train into Warminster carried this part of the reinforcement on its first leg of a long journey down to the docks at Southampton. There were to be no farewell parades, but at least the CO of 27 Cmd Wksp REME, along with some of his staff, arrived to see them off and wish them well. The next stage of the journey was about to begin.

A long trip to the Orient

The *'Empire Fowey'*, a German ship which later became a British war prize, had since been refurbished and put into service as one of His Majesty's Troop Ships. She was destined to make her maiden voyage to Korea carrying the bulk of the REME Workshop, alongside 8 KRIH, the tank Regiment supporting 29 Inf Bde. The *'Fowey'* looked quite luxurious with its gleaming paint, its long promenade decks and a full width walk around to the bows. From everyone's point of view, the ship was as good as they could ever have imagined; with excellent lounges, a fine dining room and hotel class dining. The ship was run like an Army unit and had a CO, an Adjutant, clerical staff and a roster of duty officers, sergeants, etc., in which they were all included. During the outward voyage, some weapon training was undertaken.

Within seemingly no time at all, the Rock of Gibraltar, the Mediterranean and North Africa came and went; but they were not to stop, ploughing on steadily towards the George Cross island of Malta. A daily competition was run, to guess the ship's mileage, and a daily ship's paper gave them news and information from home and around the world. There was still little news of Korea however, and even what they were able to read was not good. Finally, Malta appeared over the horizon and they were told that they would be there for twenty-four hours of shore leave, good news indeed. Mooring took place in the Grand Harbour under the walls of Valetta and the men were ferried ashore in the ship's boats. A warning was issued that anyone who had not returned on board by the time designated would be left behind and dealt with accordingly. Time ashore passed all too quickly and they were all back aboard in time for them to leave. Except that is, for four lads who were the worse for drink. Their boat chased the *'Fowey'* out of the harbour, rowed by two straining boatmen, until the ship's Captain relented and slowed enough for them to catch up.

Port Said in Egypt was their next port of call, bringing shore leave with a difference, as they were ordered to stretch their legs the hard way, with a route march and a swim. Then it was back on board, making slow progress through the Suez Canal, a highlight of the journey. They spent all day on the open promenade deck, watching the country go by, accompanied by ribald exchanges between the troops and locals on the shoreline, who exhorted them to *"Get your knees brown!"* Halfway through that Canal passing, the ship failed to make a course correction on a bend and, having clattered through a number of channel markers, they then rammed into the Canal bank. One can guess the reaction from the onboard troops - every single man cheered! In addition, a number of startled villagers on the Canal's banks scattered into the desert.

Their next stop was in the 'Bitter Lakes' and divers went down to see if there was damage, but fortunately all was well. It was getting really hot by the time that they were sailing through the Red Sea, towards their next port of call, which was to be Aden. There are many tales told about Aden. It was reckoned to be the most difficult posting in the British Army, mainly because of the heat. Little did one of the officers know that, in nine years time, he would find himself there again, under more difficult circumstances. The ship dropped anchor opposite 'The Crescent Shopping Centre', so well known by all sea travellers and those more fortunate to be posted there. Another spot of shore leave was allowed, with time to look around 'Steamer Point' and 'Crater City'. The road called 'Maala', later to be lined on both sides with blocks of flats, was only just beginning its reclamation from the sea and its new build. It was terribly hot on land and the ship was not much cooler when the men returned. It was a relief to get to sea again and have a cool breeze to drop the ship's internal temperature.

The next leg of that long journey was a long haul down to Singapore, with some relief on the way when the 'Fowey' answered a distress call from another ship. Picking up speed, she swung off course and the rumours were soon flying around deck. The other ship was found and a lifeboat was lowered to collect an injured man. Unfortunately, something went wrong and the lifeboat commenced to power around in circles for some time, while frantic attempts were made to repair the rudder that was obviously giving trouble. There were probably more than a thousand men on board the *'Fowey'*. When the situation was resolved, their cheers could no doubt be heard in their next destination, Singapore itself.

Landfall at Pusan

Upon their eventual arrival there, shore leave was once again enjoyed at 'Kepple Harbour' and 'Collier Quay', names now from the past. The troops had no sooner gone ashore than they were drowned by the onset of a monsoon. Soon, shouts of *"Taxi please"* could be heard, as well as *"Raffles Hotel, please"* – after all, where else would one start a tour of Singapore? And so onto the last leg of the journey, a long haul up through the South China Sea, unfortunately past Hong Kong and Shanghai, to the southern tip of Korea and the port of Pusan. A typhoon blew up and the ship, big as she was, was battered by huge waves and roaring winds. Clearing the decks very quickly, many were soon confined to their beds and were very, very sick. The violent movement of the ship was alarming, particularly as the sea had been like a millpond most of the previous time. Weather continued to be bad and there was a noticeable change in the temperature, with it steadily becoming colder. Men would now take one step outside, then dash quickly back inside again looking for warmer clothing. Korea! They had finally arrived, it was November 13th 1950 and it was 'bloody cold'. The troops were forty-two days from home and halfway round the world. Now, perhaps the reason for being there was about to unfold.

Another troopship, not perhaps the normal run of troopers, had left the UK in October 1950. This was the *'Empress of Australia'* and she was carrying Brig Tom Brodie, with his 29 Bde HQ and some 2,000 personnel. Len Stanway was one of them; he was a 'Tiffy' Gun/Vehicle (dual trained) and was travelling to Korea with 57 Company RASC Workshop. They arrived in Korea at Pusan after a twenty-eight day trip, the first troops direct from the UK. Like so many others at the time, Len wished he had a camera, when the Brigadier was met at the dockside by the President of South Korea, President Syngman Rhee and his Lady (a real dolly-bird, to use the modern expression!). She was presented with a large bunch of flowers, to a chorus of catcalls and wolf-whistles from around 2,000 men looking down from above. Within a few days, Len had the Workshop vehicles unloaded and on their way north. It was the second day that brought them up short, their first casualty. A man, with a Sten gun slung barrel downward from his shoulder, jumped off the back of a wagon. The piston bounced, loaded a round, fired and shot him through the foot. He became a much-envied fellow, as he was later reported to be having a very nice time recovering in San Francisco!

The unit moved north in stages, always available to give assistance when needed, moving through Taegu, Taejon, and Seoul and then across the Han River and on into North Korea. There were stops at Kaeson, Chariwon, Pyongyang and then even beyond that. It has to be pointed out there are two types of travel overseas. There is the complete package, which is the Battalion with its own Armourer and Fitters, which starts and finishes as an entity, travelling as one. Then there is the other type - the group that mainly Army Corps fall into. Here, the tendency is for an individual to move on his own or as part of a group of individuals and who, when arriving at his destination, is dispersed to an individual unit. Korean postings were no different, the fighting Battalions served approximately one year before the whole Battalion changed, taking its name with it and being replaced by a similar force, but with a different name.

In the case of the Corps, a Battalion would initially arrive as a unit with its own individual name, but made up of individuals, who would not necessarily remain with that unit throughout its service in a given theatre. The individual would, in the case of Korea, serve for eighteen months, and then be replaced in that unit by a similar trained person of equal rank. Those were the ideal situations but perhaps the next few paragraphs will enlarge on what has just been described.

A draft of thirty personnel was formed at the REME Depot in 1952. In most cases, they had come from different units. Of those thirty, two were WOIIs or (in REME terms) AQMSs, one being Mike Kinshott and the other J Parker MBE. As with so many before, they travelled by troopship but, on arrival at Hong Kong, they were off-loaded to allow a Company of the Black Watch to join its Battalion in Korea. A few days later, the REME personnel that had been-off loaded were given passage on a merchant ship to Kobe in Japan. AQMS Parker acted as the OC Troops and AQMS Kinshott was made the CSM for the voyage. After a few days in transit, their final sea trip to Korea was embarked upon. Arriving at Pusan, the draft split up and went to its respective units. By this time, 1 Comm Div had been formed so they were all members of that Division.

The experiences of Mike Kinshott

AQMS Mike Kinshott joined 57 Coy RASC LAD, the unit with which Len Stanway had embarked to Korea in 1950. It was now part of a Transport Column consisting of Canadian, NZ and British Companies. To Mike, this was something of a culture shock, as he had previously only been with Aberdeen University's Officer Training Corps (OTC). But he soon settled down, living in a tent, with the only light supplied from a 12-Volt bulb soldered to the end of a piece of wire connected to a generator! Mike's task was to keep the Bedford trucks available for detail supply to forward troops of Rations, Fuel and Ammunition. His OC LAD was a Lt Keith Fagurland, who lived in a 'house' built on a Jeep trailer. As Mike had joined the unit in the summer, he had to get used to clouds of dust. To help get over this problem, 'old engine oil' was used to help stabilise the surface – thankfully it worked well. Being an RASC Coy, transport was always at a premium, this premium being made worse by the Canadian and NZ Companies being able to repair far more vehicles 'in situ', due to their allowed depth of repair. They would change complete assemblies, while Mike would have to 'back load' to 10 Inf Wksp for assembly changes. Unfortunately, 10 Inf Wksp had the whole of 29 Bde to deal with, so 57 Coy did not get all the priority that they may have deserved. Mike eventually came to some sort of agreement with the NZASC, who used the same pattern vehicles as we did. The trade-off worked and he was able to start changing assemblies. This obviously put an extra load onto the LAD, causing a little concern, but it certainly worked and improved availability figures.

In those freezing winter months, the hot air blower, with its canvas tubes, became the most essential piece of equipment, as it was impossible to work on the vehicles due to the intense cold. Alas, they could never start work until the Company offices, housed in the back of vehicles, had been warmed up. Putting the blower onto the vehicle's radiator did this. They had their own troubles, as the *Scammell* Recovery 6x4 was rather difficult to warm up at times. As they had no shower facilities of their own, they visited the Bath and Laundry unit run by the RAOC at regular intervals, enjoying a hot shower and a change of clothing. During the winter, for those who had to work outside, the 'buddy system' was employed. This amounted to being paired off and, when outside in the extreme wind chill, one would keep your eye on your 'buddy' to watch for the first signs of frostbite. Fortunately the LAD did not fall foul of the weather.

When the troops passed each other in their vehicles they used to wave to one another. The Div Cdr thought this a good idea and requested that he be offered the same privilege. During Mike Kinshott's tour with 57 Coy RASC, the Comm Div was pulled back into reserve, being replaced in the line by the Americans. The RASC did not fully pull back, but just moved up the valley to allow the US QM Coy to move in. Their arrival was of the standard American pattern, a convoy of huge trailers in addition to the usual stores and equipment. Mike visited them and discovered they were making ice cream, as every US serviceman was due ice cream every three days in his rations! A friendship was quickly fostered and, in no time, the LAD were eating ice cream and trying out other US ration specialities.

Another much sought-after item was the camp bed, which out of necessity just had to be 'acquired'! And, of course, the US QM Coy seemed to have plenty in stock. The 57 Coy CSM, dressed up complete with pace stick, positioned himself at the head of the valley until an American truck, loaded with beds, came along. Out stepped the CSM and, with typical barrack square style, demanded *"Who goes there?"* The Afro/American driver, with his eyes almost popping out of his head, stopped and was asked to produce his ID papers. Whilst this was going on, a gang of 57 Coy drivers unloaded the rail truck of its beds and, after the drivers check was completed, he was dispatched on his way. There was no shortage of beds from that day on!

During this same period, they were also on US rations, which made a change from UK ones. The US forces are 'dry', which means no alcohol, when on active service. The UK troops had their usual supply of beer and spirits. During the winter, the beer was apt to freeze but the spirits were always drinkable. Mike recalls a US Marine Unit WO & Sgts visit, they were hard drinkers and one of them tried to drink one of ours under the table, but failed. The other Marines were so annoyed that their colleague had disgraced them that they picked him up and tossed him in the back of a truck when they left. Mike and other Mess members were invited on a return visit to the Marines' Mess. The worry was in transporting the booze, as there were plenty of US Military Police (MP) patrolling the main roads. So they put the booze in the *Scammell* recovery vehicle and used the yellow warning light. They made the journey without being stopped, just waved through at all the checkpoints. They had a most enjoyable evening with the Yanks.

Some of the officer personalities in post during Mike Kinshott's tour were:

CREME	Lt Col PG Palmer
CRASC	Lt Col Degnan
OC Comm Wksp	Maj Cowgill
OC 57 Coy RASC	Maj Patterson
OC LAD	Lt K Fagurland

When Mike's tour was over, he left Korea as an individual for a posting to Malaysia, while his unit stayed on until British forces were finally withdrawn. Meanwhile, the Chinese had entered the war and the big withdrawal south began. That was the start, many things happened after that, but eventually 57 Coy RASC ended up at Anjang, and Len Stanway left for home in March 1952.

The life of Brian Conway

Amongst others arriving in Korea was Sgt Brian Conway, who had joined the Army as a boy, intake 42A (April 1942) at the Army Technical School (Boys) Arborfield. Some of the 'Korean veterans' already knew of him from their own boys' service and, if memory served correctly, he had been in the Drum and Fife band. A further bit of background shows that Brian had met his fiancée whilst he was stationed at Tidworth. She was the 'Nanny' to the four children of the CO of Tidworth Military Hospital, Lt Col JE Snow RAMC who, in the July of 1949, gave the bride away. On his return from honeymoon, Brian was greeted by Squadron Sergeant Major (SSM) Jim Darby RTR, who took great delight in telling him, *"The honeymoon is over! You're off to Korea, Conway!"*

Brian's parent unit was 7 RTR, he had been attached to its 'A' Sqn as the commander of a Churchill ARV at Lulworth Cove. A composite 'C' Sqn, equipped with Churchill Flame-throwers and their trailers, was formed, comprising all regular soldiers drawn from the four Squadrons of the Regiment. These were supplemented by 'B' Reservists, re-called to the Colours for the duration of the Korean conflict, under the command of Maj Jack Pettingell RTR. They were to operate as 'half-Squadrons', each with their Churchill ARVs, one half under the command of Maj Pettingell, the other under Capt Freeman MC, RTR, with Sgt Jack Woodward REME commanding one ARV and Brian the other.

They were to be part of the 29 Independent Inf Bde Group, comprising Gloucesters, RNF and RUR. 8 KRIH (under Lt Col Sir Guy Lowther, Baronet), equipped with the latest Centurions, provided a full Regiment as their main tank support. Coincidentally, Lt Col Snow RAMC had now become Brig Snow and was to be Director of Medical Services (DMS) for all British Commonwealth Forces in Korea (BCFK), as well as the Commandant of the BCOF Military Hospital in Kure, Japan. Brian's wife thus returned to her previous employment with Mrs Snow, while both Brig Snow and Brian Conway were serving in Korea.

Sailing to Korea on HMTS *'Empire Fowey'*, and on their last leg of the journey from Singapore to Pusan, they had picked up a party of officers. These gentlemen had already been serving in Korea and were going to give lectures about 'The Land of the Morning Calm', a land about which they obviously knew very little*!* *"The best description that I can give you of Korea"*, said one officer, *"is that the land you will walk on will be solid s**t, the water you drink liquid s**t, and the air you breathe, evaporated s**t!"* Upon arrival at Pusan Harbour, after an almost six-week voyage, they knew what their lecturers meant about Korea, with the all-pervading stench of human excreta emanating from the 'fertilizer' used on the paddy fields. This seemed to cover the whole of South Korea, the excrement carried in buckets (inappropriately called 'Honey Buckets' by the Americans) on the two ends of a bamboo pole slung across the shoulders of Korean men. The buckets bounced up-and-down, splashing their contents over the legs of the carriers as they ran along! The world's finest rice comes from South Korea, or so it is said, so perhaps there was 'method in their madness'?

One of the most unforgettable memories (apart from the stench) as they sailed into Pusan was the sight of one particular soldier, standing at the ship's rail with a wild and angry look upon his face. He called out to them, *"To think that we spent three years in this God-forsaken hole, as prisoners of war (POWs) of the f*****g Japs, where the so-called vicious and cruel Japanese guards were in fact Koreans. And now here we are, coming back to fight for the b******s!"* When they started to unload their tanks from the freighters, tied-up alongside the jetties, they didn't get very far! Someone had forgotten to ensure that the port of Pusan had adequate lifting-gear, capable of lifting up to seventy tons or more!

The Korean stevedores were not prepared to do anything about it, so the ship's crew manned two steam-driven donkey winches, with two derricks working in unison, to lift the sheer weight of their tanks from the depths of the holds. Here, the unfortunate soldiers shackled the hawser lines to the lifting-eyes of each tank and then watched in fear, as the vehicles rose slowly from the depths. The tanks seemingly filled the whole space of the hatches, blocking-out all daylight completely, while the soldiers prayed that none of the winch-lines would snap, sending the tank crashing through the bottom of the ship – and probably taking them with it! As the weight of each tank was swung across the deck, to hang precariously over the side of the ship above the jetty, the whole ship keeled-over, with the shorelines groaning and straining to keep the ship from toppling over completely. The load was finally lowered safely to the 'terra-firma' – or 'the firmer the ground the less the terror', as Paratroopers were often wont to say!

Next came the task of loading the same tanks onto the flat-bedded railway cars for the journey to Kaesong, on the 38th Parallel, an interesting exercise indeed! The wooden flatbeds were nowhere near as sophisticated as those that they had loaded back in the UK! Fulcrum-pins on the underside of the cars simply entered fulcrum bushes on top of each bogie, unsecured, with the result that, as the first of the tanks attempted to mount the first flat-bed, the far-end tilted upwards, dislodging its bogies! This difficulty was overcome by replacing the set of bogies at the far-end, then positioning two ARVs breadth-wise across the space between each flat-car. This held them down as each tank drove on, with the ARVs interchanging along the station platform. This went on until each tank was loaded onto its own flatcar, the two ARVs being the last on. The men hoped that there would be siding platforms at Kaesong!

A comparatively short train journey, of some 250 miles, took several days. Their train was often shunted off the main line and into sidings along the way, sometimes being kept there for hours on end. It did however give them an opportunity to dismount, 'put the kettle on' and have a cooked 'compo' meal on firm land, without trying to accomplish this on the move on their swaying flat-cars. Beneath tarpaulins, which were lashed to the stern of each tank and fastened to the wooden platform of each car, would be their only sleeping quarters for the next few days! Along the way, all crews, including officers, had to provide a guard up in the turret (turret guard) during the hours of daylight, because of sabotage activity along the line. Crews drew lots for 'stag duty' during the hours of darkness. They were also pleasantly surprised to discover that officers had their fair-share of the cooking for the day!

Brian Conway's tank driver was 'Paddy' Brown RTR, a veteran of the UK's 8th Army that had fought across North Africa and then through Italy and into Germany. He had probably forgotten more about tanks than Brian would ever know and did not take kindly to twenty-three years old

THE FORGOTTEN PUNCH IN THE ARMY'S FIST — KOREA 1950-1953

REME Sergeants! The Wireless Operator was nineteen- year old Steve Hawkins RTR who, because of his age, ought not really to have been in Korea at that time! Brian's Winch Operator was Craftsman (Cfn) Gerald 'Spud' Murphy REME who, when not operating the winch from the commander's seat, was the *Besa* Machine-gunner in the hull at the co-driver's seat. One morning at sunrise as they awoke, they found all of the crew in their sleeping bags! Who then, was supposed to be on turret guard? They quickly roused the crew, to discover that it should have been young Steve Hawkins! By way of explanation, he said, *"Well Sarge, you all looked so peaceful and comfortable there, in your sleeping bags, I just didn't have the heart to wake any of you!"* They had great difficulty in restraining their mirth as Brian tried to adopt an angry countenance. He reminded Steve that they were on active service and that if the terrorists had not shot us in our sleep, then the OC would have done, had he found out! Fortunately for them, they did not encounter any terrorist activity along the way.

Additions to 'the ranks'

On arrival at Kaesong, each tank had 'acquired' an additional 'crew member' in the shape of a little Korean child, some boys and some girls. None (at a guess) was over ten years of age, these children had been found standing along the railway line, begging for food. With the OC's permission, each tank crew was permitted to 'adopt' one Korean child, who would then travel in the co-driver's seat, sharing their food and spare sleeping bags. In return, they were expected to carry out small tasks, such as folding and stowing the crew's sleeping bags and washing-up their mess-tins and 'eating-irons' after each meal. That was to last at least until they arrived at Kaesong where, perhaps, they could make other arrangements for them. One little boy on their ARV was called Won, so it was no surprise that they ended up calling him 'Two'! His younger sister was on another tank in the Squadron. Their Korean Intelligence Officer, who was the translator between them and 'their' children, told them that the North Koreans, on their initial sweep southwards towards Pusan during the early stages of the war, had shot down their parents before their eyes. They had then left the children to fend for themselves and to be taken care of by the UN forces.

At Kaesong, they were pleased to find off-loading facilities for the tanks at the railway station and used the reverse unloading procedure to that which they had used at Pusan. It was from here that they were to learn that 27 Inf Bde, the first Commonwealth Force to arrive in Korea from Hong Kong, was now enjoying a well-earned rest after experiencing what is known as 'friendly fire' from American aircraft. Having off-loaded at Kaesong, their Squadron promptly turned around to travel south, in the direction from which they had just arrived! They were permitted to keep their orphaned children on this return trip.

It was on that journey that Brian was to experience not only the perils of vehicles operating in the sub-zero temperatures of a Siberian winter, but also of the dangers of driving on very narrow roads, barely enough to take the width of one tank. Weaving along the roads between paddy fields, a weary driver could easily find his tank slipping from the road and into a paddy field, there to shed a track! This then became their most frequent recovery operation and, fortunately Cfn Spud Murphy and Brian were not often required to wade into paddy fields any deeper in the 'fertiliser' than ankle-high, singing *"Sweet violets, sweeter than all the roses!"*

Their blocking of the only main road to other traffic complicated any expectedly simple recovery task. They had to continually un-hitch their tackle and get out of the way, particularly for ambulances. At first-light each day, while the teapot was brewing, they carried out their 'first-parade maintenance', with the wireless operator 'netting-in' their radio to the Sqn Cdr's radio signals, while Spud checked over the winch and recovery equipment, as well as their weapons. 'Paddy' Brown and Brian checked the engine and the transmission oil levels, fuel and coolant and, on warming-up the engine, rocked the steering tiller-bar to-and-fro in a partial 'neutral' turn, in order to free the track links from the frozen ground.

Burning their bridges behind them?
Following upon an early visit from Capt Snow REME, the Brigade Forward Recovery Officer (no relation to Brig Snow RAMC), they learned that engine and transmission oils were to be changed from SAE 40 and SAE 60 respectively, to SAE 30 and 40. Anti-freeze was to be of a 50/50 mixture, and no ARV was to tow any other vehicle for a distance exceeding five miles in any one day! Engine and gearbox life was estimated to be no more than 500 hours, after which a major unit-change would be necessary. There was, however, a small RASC unit of Diamond-T tank-transporters in their area, on whom they could call if necessary, to help evacuate tanks to either the nearest railhead or REME repair facility. But, because of the nature of the hilly terrain, narrow roads with sharp bends and sheer drops on one side, such services were almost impossible for the RASC. They could only pray that there would be a railhead with loading ramps within five miles of them, to which they could tow the casualty. One other problem they were to confront, as they moved towards Seoul, was that the American Corps of Engineers had been ordered to destroy all road bridges behind them!

It became a part of the REME ARV commander's duties (including the commanders of the four ARVs of the 8 KRIH Squadrons) to wait on the northern side of each bridge. They would then await a signal from their respective Sqn Cdr that all 'call signs' (their tanks) had passed safely over the bridge, before they themselves could pass over and the American Engineers ordered to destroy the bridge. Indeed, it was said, that 8 KRIH did in fact lose one of their Centurions as a result of this routine, with 'all hell to pay'. It was well known that the Russians would have 'dearly loved' to have got their hands on one of those latest Centurions, courtesy of the North Korean and Chinese Forces, and here was one 'presented to them on a plate', complete and intact! It was reported that American rocket-firing aircraft had been sent to the area on a 'search and destroy mission', but no trace of the Centurion was ever found. It was known that the enemy had no mechanical facilities of their own, capable of transporting such a heavy load, so it could only be assumed that an 'Army of Chinese Ants' must have picked the tank up bodily and carried it off!

The destruction of all the road bridges created another recovery problem, with their 'soft' vehicles (particularly ambulances) becoming stranded on the steep slippery slopes of riverbanks, as they attempted to ford the shallow rivers. Fortunately, Sgt Jack Ward REME was on hand, with his *Scammell*, to assist in getting them out. Recovery vehicles thus became prime targets for the enemy T34 Russian-made tanks, with their very powerful 85mm guns. In a 'hull-down' position, these T34s would be strategically placed at bends in the road to 'pick them off' as they rounded the corner! However, with the arrival in Korea of 8 KRIH, with its full complement of Centurions and superior 105mm guns, the T34 seemed to disappear from 'the field of battle', never to be seen again. This was much to the great disappointment of the Hussars, who had hoped that they could also 'have a go' at the latest Russian T54 with its 100mm gun!

American aircraft, whose pilots seemed to have great difficulty in identifying British tanks *(nothing much has changed?)*, were now their main danger. For this reason, they displayed Aircraft Recognition Panels on top of their turrets and engine decking and, to fool the Chinese infantry, the Churchill ARVs had a 4-inch drainpipe, with a false flash-eliminator on the muzzle, welded to the front of the turrets. This was intended to look like their 'main armament', to make the enemy believe they were anything but a Recovery Vehicle! With the NKA and Chinese troops seemingly confined to the steep surrounding hillsides and with the American Air Force frequently using napalm bombs to dislodge them, this made the use of the Squadron as a 'flame-throwing' unit rather unlikely. They therefore removed their flame-guns and remounted their *Besa* Machine-guns at the co-driver's position on the hull. Ditching their trailers, they became essentially infantry support tanks, for which they were ideally suited.

It was probably at the beginning of 1951 that 29 Bde found itself consolidating its position in 'Happy Valley', just north of Seoul. At this time, only three recovery operations come to mind. The first was to extricate an Oxford Carrier, belonging to the RUR, which had become bogged-down in a paddy field and then 'frozen-in' overnight. Neither Brian nor his OC knew of their destination, except that it was north, into 'No-Man's-Land'. Brian confessed to a feeling of unease as they drove through the forward positions of their own infantry, dug-in at their slit trenches. However, it was a comfort that they were being escorted by a section of the RUR snipers, whose Carrier they were there to recover and who were directing them to it. On approaching the Carrier, they were alarmed to find the words *'Crush the British Imperialists'* painted along its hull and its instrument panel stove-in. On reporting this back to the OC on their radio, a troop of Centurions was despatched, under the command of Capt Shackleton, 8 KRIH, to protect their ARV. Provided that another armoured vehicle or a stout tree-trunk was available to anchor the ARV, they could winch themselves out from any boggy paddy field and then tow the Carrier behind the ARV. Thus the recovery operation presented no great problem. Upon the arrival of the three Centurions, they positioned one of them as their anchor, while the other two lined their main armament up on a nearby village (probably full of those enemy soldiers who had possibly sabotaged the Carrier) to 'blast it from the face of the earth'. To Capt Shackleton's dismay however, he was ordered to withdraw from that position as soon as the recovery operation had been successfully completed.

Welcome to 'Windy Corner'

The second operation was the recovery of a Centurion that had shed its track, on a 300-yard stretch of road known to all as, 'Windy Corner'! Whether this was because of the strong winds which gusted along it, or because everybody who traversed along it was 'Windy' to do so, they never really wished to know, because that particular stretch of road came under constant enemy mortar and small-arms fire. But despite this activity hampering their attempts, they got a Hollebone Drawbar onto the Centurion to tow it, and its discarded track, to safety. This was accomplished by requesting the Centurion commander to lay a smoke screen about them by firing its own smoke canisters. Brian reversed at high speed from behind the shelter of a bluff towards them, the Hollebone Drawbar lying on top of the engine decking, ready for a quick coupling-up and getaway. The Centurion and its discarded track were soon back behind the shelter of the bluff, and its track then replaced, unhampered.

The third recovery operation was the evacuation of a Light Armoured Car to the nearest railhead, for back loading to REME Workshops. What was so memorable about this particular job was that they were ordered off the road by the MPs of a US Airborne Unit, awaiting the arrival of the Commanding General of the US 8th Army, Gen Mathew B Ridgeway. He himself was an ex-Paratrooper and his entourage was about to pass through. Being British, under such circumstances, they immediately 'put the kettle on' and invited the MPs to join in a 'cuppa'. The MPs little realized that their tea was 'Gunfire'. *(N.B. For anyone not in the know, Gunfire was tea 'laced' with Navy Rum, the well-known early morning cup-of-tea, traditionally served by officers to other ranks at Reveille on Christmas Day. Just how they came by a one-gallon stone-jar of neat Navy Rum is another story! Let it be sufficient to say that the British Army in Korea received a tablespoonful of Rum each day!)* After the General had passed, they and the MPs departed to their tented camp nearby, it being now too dark to proceed further. They were all slightly inebriated, the MPs at the controls of the ARV, and the ARV crew driving their Jeeps. Between them they managed to knock down the barrier-gate at the entrance to their camp, almost crushing the Korean sentry!

The following morning, after a very comfortable night's sleep in an oil-stove heated tent and a sumptuous breakfast of flapjacks with syrup, ham and eggs, and a seemingly endless supply of coffee, they ventured to ask, *"Could we get a refill of 'Gasoline' for the ARV?"* This would enable them to complete the mission and return to their unit. They were pleasantly surprised to see a Petrol Tanker pull-up beside their ARV and fill both fuel tanks in a couple of minutes! So much easier than having to 'hump' forty-gallon drums of petrol onto their engine-decking to fill-up through a funnel!

It was about this time that their Squadron moved further south from Seoul, across the Han River, to take-up a position some thirty miles away. Here they established their own tented camp and enjoyed a period of relaxation, playing football against teams from the Royal Navy anchored at Inchon. They reciprocated by accepting invitations to visit their Battleships, where they were able to enjoy hot showers, a film show and ship's food, with a bag of bread, freshly baked in the ship's bakery, to take back to camp with them. This made a most welcome change from months on hard-tack biscuits. It was also around this time that the ARV commanded by Brian needed a new engine and gearbox. So, he and his crew moved further south by railway flatcar to a REME Workshop, to exchange their ARV for another. They then took command of *'Battle Axe'*, a former ARV of 'B' Sqn 8 KRIH, returning to re-join 'C' Sqn 7 RTR on another flat-car

. On moving forward, they were assigned to support a US Regimental Combat Team (RCT) in its activities. These were units of about three-battalion strength, surprisingly commanded by a 'Lootenant (!) Colonel' rather than a Brigadier, but with every man an infantryman, without supporting units such as artillery, road transport, armour, etc. When a RCT was assigned a specific objective, its Commander would call upon whichever support units were at hand for him to accomplish that objective - it was 'his show'. This particular RCT Cdr was Lt Col John 'Iron Mike' Michaelis, a West Point graduate and who had been a protégé of Gen Dwight 'Ike' Eisenhower, when he was Commander-in-Chief (C-in-C) at Supreme Headquarters Allied Powers in Europe (SHAPE).

A lesson in the American command structure

There was one particular occasion that Brian will never forget! The RCT Cdr had called his first 'O' Group, to brief all officers and NCOs on that day's activities. As the crew carried out 'First Parade' Daily Routine Maintenance (while the kettle was boiling), the Radio Operator, Steve, who was 'netting-in' his radio up in the turret, shouted out, *"Sarge! They're calling for you."* Brian listened in and, sure enough, there it was, *"Bluebell Sun Ray Minor, report to Sun Ray, at the double!"* ('Bluebell' was the call sign for REME and 'Sun Ray Minor' a junior commander). Strange, thought Brian, as they were not normally required to attend 'O' Groups – surely battle tactics are not the stuff of ARV commanders? They were 'on net' to the Sqn Cdr, from whom all their orders purportedly came, and from no one else. However, he decided that he had better go and show his face.

As he approached, the Colonel, who was as ever immaculately turned-out whatever the weather, and surrounded by his officers and NCOs, glared at him. *"Sergeant! Did you hear a message at 0630 hours today, calling ALL Sun Ray Minors to an 'O' Group briefing?"* *"Yes, Sir!"* Brian replied. *"And are you a Sun Ray Minor?"* enquired the Colonel menacingly. *"Yes, Sir!"* again Brian replied, by now wishing that the ground would open and swallow him up. *"Well! Why did you not comply with that command?"* barked the Colonel. *"Well, Sir, in my Regiment ...."*, Brian began to explain. *"You are NOT in your Regiment NOW! You are in mine! And you will be the FIRST soldier to appear at all future GODDAM 'O' Groups!"* (Would even Errol Flynn ever have spoken like that to his men?).

"And, while we are on the subject of MY REGIMENT", the Colonel continued, *"I have observed that UN Soldiers are not paying compliments to my officers, the excuse being made that they are unable to distinguish the various ranks used in the United States Army. I am now going to tell you how to recognise the various badges of rank of my officers. And herein after, any soldier failing to salute any officer will answer to me. Now Gold is found lower in the ground than is Silver. Therefore, Gold badges are lower in rank than are Silver. One Gold Bar is a Second Lootenant and one Silver Bar is a First Lootenant. Two silver Bars is a Captain. Now, above the ground are the trees and the trees have leaves. Therefore, a Gold leaf is a Major and a Silver leaf, LIKE I'M WEARING, is a Lootenant Colonel. Now, above the trees are the Birds - the Eagle, the Silver Eagle. And that denotes a Full Colonel. And above the Birds, are the Stars - Silver Stars, and they are the Generals, one Star being a Brigadier General, two Stars a Major General and so on. AND DON'T YOU FORGET IT!"*

Brian always tried to be first to appear at all 'O' Groups thereafter, saluting every American officer with both hands, just to be sure! He has related this story to many American friends since then, including a former 'Lootenant' General with whom they worked in Saudi Arabia, some thirty years after the Korean War – and they all admitted to have never heard of the American officer ranks described like that! 'Lootenant' Col Michaelis went on to become a Brigadier General at SHAPE after the Korean War.

As the UN Forces moved north, towards Seoul, the Squadron occupied a position on the banks of the Han River at Yongdong-Po, a southern suburb of Seoul. For some unaccountable reason, Brian's crew found themselves and their ARV on a railway platform at Seoul railway station! Just them, no one else! Their orders had been to report to a US Signal Unit, housed in a building across from the station. As they walked across the square, hand-in-hand with Won (Two), their little Korean orphan, Won took them to a large dilapidated house that had been vandalised and looted. Won pointed to a sign over the doorway and then to an identical sign on his box of paints, his only treasured possession. On meeting-up with our Korean Intelligence Officer at a later occasion, Brian had it explained to him that the house Won had shown him had once been a fully equipped, modern private hospital. It had been owned by Won's parents, both of them surgeons, whom the North Koreans had shot in front of Won and his sister, before ransacking the hospital and destroying all the medical equipment. Brian still wasn't too sure what they were supposed to be doing on a station platform in a deserted city, reporting to an American Signal unit every hour, on the hour.

Shortly after this, Brian's crew was detached from 'C' Sqn and assigned to 'B' Sqn 8 KRIH, which was then camped in an orchard north of Seoul. This meant leaving the Korean orphan in the care of their 'B' Echelon until their return. They were not quite sure why 8 KRIH had not used their own REME ARV commanders and, come to think of it, what had happened to their REME colleague, 'Jack' Woodward, and his ARV? For the next few weeks, each Squadron of Hussars took fortnightly turns of duty. But not for them, as 'C' Sqn relieved 'B' Sqn, although they did enjoy the experience of serving with various Squadrons. They were particularly impressed with 8 KRIH's use of their SSM's tank to escort and protect their AFV. The SSM of 'C' Sqn was 'Jimmy' Marshall, a character well known in RAC circles because of his very distinctive voice, caused by a speech impediment. Wherever Brian's ARV went, 'Jimmy' Marshall's tank went too, answering to the 'call-sign', 'Bluebell Sun Ray Minor Able' - aid to the REME ARV commander.

They were not certain if it was a general rule for all units of the RAC, when travelling in 'line ahead' or 'line abreast', that there must always be one round 'up-the-spout' of their main armament. The story goes that, on one occasion, 'Jimmy' Marshall's gunner turned the turret through ninety degrees and lowered the main armament towards the ground, in preparation for cleaning the barrel.

He inadvertently stepped on the firing lever to send a round into the ground, which fortunately was not High Explosive (HE)! Now at about this same time, there was a very popular song going the rounds in the UK, the words of which were, *"I didn't know, the gun was loaded"*. Thus, as the Squadron later moved along the road, a voice would be heard over their radios, using 'Jimmy's distinctive voice, *"I didn't know"*, to be taken-up by another voice, in mimicry, *"The gun was loaded"*. This was shortly followed by 'Jimmy's outraged, unmistaken voice over the air, *"Are you taking the f*****g piss?"*, with the CO's voice, in an endeavour to bring things back under control, finally ordering, *"Use the proper procedure"*!

On the eve of St George's Day 1951, one of their Centurions had developed engine trouble, attended by the Squadron Mechanist Sergeant, with Brian standing-by with the ARV to lend a hand if necessary. The repair carried on into the hours of darkness, before they could return to base. It was at daybreak of the following day, 23rd April, that the Chinese spring offensive began, with hordes of Chinese infantry seemingly appearing from nowhere. For more than two weeks, the Squadrons had searched that particular area, with American aircraft carrying out reconnaissance flights, without a sight of the enemy. Yet there must have been several Divisions of Chinese infantry in that area at that very time. For Brian and the crew it was a sobering thought to reflect that, only a few hours before, just one Centurion tank and one Churchill ARV stood between several Divisions of Chinese and the UN Forces!

As their Squadron moved forward in support of the infantry, their progress was impeded by an American tank, believed to have belonged to the Philippines UN Force, which had caught fire and been abandoned by its crew. Brian's ARV, at the rear of the column, had stopped to lend assistance to a Centurion which had slipped from the road and shed one of its tracks. This was a simple enough task but, once again, their winch-rope was stretched across the only road, thus impeding the free movement of ambulances and other soft vehicles moving south. With both ends of the road being blocked, they were ordered to discontinue the recovery operation, for the time being. Eventually, during an appropriate lull in the movement of traffic, they were allowed to continue pulling the stranded Centurion back onto the road.

In the line of fire

On attempting to attach the winch-rope to the Centurion, they and Spud Murphy came under small-arms fire from the hills above them. Tracer bullets could be seen going towards Steve, their 'Wireless Op', sitting up in the turret, engrossed in reading a magazine and oblivious to the danger he was in! Calling up Jimmy Marshall on their set, they asked if he could see where the small-arms fire was coming from, to which came the reply, *"Do you think I'm blind?"* Promptly he placed a HE shell in amongst the enemy positions, scattering them in all directions and then opening-up with his own Co-axial MG. The enemy small-arms fire subsided for a while and Brian was able to get a line to the Centurion. He began to inch it out but, unfortunately, they were blocking the road once again, not only for the ambulances, now full of the wounded from their Brigade, but also for their returning Squadron, whose attempts to reach our infantry had to be aborted.

By this time, enemy infantry were within 300 yards of the ARV and they had come under enemy small-arms fire. The Hussar Lieutenant who commanded the 'ditched' Centurion brought his own Co-axial MG into play, as did Jimmy Marshall, acting as 'his shadow'. With a small band of their own withdrawing infantry manning the Bren Guns that are carried on top of the fixed turret, Spud Murphy and Brian then unhitched their winch-rope to get out of there! As the last tank up and the first tank out, what a 'Golden Opportunity' the Chinese would have if they could knock them out and block their only escape route.

As they sped along the road (at a top speed of eighteen miles per hour!), carrying about half a dozen of their infantry boys on the engine decking, they noticed several odd-looking soldiers, lying on the edges of the paddy fields, on each side of the road. They appeared to be throwing large stones at the passing vehicles. Suddenly, a large flame shot through the winch-rope opening at the bottom of their turret, level with the engine decking. It burned a large hole through Brian's tank over-suit, windproof clothing and battle-dress, leaving a very painful blister on his backside. It was then realized that these odd-looking characters were not at all friendly, but were in fact Chinese soldiers throwing grenades! One of these, a phosphorous grenade, had landed on their engine decking, with some of their infantry passengers taking the full blast and being severely burned about their faces and eyes.

The Chinese forces had apparently encircled 29 Bde, but how were the Allied forces supposed to distinguish the North Koreans from the Southern, the Koreans from the Chinese or, for that matter, from the UN Thai or Filipino soldiers? Apart from administering morphine injections from their First Aid Kits to the injured infantry on their tank, there was very little they could do for them until they got well away from the hostile forces. They were then able to hand-over their wounded men to the nearest FAP. The dead had been carried on their engine decking, covered by Aircraft Recognition Panels, until they could be placed in an appropriate area for later burial. At the end of the day, their Squadron re-assembled and laagered some miles further south. They established 'listening-post slit-trenches' around the outside of their laager perimeter, with Brian and his crew taking their turn for a one hour 'stag' in one of the 'listening posts', along with some of the remnants of the infantry units who were sheltering with them. The sound of battle raged about them and the flares lit up the night sky.

Brian can remember his Sqn Cdr (who was later to be awarded the Distinguished Service Order (DSO) for his part in the Imjin River Battle) telling them that, as they went to the 'listening-post', to whistle the refrain of a well-known English song. If they did this as they approached the laager at the end of their 'stag', it would rouse their relief. But, being unable to whistle through their dry and anxious lips, they waited in fear for a hail of 'friendly-fire' to greet them from the laager! They needn't have worried however, the whole Squadron had been roused and stood-by, for the last hour. They hadn't heard a sound from them, or, thank God from the enemy! As they moved further south, they were allowed to join their own Squadron of 7 RTR, for a welcome reunion with Won, their Korean orphan. But, within hours, along with the remnants of their Brigade, they were sent to Tokyo for a one-week spell of Rest and Recuperation (R&R). They to re-join their Squadron at Inchon, where they were accommodated in a former Health and Holiday Complex, complete with natural hot-spring baths.

R&R at the hot spring baths

Chapter 7

10 Infantry Workshop REME

November to December 1950

Every morning, the officers of 10 Inf Wksp REME breakfasted together in their unique marquee dining room with its extra thatched roof. Korea's climate varies from extreme cold in winter, with temperatures dropping at night to less than minus twenty degrees centigrade, to steamy sub-tropical heat in the summer. That thatched roof set this tent apart from all the others in the unit and its insulation qualities were a godsend. There were seven members in the mess, including the OC, who had spent much of WWII as a POW, some of it in the infamous Colditz Castle, where his engineering skills had been much in demand. The only regular, he was a quiet, reserved man who smoked a pipe. The two REME Captains were both short service officers. The Workshop Officer owned a racing *Bentley* that dated back to the early thirties and his main aim in life was to race it once more at Le Mans. The Administrative Officer (AO) liked to be known as 'The Adjutant'. He also liked gin but did not like women; somewhere down the line he had suffered a failed marriage. He delegated every job that came up to one of the two subalterns, usually Lt KL Webb. Not surprisingly, they didn't get on.

Charles – the misfit

Then there was Charles, the Officer-in-charge (OIC) of the RAOC section, responsible for providing all the spares that were utilised to keep the Brigade's transport on the road. As Jeep engines wore out at about seven thousand miles in Korea's dust - and most other parts just as quickly - he was a busy man; but Charles did not fit in. The REME officers were all southerners and engineers, but that did not make any difference to their Mess life. Charles came from Yorkshire and spoke with a broad accent but, worst of all, he had no taste refinement at all. He ate cheeses with apple pie! Now, the one thing that the Mess cook was good at cooking was apple pie and they had that every time apples came up with the rations. Thanks to the Americans, who normally never go short of anything in battle, six of them ate their apple pie with a generous helping of cream, while Charles had cheese with his. No amount of comment, ridicule or mirth could make the man see sense, it came up in every conversation. If they needed a butt, they had a ready-made one!

Charles differed from them in another way that no one had ever found reason to comment upon. One very, very cold morning six of them assembled for breakfast as usual, but there was no sign of Charles. Tent walls are thin and his tent was well within earshot. *"Come on Charles, hurry up, the porridge is getting cold."* Strangled mutterings from his tent did indicate some life, but still no Charles. *"Come on Charles, the bacon is getting cold"*, they all yelled, still no sign of him. They had all learned to eat quickly, as food transferred from the cookhouse, some twenty yards away, soon congealed in several degrees of frost and they were always ravenous - the Korean climate necessitates a lot of carbohydrate in winter.

Finally, with the toast, Charles appeared. He looked terrible, something seemed to have happened to his face. *"What is it Charles?"* they enquired. He raised his hand to hide his mouth and muttered out the reason. *"My bloody batman forgot to put my teeth on the stove when he woke me"*. They were convulsed with laughter. Charles had put his teeth in 'Steradent' each night and inevitably they had frozen into a solid block of ice, which had to be thawed out in the morning. They hadn't known until then and Charles never lived that down. A broken man, he remained with them for a few weeks until posted and they never heard of him again.

Page 31

THE FORGOTTEN PUNCH IN THE ARMY'S FIST — KOREA 1950-1953

Tent walls are very thin and don't offer much thermal insulation!

Christmas Day in Korea in 1952 started rather badly. As one of probably only twenty or so who wished to attend early communion, some miles away at Div HQ, Lt Webb walked down to the transport area to pick up his Jeep. It was about seven fifteen and bitterly cold. From the drivers' tent emerged a fully dressed, unshaven figure clutching a nearly empty bottle. He, one of our Scots, had obviously been celebrating all night. His eyes were so fogged that he probably did not recognise the officer, but he still represented authority in his red-rimmed eyes. With his left hand still clutching the bottle, he staggered closer and aimed a wild blow at Webb's head. *"You're a f***** b*****d"*, he yelled but, missing him by about a yard, the effort was too much and he fell over backwards as if pole-axed.

The normal ration of drink was somewhat exceeded that day. The *Daily Express*, as well as the NAAFI and at least one more out of PRI funds, had each contributed one large bottle of the Japanese *'Asahi'* beer per man. When added to the illicit hooch available from the locals (which blinded more than a few in the Div, as it contained methyl alcohol), and those bottles sent as presents from home or acquired from the NAAFI stores at Tokchon, there were all the ingredients for a disaster. Fortunately, they were a full ten miles from the front line.

As was the norm, Christmas lunch was to be served up by the officers and NCOs. The unit had one big mess tent and the cooks had done a sterling job on the mainly American rations. They had turkey, ham, sausages, vegetables and some enormous Christmas puddings. They were to be joined by CREME who was, as CO of all the REME troops in Comm Div, visiting as many units under his command as he was able to. But the meal was a disaster. Having their first day off in months, hardly a single man was anything other than outrageously drunk. Those who were serving the meal did their best and turned a blind eye to the collapsed figures and the uneaten platefuls of food. Every man had several bottles in front of him, by then mostly empty.

10 Infantry Workshop REME 5th November to 3rd December 1950.

But where was CREME? He had promised to drop in, giving his driver the day off so that he could enjoy his Christmas at Div HQ. So CREME drove his own Jeep himself. He turned in off the main road and approached the Workshop barrier. This normally rose as if automatically, always opened by an immaculately dressed sentry, who would salute as he passed. But not that day! CREME, Col Palmer REME, waited and waited. Then he impatiently sounded his horn, but still no response. Finally, in a fury, he got out of his Jeep to investigate. In the guard tent lay the guard, flat out on a couple of packing cases doing duty as a bed, head back, a bottle in his grasp and snoring loudly. Col Palmer, dead sober as he was, was none too pleased. The Workshop took a long time to live that episode down.

The Officers' Mess was perched on top of a small hill, overlooking a tiny Korean hamlet and its many paddy fields. The unit boundary, a single strip of barbed wire, provided no deterrent to the hungry local peasant looking for food from the mess or anything else he could steal. It was still winter and, in those tents, the double sleeping bags were very necessary. Temperatures at night dropped to less than minus twenty Centigrade. They had done what they could to improve their lot and the wooden crates that the *'Asahi'* beer came in, were pressed into service as floorboards. Feet could stick to the bare floor, as that froze solid.

Lt Webb's nervous night!

They were all armed of course but never bothered loading their .38" revolvers. Never, that is, until their OC woke one night to find a Korean rifling through his trousers! After that, things changed. A few nights later, Lt Webb woke to hear a noise in his tent. His immediate thought was that someone had come in. Two sleeping bags were very, very constricting and his torch and revolver were under the pillow for security reasons. Very slowly, and making as little noise as possible, he felt for both. No easy task as he was lying on his back and was certainly no contortionist. Finally he had both torch and revolver in his hands and managed to roll over sufficiently to be able to fire at the intruder. Now it is one thing to open fire in the heat of battle, but quite another to know that the moment you turn on your torch, you are very likely going to have to kill someone who is possibly armed and so near that you could probably touch him. REME officers, although receiving full infantry training at the Officer Cadet Training Unit (OCTU), did not expect to have to face that sort of emergency!

The adrenaline built up somewhat. Gritting his teeth, Webb turned on the torch and thrust out the revolver. Nothing! The tent was empty. With utter relief, he replaced the torch and revolver and went back to an uneasy sleep. Then, some time later, it happened again. This time there was **definitely** someone in the tent and again, he laboriously armed himself. Having a large chest, he was more than usually constricted by the sleeping bag, but finally made it. In spite of the cold, he had begun to sweat and was wringing wet. Once again he braved turning on the torch, ready to kill the intruder. Nothing! Again the tent was empty. This time sleep was slower coming. He really had heard something, had he not? Doubt s began to creep in until finally he fell into a fitful sleep.

There it was again! This time he was awake in a flash, both revolver and torch at the ready inside the sleeping bag with him. Slowly and silently he rolled over ready to fire. On went the torch and his eyes went at once to the cause. One of his beer case floorboards had a knothole in it and one of his airmail letters was being tugged down into the hole! It was the rustle of the paper that had woken him. He never did find that bloody mouse, but he, or more probably she, had shortened Lt Webb's life by several years. Drenched in sweat and heart still pounding, he slept no more that night!

Chapter 8

Advance to the north

The early engagements of 27 Infantry Brigade

September to November 1950

On September 16th 1950, American troops attacked in strength in the Taegu area. By September 18th, 24 US Div had crossed the Naktong River west of Taegu and was fighting its way north astride the Taegu-Seoul road. As part of these operations, 27 Inf Bde – under the command of 24 Div – left its defensive positions and moved north. With the crossing of the Naktong River, some five miles south of Waegwan, and the advance on Songju, a small town about seven miles to the west, this operation was designed to protect the left flank of the American advance.

Upon its arrival in Korea, 11 Inf Wksp was located just outside the town of Taegu, about six miles behind the Brigade. After off-loading a couple of vehicles, the advance party set off in the direction of Taegu via the east coast route. But they had to return, having been barred further progress by US Army MPs, who reported that the road had been cut and that the enemy was in possession of Kyongju. Back they went to Pusan, where the vehicles were being unloaded, and there followed a two-day move by road and rail to a riverbed that lay a mile south of Taegu. Here they established their first contact with 27 Bde, at which stage they were put in the picture and were finally able to obtain some maps of Korea. The Brigade Electrical and Mechanical Engineer (BEME) was able to brief them on the Brigade's technical problems and it was a case of down to work without further delay.

'The 88 Outfit'

Being located in the riverbed just off the main axis, the Workshop was of some interest to the Americans, whose appreciation of the arrival of 27 Bde seemed to be out of all proportion to its strength. Friendships quickly sprang up between Workshop members and the MP Coy of 24 Div, which shared the riverbed with them. Hereafter the Workshop was always known as 'The 88 Outfit' to this Company, '88' being the tactical number that was on a large double-sided unit sign, on the tallest jointed flagpole in Korea. Since camouflage did not exist, these flagpoles became landmarks. They were always carried by the advance party and, once erected at a new location, acted as a homing device not only for the unit but for its customers as well. There was a great deal of work to be done so that each day was like any other. From this grew the custom of flying the tactical flag on six days a week and the Corps flag on Sundays. The Corps flag very soon became known as the 'Sunday flag' and was often the only reminder that it actually **was** Sunday. *(This flag is now in the Corps Museum at Arborfield.)* During the stay of over two weeks at Taegu, there was an opportunity for re-planning men and equipment dispositions for move purposes and to shake down into a really mobile role.

Shortly before moving on to Waegwan, the 'Aldershot shelter' was being lowered (to ironic cheers) when the President of South Korea called in to see them, accompanied by several of his ministers. All were dressed in US fatigue dress except for one splendid looking Aide-de-Camp (ADC). Introductions were made and the President, Syngman Rhee, said how grateful he was that British troops had now arrived. He left to more cheers, this time they really were intended for him and he became known as 'Signalman' Rhee from that time on! Before finally moving, the motorcycles, 7.5-ton trailers and the Aldershot shelter were all back-loaded to Pusan as being

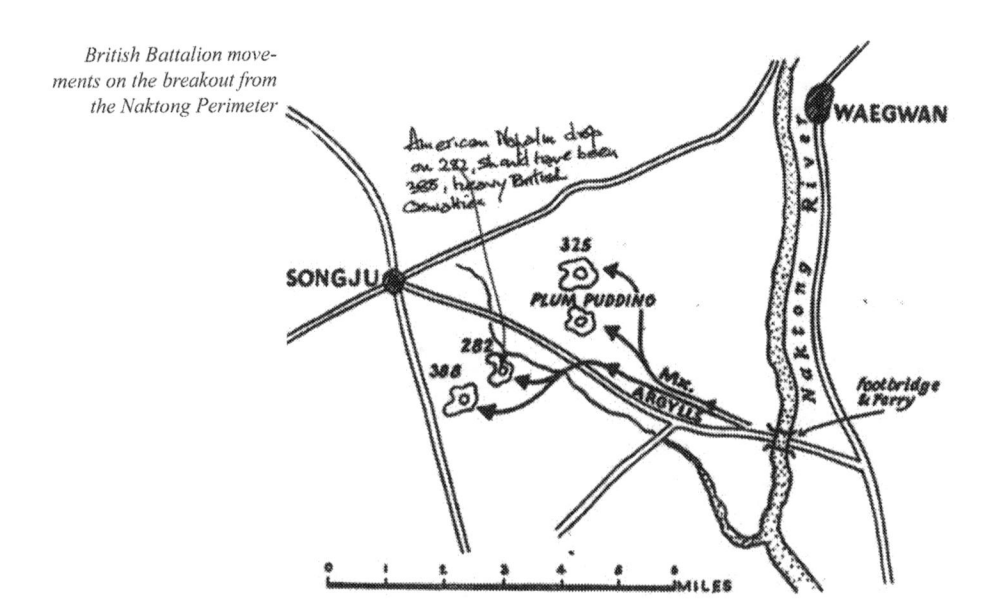

ADVANCE TO THE NORTH — SEPTEMBER TO NOVEMBER 1950

British Battalion movements on the breakout from the Naktong Perimeter

unsuitable for use in the conditions being encountered. During this period, more US troops were coming in, the position was being stabilized and, in some sectors, their perimeter was being pushed out. It was about this time that a Platoon from one of the Battalions suffered several fatal casualties.

Protected by troops of 24 American Div here, a river crossing took place on September 21st, led by the Middlesex by way of an insecure footbridge. The transport was ferried at first and, when this broke down, manhandling of ammunitions and heavy weapons had to be resorted to. The Battalions lost a few men from shellfire during that perilous passage across the river. But, by the early hours of September 22nd, both Battalions were across and ready to attack the enemy, now known to be holding the high ground on either side of the road to Songju. The advance began at dawn, led by the Middlesex on the right of the road. The ASH followed and later deployed to the left of the road. Supported by two American tanks, a Platoon of 'B' Coy of the Middlesex soon captured 'Plum Pudding' hill. This was followed by a successful attack by 'D' Coy on Pt 325 ('Middlesex Hill'). This attack was also supported by American tanks and by the Battalion's own machine guns and mortars, but not by artillery fire. The Battalion then occupied the whole feature and heavy losses had been inflicted on the enemy at very little cost.

Meanwhile, the ASH had advanced up the road, preparing to attack Pt 282 before a further advance towards Songju, supported by five American tanks and a battery of American artillery. 'A' Coy captured an intermediate feature on the afternoon of September 22nd, while 'B' Coy, along with 'C' Coy and after a night advance, occupied the hill by 0630 hrs on September 23rd. 'C' Coy, on the left, was then ordered to secure Pt 388, but the enemy reacted strongly. The Battalion was shelled and mortared and enemy infantry began to move in strength left around the rear of all three Companies. With the steepness of the hill and a lack of men to act as carriers, a combination of heavy enemy fire and the slow supply of ammunition, together with the evacuation of wounded, things proved very difficult. The Second-in-Command (2IC) was successful in taking forward a party with additional ammunition and stretchers. However, the situation continued to worsen and

Page 35

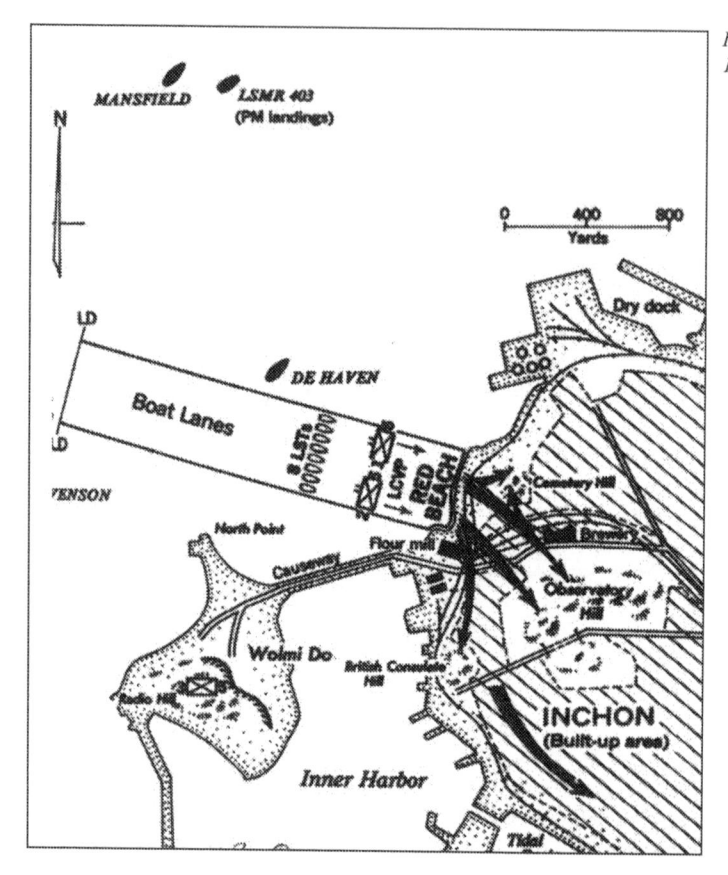

*Red Beach Assault
15th September 1950.*

an air strike on Pt 388 was arranged. This was carried out soon after noon by three American planes but, unfortunately, their napalm firebombs fell on 'B' and 'C' Companies on Pt 282, instead of on Pt 388. The pilots were under the impression that the enemy had already overrun Pt 282. Together with the earlier casualties, this action reduced the fighting strength of the two Companies to about forty uninjured personnel.

Almost at once, the enemy counter-attacked, resulting in a temporary withdrawal from the crest of Pt 282. The situation was quickly restored, however, when Maj Muir, who had taken command of both Companies, gathered some thirty men and led them back. Fierce, close-quarter fighting followed, in which Maj Muir showed the greatest courage and resourcefulness. He was eventually mortally wounded and later posthumously awarded the Victoria Cross (VC) - a very gallant officer. There were barely twenty men left unwounded in the two Companies and it proved impossible to hold Pt 282. At about 1400 hrs, Lt Col Neilson reluctantly gave permission for the withdrawal of the remnants of both Companies. In this engagement, the ASH lost two officers and eleven other ranks (ORs) killed, with four officers and sixty-nine ORs wounded.

Pursuit and Advance to the Yalu 7th - 26th October 1950

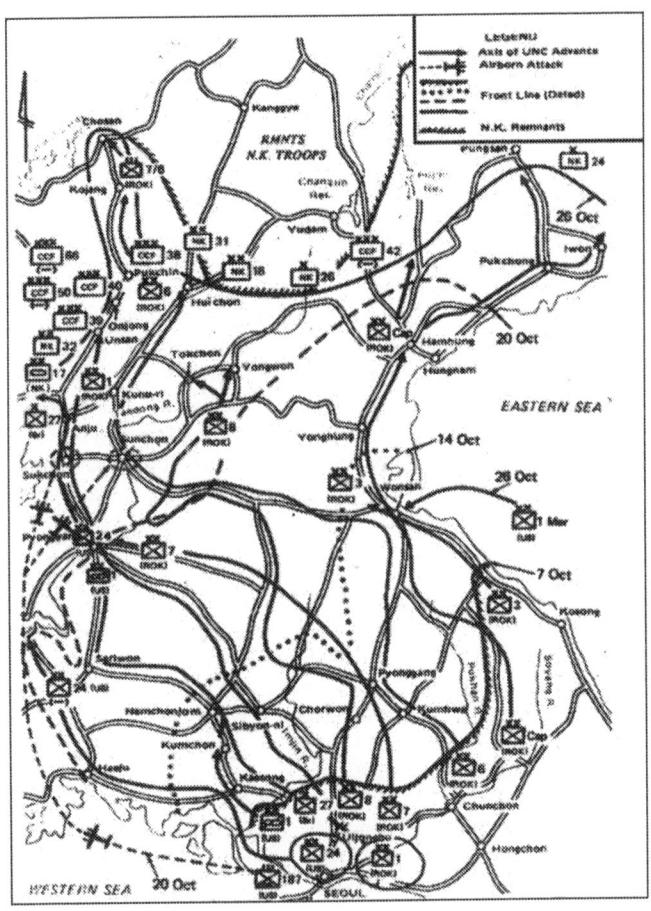

Across the 38th Parallel

On the 27th September, 27 Bde moved to the outskirts of Songju, which the Americans had by then captured. As the Brigade moved forward, 11 Inf Wksp moved to Waegwan and set up a repair facility, which lasted in this location until October 9th. Just before their next move, the RAOC OFP that had been set up in Singapore started to trickle in. On the 28th September, 24 Div occupied Taejon. The Eighth Army was now on the move north, where it joined X Corps, which had landed at Inchon on the western coast, reaching the outskirts of Seoul on September 20th. By September 30th 1950, all of Korea south of the 38th Parallel was in UN hands. With this success, Gen MacArthur was faced with a political and strategic problem of the utmost importance. Should he remain on the old frontier of the 38th Parallel or continue in pursuit of the enemy and thereby risk Chinese participation in the struggle? The General considered that Chinese intervention was unlikely so long as his own force did not go right up to the Yalu River. And so, supported by a resolution of the UN General Assembly, MacArthur decided to continue the advance and, on October 9th, UN forces crossed the 38th Parallel.

The Forgotten Punch in the Army's Fist — Korea 1950-1953

September 8th brought the arrival of 3 Btn RAR in Korea. On October 1st, it joined 27 Bde, which was immediately renamed 'The 27 British Commonwealth Infantry Brigade'. The arrival of this Australian unit, up to full fighting strength and well equipped, was most welcome, for it gave the Brigade the tactical scope, which had been lacking with only two Battalions. On October 4th a message was received, indicating that the whole Brigade was to be flown to Kimpo airfield, near Seoul. After relief in the line, a MT move of twenty-five miles, over very bad roads, was made to Taegu airfield. Here, one American and one British Staff Officer supervised the enplaning of 2,000 men. Brig Coad later recorded that not a single piece of paper was written and that the move was accomplished without a casualty or hitch of any kind.

On October 6th, fighting personnel of the Brigade had deplaned at Kimpo, with the transport following by road. The Brigade remained in the area of Kimpo airfield for a few days awaiting its transport, before moving north by road. Between the 10th and 13th of October, 11 Inf Wksp REME moved forward, through Taejon, Suwon and Seoul, to an area two miles north-west of Kaesong and to within a mile of the 38th Parallel, the international boundary between North and South Korea. While settling into this location, a Bde HQ representative came along with the request for them to move back, as the Bde Cdr preferred to have his infantry lead the advance rather than the REME Workshop! So, after a mere four hours, their shortest stay anywhere, they moved back to a riverbed south of Kaesong.

The fighting cook!

The Workshop stayed in this location from 13th to 17th October and it was whilst at this location that one of their Army Catering Corps (ACC) cooks, Pte Harwood, went absent. He was to give himself up six months later, having been slightly wounded. In evidence, it was found that he had absented himself in order to 'see some action'. He had gone forward and 'attached himself' to 1 Cavalry Div, professing to be a Canadian who had hitchhiked to Korea. He was thus attached to a Combat Platoon. He was kitted out by them and carried on as a Rifleman throughout the advance and the subsequent withdrawal. He was well reported on by the American officers and NCOs with whom he served. At his subsequent court-martial in April 1951, he was found 'not guilty' of desertion but 'guilty' of absence without leave. He was awarded twenty-eight days detention, which was promptly remitted by the confirming officer.

On October 11th, the Workshop advanced to Kaesong, now under command of American 1 Cavalry Div. On the 15th, instructions were received for a forward movement, in conjunction with 1 Cavalry and 24 Div. The role of 27 Bde was to advance from Kaesong, through 7 American RCT and then to lead the Div up the Sariwon-Pyongyang road. The objective was Sariwon, thirty-four miles distant and reputed to be an important NKA military training centre. For two days the advance continued without opposition, each Battalion in turn acting as vanguard.

By October 17th, the ASH, who were leading and being supported by American tanks, encountered some slight resistance a few miles south of Sariwon. This was quickly overcome and the Battalion spent the nights of the 17th and 18th October in the town. 3 Btn RAR advanced through Sariwon before dark, taking up positions on the northern outskirts. As darkness fell on the town, which had been heavily bombed, small parties of the enemy attempting to escape to the north were captured. In total, some 2,000 prisoners, who had blundered into UN positions, were taken. Later, some 125 of the enemy were killed by the ASH in the town. On the 18th, the Middlesex cleared the town and passed through. It is estimated that another 2,000 prisoners had been taken and about 150 enemies killed. The Brigade moved forward again, with 3 RAR leading. In order to keep up with the Brigade, 11 Inf Wksp moved forward to Hwangju and remained in that location till October 21st.

ADVANCE TO THE NORTH — SEPTEMBER TO NOVEMBER 1950

The previous day, South Korean troops had entered Pyongyang from the east, followed later by the leading Battalion of 27 Bde, the Middlesex, from the west. The Brigade was placed under the command of 24 American Div and ordered to lead the advance on Chongju, via Sinanju. It was hoped to reach the former place by the evening of the 21st. A further move by 11 Inf Wksp brought them to Yongyu, where they stayed until October 23rd.

After the capture of the North Korean capital, a further advance was not anticipated, but nevertheless, the forward movement continued. On October 21st, the Brigade crossed the River Taedong at Pyongyang. Some delay was caused by congestion with competing American troops but, after meeting slight opposition, the leading unit of ASH approached Yongyu. 24 Div had not crossed the river, so Brig Coad decided to halt for the night south of the town. Some American airborne troops were in the northern outskirts of Yongyu, so the ASH made contact with them, before taking up position about 1,000 yards south of the town. At about 2230 hrs, a furious battle started in the town, between the Paratroops and North Koreans. The encounter lasted most of the night, with the ASH taking some casualties.

At first light on October 22nd, 'A' and 'C' Companies of the ASH moved in to clear the town, while the Middlesex took up defensive positions on the northern outskirts. At this juncture, 'C' Coy of 3 Btn RAR became involved in a sharp engagement of the kind that had come to be associated with Australian infantryman. They were moving slightly in advance of the Middlesex. The advance continued, with Sinanju being entered on October 23rd. The Middlesex then made an unopposed assault crossing of the formidable Chongchon River. Difficulties were met, owing to the tidal nature of the river, with craft being carried seawards or inland, according to the tide. The Australians gained a bridgehead across the next river, the Taeryong, where they were reinforced by the ASH, who had crossed at Pakchon. The Middlesex struck west towards Kasan, where they came up against strong opposition. A Battalion attack, supported by US artillery and an air strike, was successful in bringing the Battalion to the outskirts of Kasan.

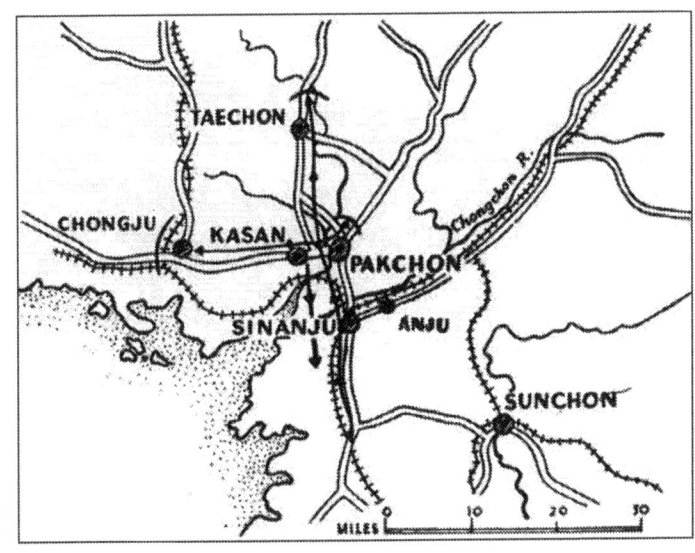

Chongchon River crossing

The Workshop had followed the Brigade, stopping several times for three or four days to clear up the outstanding vehicle repairs. It arrived at Sinanju on October 27th, thus between the 9th and 27th, 11 Inf Wksp had moved eight times and advanced approximately 300 miles from Waegwan to Sinanju.

On October 29th, the Australians and ASH passed through to the west, the Australians encountering very heavy opposition just east of Chongju. The enemy opposing the Australians occupied a mountain pass, held by well dug in infantry, supported by tanks concealed in woods and undergrowth. An attack by 'D' Coy, supported by an air strike and American tanks, succeeded in opening the road. 'D' Coy, now supported by 'A' Coy and the fire of American 155mm guns, continued the advance against stiff opposition. By nightfall, they were on the high ground overlooking Chongju. The following day, the ASH entered Chongju, while the RCT of the American 24 Div passed through to lead the advance. 27 Comm Bde now went into reserve for the first time in eight weeks; for the past two weeks it had led the advance, to within forty miles of the Manchurian border. That evening, the Brigadier was ordered to send a Battalion to Taechon. The Middlesex were detailed but, owing to a shortage of transport, the move took two days, as the troops had to be sent in relays.

By the end of October, the NKA had not only been defeated, but also completely destroyed. It was no longer an effective fighting force and it appeared unlikely that it could be resuscitated. At its peak, the NKA had numbered about 350,000 men. Of these, 145,000 became POWs and about 150,000 were estimated to have been killed by the end of October. It seemed that the campaign was over and, even in the highest quarters, the talk was of being *"home by Christmas"*. That optimism resulting from success was, however, short-lived. It was, of course, known that large Chinese forces were concentrated in Southern Manchuria and the possibilities of their participation in Korea had not been overlooked. This was not considered very likely, however, as long as the UN forces remained south of the Yalu. The deployment of the Chinese troops was regarded as a threat, but no more than that.

The Chinese enter the conflict

The first reports of Chinese troops in Korea came from local inhabitants in the north, through agents to the American Intelligence service. In the meantime, X Corps, which landed at Inchon and captured Seoul, moved by sea to the east coast, then advanced through the mountainous Choshin Reservoir area towards the Manchurian border. During these operations, 41 Royal Marines Independent Commando was attached to X Corps. The last days of October brought reports from patrols, aircraft and local inhabitants that a strong Chinese force was converging on Taechon. It was apparent, if reports of their strength were correct, that the Brigade would be in a precarious position, should the enemy by-pass Taechon and make a drive on Pakchon from the west or the northeast. A withdrawal to Pakchon, or even to behind the Chongchon River, was clearly indicated.

After the occupation of Chongju, 27 Bde had come into reserve on October 30th. Some supplies of equipment and clothing, including battledress, had arrived and were issued. But the Chinese threat sharply ended this brief rest period. On October 31st, acting on orders, the Bde Cdr moved the Middlesex to Taechon, forty-two miles distant. The next day the rest of the Brigade withdrew to Pakchon and then the ASH moved north to join the Middlesex at Taechon, a very isolated position some twenty-five miles from any other friendly troops. Here, for the first time, the bodies of some dead Chinese soldiers were found.

Chapter 9

The advance of 11 Infantry Workshop REME to Sinanju

During the long advance, the Brigade transport had been severely pounded and a lot of work was required to put things right. This was the Workshop's first priority, but it was accompanied by problems that were aggravated by a shortage of some essential spares. At this time, the nearest REME support behind them was in Hong Kong, although some spares were being sent over to Pusan via Japan. Despite the fact that American railway engineers were doing a fine job of repairing the track and bridges, the line was only working up to Munsan. About twenty-five miles north of Seoul, the blown bridge over the Imjin River prevented further progress without a major repair effort. This being the case, 27 Bde had to establish a railhead at Munsan, by which they could receive and sort out Brigade supplies from the trainloads of stores arriving there. This task fell to 11 Inf Wksp and became the responsibility of the OIC RAOC Stores Section, Capt RK Hind. A small detachment of some of his staff, plus the few REME tradesmen that could be spared, established themselves at the Munsan station. There were guerrilla activities in the area, but a lot of it was by a rather hungry local population foraging for food.

Thus it became a major operation, as Capt Hind not only had to organise the activities of a mixed bag of nationalities, but to take control of the station and also run its defences. At one time, he was commanding over a hundred men of about seven different nationalities, a command that amazingly appeared to be acceptable to all. In their location, about a mile south of Sinanju, they gradually caught up with the work but by now the weather was getting quite cold and the Brigade was still in 'Jungle Green' tropical kit. However, there were some very good scroungers in the unit so, gradually, American-pattern winter kit began to appear and, by the time the official issue eventually arrived, most men had acquired the essential 'parka' jacket and windproof trousers. The winter hats with ear and neck flaps, as well as a turndown peak, were especially welcome; but where to put the cap badge was a minor problem!

Captain RA Newman, 2IC and AO to 11 Inf Wksp, had given some thought to the move prior to leaving Hong Kong. His Army service had started long ago in 1928, during which time he had served in India, on the Khyber Pass area. That location could also be cold when it liked! His early training saw five years apprenticeship as an Armourer and he remembered problems that raised their heads then, with firing-pins in MGs breaking because of the intense cold. Thus he had made a visit to the RAOC Stores section in Hong Kong. Here, he

Moving into a dry river bed location

Page 41

"The 88 Outfit"
in a Riverbed location just off the Main Supply Route

had obtained a hand full of firing-pins for the *Vickers* MG, taking them back to the Armourers' shop, where he instructed that they were to be annealed and re-tempered. This process was repeated until finally annealing to a 'dark straw' colour, then re-tempering proved to be the most satisfactory solution when retried in a weapon. These pins then travelled to Korea with the Captain.

As the Korean winter intensified and technical visits to Battalions were made, Capt Newman found their defences suffering, because the *Vickers* MGs were out of action with broken firing-pins. He had the Battalion Armourers remove those damaged items and replaced with the re-tempered ones. They proved to be satisfactory and an order was made that all firing-pins were to be immediately modified in a similar manner throughout the Brigade.

Thirty miles from China

As previously explained, 'The 88 Outfit' was the name given to the unit by the Americans. The most recent advances had put the Brigade about thirty miles from the Yalu River and the border with China. As the Workshop was now a little too far behind the Brigade, it was planned to move to an area near Taechon. The officer who normally went on the advance party did a recce and reserved a suitable site for the Workshop to move on about November 29th, a time at which it was thought they would be lightly loaded with vehicle repair work. However, the South Korean Divisions in the centre of the front were already reporting that some of the enemy they were running up against were Chinese. Almost overnight, this turned into a full-scale attack by the Chinese.

As this news was received, they had a visit from Brig Brodie, Cdr of 29 Inf Bde Group, which was in the process of landing at Pusan from the UK. He was provided with transport and escorted to Bde HQ. It appears that the Workshop created quite an impression with him because, immediately on his return to his Brigade forming-up area, he arranged for an officer (Capt Husband) from 10 Inf Wksp to visit and stay a few days with them. In late November, being on American rations, they celebrated their 'Thanksgiving Day' with a roast turkey dinner and all the trimmings, a lavish spread, which their cooks prepared and served as is normal at the British Christmas.

With the arrival of 29 Bde in Korea, it was the intention that 27 Bde would return to Hong Kong; in fact loading tables had already been prepared and provisional dates for embarkation at Inchon had been decided. This was one of the reasons why no provision, for the issue of UK pattern winter clothing to 27 Bde, had been made and was why they started with the US pattern. Needless to say, the entry of the Chinese into the campaign made the departure of 27 Bde from the theatre of operations quite impossible.

Chapter 10

29 Brigade Group & 10 Infantry Workshop REME

November 1950 to March 1951

During November 1950, the UK reinforcements had started to arrive; indeed that month would see a considerable force landing on the shores of far-distant Korea. They came in a steady stream: 8 KRIH, 1 Btn RNF, 1 Btn Gloucesters, 1 Btn RUR, 45 Fld Regt RA, 55 Field Sqn RE, an Ambulance Car Company of the Royal Army Service Corps (RASC), 10 Inf Wksp REME and their supporting Arms - RAOC, RASC, REME, R Sigs, RMP, ACC and many more. They all disembarked from the troopships, HMTS *'Empire Pride'* and HMTS *'Empire Windrush'* and the SS *'John Star'*, carrying some of their transport too. There were several other ships, mainly carrying equipment and vehicles.

Brian Worthington – 'the REME bloke'

Amongst those from the *'Windrush'* was Brian Worthington, an 'ex-boy' Vehicle Mechanic (VM) and attached to the Gloucesters' Mortar Pln for his sins. He was later to find out that the 'REME bloke' was rather taken for granted, in that he was expected to know all about petrol cookers, the 19, 39 and 88 radio sets and field telephones. He would also be able to stand in for any member on the 3" mortar, be in command of the Pln HQ Bren-gun and also take turns on the nightly one-hour guard stags. On top of all this, he was available to 'stand to' from dawn to dusk and cook the Pln HQ compo rations - and all this before they even sailed for Korea!

That day arrived and the sea trooping started, with all its shipboard routines. However, a slight variation took place when they reached the Suez Canal. On board was a young Captain, now today better known by the name of Gen Sir Anthony Farrar-Hockley. As its Adjutant, he had decided that it would be a good idea for his Battalion of Gloucesters to march along the canal road for exercise, as the ships only moved at about 5 mph whilst on the Canal. Most of the young soldiers, who had never been away from the UK, grew up quickly in their visits to the 'ports of call', the ship's first indication of nearing Korea was the smell in the air, still twelve hours out and they could 'smell' it.

His Majestys Troop Ship the Empire Windrush

The Forgotten Punch in the Army's Fist — Korea 1950-1953

On disembarkation, the Battalion moved north by train, leaving its drivers and VMs to collect, service and then drive the vehicles to join the Battalion somewhere in the north of Korea. This drive took three days, using the same main supply route (MSR) along which the Americans had recently made their rapid advance into the Yalu River border area. As they had pushed forward, little thought was given to NKA stragglers left in the hills and they were by passed. Unfortunately, many of these 'stragglers' then became guerrillas, who constantly harassed the road transport and made night guard a very creepy experience.

During the journey, the destroyed villages and towns, with burnt out tanks and trucks pushed to the roadside, brought home to them the fierceness of the fighting that had gone on. They found the Battalion in a small valley about twenty miles south of Pyongyang, with orders to clear up the stragglers of the NKA. Brian Worthington rejoined the Mortar Pln as they were digging in, but this came to a sudden stop when they realised they were digging into a mass grave of civilian clothed men, women and children. These unfortunates had obviously been shot and put into the grave - but by which side? With no way of knowing, they hastily covered up the grave again and moved further up the valley.

Next day, they loaned one of the Battalion rifle companies six of their carriers for a fast patrol but, within half an hour, the leading carrier blew up on an anti-tank mine. The patrol was ambushed, taking several casualties, two killed and the one carrier destroyed. Nobody had told Brian about this at Arborfield! Before they could recover the carrier, the Battalion started to move north to a position on the Chong Song River. During the journey, their 3-tonner QL transfer-box disintegrated. Brian suspected that the driver had deliberately abused the transmission, so that he would be sent back to 10 Inf Wksp. The incident left them with only a 15-cwt for soft transport and one carrier. With the one 3-tonner wrecked and their motorcycles left in Pusan, having been considered 'useless', Brian's charges were getting fewer, as no replacements were forthcoming.

The nights were now so cold that their turns on guard were reduced to a one-hour period. They were detailed to keep in pairs and remain in close contact. As well as watching for the enemy, they were to watch one another for signs of frostbite or falling asleep. On one such stag, Brian's partner, known to one and all as 'Jonah', swore he knew that the CQMS carried two water bottles on his webbing, both filled with issue rum. So, with the stealth that would have earned full marks in training, they crept up to the 3-ton *Bedford*. Brian was to quietly open the door, while Jonah was to grab the webbing. The door handle was gently pressed down and the door eased open. Jonah duly grabbed the webbing and pulled but, to their alarm, out tumbled the CQMS who was still wearing the webbing! They jumped back as he started shouting, *"Stand to! Stand to!"* at the top of his voice. And then, to really put the 'fat in the fire', the CSM, who had been sharing the cab as a 'cushy billet', leapt out of the other side of the cab, also shouting the alarm.

The ultimate then happened of course, because, as the CSM jumped out, he grabbed for his Sten-gun, which snagged and fell to the ground. Of course, as Sten-guns were apt to do, it immediately fired! The commotion had to be seen to be believed, with the Company dashing about in the dark to their 'Stand To' positions, a few more shots at 'moon shadows', then Battalion on the Net wanting the latest situation report (Sitrep). Thus Jonah's and Brian's hopes for a drop of rum caused a thousand men to stand to in the freezing cold, lose their valuable sleep, and a certain amount of panic at HQ. For days they expected at least to be lynched, but it passed off with only the two of them knowing the truth of the epic 'Battle of Chong Song'!

They moved steadily north without further incident until they came to a river, which they believed to be the Manchurian border. Here they dug in on the south bank, near a pontoon bridge built by American Army Engineers. Everybody knew that, because a very large signboard said so, in very large print! It was supposed to be the first major 'Air Lifted Bridge', but nearby was a similar bridge, with a small notice board announcing *"All in a days work - Royal Engineers"*!

Brian was getting used to his new life in an infantry role, *"Move up, Dig in, Test weapons, Range mortars, Stand to, Stand down, Brew up at all opportunities"*.

The cold was a killer, it numbed the body and mind, seizing up automatic weapons, tearing off ones skin, if it contacted bare metal, and made the normal bodily functions something of a master performance! Hammer heads shattered, tyres went down and, would you believe, only armoured vehicles qualified for an issue of anti-freeze. Because it was in such short supply, the 'soft skin' vehicles had to be started up every half-hour or so, until enough ethylene glycol was eventually 'liberated' from the Yanks.

From advance to retreat

So here they were, waiting for MacArthur's 'big push to Peking', covering the crossing point, while armoured patrols went over to scout their front. Then suddenly the mood changed, the Chinese were coming, apparently millions of them (well somebody had seen at least a dozen), but they moved fast and that was the start of 'The REAL Panic'. A returning Centurion of the 8 Hussars got stuck on the north side of the river and was abandoned just before the 'World's first air-lifted bridge' became airborne once again, as it was blown up! For three days they watched attempts to destroy the tank by artillery and air strikes, as it seems it was still on the 'secret list'. By now all sign of American and South Korean forces had disappeared in the 'great race south'. It is believed that the SKA won that race by a short head – but then, of course, they were fitter!

Brian and his mates still sat, all peaceful and looking north, awaiting the next orders, as was their wont. Eventually that word came, *"Move south"*. The withdrawal was to be through 27 Bde, who would themselves then retreat through 29 Bde, who were covering the rear of the UN Eighth Army. But still no Chinese, only plenty of rumours. So the 'Order of Retreat' (sorry, 'strategic withdrawal') was set and looked like taking them back to Pusan. It was the Yanks and all and sundry well in the lead, then 27 Bde and 29 Bde alternating. Within 29 Bde itself, it was the RNF, the RUR and the Gloucesters alternating. To the rear of the Gloucesters came Support Coy with Rear Pln, with their 3" Mortars, in the last vehicle, in pride of place to pick up stragglers.

"The poor bloody REME fitter! No matter how hard he tried to explain about REME, how the Corps was of service troops, not fighting troops; how difficult it would be to replace him, how much it had cost to train him; 'boy soldier' just setting out on a long career, etc, etc. It all made no difference, he was to just sit in the last Carrier, with a Bren-gun mounted, looking back along the road and, if anything breaks down, just jump out and fix it! Then, and only then, would he be allowed to catch up with the convoy!" These were Brian's immediate thoughts. Following that, Brian thought it showed either what remarkable faith the 'Swedes' (Gloucesters) had in the REME types, or that they just bloody expendable! Anyway, it turned out to be an uneventful journey really, to another riverbank position, just north of Pyongyang.

Then it was *"Dig in, Range weapons, Brew up"* - standard procedure, with a couple of days to re-fuel and service the vehicles. They got news that a supply dump at the Pyongyang railhead was being prepared for demolition, so a few of the blokes went to see what, if anything, could be saved. Soon they were back, highly excited. The dump was absolutely massive, with anything and everything in it. So they all rushed back with the first few, leaving only a few guards behind them. What a sight! Apparently, the Yanks had been rushing up supplies as fast as they could, ever since Pyongyang had been taken, ready for MacArthur's big push to Peking, no doubt. And now, there it was, theirs to take before it was destroyed. The American demolition team was already at work and in a great hurry to get the task completed.

The Yanks couldn't understand the British desire to grab what they could, it would only slow them down, they said. The dump was like a small town of terraced houses in rows, but the rows were not houses, but great mounds of winter clothing, sugar, butter, tinned meat, beans, tea, coffee, milk, petrol, even arms and ammunition. After initially trying to grab everything at once, they calmed themselves down and found vehicles, *GMC, Dodge, Studebakers, Chevrolets*, Jeeps - just *"Help yourselves"* they were told and this they did. Drivers were trained on the spot, and drove back to their positions in second gear. Then they looked at it all, their ill-gotten gains, and wondered what could they do with it? Nothing really, it was just as the Yanks had said, it would get in their way and slow them down. Reality set in, so they stowed what they could and destroyed the rest, at least they were now well dressed and would in future be over fed! Later that same day an order came from Brigade, supposed to be from 'Brodie' (the Bde Cdr) personally - *"Get rid of all surplus vehicles, there is not enough petrol for a vehicle each".*

Bringing up the rear

Soon the order came to move south once again, using the same order of march, with Brian at the rear. One bit of excitement - Pyongyang was ablaze, the engineers had destroyed everything that may have been of use to the enemy but, somehow, everybody had missed the fuel dump at the airfield. It was then suggested that the drums contained jet fuel, similar to paraffin, and should be set alight by them as they passed, last in the column, by firing tracer rounds into them. Of course someone had got it wrong again, it was not jet fuel, but high-octane aviation fuel. It made a wonderful sight as the fire took hold and forty-gallon fuel drums leaped into the air before exploding into a display that Guy Fawkes would have been proud off. Weeks afterwards, Brian was to read an article, he thinks it was by reporter Arthur Helliwell in a Sunday newspaper, describing the evacuation of blazing Pyongyang, amid the crash of mortar bombs and the rattle of small arms fire!

Brian didn't think there was an enemy soldier within thirty miles of them, why should the enemy bother; they only had to follow at a safe distance and pick up the booty! Now, the main thing was just to get south in as orderly manner as possible. Just to keep going and, if anything breaks down, either fix it quick or tow it behind. This despite the fact that the roadside was already covered with abandoned American vehicles and supplies, pushed aside to keep the road clear. In true 'Brit' style, the Gloucesters didn't leave a single vehicle or piece of equipment behind, thinking that they would probably end up paying for it! Brian did see one 3-tonner of their MT section off the road, burned out, he learned later that a phosphorous grenade had accidentally been set off and burned the truck before it could be saved.

Refugees were now becoming a major problem, walking and carrying what they could save on their heads and backs. They would walk 'off the road' wherever they could, but getting back on and causing blockages where the road was the only footpath available. Of course everyone knew the pecking order of a Korean family – Granddad first, then Dad, followed by the sons, Mother and finally daughters. But watch out when the girls are sent out in the lead, the path is probably mined!

The endless trail of refugees, passing an abandoned anti tank gun, slightly the worse for wear.

Their next stop was Seoul, on the northern side of the Han River, in the remains of an agricultural college. Here they made a stunning find - potatoes, one of each species, all still mounted in their glass display cases. Out came the Dixies, fires were soon got going, a tin of bacon was opened for the fat and the spuds were soon transformed into 'chips'. These were the first they had tasted since the troopship. Although the potatoes were soft and rubbery, the chips tasted just wonderful. A pity though, no bread and butter, in fact they had not had any bread either, since leaving the troopship.

Their joy at sleeping inside a building, albeit with its roof full of holes, courtesy of the American Air force, was short lived - next day they found themselves dug in, in a graveyard just north of the city! They spent a pleasant Christmas in amongst the burial mounds, with lots of extra rations - rum, *Asahi* beer, tinned turkey and Christmas pudding (which was really compo ration rich cake mashed up). Brian's contribution was to make the baking tins out of old 'hardtack' biscuit tins. Being 'the REME bloke', you must be an expert in the tin bashing field, according to the infantry mind. Anyway, a good time was had by all and, for once, all of Support Coy was together again, instead of being split up in support of various Rifle Companies. Higher Command, in its infinite wisdom, had decreed that as the *"fiendish and devious Chinese"* knew that they would celebrate on the 25th. Being foreigners, with no sense of fair play, the Chinese would probably attack while the Battalion was less than fully alert. So they were told to have Christmas Dinner on the 24th, clever eh? Of course the Chinese knew that we knew that they knew etc.

The few days 'at rest' were quite good. The weather was dry - forty degrees below, mind you - but dry! By day they had caught up with some vehicle servicing and managed some of the 'monthly tasks', such as track removal to take out links, brake drums off to check and service brake shoes and linkages, as well as oil changes, when they had enough oil. Tracks were becoming quite a problem, with their constant use the links and pins were well worn and replacements just about unobtainable. Another recurring problem Brain had was with the sealed 'cut-out' in the electrical charging system. Their Carriers were of the universal type, adapted to 3"-mortar use, with the American *Ford* 80 BHP V8 engine. These had *Delco-Remy* electrics, where the voltage regulator assembly and cut-out were separate sealed items, and it was the latter that kept 'cutting out' permanently. Brian managed to get hold of a couple of spares, so in his 'spare' time he prized open the faulty units. He found that a piece of fine wire was burning out, this was the problem. His 'cure' was to get a length of fine signal wire, then to hold it across the gap and put a six-volt 'dead short' across it! The hope was that it would 'weld' itself into position. It was a tricky operation with frozen hands, but he had amazing success and saved them from flat batteries.

That problem, along with frozen petrol (or was it water in the petrol?) and broken bogey tyres were the main problems on the Carriers. The poor *Bedford* 15-cwt 4x2 struggled on manfully under conditions that its designers had never envisaged. The Jeeps were no problem except that they were always issued with *Ford* spares for their *Willy's* Jeep, but never mind, they would just roll it on its side, change the clutch plate, and carry on. Anyway, now the 'easy time' was over and it was 'back on the road' again. There was just one thing wrong, because when they got back on the MSR, they turned north! There must be some mistake, they thought, we're supposed to be heading south in easy stages, to Pusan then Japan or Hong Kong - or so the 'latrine generals' had said! They definitely headed north a few miles, to where the road ran through a very deep valley a mile or two long. It had steep hills either side and a river at the bottom opening out at the northern end to a bit of flat land with a few houses and a school. The RUR called it 'Happy Valley' must have been down to the Irish sense of humour. With the RUR and RNF up forward and the Gloucesters in reserve, they dug in as best they could and settled down for a cold night.

After 'Stand To' the next morning, the OC Pln asked if all the vehicles were fit for duty. Careful, Brian thought, there must be something dodgy in the air if he is showing interest in their problems!

So he started to tell the OC all his woes, but was cut short by the OC retorting, *"Well, if you're not busy, go along with Sgt Northey and put in a phone line to his forward observation post (OP)"*. *"Ours is not to reason why"*, thought Brian, as he found himself struggling over the adjoining hills with a HQ Signalman and a damn great drum of assault cable. They found that they couldn't get an 'earth return' in the frozen ground, so they were using American twin-core assault cable instead of their own much heavier 'DON 8' single core. Brian later found out that all this work was due to the interference caused by the hills, between the OP and HQ, affecting radio contact. When they eventually got to the OP, it was almost worth it, a panoramic view of the northern plain, with snow covered hills and the little village with its school to the RNF front.

With the phone tested and working, the next job was to get some ranging shots from the mortars to the pre-arranged target points, those most likely as where the enemy would attack. So the OP Sgt gives the estimated range and location, then watches for the fall of the bombs, ready to correct if necessary. So off go the mortars, but it was a pity nobody told the OP that the RNF had decided to 'recce' (reconnoitre) the village and school at that moment. The sight of the tiny 'stick men' darting about would possibly have been funny in other circumstances, but not now. Luckily, the first shots were wide, all based upon unreliable maps, so no one was hurt.

During that afternoon, Brian got back to the Mortar lines, down near the river below the shelter of the bank. A shout from a small bridge above him turned out to come from his old mate Wally 'Robbo' Robinson, a REME VM attached to the MG Pln. Robbo had found himself detailed off to be 'No.1' on the Bren-gun covering the approach to the bridge. He told Brian that he had seen Bob Mathews on a similar suicide mission farther up the road, Bob being the VM attached to the Anti-tank Pln. The firing to their front was getting heavier and the mortars started firing in support of the RNF at 1800 yards – it certainly seemed to be *"No place for REME!"*

Load up and get out

Later in the same afternoon, they saw what they took to be remnants of the SKA troops, who they knew had 'done a bunk' somewhere on the left earlier; they were now being herded back by what seemed to be MPs, all very amusing to the astonished onlooker. But nowhere near so incredible as the truth, they were in fact Chinese troops who, having previously gone around them, captured many of the SKA personnel. Then, dressed in SKA clothing and equipment, they walked back up through their line to await darkness, which they planned to use to surround the RUR. As darkness fell, the RUR, who had taken most of the Chinese attack all day, now started to fight their way back to the Gloucesters' position. As the moon came up, it was as bright as day and even colder than usual. When they got the order to pull out (a bit early, some thought, as the RUR hadn't by any means fully withdrawn through their lines), they were still fighting their way back. *"Load up and get out"*, came the command. But that was easier said than done. The mortar base-plates were frozen solid in the ground and could only be freed by fixing tow chains and getting the Carriers to pull them out. All this while ammunition was being re-loaded onto the Carriers and their crews were trying desperately to get everything else on board.

Now they had to climb a steep bank, which soon became a sheet of ice. Track-laying vehicles are hopeless on ice, they skidded and slewed, over revved, then tried to 'creep', until they managed to get two over the top of the bank. This was accomplished by using their camouflage nets and tarpaulins as 'sand mats', thanks to the expertise of their 'ex-Desert Rat' reservists. With the two vehicles now on top, pulling on two ropes passed down to the ones yet to come up, they managed to save all but one, but by this time they were being fired at from the hills to their side and rear. The Carrier they lost was an Ammunition Carrier, which made it heavier than the Mortar Carriers; it slewed sideways down to the river and literally burned out its engine, trying to get out. It may have succeeded, had not some young zealous officer with a loud voice, but no technical know-how, overridden all skilled advice to the driver and bullied him into revving the engine to death.

After setting fire to the abandoned vehicle, they withdrew slowly down an icy, brilliantly moonlit road, being shot at from both sides. Brian had been frightened before and has also been frightened since, but that night he knew real fear. Just one bit of levity here. Halfway out, they came across some men struggling on the roadside. Thinking that they must be survivors of a skirmish, they stopped to pull them aboard. They were three RUR soldiers, one

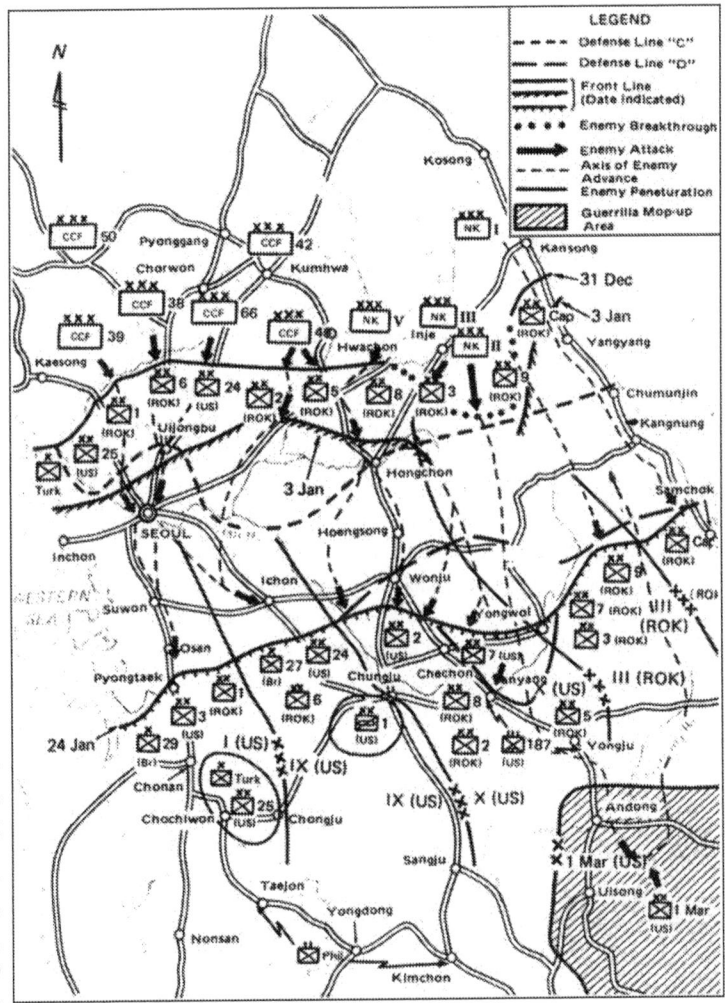

Communist New Year Offensive 31 Dec 1950 - 24 January 1951

slightly wounded and all three fighting amongst themselves over some, probably imagined affront, that had taken place back in Colchester. Only the Irish could fight amongst themselves in such a situation, thought Brian. As if to rub salt in the wound, the wounded chap, by some great injustice, after his hospital confinement, was sent by the replacement Depot to join the Gloucesters. He was to blight Brian's life for the next five years!

And so it was back to 'Happy Valley'. They carried on down, now laden with those three extra bodies on top of the engine cover, until near the mouth of the valley, they again came under heavy fire. Luckily, somebody spotted that the fire was coming from tanks straddling the road. As the Chinese had no tanks, it was assumed that they must be theirs, so they immediately switched on their headlights. This stopped the firing and thankfully their vehicles were now recognised. It seems that the batch out before them had told the tank crews that they were the last. Brian explained to them, in 'simple soldier language', that the 'Tail-end Charlie' was sure to be a daft REME fitter! And, of course, they had hung back to pick up those three RUR soldiers. It wouldn't have been so bad had they been proper tanks firing at them, like 8 Hussars Centurions, but to add insult to injury they turned out to be bloody old Churchills!

.After that it was just a case of moving at top speed. They nearly caught up with the Yanks and SKA, crossing the Han River just in time, before the last bridge was blown. Then it was 'hell for leather' down the road south, with just one breakdown, caused by a dead battery. They screwed up the slow-running screw to keep it charging as best possible and tow started it. They then went flat out until they reached a place called Pyongtaek-Ni, taking up position behind a railway embankment, in a granary. With most of the Platoon still intact, it was a small miracle out of the night's confusion. They hastily made some sort of defence position. The ground was too hard to dig, frozen solid, and so they piled sacks of rice into nice little posts and waited for dawn. When first light arrived, they saw that the road ran through their centre, with a railway embankment to their left and another railway branch and station to their right. They were in the granary, surrounded by a few houses, right in the middle of what must have been the one sizeable flat plain in Korea.

No matter, it was time to get the brew going, to set up the mortar line local defence and have a scrounge round the buildings, most of which were in fair shape. The vehicles had done exceptionally well but had obviously suffered during the long hard run. The worst casualty was one of the Mortar Carriers, with its big end gone. There was no cure and no hope for that one. Then they realised that all the tracked vehicles were stuck solid to the ground. They had parked with hot tracks at the end of the day on wet surfaces and the night's drastic temperature had frozen them down hard and fast. Before they eventually gave up trying to rip them free, one Carrier had smashed its gearbox. For the rest of them, it was a case of breaking their tracks, rolling the vehicle clear, then pouring petrol on those parts of the track that had been at the bottom and were still frozen. They then set fire to the petrol until, with picks and crowbars, they could free the track and re-assemble the tracks to the vehicle. This took all of the free men nearly all day to accomplish, it's a good job that the Chinese weren't too hard on their heels.

And now, with three Carriers and one 3-tonner lost, things were getting critical, the only spare Carriers were those of the Assault Pioneer Pln. But as these were 'Wasps', with flame-throwers on the front and big Napalm tanks at the back, they were hardly ideal for other tasks. So it was on to 'B' Echelon for help. Here resided the Technical Stores wagon, but they found nothing for them. But it proved a nice visit with the chance to meet up with ex-boy Sgt Garry Thompson REME, Jack Commons and John Musgrave, who were both VM's, as well as George Harold and Robert (Bob) Holles, both ex-boys and Armourers by trade. *(N.B. In the case of Bob Holles, he later became an author in his own right. In 1952, he wrote and had published a book called "Now Thrive the Armourers".)* A mini re-union was thus had by all and Brian did manage to make a contact with 29 Bde LAD, who offered facilities for making one good Carrier out of the two that they had, which had been sentenced Beyond Local Repair (BLR). This meant Brian going with them and doing the job himself, so off he went. Using their lifting gear and with the aid of some hard work from the detachment Artificer Sergeant Major (ASM), they managed to swap a good gearbox onto a good engine and drive back to their position, all in two days - no mean feat under the conditions at the time

29TH BRIGADE GROUP 5TH NOVEMBER 1950 TO MARCH 1951

Scenes of utter confusion

Meanwhile, back at Pyongtaek, the scenes were ones of utter confusion. Literally hundreds of thousands of refugees had completely swamped the area and it proved a continuous struggle to keep the road open. It was heartbreaking to hear the cries of hungry lost children and the plaintiff wail of *"Amoni! Abogee!"* (Mother! Father!) from those who had become separated from their families. Amongst all this chaos, they had to do random searches for arms, with suspects initially being passed to SKA MPs - until the lads found out that they were being promptly shot. It was also here that some of the lads reported seeing a mother actually drowning her children in the river to save them further suffering. In the railway station, these human flotsam fought for a place on a train that was stood there, clinging anywhere they could. They were all over - in, on and under the boxcars. They didn't know, or wouldn't believe, that the train wasn't going anywhere, as all the bridges had been blown at least thirty miles south of them. One more lesson was learned here - all these thousands of desperate people were fleeing southwards. Most had tried the Communist way and preferred the suffering of trying to get away to anything they had before. One thing nobody ever saw was a refugee fleeing north, which did tend to make one think.

The granary, as it turned out, had also been a distillery and, lying in the vat was still a fair amount of *sake* (pronounced 'sah-ki', a rice-based wine), which of course had to be controlled. But the supply was still there and so 'trade' was established. Water cans were at a premium until suddenly the tap stopped providing its heaven-sent liquid. A blockage was the obvious verdict. Now those vats were built right up to the height of the building, through all floors and to the roof ventilator. Off went some volunteers to investigate the problem. The roof was found to have been riddled by strafing aircraft and, when clearing the debris from the vent, top they were able to shine a light down and peer into the depths of the vat. It was then that they saw what had caused the blockage. They drank no more sake after that, but they did know what had happened to the lookout during the last air raid!

Life started to settle back into a routine, now that the numbers of refugees were thinning out, their equipment was in reasonable order and there was still no sign of the Chinese catching up. So all was now ready for the next phase of the move south. The Yanks must have stopped and established a line by now but then it all went pear-shaped. The General who took over from MacArthur to mastermind the retreat got out of his Jeep a bit clumsily and was killed. So now they had a new Cdr, one who wanted to make a name for himself. The order of the day became, *"We will stand firm, we will not give up another yard of ground, we will push the enemy back to where he came from"*. Thus said the great man from his office in Tokyo, while the troops on the ground thought, just like Tonto, *"Who's the we, Kimo Sabe?"* To Brian and his colleagues it seemed a good idea to just settle where they were, while the 'powers-that-be' worked out their new master strategy for the conquest of Asia, or how to keep Japan safe from those nasty 'Reds' (communists).

Things were certainly now getting altogether too organised! Baths, haircuts, a change of socks, vests and shirts, even clean long johns. One or two of the more confident even started taking their boots off to sleep; why, much more of this pampering could make them soft! All their vehicles had been serviced, all fairly roadworthy (or as near as is possible) again - they have even got back their 3-ton *Bedford* QL. But, in the greater scheme of things, the decision has been made - they were going to re-take Seoul, Inchon, Uijongbu, Kimpo and Kaesong and anything else that they had so freely given away. The American 1 Cavalry was going to spearhead the move, which should be good for a laugh thought some. So the RCT moved through them a few days later, all shiny and clean, with nice new tanks, their turrets open so that their crews could show off their yellow cravat-style scarves, highly polished boots and *Colt-45* revolvers in open holsters – they made a truly beautiful sight. The RCT was followed by a Battalion of American black infantry, at last being allowed to take part in combat as equals. The funny thing is that they didn't look all that pleased about it!

Contact was finally made with the Chinese and that certainly nullified any 'gung-ho' attitudes somewhat. As the 'great Hollywood epic' stalled, 29 Bde (with a Turkish Battalion attached) was moved up to clear the hills, their holiday was over. There seemed to be several ominously steep hills between them and Seoul. Brian was under the impression that they were to go in after the Americans and the Turks, but things had got a little confused, as the American Cavalry kept losing their objectives and the Turks had to continually help them out. This went on until the Turk's got fed up with being fired upon from high ground positions, which they thought had been cleared by the American Forces, so they got a bit shirty with the Yanks and announced that they were going home! Only a last-ditch promise that they would be flanked by British or Commonwealth troops saved faces, or so the very good 'latrine gossip' had it. It had started getting a bit warmer by now, so they were now back to a dress of cap comforter and heavy-duty pullover, making physical movement a lot easier.

So it was then on to their next set-piece battle, after an early morning church service, after which Brian confesses he has been atheist ever since. Up to the 'start line', with air cover provided by *'Mustangs'*, which Brain reckoned were piloted by Australians, then the pounding of artillery - both 25-pdr and 5.5". The riflemen walked in, and then Support Coy dashed into position. With the mortars in the riverbed to the left of the base of the hill, there was a track leading straight at the hill through a ford and then round to the right. As one of the Ammunition Carrier drivers was not too well, Brian found himself volunteering to follow up with spare bombs. So with the lower slopes cleared, they could see where their Rifle Companies were, as they were laying out aircraft recognition panels as they went. Then the mortars were heard to start up so off they went, with Brian driving and a mate in the cupola with a Bren. He drove as fast as he could, across the ford, following the track, easy now, until they seemed to be on the crest of the hill. To their left, a lot of small figures were running down the hill, so his mate with the Bren decided to have a pop at them.

That was when Brian realised that the track he was following ran round the hill to the right and the mortar position, as it turned out, was over the ford to the left. This meant that the 'retreating' enemy was actually advancing towards them, and very annoyed they appeared to be too! Brian now joined in the firing with an American carbine that he had 'found' whilst in the north of Korea and had become quite pleased with. It was hard to tell if they actually hit anything, but it gave them a breathing space, enabling Brian to spin the Carrier around, praying that it would not shed a track, and then fly back down the hill and find the mortars. They had supposedly done their job but had not seen any Chinese, so it was the REME guys who told them what they looked like. Brian thought that, even if he didn't know his left from his right, he was still sure it was the mortar men that got it muddled up.

They did not take many casualties really for such a big hill, but one of them was quite bad. Coincidentally, Brian had previously known him in Wokingham, through the casualty's sister, during his time on boys' service at Arborfield. Brian was told that he had died but was glad to later meet up with him again in Japan, still in a bad way, but alive. After a bit of a rest, they started north again, up to Seoul, which was really battered by now, the Air Force must have had a field day. Then it was east to Ichon (not to be confused with Inchon), a comparatively easy journey, as all the vehicles behaved. They were held up a few times by firing from the hillsides, but nothing too serious, and they reached their position about noon the following day. Mortar Pln was quartered in what had been the local bank. Brian, a driver, and a recently joined Signalman, found themselves sleeping in a sort of cloakroom. They settled in and then went a mile or so in each direction, but there seemed nothing to be seen but a few 'Gooks' (the derogatory term for all Koreans apparently, either friend or foe!). Those they did come close to were very jumpy and did not want to be seen talking to them. That meant 'keep your eyes open', as the locals obviously knew something that they did not.

They were quite snug in the bank, some of the lads had managed to get both the vault and safe open; both were empty of course, but provided a good bunker. It brought with it the thought that they were getting soft again. The only cover they ever usually had were the odd buildings they came across intact, which were few and far between, it was more often the case of a sleeping bag under the stars. Certainly, if there were any tents or the like they never saw them, their best was a tarpaulin stretched between two Carriers when they could park them close enough together or, as has been mentioned previously, sat up, cold and uncomfortable in a vehicle cab. Come to think of it though, Btn HQ and the Regimental Aid Post (RAP) always seemed to have tents!

Brian gets knocked out of the action

Three or four days later, the 15-cwt driver reported his 'brakes were dodgy' so, making sure that the truck was not going to move, Brian stripped down the brakes to find the shoes were 'down to the rivets'. He got on to 'B' Echelon for replacements and went for a brew. In the little billet that Brian shared with his signalman, there was already a brew on so he got a cupful and sat down. Almost immediately there was a mighty bang and he was knocked backwards, as though hit by a big hot heavy blanket. He 'came to' among all the usual confusion of people diving about, with shouts of *"Stand To"* and then found himself being carried off. Somebody was messing about with dressings and cutting off his clothes. He had got new boots at the last issue and he remembers seeing them cut up. And then he was in the back of an ambulance (a Jeep, he guessed) on a very bumpy road, with someone screaming in the opposite bunk. Brian can't remember how long it was before the screaming turned to gurgling and he himself was shouting for help. An orderly came from the cab, looked at Brian's companion (who he found out later was the poor signalman) and said something like *"Too late!"* The orderly then covered up the body and went back into the cab, no doubt it was warmer in there!

Brian himself spent some time drifting in and out of consciousness, in tents, on tables, with people fiddling and probing until, a funny thing, he was sailing gently through the clouds and up towards the stars. He thought, *"Oh well, that's it, my Mum will go mad when she gets the telegram"*. His Mom had always been against him joining up in the first place. Then, as he gradually became more conscious, he realised that he was looking up at the cabin and rotor blades of a helicopter. He was strapped on the outside stretcher rack, to his utter and profound relief! Then came the biggest farce of the lot, at an American MASH. In the Fifties, the average lad had little knowledge of 'queers' or 'homos', call them what you will; maybe a story in the *'News of the World'* now and again and, anyway, it was against King's Regulations! But here it was cases of defend oneself at all times, as all the nursing staff appeared to be both male and queer. Anyway, Brian was soon patched up and on his way by train to Pusan, breathing sighs of relief. He was now ensconced in Third Station Hospital, 'all American of course, in fact it was a large school, taken over and converted into a hospital. The room to which Brian was allocated had eight beds, with one of his companions an Australian from York (England). This Aussie had answered a newspaper advert to join the Australian Army and get £20.00 a week. Brian didn't know if he got his £20.00, but he certainly never saw Australia, they only took trained soldiers. He had been sent straight to Japan as part of the occupation forces and then to 1 RAR in Korea. Here, he had been shot through the thighs and the doctors wanted to take one leg off. This, he was discouraging by waving a *Colt-45* automatic at anybody who came near! On learning that Brian was British, he handed over the automatic and asked Brian to guard him while he got some sleep and waited to see a British doctor.

Give that man a medal!

The rest of the beds contained some very sad American soldiers suffering from such things as traffic accidents, diesel-stove burns, wood alcohol poisoning and venereal disease (VD), they were all from the Pusan Garrison. The reason this information is included is to highlight the farce that took place the next day. Korean orderlies came in and tidied up the beds, followed by a full-blown American General and his entourage. They stopped at the foot of each bed and, with great panache, gave a speech about 'valour and duty and all things nice'. Then, from a tray held by a beautifully dressed minion, the officer presented a Purple Heart Medal, that is until he got to the Aussie's bed. Our colonial friend listened to the officer's speech then told him in no uncertain manner where to stuff his medal, pointing out that he was Australian/British. The General, somewhat taken aback, tried a repeat performance on Brian and, with cameras ready to click, Brian had to explain, not quite so colourfully, that he also was British.

There was a short conference, with a lot of *"Yes Sir! No Sir! Three bags full, Sir!"* then the General, to his credit, declared, *"I don't care what Goddamned outfit you were with, you got f*****g well wounded, so you get a f*****g medal!"* He then threw the medals on the beds and stalked out, it really broke the monotony of a boring day! (Brian later swapped his for a fleece-lined raincoat.) Next day he and the Aussie were both wheeled out and loaded on a *Dakota* aircraft for Japan. After taxiing round the perimeter runway for ten minutes, the undercarriage collapsed, so the slightly wounded now became seriously wounded and the seriously wounded more so, happy days. Another *Dakota* was found, they were checked over and re-stowed, then off to Japan. They then journeyed on a very fast train, with food, drink and sympathetic orderlies, to Kure. *"Get those filthy people bathed before they're put into my clean sheets! Doctor's rounds in ten minutes!"* There she stood, Matron, the Queen Alexandra Nursing Service's answer to RSM Brittain. This wonderful lady made everyone feel right at home. After all that sloppy American treatment, they could now lie blissfully to attention in clean white sheets with starched hats and red capes all around them, even York's/Australia's finest kept quiet!

After this stay came convalescence on Mia-Jima, then it was back to duty with JDRU, Kure Dock Guard. But inevitably there was 'a flap' on in Korea, so Brian was sent back, first to 10 Inf Wksp and then on to 1 Gloucesters. A lot had happened while he had been away, all his mates had gone!

Sid Blake's memories

A soldier's memory to cherish - Cfn Sid Blake was first ashore from the *'Empire Pride'*, with the baggage party. He remembered the date well because an ammunition truck blew up at the far end of the docks. It was November 6th 1950 and 10 Inf Wksp, which had a very large establishment, split itself into two groups. Sid was in the first party, consisting of five officers and eighty-five other ranks, who left by train. They travelled for the next three days in the baggage van to Suwon, where the advance party was waiting. The second group, of two officers and 107 ORs, remained in Pusan as the vehicle party. November 8th saw a travel-weary party arrive in Suwon, to be met by Capt Husband, the OIC Advance Party, who guided them to their first location in Korea. It was an Agricultural Research Station and a shared location, as the LAD to Support Troops was already there. They then had to wait for the transport, so spent the time sorting their accommodation out. They moved out from the location during the early hours and liberated their interpreter, who was going through a bad time with the local 'Old Bill'. His name was Kim (weren't they all?), he could speak a couple of languages, and was being accused of being a 'Collaborator'. Anyway, Kim eventually finished up being the 'Best dressed person in the unit'.

November 10th saw the arrival of the first vehicles, four 3-ton stores lorries and one office lorry

RAOC. However, they found that the stores bins had been removed and the lorries converted to 'general service' (GS). Apparently this had been done at Tilbury docks, but no one seemed to know why. Presumably the stores had been returned to Chilwell, and they worried that this loss might prove to be vital in the near future. A few days later, a sudden frost that had not been forecast caught most of the Brigade vehicles. Completely frozen up, there was great difficulty with water pumps, radiators and cracked cylinder blocks. The work had started in earnest! On November 26th, a warning order was received to move on the 28th so now the learning curve began, packing all their 'goodies' into the vehicles

November 28th saw the Workshop on the move north to Kaesong; at this time its command structure was:

OC	Maj J Christie Smith
QM	Capt M J P Wallace
AO	Capt F C D Tinkham
Wksp Officer	T/Capt J S Husband
Recy Officer	Lt M C Snow (Recovery)
Tels Officer	Lt A Cribb (Telecommunications)
Assistant Wksp Officer	2/Lt R Spittle
Ordnance Officer	Capt J Nicel RAOC

They just about had time to unpack the vehicles and settle into the grounds of this big school. It was while they were there that Sid Blake obtained a pedal powered organ, while Bill Bechelli got himself a piano, which probably remained with the unit. Bill was going to teach Sid to play but, the next day when they awoke in the morning, it was found that some of the lads had burned the organ to keep warm! The weather was turning cold - ruddy cold – and they didn't have the luxury of Arctic clothing to keep it at bay. They moved again, crossed the 38th Parallel, and set up a couple of miles south of Pyongyang on December 2nd, they didn't know it at the time, but there were to be five more moves on the cards for them before the New Year.

The Yanks had 'bugged out' (rapidly withdrawn!) and, down at the airfield, their rearguard was burning everything – stores, vehicles, planes - nothing was going to be left for the Chinese!

Believe it or not! This is a main road after some rain in March 1951.

Photograph taken from the hillside behind the Administrative tents looking across the workshop Vehicle compound, towards the A & G section. The Instrument section is on the far hillside behind the long shed. Blacksmith's section is on the left, tucked in behind the middle distance trees.

Meanwhile it was the RNF that had prepared to defend the town. 2/Lt Spittle gave Sid permission to take a 3-tonner into town and see what could be scrounged. A small party of them descended on the airfield and came back, after a couple of trips, with camp beds, parkas, rations, Jeeps and even a *GMC* 2.5-ton and a half-track! *(GMC was – and still is – the American General Motors Corporation.)* Sid remembers that there were some heavy explosions during the night. The Blacksmiths shelter had been assembled and the 'Old Sweats' kept asking, *"Are you OK, young Sid?"* while he was actually dying to go outside to see what was happening! (Since disembarking at Pusan, young Sid had celebrated his twentieth birthday, but he was still 'young Sid'.) It was again about 0200 hrs, when they were told that the unit was going back to Kaesong, to leave a clear road for the RNF, who would be looking for a fast move south. It was snowing heavily and it was only the first week of December 1950. They had drained the radiators and were desperate for coolant. Anyhow, Artificer Quarter Master Sergeant (AQMS) Sam Dixon hooked up a 2-ton servicing trailer to Sid's 3-ton truck and said "Go to Kaesong". They were thus to travel independently, under their own steam so to speak. And so, as dawn broke, they had a lovely breakfast, tinned bacon, hard tack and tinned bangers (pre-cooked) and warmed on the five pint brazing lamp.

Sid's companions on the trip were Corporal (Cpl) Harvey, Cfn Len Parke, Charlie Littlewood, Cfn Ted Fordyce and Cpl Stan Fillis. They were therefore all reservists, except for young Sid, but they had loads of faith in him, despite his inexperience as a driver. About the same amount as he felt safe with such old sweats! The unit arrived in Kaesong in 'dribs and drabs' that day, but as everything was on the move, they didn't bother setting up shop. Inside of forty-eight hours, they were back on the MSR again – still going south. Eventually they withdrew as far as Taegu, but were immediately ordered to *"Get back up here!"* So off they jolly well went again and settled around Pyongtaek. It was now almost Christmas and they wanted to settle for a couple of days to have a bash at their *Asahi* beer. They were in an old factory and got their camp beds made up inside a solid building with a couple of pot-bellied stoves (gas-oil and water) that they had obtained from the Yanks.

After Christmas 1950 and then New Year 1950/51, they seemed to be continually 'setting up' then 'packing up', moving to various locations - the names have mostly disappeared from memory. At one time they were on top of a flat-topped hill beside a railway line, from where they used to watch the daily hospital train passing. On the other side of the line was a war graves collection point and there were always vehicles going there with their casualties.

The unit suffered greatly from the rainy season, when the MSR was a foot or more deep in churned mud and they stood on guard. It was a case of holding one's Sten-gun under your poncho (waterproof cape), water pouring off your jungle hat and thinking to yourself *"Why am I here?" I didn't have to join!"* It was during one of their moves that Cfn Jim Meadows, their *Scammell* recovery vehicle driver, came a cropper - or rather his *Scammell* did. As usual, Jim was trundling along with three or four casualties on rigid tows to their next location, when they were flagged down by a Yank. His *GMC* was stuck in the paddy and he asked could Jim pull him out. *"No trouble mate"*, says Jim, as he unhooked the broken-down tows and backed across the paddy field. Unfortunately, at that point, the vehicle's back wheels were blown off on a mine! The Yank then managed to get a tow from his own side and Jim was left stewing in the paddy-field all night, 'on his tod' and listening to every little rustle! Later on, after the necessary pick-up and repair, Jim and Sid drove down to the Han River to wash the *Scammell*, got it stuck and had to send for a Cromwell Recovery Tank. They looked like shipwrecked mariners, almost submerged!

Eventually, after a spell in Uijongbu, they arrived at Tokchon crossroads, where they were within easy reach of Seoul and Inchon. They stopped a US Jeep one night to ask the way to the Yanks' cinema in Seoul, and it turned out that Sid was addressing Mathew B Ridgway, the US General as 'Mate'! Sid and his party got settled at Tokchon, where they had a rat hunt, celebrated his 21st birthday party and enjoyed some R&R leave. They built a large wooden structure (later used as a cinema, church, dining-hall and for ENSA shows) and Sid was charged with a misdemeanour - it all happened there. His birthday party went well for someone that was skint. All the lads had a 'whip-round' (he was in debt) and asked nicely at the bulk NAAFI for booze. They got Bechelli's piano inside two blacksmiths' shelters and had a great night, which included a visit from the CREME, who was curious as to the outburst of 'jollification'. Sid also went to Japan, the first time he had ever flown. He thought the pilot had something of Spencer Tracy about him – and remained apprehensive about flying ever after!

AQMS Bill Saunders - a great guy according to young Sid - says to him one day, *"Don't stand around scratching your bum. I've got a 25-pdr gun barrel, it had a 'premature' in the muzzle brake, so get a hacksaw and tidy it up for me"*. So of course 'muggins' tried this impossible task, amid howls of mirth! Sid eventually wrote a requisition and signed it, with Bill then having to countersign it. Sid took it to the Signals people, it was ordered *'Red Star'* and, 'Hey Presto', they had a new barrel within the week. Then came the admonition – *"Not the way to do it Corporal!"* Sid found himself 'marking time' on CO's orders. The requisition should have been sent via CQMS, CO, CREME and CRAOC – not direct from a clever-arse Lance-Jack! Nevertheless, the gun was back with 45 Field Regt a lot quicker, doing it his way! Sid was a renowned scrounger. He once managed to 'trade' a dozen 8x4 sheets of Plexiglas for five bottles of beer, the sheets going into the manufacture of the Bde Cdr's mobile Office/Caravans.

Sid certainly enjoyed his Army service. The nearest he ever got to being a 'front line' type of soldier was when he was loaded into a lorry and sent to help rescue 1 Btn Gloucesters on St George's Day 1951. They didn't manage to get there! They were too late and were turned back, much to their relief. S part of the Armament and General (A&G) Section, he was nominated to be A&G fire chief. He recalls that Cfn Beale was the first aid orderly. One morning in the very early hours (isn't it always?), the Armourers' lorry was found to be on fire. The Corporal Armourer was in the side-shelter attached to the lorry, his 'mozzy' (mosquito) net in flames. Young Sid dashed in and got him out, badly burned, and sent him off to the nearest MASH with 'Dolly' Gray, the CO's driver. Meanwhile, Staff Sergeant (SSgt) Robbie Robertson reversed the lorry, still in flames, into the stream that ran through the middle of the workshop compound.

They also once had a fire in the Company Office vehicle, just after the unit had been paid. All the pay aquittance rolls were burnt and lost. CSM Jock Mullhern pleaded with his men, *"Come on lads, be honest, come and sign again"*. (Must be joking!) The day (Christmas 1951) arrived at last, many of Sid's mates, the reservists, had gone home. But by now SSgt John Dutton was there, in the posh Mess dining tent with seats, but it burned down around his ears that Christmas. By then, the remainder of 29 Bde Group had arrived, with the Armour and other Battalions. What follows is perhaps in some ways similar to what has already been written, John has tried to blend the relative aspects of the Corps moves, but it loses a great deal of detail in the attempt.

5 Med Wksp moves 'up country'

November 13th, arriving on deck, Korea was visible for the first time and it was not really an impressive sight. 29 Bde Advance Party greeted them and passed on the information that 5 Med Wksp REME was to move 'up country' as soon as possible to a town called Taegu, some eighty miles by train. The Workshop personnel had arrived in Korea ahead of their vehicles and stores, so there was little for them to do other than look after themselves. The train that was allocated to them stood in a nearby siding. So, gathering their personal kit and 'Not wanted on voyage' baggage, they moved off to board their transport. They soon found out that it was a cattle train, the wagons having sliding doors on either side. Within minutes of boarding and stowing their kit, the hydro-burners were unpacked and filled with petrol, pumped up and alight, roaring out their tongues of flame to produce their very first brew. A foraging party was despatched to the sheds around the dock, to see if anything of theirs had been missed or had already arrived and placed in storage. A helpful American MP greeted them, who was as interested in meeting them as they were he. He advised them that he had seen some 'Brits' unloading cases, which had been marked with *"A fat-arsed duck and K One W One"*. Not theirs of course, but there were obviously some New Zealanders (Kiwis) around!

Some very small boys, wearing nothing more than a big grin and a few rags, had gathered around to watch the new arrivals and to practice the English they had already learned. It seemed to mainly consist of the term *"Chocolate and Cigarettes"*. These children didn't seem to feel the cold. This was 5 Med Wksp's first introduction to Korean poverty, so the children got their chocolate without too much trouble. An engine had eventually hooked on to their wagons and they trundled slowly off into the gloom. The eighty or so miles to Taegu took many hours, with many stops. As it got light, they could begin to study the country with more interest. Korea was mainly mountainous and very barren, with little sign of life. A few small clusters of mud houses and dirt roads built up on dykes, surrounded by what were obviously rice paddy fields. What trees they saw were small and spindly and looked as though they had a tough time staying alive. They never saw Pusan at first but some months later, on a return visit, they found that it was a very run down town. It had little or no amenities and was packed to bursting with refugees, who were themselves in a very sorry state indeed.

The Workshop arrived in Taegu, still with no sight of the sun. The railway station was a small insignificant building, but there were many lines and a fair number of trains. Taegu was clearly a major marshalling area in the train system. The advance party had done well and found an abandoned school, which had at least one reasonably weatherproof building that would house them. There was also a large school yard in which they could set up to work when their vehicles arrived. The Workshop personnel did exactly what the British Army always does - made themselves as comfortable as possible in quick time and brewed more tea! 5 Med Wksp had been provided with a Korean interpreter by the name of Kim. *(All Koreans seemed to be called Kim, so life was somewhat confused at times!)* This Kim's command of English was rather patchy and, at that time, not a single soldier could speak one word of Korean. Like all Asian languages, they were to find the hard way that reading it was impossible and understanding it just about the same. However, despite this, they soon found ways to make themselves understood, one way or another.

Taegu turned out to be the usual mixture of one or two reasonable buildings but, in the main, a warren of frail houses and shops with very little to offer. Cleanliness was not too evident and there

29TH BRIGADE GROUP 5TH NOVEMBER 1950 TO MARCH 1951

were more dogs around than they had ever seen before. They soon discovered, to their universal disgust, that dogs were part of the food chain and were slaughtered and sold in the open markets. The British troops' food was entirely confined to 'Compo' (composite), which although as it turned out was ideal for the cold climate, was not all that popular. It came in cardboard boxes, each one of which contained sufficient tins of food to feed ten men for one day. The food was actually very good quality but tended to be heavy and rather stodgy. Also included in the boxes were cigarettes and matches, toilet paper, excellent bars of chocolate, steam puddings, rolls of very fatty bacon, meat stew, oatmeal biscuits, etc. and of course tea, coffee, sugar and powdered milk. Army cooks could, and most of them did, produce good food, so no man could complain that he went hungry. The Americans flew in fresh food from Japan and there was soon had a barter system in operation, exchanging our Compo for their 'K' rations. These were lighter and contained such things as fresh eggs or anything that would add variety to the day. There was nothing available from the locals and, having seen the unsanitary arrangements in the town and villages, our lads soon learned to stay clear of the local produce.

The Workshop had one field telephone coupled into the civilian system, which had operators who spoke some English or, to be correct, the American style of English. And there **was** a difference, as they were to learn all too soon. The Workshop's main concern was to get their vehicles, tools and equipment, so that they could start work. They therefore took turns on this field telephone, attempting to 'get through' to Pusan and so to the docks. This tenuous eighty-mile land link was not designed for efficient use and literally they would spend hours at this task, shouting in to the phone, requesting a connection to freight movements at Pusan. When one tired of the task, another took over. The days passed slowly, with still no news of their vehicles etc. To all intents and purposes they were alone in Taegu, with no orders and very little to do except try to keep warm. Then one day things started to improve. The telephone seemed to be giving them some joy at last and they gathered around whoever was trying to 'get through' on that occasion. He waved his hand in the air and indicated, with a wide smile, that he was indeed talking to Pusan. However, the smile soon vanished. The Korean 'American- speaking' operator had cut in and asked if they were through, to which his reply was an obvious and grateful *"Yes"*. Whereupon she immediately cut the connection! Still, perseverance finally won the day and they eventually heard that their vehicles had arrived and that they could collect them.

The return road journey turned out to be an endurance test for the poor old trucks, they ground slowly along in a very long line, eventually into the school-cum-workshop. And so, at last, the Workshop was more or less complete, if not yet ready for work. It was still 1950, if only a few days left of it. Taegu was destined to be a difficult location for 5 Med Wksp REME. Not only was the weather bitterly cold, making outside work a very slow and painful process, but also within hours they had what surely must have been the first REME casualty in Korea. No sooner had they established themselves in the old school buildings than there was a mains supply power failure. One of their Staff Sergeants climbed the pole carrying the power lines to investigate, whereupon he must have come into contact with a live power line and was instantly killed. This was a most unfortunate accident and a savage blow to the Workshop staff, and then there followed the miserable procedure of arranging for the disposal of his body and writing to his family.

When all else fails – improvise!

A small selection of vehicles had appeared for repair and a start was made, to get work in hand. The repairs were all of a fairly minor nature - not the sort they had been set up to do, but none the less important. No one had had experience in operating or repairing vehicles and equipment in such low temperatures and they were faced with many problems. The tradesmen found that attempting to

Page 59

work in the open, in the bitter cold and with even the slightest wind, their hands became numb and work just about impossible if not dangerous. Picking up a steel tool with bare hands could result in the tool immediately freezing to one's skin and tearing it from the flesh. This was very painful and

---

SECRET
BRITISH COMMONWEALTH KOREAN BASE
OO No.1

KB 1027 G
5 DEC 50

Ref maps Korea 1/250,000 sheets 1 52 B, J 52 C, J 52 T, J 52 U. KOREA 1/ 1,000,000

INFO

1. One lorry three ton, accompanied by 4 OR of Cable and Wireless Coy. has broken down at CHINNAN (CQ 5861) and are now with det 11 ROK Div.
2. It is understood that, the lorry CANNOT be moved unless the gearbox is changed.
3. Guerrillas are op in area between TAEGU-CHINNAN-TAEJON. They op chiefly by night but have been known to attack small parties by day.
4. Roads to CHINNAN are mountainous and in bad condition and not fit for towing.

INTENTION

5. To evac Cable and Wireless pers and lorry three ton if repairable.

METHOD

6. Composition of rescue party.
    (a) Comd Offr to be detailed by OC "K" RHU.
    (b) Escort One pl "K" RHU min 24 men.
    (c) Repair Party As detailed by OC 5 Med Wksps.
    (d) Guide Offr to be detailed by Cable and Wireless.
    (e) Interpreter Under arrangements this HQ.
7. Vehicles
    (a) For escort and guide 2 x lorries three ton 4 x 4 provided by 23 Hy Rec Sec.
    (b) For repair party veh as detailed by 5 Med Wksps
8. Repair Stores
    Spare gear box and necessary repair equipt.
9. Weapons
    (a) Escort 3 LMG with six mags per gun.
        NCOs to carry stens and four magazines.
        Other OR rifle and 50 rds per man.
    (b) Repair party – personal arms and amn.
10. Reg Amn
    Following will be taken under arrangements "K" RHU.
    One box .303 ctn
    One box .303 bdr.
    One box 9 mm
11. Route
    TAEGU – YONGDONG (CR 9003) CHINNAN.
12. SP and time passed SP
    (a) Sp Area 6
    (b) 0700 hrs 6 Dec 50.

---

would quickly result in an open wound. The solution proved to be in a supply of 105mm brass shell cases. These had their base-plates cut off and then four or five were stacked to form a chimney. Diesel fuel was drip fed into the base of the chimney, which was then ignited with a petrol primer charge, producing a roaring flame which heated the whole chimney and radiated a good deal of heat. Initially, this type of heater was pretty crude but it soon became quite sophisticated, with the addition of a control tap (in the shape of an engine-block drain tap) and a form of carburettor, made from a round fifty-cigarette tin, as supplied in the Compo packs.

Page 60

29th Brigade Group 5th November 1950 to March 1951

The Americans, of course, came with wonderful petrol-fired space heaters of all sorts and sizes, including one especially made for their Jeeps and other vehicles. It is no secret that the American forces were not supplied with hard liquor, whereas the British (through NAAFI) were, and thus many of their problems were solved in the age-old fashion of barter! As a Medium Workshop, they had tradesmen the like of which no longer probably exists in REME. Sheet-metal workers, carpenters, turners, instrument mechanics, watchmakers, textile fitters, sign writers, etc. They were thus able to make almost anything that was needed for their own comfort and this they did. The cooks needed an oven and the men needed showers with hot water. With a clever combination of fifty-gallon drums, piping, rudimentary heaters and gravity, all these essentials gradually evolved.

While writing this chapter, a copy of a secret document has come to hand, referring back to early December, just after 5 Med Wksp arrived in Taegu. It was issued by the BCKF Base, dated December 5th 1950. It has been kept, because it was the first Operational Order issued and involved 5 Med Wksp REME. Communications from Korea to Japan and UK were the responsibility of a civilian detachment of *Cable & Wireless* (C&W). This detachment comprised of two 3-ton trucks fitted with wireless equipment and their own generators. Needless to say, when one vehicle from this critical unit was lost in the mountains, somewhere outside of Taegu, there was a minor flap at Base HQ (which was actually in Pusan). A joint repair and recovery operation was launched in true military fashion. 5 Med Wksp was called upon to provide both recovery and repair, to be supported and guarded by a Platoon of twenty-four men. They also had an interpreter and a guide from C&W, who presumably knew where the vehicle was. Capt Victor 'Vic' Moore was to command the REME section, so they provided a *Bedford* 3-ton QL, with a couple of fitters and some spares, in order to deal with the reported gearbox fault. For their own reassurance and good measure, they took a good old reliable 6x4 *Scammell* diesel recovery vehicle with them. Designed in the Twenties, it certainly looked it! Terrible to drive and operate, it had an open cab and was pure misery in the cold conditions.

So off went this military operation into the hills beyond Taegu, totally barren but reportedly overrun with North Korean infiltrators. They never did see any of the enemy, but that did not stop them from being somewhat apprehensive. Having found the broken-down vehicle, it soon transpired that it had merely lost the drain-plug from the gearbox, but was otherwise roadworthy. The gearbox was quickly plugged and the box filled with engine oil, because that was all they had with them, and then night fell. They were under orders not to move by night so their trustworthy guards spread out and took cover, while the REME lads made tea. The day had been cold but the night was worse and they were all suffering badly. There was no heat anywhere and, in the early hours of the morning, one of the crew began to act strangely and was clearly very ill with loss of body heat. In desperation they removed a spare wheel from one of the vehicles, placed it on the road and set it on fire. With the heat from the fire and by making him walk, they kept their colleague going until he showed some visual signs of an improvement.

To their surprise, they then heard a vehicle climbing up into the hills towards them; they immediately took up positions in the ditches beside the road. The vehicle that came into sight was an American 2.5-ton truck that should not have been anywhere near this area. The sight of the British recovery sergeant, standing in the road and menacingly pointing his Sten-gun, was very effective, the truck stopped dead! The black driver was terrified until they convinced him that they were on his side and they then had no difficulty in liberating a fifty-gallon drum of 'gas', which all American truck drivers seemed to carry in the back of their vehicles. Tin hats, filled with soil and doused with the petrol, soon provided a most welcome warmth until the following morning, when they made their way out of the mountains and back to Taegu. They had been lucky that the enemy was not in that area with all their fires burning.

Life in a cold climate

The cold was a subject that would dominate the lives of every man in Korea during the winter months, particularly so during their first winter, as they were completely devoid of suitable clothing to cope with the this very extreme climate. Added to that was the fact that the winter of 1950 was, by all reports, particularly severe. Not only did the troops suffer from the cold, but so did their vehicles and equipment. They had arrived in that far-off oriental land, still issued with the WWII woollen battle-dress, webbing equipment, ammunition boots, overcoats and berets or caps that had been a standard issue uniform for Europe. A good heavy wool pullover was issued as 'an extra', but little else. Gloves were an essential, but woollen gloves are little protection in a wind and quite impossible if one is working on a repair job. It was after the Christmas of 1950 that the cold weather settled upon Korea and highlighted the grave deficiencies in their equipment. Water separated out in the petrol tanks, froze and immobilised their engines. Lubricating oil became increasingly viscous until it reached the consistency of butter and no longer lubricated. Guns failed to recoil correctly, small arms seemed to be glued together and even diesel oil refused to flow.

The Americans were better used to this cold weather from their own country and had arrived equipped for everything, including portable heaters and hot air blowers, which could warm tents and vehicles and thaw out frozen items in quick time. Examples of the effects of abnormally low temperatures on equipment were many but, to illustrate the point, on one occasion they were unable to start the *Scammell* recovery vehicle. The diesel was so thick, it had literally frozen and the batteries' power output was low, having lost a great deal of their charge due to the cold night. Being near a troop of Centurions, they asked for a tow and, when even this failed to start the *Scammell*, they investigated further. To their amazement, they found that the valve gear on the engine had become so stiff with the cold that, when the engine had turned over while being towed, the process had bent the valve push rods into a neat S-shape. The nearest replacement push rods were held at a depot back in the UK and, at the very least, two months away. Improvisation was the name of the game, the rods were eventually straightened, and the poor old *Scammell* put back to work. After that, it became common practice to obtain a large cooking pot from the Koreans and fill it with sand, pour in petrol and light it under the engine to warm everything up. This was a crude but very effective solution, but also time-consuming and messy.

Tracked vehicles froze into the mud at night and their unsuspecting drivers, attempting to break their vehicles free with the engine power, could only succeed in breaking the drive shafts. The Oxford Carriers and Bren-gun Carriers severely suffered from this, until the crews learned to sit their vehicles on straw, some other material or, if available, on a dry hard standing. When the gearbox on the Jeep finally failed during the second winter, it was interesting to see that the cause was that the oil in the gearbox had been reduced to the consistency of soft cheese. Bearings had failed and one gear had ground its way through the side of the box. Even the simple process of collecting water in water tankers from water points became a problem, as the taps froze by the time the tanker was back to its unit. For forward troops, this was a major problem. In the Workshops and LADs, at least they had gas-welding equipment, which was quick and convenient. Water in jerry cans froze solid and a great deal of effort was required to obtain drinking water. As any engineer will know, the cold weather affects metal and it becomes brittle, many failures were attributable to this. The ground froze rock-solid and, in many cases, it was only with great difficulty that latrines could be dug. Driving wooden tent pegs into the ground proved impossible. One way that was found to break up frozen ground was to explode a slab of gun cotton, which fractured the icy surface.

The Americans again came to the British aid with their well-designed heaters. Their field kitchens made the British equivalent look ridiculous. They had stainless-steel boilers with immersion heaters amongst other things, petrol fired and very effective. These became favourites with the British and were obtained at every opportunity. During the second winter, they had some very cold weather while they were with the Bde LAD. Getting water from the water point was still a long and tedious process and the water trailers inevitably froze. Obtaining an immersion heater by bartering for a bottle of gin, they fitted the heater into the top hatch of the water tanker. The subsequent sight of their tanker, with the heater sticking out of the top and trailing smoke, caused some amusement, but at least they had running water on its arrival back at the Workshop area.

Any soldier from the forward areas will tell endless tales of how cold affected them. The Infantry Regiments had a very tough time indeed, apart from dealing with the enemy. REME problems were really nothing compared to the infantry's daily existence, living in trenches with only the most basic of cover and clothing. During later months things did improve, with the issue of 'combat clothing' and warm parkas. The combat dress was never that popular, as it was cold to wear and very quickly became dirty and greasy. The Canadian parkas were far superior to the British issue and they did not have that long tail that, although sensible for despatch riders on motorcycles, or when travelling in an open vehicle in cold weather, made everyone look like a duck! Obviously the subject of much ridicule. Keeping one's feet warm was a problem and, although there were some cold-weather boots around, the old issue boot with gaiters remained the standard dress for most. Leather jerkins were great if you could get one. The tank crews had a fully lined coverall, which was very good for stopping the wind but proved difficult to work in. The favourite trick was to pull a normal working overall over everything one could get on underneath! Provided it was dry, it worked well.

As a complete contrast, summers were hot, dry and very dusty. Any rain that then fell would turn roads, tracks and work areas into a sea of mud. Roads, which were almost without exception **not** hard-topped, rapidly deteriorated into mudslides. While they were dry, they threw up enormous trails of dust, which percolated into every nook and cranny and made driving behind any vehicle a nightmare. The roads eventually became very dangerous, as they developed a deep washboard ripple surface that pounded vehicles and passengers alike. It encouraged driving at high speeds to reduce the shaking, but drastically increased the accident rate. Most of the roads were narrow, lined with trees, and ran high above the surrounding rice fields. Any error of judgement quickly resulted in a serious accident.

5 Med Wksp was now complete, along with its RAOC Stores section, and reasonably capable of doing plenty of repair work. The war, as they now knew, was over two hundred and fifty miles north of them and there was no reliable method of back-loading equipment to them. The route from Taegu to Seoul was the MSR, consisting of one narrow road, in very bad condition, congested with both civilian and military traffic. For mile after mile, it offered columns of pathetic looking refugees, desperately fleeing the war that was overtaking them. The train lines, which ran alongside the road in many places, were of little use, as the SKA had blown most of the bridges after the original onslaught. 23 Heavy Recy Coy did their best to salvage equipment and bring it into the Workshop, but it was a trickle at the most.

Out on detachment

Shortly after the recovery of the C&W vehicle, Capt Vic Moore was detailed to go north, with a detachment from the Workshop and to report to 29 Bde HQ. As far as they were aware, the Workshop had had no contact with the Brigade, and it was prudent to let them know what they were doing (or to be accurate, not doing!) and to obtain what information they could for themselves. They had no small vehicles, so they took two *Bedford* QL 3-ton trucks, about fifteen men and supplies, then set off on the MSR out of Taegu. The journey north was to take three days and two nights under the most difficult conditions. They were still not fully aware of the disaster that was taking place ahead of them. But it soon became evident that things were not good, as the road

The Forgotten Punch in the Army's Fist — Korea 1950-1953

Suwon, the old entrance gates

was packed with vehicles, as far as the eye could see. As well as that, the roadsides were filled with thousands upon thousands of refugees, walking south carrying their pitiful belongings and wailing children. They had never seen or imagined anything like this and were appalled at the misery and suffering. The MSR was in a very bad condition and they crept along in one huge convoy, unable to gauge just how far they had gone.

Just north of Taegu is the Naktong River, which not long before had been the front line. The bridge had been destroyed, but was now replaced with a pontoon bridge. That day they reached a point somewhere between Kumch'on and Taegu and pulled off into the remains of a village in which many other vehicles were laagering for the night. It was dreadfully cold and they all slept in the truck together amongst their kit. At first light, they had a meal and a brew then pushed their way into the seemingly endless line of vehicles. Beyond Kumch'on, the MSR crossed the Kum River, which was very wide and had once had both a rail and a road bridge. Here, there was much evidence of heavy fighting, including the hulks of two Russian T34 tanks, of which only the turrets showed above the mud on one bank. The long pontoon bridge afforded only one-way traffic and progress was slow. The second day found them in the remains of a town called Osan. These Korean towns had been reduced to rubble as the war had passed over them, by this time not just once, but twice. Now it was usually only the town bank that stood and was still recognisable as a building. Another night in the truck and next morning they drove the short distance into the town of Suwon.

It was December 14th 1950 and 5 Med Wksp Detachment had arrived at 29 Bde HQ, the signs of war all around them. The situation throughout this period was desperate and very fast moving; it must be speculated that REME, wherever it was at that time, was hard pressed to maintain the units it supported. Once again, back loading was out of the question, thus rendering the repair capacity of the largest REME unit, to all intents and purposes, useless. The lesson to be learned again was that the principle of 'repair as far forward as possible' was the way to go. The only two things clearly remembered about Suwon are the old entrance gates to the ancient city, which were still standing, and the railway station. There wasn't much else to see in any event, as this major town, just twenty miles south of the capital, had been fought over twice in a period of six months, and largely reduced to rubble in the process. Once a cultural centre of Korea, Suwon was now just a difficult place to get through on the MSR to the north. The railway station construction was more substantial and was still standing. There were freight-train wagons in the sidings, presumably stranded there and then abandoned, due to the loss of bridges both to the north and the south.

It was an obvious place to stop and look around to gather their bearings, so they deployed in the rail yard. It was here that they had their first contact with a 29 Bde unit since they had left the UK in September. This was the 29 Bde Support Troops LAD, commanded by Capt Gordon Ewing, who had made his billet in the station entrance hall. Having got this far, it was not too difficult to find their way forward to Bde Rear HQ and report to the Deputy QM, Maj Hugh Beech. He was able to give them a short briefing on the situation, which, needless to say, was not very encouraging. They set up 5 Med Wksp in some ruined buildings and were able to provide running repairs to a number of vehicles moving on the MSR, for a few days only. Their sharp-eyed lads had taken the opportunity to investigate some of the wagons in the rail yard. To their intense pleasure, one was found to contain American combat uniforms and some very welcome parkas. A selection of these were immediately 'liberated' and put to good use. On one of their daily trips up to Brigade Rear, to their utter astonishment they encountered a party of British troops at the road side, dressed only in olive-green summer dress and very cold indeed. It turned out that they were some Gunners from 27 Bde, who had been separated from their unit and were moving south, as best they could. It was soon able to provide them with some more suitable clothing, thanks to the Americans, then to feed them and put them on some British trucks on their way south.

As the days passed, it became more and more evident that the war was not going their way. The MSR was jammed with American units moving south, in what can only be described as 'some haste and confusion'. They were quite unaware of the seriousness of the situation at the time; the front line had rolled south to the Imjin River, north of Seoul, and, by January 7th 1951, fourteen days later, was to reach Pyongtaek, twenty miles south of their present location. The 'Bug Out' was in full flood and it was time to be gone.

So it was that, a short week after arriving in Suwon, they had packed and forced their way into the great mass of vehicles creeping down the only road there was to the south, and away from the dreaded Chinese. The next three days were a repeat of their journey north but, if anything, progress was much more difficult. Every river crossing was a long delay, while the American MPs struggled to control the crush of vehicles and equipment, waiting to drive over the pontoon bridges. They also had to hold off the thousands of Korean refugees, whose only escape route was that same bridge. The ice on the river was treacherous and many refugees did cross that way, but many were also to die in the attempt. The Workshop came across the odd British vehicle on the way. They did their best to repair what they could and take them along with their lot, but it was only a token effort. The MSR was in an even worse state now, with discarded vehicles pushed off and abandoned in the rice paddy fields on both sides as they broke down. These were the classic signs of an Army in full retreat.

The detachment arrived back in Taegu in time for Christmas. Nothing much had changed during their relatively short time with the Brigade, there was more work in hand in the workshop yard, but little to indicate that the general situation was not getting worse. They celebrated Christmas in the usual way and made the very best of their own rations and those they had exchanged with their American allies. As the Workshop was situated in the middle of the town, security was important. Apart from other efforts, a barrier had been erected at the Workshop entrance, utilising a steel pole that had at one time been part of the school playground swings. This pole had been raised to allow a truck to leave and, when the canopy of the truck caught the pole, it had been snapped off at the base. Capt 'Chuck' Hesketh just happened to be there as the pole fell; sadly, he was hit on the head and killed outright. This was the unit's second death in two months and they had lost yet another popular and invaluable member of their company. It was such a stupid accident and it put the whole Workshop strength into a depressed mood. They had lost a friend and, as he was a reservist officer, this seemed to somehow make his death even more tragic. Chuck was buried in Yokohama (Japan) and the record shows he was killed on January 8th 1951.

This was a bad start to the year and, unfortunately, they soon had another serious problem to come about. The Officers' Mess in the schoolhouse had settled down well, with each officer having his own space, with its camp bed and kit box. Maj Desmond Gadsby, the CO, had his own little area, to one end of the room in which they all lived. One morning, they had all had breakfast, except for the Major, who seemed to be having a late morning and had apparently not woken as yet. They grew concerned and attempted to wake him but to no avail. Clearly, Maj Gadsby was ill, his eyes were open but he did not respond at all to their questions. A doctor was summoned and, in a very short time, their CO was evacuated, never to be seen again. They never did hear what was wrong with him and, of course, there was no question of an early replacement. Further research has revealed that he must have recovered, as he served for quite a few more years. So that was two officers and a senior NCO lost to their unit, in less than two months after their arrival in Korea. They were sorry to lose the Major, but life had to go on. It was agreed that Capt Dennis, the senior officer amongst them, would take over command of 5 Med Wksp REME until such time as they were told otherwise.

So January passed and they were now into February 1951. The weather had become steadily colder. Although the tradesmen were getting used to working in such difficult conditions, it was very uncomfortable for everyone. Trying to recall the exact sequence of events, as they related to movements, has been very difficult after some forty-six years. However, that sequence has been helped by the fact that Capt Moore had become interested in photography whilst in Korea and still had over two hundred photographs that he took whilst serving in that Campaign. There was one tradesman in 5 Med Wksp who was a photographic enthusiast and had managed to obtain the necessary chemicals to do some developing and printing. The results were not always as good as one can achieve today, to say the least. But their strength lies in the fact that many of these photos are dated and located, indicating the Workshop's whereabouts from month to month. It is known for a fact that they were in Suwon in December 1950, with their small detachment, and back in Taegu for Christmas. It transpires that they were back in the Suwon, Taejon and Won Chong areas in February, then back in Pusan in March 1951. Many personnel were unable to remember this period clearly but they must have taken the detachment north again. In some of the photos of this time can be seen one of their old *Scammell*, with trailers and vehicles on tow, and what is shown very clearly is the dreadful condition of the roads and river crossings. Refugees, as always on foot and crammed into every possible means of transport, contributed to making every movement very difficult.

Entertainment was provided by both British & US Concert Parties

29TH BRIGADE GROUP 5TH NOVEMBER 1950 TO MARCH 1951

They must have had a bigger detachment this second time around, as their vehicles included a recovery *Scammell*, two 7.5-ton recovery trailers and a big American Diamond-T Tank-transporter, capable of hauling a Centurion Tank if required. The trip north was again a fight against the MSR and the traffic, both human and mechanical. Wherever they stayed, they undertook what work they could but as before, if the vehicle was not repairable by the unit REME tradesmen or LAD, there was little or no chance of getting it out of the area for repair. Nevertheless, there were many casualties that they could deal with and this they duly did. Although they were again in the Brigade area, they saw little of the war, although they could hear and see some of it from time to time. They set themselves up near Suwon airstrip and it was from here that American *'Sabre'* jets took off, constantly screaming low over their heads. They thought this would be a reasonably safe area to be and reasoned that they would have good warning if they had to move quickly. The weather was still extremely cold but by this time they had adjusted to it and were keeping reasonably warm and well fed. Working in the open as they did was still no easier, but the men worked well and they do not remember any complaints or grumbling, nor for that matter any form of indiscipline. But the only question permanently on everyone's lips was, *"When are we going home?"*

The situation on the front was still very unstable and they became increasingly concerned, especially because the detachment was hardly an integral part of 29 Bde and very much on its own. Brigade agreed that they would be better out of harms way, if things got worse, so eventually it was left to them to go when they felt the time was right. What had to be borne in mind was their limited ability to work efficiently and the difficulty anyone would have in getting to them. Capt Moore finally decided that they should move back and rejoin 5 Med Wksp. They were advised that 5 Med had itself moved back to Pusan and would soon be moving to Japan. It had been detailed to set up there in support of the new Comm Div, which was being formed from 28 and 29 Brigades.

A difficult return journey

The move back to Pusan was along a difficult journey down the only road available to them, the dreaded MSR. It was 250 miles of long slow tedious driving, with all the constrictions and dangers as previously described. Because the road was so congested with vehicles and refugees, there was very little hope of repairing or recovering your vehicle following a mishap, and it was just a case of abandoning it and hitching a lift. This appeared to be common practice with the American forces but, for the British at least, it was a tragedy to be avoided at all costs, as a replacement was just not available. At places, the MSR virtually ceased to exist and it was a question of 'follow the leader'. All the permanent bridges across the very wide rivers had been destroyed and, in some cases, they were able to wade the river or literally 'skate' on the ice. At some locations however, the Americans had done a grand job and erected huge pontoon bridges. The American Engineers were good, there was no doubt about that, and seemed to be able to provide masses of bridging equipment, without which the whole Army would have ground to a halt, with even more tragic results. Everyone suffered from frayed tempers, and the SKA had to be treated 'with care', despite the fact that they were there to help them. American MPs were not to be argued with, as they were not averse to pulling a gun if one did not respond as they wished.

At one point, there was a difficult hill to climb and they were stopped by a British *Austin* ambulance, which had obviously been in a collision and now had its front wheels going in opposite directions! Its driver was bravely defending his vehicle against a young American officer who was about to have the vehicle pushed off the road. Capt Moore became involved and, by using his rank, persuaded this young officer to let them recover the ambulance and get the road clear. All this was in the middle of the night and, to their amazement and amusement, this young officer, who was wearing dark glasses of all things, produced an automatic pistol and proceeded to empty the magazine into the dark. On another occasion, their convoy ground into a village to find the MSR, the only MSR, completely blocked by a long line of very clean SKA vehicles. These were filled with smart soldiers and immaculately dressed officers, on their way to the battle no doubt, but definitely taking their time. As it so happened, the 5 Med Wksp detachment always had their big Diamond-T Tractor as its lead vehicle and, when they went forward to find out what had stopped them, Capt Moore was confronted by a very pompous SKA Major. This gentleman was in no mood to get his convoy out of the way, as he quite clearly had no idea what chaos he was causing for many miles to the rear. The Workshop detachment were tired, as were everybody in the convoy, and so they resolved the problem by putting three men on the front of the Diamond-T, with weapons, and indicated that they were about to drive on. The Korean Major hesitated so they did drive on and, none too gently, pushed the leading SKA truck off the road. That certainly changed his mind and there was a rush then to get his other vehicles out of their way and let the dirty, tired, but determined British and their convoy on their way. It cannot be recalled how many days that journey took, but it was definitely too many! They were finally relieved to cross the Naktong River and lumber into Taegu, only to find that 5 Med had indeed moved on. The last eighty miles to Pusan were relatively easy. On the way there, they had managed to repair one or two roadside breakdowns. They also had on tow two loaded 7.5-ton trailers and a number of wrecks, which they fondly hoped 5 Med would be able to cope with. And so they trundled slowly into the outskirts of Pusan, still in open country, until by the roadside they saw their Workshop sign and, behind it, a tented, semi-permanent camp. With thoughts of a hot bath and the luxury of a hot meal, at a table, they turned in and came to a halt. Goodness knows what they looked like, scruffy and dirty and not exactly 'parade ground' soldiers. And there, standing in front of them, smartly attired in well-pressed battle-dress and a nice warm winter parka was the new OC of 5 Med Wksp. Was his name Jolly? Memory cannot recall.

A brief reunion

They settled in and told their story. In turn, they were told that 5 Med was off to Japan, but the detachment was to stay in Pusan, to act as a LAD for the British Forces Base and to service the new arrivals. And of course that was now Vic Moore's project. As it so happened, he was not too keen to go to Japan - if they were to be here on the 'other side of the world', he preferred to be in Korea and have his own unit, such as it was. Two interesting things happened during his very brief stay with 5 Med Wksp.

Firstly, the whole area was a sea of mud and it was just about impossible to move. Now just across the valley there happened to be a very large POW camp, with thousands of North Korean and presumably Chinese prisoners. It was arranged that they would have help putting down some hard standing and, one morning, they watched with growing amazement (and in some trepidation), as a long column of prisoners, about ten abreast, marched out of their camp. Their first destination was to a local stone quarry in the area and then they headed towards the Workshop. It cannot be imagined how many there were but it seemed like an endless snake coming towards them and very few guards with it. Then, as it got near, they could see that every man carried a rock in front of him. At the entrance to the Workshop area, the lead files of prisoners dropped their rocks and walked over them. The next file did the same, and so on. In no time at all they had an instant road wherever they indicated. They had never seen anything like that and probably would never do so again.

The second thing was that they had a hurricane! It was a tremendous storm and absolutely flattened the whole Workshop. A few of them remember taking shelter in a tank and they could actually feel the whole thing rock. 5 Med Wksp was not having the best of times, what with one thing and another, so the detachment gathered together their little unit and set off to find a home for themselves in Pusan. It was now March 1951 and the weather was improving, just a little.

Chapter 11

45 Field Regiment Royal Artillery

The LAD REME

Ron Stevens tells of his experiences

SSgt Ron Stevens had left regular service in 1948 and transferred to the 'Class B' reserve. He had joined the Army as a 'boy soldier' in July 1936, apprenticed at Chepstow as a Fitter and then served throughout the 1939/45 War, finally taking 'Tiffy' course No.10 to become a Vehicle Artificer. He was recalled to serve in Korea during August 1950, one of the many 'Z' reservists who were also recalled. He reported to Poperinghe Barracks, Arborfield, and was told he was posted to the LAD REME, 45 Field (Fld) Regt RA. He joined this Regiment of Gunners at Colchester, to become part of 29 British Independent Inf Bde, under the Command of Brig Brodie. His immediate superior was ASM 'Dolly' Gray, 'Tiffy' Guns, and the Armourer was a Sgt Howard Stokes. These personnel, together with a Sergeant & Corporal (Vehicles), L/Cpl (Welder), *Scammell* Recovery driver, six fitters vehicle, one electrician and a storeman, made up the working strength of the LAD.

The Regiment and LAD sailed from Liverpool in October 1950, in the *'Empress of Australia'*, with the Bde HQ and others. The accommodation on board was varied; officers and senior ranks had cabins, while the ORs had mess deck with hammocks. The officers and senior ranks dined in the first class saloon, fully emblazoned with tablecloths, with waiter service, three course breakfasts, lunch, dinner and afternoon tea - luxury beyond their dreams. The ORs had mess deck accommodation with their mess orderlies. Ron Stevens and Howard Stokes shared a cabin, which was equipped with bunks and a shower.

On November 3rd 1950, with the pennant of 45 Fld Regt flying from the ship's yardarm, they docked at Pusan. The dockside appeared a long way down from the main deck; it was a high tide, so the gangway was exceedingly steep. Especially so for men in full kit, each with his rifle and balancing a kit bag across his large pack. They precariously made it down to the dockside, while at least one kit bag went into the sea from an unsteady shoulder. Upon descent, each was presented with a large apple by a sweet young Korean girl. Then they were marched to waiting open-sided articulated trucks, where they were all jammed in, standing ready for the short journey to the transit camp. They came 'down to earth' to occupy Indian pattern tents, on the side of a gently sloping hill; all the tents had folding camp beds. That night it rained so hard that little rivers began running through the tents. Poor

Keeping the water out!

Page 69

The Forgotten Punch in the Army's Fist — Korea 1950-1953

Dolly Gray had his battle-dress soaked and had to wear his khaki drill (KD) whilst it dried but, before it did, it was stolen! He then had to spend the first part of that winter in tropical kit. Howard Stokes and Ron spent a good part of the first morning digging drainage ditches round their tent.

'B' Echelon of 45 Fld Regt RA, along with its LAD, stayed in Pusan for about two weeks, until all their vehicles and guns had left the dockside, before moving north to join the Regiment, which had already gone by train directly on landing. They were called the '*Rolls Royce* Brigade', because all their vehicles etc were supposed to be new. In fact they were all reconditioned and the LAD's first job was to replace a slipping Jeep clutch disc, which they had to scrounge off the Yanks - a forerunner of what to expect. Before their tour in Korea was to finish, they would be able to change a Jeep clutch in two and half hours, it being quicker to remove the engine manually.

There was a POW camp close by, with SKA guards; the prisoners were working on the railway track. It was noticed that the guards were goading the prisoners of war to make a run for freedom, so they could be shot as escaping prisoners. This was something that was difficult to come to terms with, but such was the local low regard for life. Eventually the party followed their artillery pieces on the road north, through some breathtaking mountain scenery. They had to ford the Naktong River, where their Jeeps stalled with flooded exhausts, the LAD's first recovery task. Ron remembers those raised narrow roads, crossing paddy fields like causeways. There was one instance when they had to climb a causeway to cross the railway track, a slow bumping process, which was suddenly made more urgent by the arrival of a train. They just got over with their water trailer in time as the train passed behind them. It then stopped and reversed, in order to let the rest of the little convoy cross in safety.

They soon joined the rest of the Regiment in Seoul for the space of two days. Then, minus the kit-bags that contained non-essentials, which they had put into store at Pusan Transit camp, they made their way firstly to Kaesong, then on to Pyongyang and beyond. While going through the North Korean capital, the American Army was coming south with some of their tank crews making remarks such as, *"Gee, Limey it's hot up there"*. They thought they had arrived at their destination, with a fine snow blowing a welcome into their faces. They were just about to unload in a frozen field, to set up their camp and get some food, when they received the order to pull out.

Earlier, Ron had decided to try out the benefits of his string vest, which he was now wearing. They had been driving north all day, but now they joined the queue going south, nose to tail like a holiday traffic jam. They eventually got south of Pyongyang and pulled off to the side of the MSR. It was now about 0200 hrs, not much sleep time left, but Ron was not worried, it was his turn as Guard Cdr. He found that his backside was indented like a fish net from the mesh of his string vest! They had been issued with light wind-proofs for winter protection, consisting of smocks with hoods and over-trousers. These went over their denim boiler suits and they proved invaluable. As dawn arrived and nature called, by coincidence Dolly Gray had also got the same call. The adjoining field beckoned but the ground was too frozen to dig. An icy wind blew unchecked directly from China and, as realisation dawned on them that they had to strip off their wind-proofs and drop the tops of their boiler suits as they faced into the cold blast, they passed the quickest motion ever, instantaneously agreed and carried!

Their run up north was not without mishap, the bottom tank of their *Scammell* radiator froze. They resorted to lighting a small fire under it in order to thaw it out, but it had fractured. The Americans wanted to blow the vehicle up but, luckily, the LAD managed to effect a weld repair. Then the *GMC* Armoured Personnel Carrier (APC) cracked its cylinder block. They managed to scrounge a replacement engine from the Yanks but the clutch-operating lever was for a left-hand drive vehicle, leaving them no alternative but to stow the engine in the back and tow it all the way south to Kaesong. This had taught them to use a stronger mixture of antifreeze for their engines.

While outside Pyongyang, they learned of American plans to blow up a massive dump of stores, including vehicles, clothing, food and cigarettes. They found beautiful great coats and parkas, masses of individual packets of *'Kellogg's'* cereals, and cigarettes, with various American brands. While in Pusan, during the idle evenings, they had played a card game called *'Shoot'* and, because money was useless, they played for cigarettes. Ron lost over a thousand, while Howard was able to pay off his debts with interest. For the three days there, they watched the American armour going south and the capital burning just to the north. The MSR was clogged with refugees and, in one case, a string of prisoners tied together by their wrists.

The frozen dirt road was throwing up clouds of debris, giving the strong image of a defeat without a battle! They later learned that two Battalions, the Gloucesters and the RUR, two RA Batteries of 25-pdrs and a Squadron of Centurions with some Churchill Flame-throwers were the rearguard for these divisions, was it their task to delay the Chinese armies? They were actually witnessing - and were soon to join - the great 'Bug Out', their destination was to be Kaesong. They didn't realise the significance of all that armour going through them until two days later, when the stragglers joined the procession. They had left Pyongyang well behind them as they caught up with the queue of traffic going south. The endless stream of refugees was forced off the road, because they were impeding the flow of military traffic. That was a strange paradox, when the very people who looked to them for saviour were now in the way of this great war machine, which was in full retreat, if only slowly. They eventually came to a halt at a bridge over a frozen stream. Down the bank, a party of RE 'Sappers' was waiting, with charges laid to blow it up. So as not to be too idle in the cold, like all good soldiers, they had got a brew of tea going. Also, in the pervading spirit of comradeship, they offered to share their brew with them, in the cab of a *Bedford* QL. Goodness knows how long they had been in that lorry but they were dusty and thirsty, so such an offer was heaven blessed. It was strong, sweet and hot with a good layer of tealeaves in the mug that Ron had handed down to him. Of course Ron shared the brew with Ginger, the driver. At the time, Ron was sporting a protective moustache, so he used that to filter out the tealeaves. Ron will never forget those engineers and often wonders how long they had to wait.

American Armour going south on the MSR which was clogged with refugees.

They spent the night just south of Sariwon, in a farmhouse compound. The poor driver of the engine-less *GMC* personnel carrier was frozen and covered in dust, it having broken three towropes on the road south. But at least for this night they would sleep with a roof over their heads and on the camp beds they brought with them from Pusan. Ron was given the job of taking round the rum ration, so he started with the senior ranks, and went round the rooms, which formed three sides of a square. Just as he was going to return the jar to the QM, some sergeants claimed to have been missed, so the jar went round again. Ron had earlier started a letter to his wife, writing quite well, but now it did get a little illegible towards the end! Ron was never trusted with that 'rum job' again.

Next day they were back in Kaesong, to learn that the battery of 25-pdrs they left behind with the RNF had been in action against those North Koreans who had stayed in the hills, while the advancing troops had stuck to the roads on the rush north. This was evidenced by one of the *Morris* trucks bearing several shrapnel holes, from mortar fire. The North Koreans had approached the guns from their rear, but because they were on their circular platforms, they could be traversed 180 degrees and fired through open sights. As the enemy took cover in a house, a shell followed them through the door, so they caused no further trouble. At around that time, the clutch bell housing of the *GMC* was sent to Bde Wksp for modifying, for the right hand drive control.

Summoned north again

Next day they were summoned north again, to be available to nurse the Regiment back to Kaesong. Once again they were on a raised causeway, with paddy fields on either side, when they met the Squadron of Churchill tanks coming south. There wasn't much room to pass, so their stores *Bedford* QL, with its fuel tank behind the cab on the passenger side, was hit by a projection on the Churchill. The fuel tank was fractured and the gushing petrol from the full tank ignited on contact with the exhaust from the *Bedford* Liberator engine. In a flash (literally!), the whole QL was ablaze. Their RA stores sergeant, Ken Stone, swore he got out of the driver's door before the driver. The men in the back jumped out and stumbled down the embankment. Ron was the passenger in the following QL, but his driver was gone. So, just in case that too caught fire, Ron transferred to the driving seat and reversed the lorry out of danger. In doing so, he nearly put it in the paddy field on the other side of the road, leaving it with two wheels off the road and tilted at an alarming angle. Very soon, a RE armoured bulldozer, a Cromwell chassis, arrived on the scene, pushing their burning lorry off the road, along with all the FAMTO gun spares, their PIAT (anti-tank weapon) with ammo and personal weapons, all still on

Loss of FAMTO after Bedford QL goes up in flames

The LAD REME, 45th Field Regiment, Royal Artillery

board. That was quite a loss to them. The bulldozer then attached a cable to their listing remaining QL to prevent it toppling down the bank until it could be returned to the road. So they were able to resume a journey north through the refugees that were fleeing to South Korea.

At some point they met the guns, but had to continue north in order to turn round in a staging area and back onto the MSR. They encountered an MP directing traffic, who

RE armoured bulldozer recovering REME Beford QL

indicated that they must go down a right fork, where they soon found themselves with HQ Coy, RUR. That Battalion had been diverted west to investigate some unidentified troops seen on the road there. So they were stood-to late at night and until early next morning. Happily, there was no action and they went back along the road to join the MSR. Before they got back to it, they encountered the 'unidentified troops', who turned out to be just another column of refugees. The gunners made it back to Kaesong without their help, but their *Scammell*, which had been left with them, had been put to use by Col Maris Young. The prisoners they had seen tied together from Pyongyang had been escorted by South Korean guards, who had later become bored with their charges and so they shot them all! The guards themselves were taken in charge and disarmed. Their rifles were laid out along the road for the *Scammell* to drive over and destroy. The guards were subsequently released, what else could one do?

Somewhere between Sariwon and Kaesong, the LAD camped for a couple of nights, during which time some enterprising individual had constructed a urinal for their use, from a piece of guttering which even had a hole with spigot for a down pipe. They didn't have the down pipe itself, so the urinal dripped into a hole lined with chloride of lime. The funny side of it all was that the drips froze into a most impressive icicle. *(Now we know what 'A Long Streak Of Piss' means!)* That was one convenience that they left for the North Koreans. Back at Kaesong, their *GMC* clutch bell-housing had been modified and returned so the vehicle was road-worthy again and once more they were on the move to somewhere astride the MSR. They found themselves about twenty miles north of Seoul, in a compound with a roof over their heads again and fire heating under the floor. There wasn't enough room for all LAD personnel, so their storeman and welder slept in the welding shelter across the road, with the vehicles, in a frozen paddy field.

Soon afterwards they were able to enjoy the luxury of a mobile bath unit, which set up a shower with a curtain for a door. That west wind was still freezing them with its load of fine snow but, after that shower, the first since they left Pusan, it gave there skins a strange clean feeling, free of the fine dust that permeated everything. The next day more luxury, as they were issued with sleeping bags; an inner kapok-filled one and a waterproof outer bag for extra warmth. Once again Ken Stone escaped from a fire, self-inflicted this time from smoking in his sleeping bag. It started as a quiet roar, as the draught went through the kapok. Luckily neither he nor his sleeping bag suffered any serious damage. It was in the frozen paddy across the road where Ron had one of his coldest jobs.

Page 73

The Forgotten Punch in the Army's Fist — Korea 1950-1953

That *GMC* was in trouble again, this time with a frozen fuel line that ran under the belly of the Carrier from back to front. He used a small petrol fire to warm his spanners in case they stuck to his hands then, undoing the unions of the pipe, the petrol dripped onto his hands and evaporated in that same westerly wind with its fine powdery snow. Ron can still feel the chill to this day.

The next day, in their *Bedford* 15-cwt, Ron went with Sgt. Howard Stokes, the Armourer, up to a forward American artillery unit. 45 Fld Regt RA was in liaison with the American 'Heavies' by exchanging OP officers. The Yank instructions to our gunners were in the form of, *"Up a bit, no, down a bit - now to the left"* - and so it went on until the target was hit. In contrast, the American gunners were amazed to hit their target, for the first time in three shots. To their credit they did learn to improve accuracy and rate of fire. That night, Howard and Ron slept in the back of the 15-cwt, well at least they 'tried' to sleep, because they could hear the American shells going over and of course it was bitterly cold. By morning, there was a thick layer of frost inside the canopy and the outer sleeping bag was frozen to the inner, so you can appreciate that they were glad to get back to their cosy billet.

A memorable Christmas

Some Christmases you forget and some you remember. Christmas 1950 is one they will always remember. On Dec 24th, they were able to buy their first liquor ration. The ORs got their *Asahi* beer plus a bottle of spirits, so they got all the LAD into their cosy billet and pooled the booze to settle down to a celebratory evening. Before long it was time to turn in, but of course two of their boys were sleeping across the road in that welding shelter on that frozen paddy field! In view of their unsteady state, Ron escorted them to their beds then, while hanging around his shoulders, one of them declared, *"Well, Staff, you're not such a bad bastard after all."*

Christmas morning they rather over-slept, to be woken by the Medical Sergeant with the 'Gunfire' - an early morning cup of tea laced with rum, a tradition of the British Army. This Ron could face, especially as he should have been one of the servers! It was a dry bright morning, without that fine powdery snow. They were enjoying a little sun on the south-facing veranda when they suddenly heard the whine of a bullet passing over. Instead of being sensible and taking cover, they all donned helmets and tried to spot the sniper who, luckily for them, seemed to be a bad shot. Of course they couldn't see anybody or the glint of a weapon so, when the shooting stopped, they went about their business. The sergeants went off to the cook's area to peel the spuds. Yes, real potatoes, not 'pom' or tinned, but fresh spuds that cooked in superbly fluffy fashion to go with the roast turkey. It was the senior ranks' pleasant task to serve the troops, a further part of the British Army Christmas tradition. This also included HQ Battery,

Margi

who sat at tables with benches in the open; but all too soon it was over and shortly they were moving south again.

This time it was to a school just north of Seoul, with all LAD members sleeping in one room. This was where 'Margi' came on the scene. She was nine years old, small for her age, with a face you cannot forget. She wore ragged clothes that were dirty and lousy; she was orphaned and all alone. She was a pathetic little creature, much in need of friendship, love and feeding. Tom (Dolly) Gray agreed for them to adopt her. They had her take a bath, which she did very privately, preserving her pride and dignity for one in such unfortunate circumstances, while her rags were incinerated in the boiler. One of our rougher fitters had once been a 'matelote' (sailor) but, surprisingly, he took a soft khaki American blanket, previously rescued from the Pyongyang dump and made for our little waif a type of boiler or siren suit. The lads clubbed around for bedding, so she was soon safe and snug, then fast asleep. They also adopted a Korean boy, also orphaned, named Hung Chang Poi, *(or well-Hung Pee Hole by some of the less kind wags!)* but he eventually became known more comfortably as Chang.

Rancid and Ringworm

45 Fld Regt RA had two 'white' half-tracks called *'Rancid'* and *'Ringworm'*, high sided and armoured, which housed mortar-locating equipment. Their job was to pick up on incoming mortar bombs, plot their course and calculate their source, so that the guns could silence the mortars. These vehicles were one long headache and the equipment, being very innovative, kept on breaking down. But when they actually worked, they did well. *'Rancid'* came to them in need of repair, with a busted taper roller bearing on a front wheel. Along with Tom Gray, Ron went to all the local American stores units to try and get a replacement bearing. They even had to go to Yongdong-Po, across the frozen Han River. Here they met a man who must have had the coldest job in Korea. The river was crossed using a pontoon bridge, at least 100 metres long, completely exposed to the west wind, which was funneled between the banks over the frozen surface. On this bridge was the biggest black American foot soldier (General Infantryman – or GI) Ron had ever seen. He had a great big crowbar, with which his job was to keep breaking the ice around the pontoons. Ron and Tom were frozen, even in the Jeep, so they hoped he was only there for short spells.

Unfortunately, their trip was to no avail, they couldn't get a new wheel bearing. Not to be beaten, our resolute welder brazed up the broken cage that kept the rollers in place and *'Rancid'* went back to the guns, that was on New Year's Day 1951. The operators were feeling 'over the moon' by tracking their first mortar in the 'Happy Valley' battle in January. That enabled the guns to put paid to it and they all felt better after that. Before that battle, they had to move out again to settle in a university building in Seoul. Ron could never find the place again, but the part they were in must have been for medical training because they found a complete human skeleton that

Pontoon crossing over the Han River

THE FORGOTTEN PUNCH IN THE ARMY'S FIST — KOREA 1950-1953

When the unstoppable meets the inmovable!

they borrowed and put in the RSM's bed! The unfortunate recipient was on a self-appointed mission to rescue the coat of arms from the entrance to the British Embassy. RSM Ward, proud owner of the Military Medal (MM), was racing through the burning streets of the capital to save the Embassy's honour, he couldn't dream of letting the Chinese secure such a trophy. After his mission, he came back flushed with success, but anxious to get to bed. Then he exploded and the skeleton hit the ceiling, its bones scattering all over the floor. Our PT-cum-postal Sergeant spent most of the night trying to re-assemble those bones.

Next morning they had to pull out, leaving that university building ablaze. Ron doesn't know how the fire started, but it was going well when they left. And so they crossed the Han River once again, no sign now of that GI with the crowbar, only the great queue of traffic going south, blasted by that same wind, laden with powdery snow. How they praised the Lord for air superiority, because without it they were just 'sitting ducks', a very dodgy situation encountered so often back in WWII. They moved all the way back to north of Suwon, where they got news of that battle of 'Happy Valley', that took place on January 3rd and 4th 1951. At about that period, 45 Fld Regt had a troop of five Cromwell tanks, whose role was as armoured OP's, under the command of Maj Howe, so they were collectively known as 'Howe Troop'. Due to the battle situation, these Cromwells were committed as battle tanks in support of the RUR. However, all of these tanks were lost and only Maj Howe and his crew made it back to Brigade. To a man, the rest were either killed or captured.

On January 3rd, in order to get vital gun spares, 'Chalky' White (Tom Gray's driver) took Ron in the Jeep to the OFP at Suwon, where they were lucky to find a market in which they bought some clothes for Margi - a kimono, socks, leggings and shoes. Later Ron's wife sent more clothes, including shoes and a handbag. Next day they were on the move again, back south to Suwon, where they bivouacked overnight before travelling on to Chonan on January 5th. Here they set up a hasty billet in a warehouse. They had a slight thaw, but that only gave them more problems, with the Gunners getting their vehicles stuck in the mud. Finally their *Scammell* returned, with two 'Quads' on tow. *(N.B. A Quad was a vehicle used for towing field artillery pieces.)*

On January 6th, ASM Tom Gray found them a very good situation, on some high ground overlooking Chonan. This was to prove an excellent choice, the site itself comprised two buildings that appeared to have been previously used for local government. The one was occupied by 45 Fld 'B' Echelon, with the Captain QM and the ASM. The second building had a large room, where they installed their camp beds around a central slow burning stove. The side facing the town below them held some small offices. Their first task was to find fuel for the stove, so Howard Stokes and Ron set off to scour nearby buildings. They blundered into one occupied by some Turkish soldiers. Not wishing to upset them, they explained the cause of their search and, to their surprise, were offered a supply to fulfill their needs. On a few previous occasions they had gained the friendship of these fearless warriors by repairing the odd Jeep radiator and doing other minor work as required. So they returned to their nice but cold building, which was separated at right angles to the other one by an ample area of hard standing, sufficient to contain their vehicles and any that came in for repair. That evening, an American from 25 Div paid them a social call and remarked on the lack of heating. Ron told him not to worry, that the Turks would be providing 'the necessary'. At this, the Yank scoffed, *"What, the Turks? You'll get nothing from them"*. His face was a picture when two Turks came in with a huge sack of charcoal, which was put to good use straight away.

On the next day, a Sunday, they got down to some serious repair work. The Quads were due to go to Workshops, Ron's diary records, and they then received one with a busted radiator. He had to go up to the guns to deliver stores and a gun platform to 70 Battery (Bty). Later came a night trip to Howe Troop's remaining tank, with a 'duff' cocking link. This fault saved it from the January battle of 'Happy Valley'. Ron had quite a game trying to find the Cromwell in the dark, avoiding flare trip wires. He got back late but still found time to write home. On Monday 8th, a Jeep with a new clutch was returned to its unit while the Quad with a new radiator was delivered back to 176 Bty. Another Jeep was back-loaded to Workshops with a useless gearbox. That same day, Ron managed to open a safe in one of the offices, where he found some Japanese occupation 'Won' (currency notes), a few of which he still has. They also did a few jobs for their friends in the Turkish Battalion.

Return of 'the freeze'

The thaw was short-lived as the freeze returned with a vengeance. Their water-trailer was constantly frozen, the taps being long since fractured with the ice inside. To get their water, for whatever purpose they needed it, meant climbing up on top of the tank with a crowbar to break off sufficient ice for their needs. In the billet, Ron's bed was about eight feet from their charcoal-burning stove, so he made a mug of hot tea and sat on the end of his bed to write home to his wife, Lillian. He put the mug down on the floor at his side, wrote a few lines, then bent down for his tea, only to find it frozen. It then had to go on top of the stove to thaw out. Ron remembers one chap trying to shave in the open, using his lathered brush that froze as it moved from shaving-can to face. The Oxford Carriers in for repair had their tracks frozen to the ground and the steering-brake rods embedded in solid ice in their bellies.

When they had to go back to the Workshop or to the OFP, Ron would usually go with Ginger, one of their fitters, they never travelled alone. They would use Ron's *Bedford* 15-cwt for comfort and security. Often the bridges over streams would be down, so a ford was the answer. But as vehicles coming out of the water climbed the bank, water would run off and instantly freeze, making the slight climb yet another hazard. One good feature on the *Bedford* was a small flap, low down on the engine bulkhead, which opened to give access to the dipstick; it also allowed warm air to pass into the cab! They did appreciate those little luxuries, even if they had no side-windows. They would take turns from driving, to snuggle down by that opening to thaw out.

There was one big failing with the 15-cwt, their front springs were not standing up to the hammering they were inevitably getting. The first such casualty was Howard Stokes' truck, when a main leaf on a front spring broke. He was making regular trips to the Batteries, to attend to their small arms problems. Main leaves or springs for the *Bedfords* were unobtainable, but *Morris* 15-cwt springs they had to spare. These they found were the same length as the *Bedford's*, so they thought their troubles were over. Having fitted Howard's *Bedford* with the *Morris* spring, his steering was haywire, so they had to look again. The *Morris* spring central bolt-hole was dead centre, but the *Bedford* was one and a half inches offset. Spring steel is not the easiest of metals to drill, needing a slow speed and a good pressure. Luckily, during their first run up, they found a manual bench drill in a workshop in Suwon. This was ideal for the job, so the new main leaf was soon modified and Howard was back on the road. His improvised repair was the precedent that became the established drill, until *Bedford* springs became available. During this period in Chonan, they were treated to fresh eggs, potatoes and cabbage. They also had American ground beef, which was a chunk of minced beef, pressed into a loaf of six-inch square cross section and about twelve inches long. It proved very tasty, roasted en-bloc and carved like a joint.

Their *Scammell* developed a baffling 'knock', which defied all their faultfinding. After changing injectors and adjusting tappets then, while taking it on a test drive, they came across another *Scammell*, broken down with a busted rocker-shaft. They took it on tow to the Workshop via 29 Support Troops LAD. They had a problem negotiating a bridge, because that *Scammell* was also towing a Carrier. Then they found 10 Inf Wksp located in a paddy field and hoped it didn't thaw for their sakes! Another day dawned and their *Scammell* broke a rocker-shaft. Their Support Workshop had moved into Chonan, so they used their facilities to get it welded, until a spare became available. That evening and after a hard day, using an empty biscuit tin, Ron heated enough water on the stove to allow for a bath and to wash his underwear. But that knock in the engine still plagued their *Scammell*. Finally admitting defeat, they took it into the Workshop and, to their gratification, they were also baffled. Ron's ego was consoled, but they would still rather have had a healthy recovery wrecker. Now Ron developed a severe toothache, so off he went up to the MO at Regimental HQ. That gentleman sent Ron back to the Brigade dentist, who diagnosed a wisdom tooth emergency, so he cut away the gum to make life easier for both it and the suffering Ron.

On January 27th, looking down into Chonan, they saw that a cinema, a large wooden building, was on fire, but quickly decided that it was not their problem! So they carried on repairing the vehicles they had in their 'Receipt Park'. Chonan's, and most of Korea's, housing of the day was mainly built of timber, so one cinema on fire soon became one town on fire. By later that evening, the fire was up the hill and the heat was such that the timber cladding on their building started to steam. The LAD was forced to turn out, to throw their available water onto the hot woodwork. And so they survived, but there wasn't much left of the town the following morning, when they started moving north again, this time to a brick built vicarage at Sudung-Ni. Here, waiting for them, was a considerable and most welcome amount of surface mail, which meant parcels, papers and magazines from home.

After only one night they were on the move again but, before they set off, they watched from their elevated location as 8 KRIH moved through towards Suwon. They loaded their vehicles and moved to set up just south of Suwon, near the airstrip that was still unused. By knocking down part of a wall, in the building that had been allotted to them, they could get the vehicles that were in for repair under cover. They had acquired a small generator and lighting equipment; which they used to light their billets. Although they were nearer to the guns, they could not be seen, but could hear them firing all night, mainly as harassing fire. The next day Ron's *Bedford* 15-cwt decided that one of its front springs had lasted long enough, so it had to be replaced. One of their fitters, by the name of Steve, reported sick with sore eyes and warts, so he was first taken by Ron to see an eye specialist, then to the MO. Here, his warts were removed – the quick way! - and, he hoped, for good. Tom Gray and Howard Stokes went to Chonan to get replacement filled welding bottles from the Advanced Ordnance Depot (AOD) and, while they were there, they found an electric arc welder and brought that back to the unit as well. Later, Steve was sent to Japan for treatment to his eyes, a small compensation for his ailment.

One of your prayer books is leaking!

By February 10th, they were having trouble with the generator again from *'Ringworm'*, the half-track. This was needed to charge the batteries that powered all the radar equipment. The 'starter' was a knotted rope wound round a pulley, which normally responded to a good hard pull, but was now being awkward and simply refused to co-operate and start. They stripped down the magneto and fixed the impulse settings, but it still failed to cooperate. Next morning, the LAD had to move with 'B' Echelon of 45 Fld Regt, as the Gunners were detailed to support the Americans, Turks and Koreans. There were just so many different assignments. The Padre had a couple of the LAD boys help pack and load his gear onto his truck. A box marked *'Booth's Gin'* was being carried on one of the boy's shoulders, when the Padre spotted its precarious position and called to the lad, *"Be careful with my prayer books"*, to which the lad replied, *"Sorry Sir, but one of them is leaking"*! The LAD moved up to Anyang-Ni, leaving Ron and another colleague behind to fix that little charger. Despite all their attempts, it only coughed a few times, but that was all the response they got. That evening they had to feed themselves, so they cooked what rations they had. This consisted of bully beef, which they fried, and they also made tea with well-water and sour milk. The LAD joined them again from Anyang-Ni, then they all moved off again. Howard and Ron went off in another direction, back to Osan, where they knew a burned-out *Bedford* QL had been abandoned.

At this time the town was quarantined because of a cholera outbreak, but that QL was important it had a transfer gearbox that they needed. Due to a late start, they had to work in the gloom of evening. Ron had removed all the bolts except one, so he asked Howard to support the box, while he took that last bolt out. Howard said there was no need, because the cross-member would support it, so out came that last bolt and the box dropped onto the cross-member. But it also fell onto Ron's head, fortunately just a cut and a bruise above his right eye, which felt a lot worse than it looked. They loaded the transfer box into their 15-cwt truck, which had now started to misfire, but they made it to an American FAP in Suwon, where Ron took precedence over a queue of Chinese prisoners to get his head cleaned and dressed. They then spent another night in the back of the truck as guests of the RASC, though they didn't get their heads down for sleep until 1am.

On February 13th, they set off to rejoin their unit just outside Suwon, but stopped for a lunch of bully beef (corned dog!) sandwiches. Alongside them they discovered two lumpy rice-straw mats. Howard jokingly suggested that a body was hidden under them; in fact there were two, a poor civilian and his lady. They could do nothing for them, so they got on with their lunch. By now Ron's eye had turned a nice purple, so they could expect the usual banter when they got back. At the same time, the *Bedford* was crying out for attention and, if they wanted to see their unit today, they had to get busy and find the trouble. Under the dust that coated the engine was the distributor. They gave it a clean up, only to discover that the cover was cracked. They had no option but to put it back on and, after its clean up, it behaved reasonably well. Well enough to get them back to their LAD location in the paddy field, so that the lads could use the transfer box and get the QL back in service. Tom Gray brought a spring for one of the Quads, so they had to get busy again to fit it, finishing it at midnight. *(He really ought to talk to his Union about the long hours!)*

On Valentine's Day, Ron was sorry but there was no card to send to his wife. The Quad with the new spring was sent back to the RA Battery, but it was a case of 'one out, another one in', as a Quad with gear box trouble arrived. This one was found to be suffering from a broken tooth on a lay shaft gear. Luckily, the charging generator for *'Ringworm'* had finally been fixed and it was back into the action. It was a busy life, as the LAD still had all the routine jobs, such as Jeep clutches and *Bedford* cylinder heads, broken springs and leaky radiators. Ron was 'out and about', around the RA positions, when he came across a wrecked *Morris* that had a good gearbox. He sat down and brewed a necessary mess of tea, to get over the shock of his discovery. Tom Gray must have smelled the tea

Able to smile in spite of the wet and cold!

because he turned up for his share. Between them, they removed the gearbox and took it back to the LAD and were treated to a turkey dinner. No questions were asked, but the recipients were simply grateful.

That same day, February 16th, they managed to fix the Quad with the replacement gearbox and then, as if to ring the changes, an American Major came in with a minor problem on his Jeep. As busy as they were, they didn't like refusing anyone that was in trouble. They also had a Carrier with a fuel pump problem that was soon fixed, giving them the opportunity to give Margie and Chang an exciting outing in it during a test run. Those two children had made themselves useful by taking care of mess tins and cutlery, seeing to the beds and the clothes washing, which they hung up for 'freeze-drying'. The men rationed Margi's toilet paper to three sheets of 'Army Form blank' (toilet paper). One to wipe up, one to wipe down and one to polish, she soon got the idea! Later, on her behalf, Chang would dig her own private lavatory, and then they got a single seat box, complete with screen, made for her.

The *Morris* Quad at last went back to its Battery on Sunday, as good as ever. The winter was now on its last gasp with the ground starting to thaw. Luckily for them, they had recently received an issue of American over-boots that really kept their feet dry in the mud. They also befriended two young orphan boys, cleaning them free of lice, burning their rags and kitting them out with gear much too big for them. One they called 'Charlie Harry' and he became Tom Gray's house-boy, but the other little fellow, about seven years old, went to an orphanage. Later, Charlie Harry went off as well, with a bag of clothing.

During this time of probing forward to find the enemy, instead of reeling back as was expected, the Gunners supported their own 29 Bde for only ten days until April 16th, the rest of the time shooting from every available kind of situation. They were supporting Americans, 1 ROK Div, Turks, Belgians, Thais and Puerto Ricans. These disparate troops all had different ideas and of course a language problem, creating a situation unique in warfare. They were moving occasionally during the night and with hardly a day going by without firing in support of someone, much of it in heavy concentrations. Gen Ridgway adopted the 'meat grinder' slogan, no more speedy dashing up roads, ignoring the land in between, but a steady advance along the whole front, clearing the ground of all enemies. The Gunners were the admiration of all they supported, making many new friends. The Koreans particularly wanted those 25-pdr guns and the Turks would take on anything, knowing that 45 Fld Regt would not let them down. The Regiment's establishment consisted of about two-thirds reservists who, during WWII, had served on all fronts and campaigns, some were ex-POWs. Whilst in support of the American 25 Div, the guns were firing at their extreme range, which resulted in the circular support platforms being given quite a hammering, so it meant more work for the REME lads. Later, they were so close to the sharp end that they used 11 Light Anti-Aircraft Bty, with their mobile 40mm *Bofors* Guns, for their perimeter defence. No praise was good enough for those Gunners.

Candles and misery

With the thaw, inevitably came the rain. Bde HQ had set up in a dry riverbed, but what was dry now became a torrent, they were lucky to escape unscathed as the roads turned from dust to mud. They just had to get on with the work in hand and get wet. In a hut where they had their beds they had to rig up shelters to sleep dry. The walls of the place were mud and wattle, which was fine when they were protected by the thatched roof. But this had become damaged, allowing the rain to beat on the walls that were actually disintegrating and returning to liquid mud. On top of that, their faithful chore-horse generator just gave in under the strain, so it was back to candles and misery.

Next day, most of the bridges had been washed away, but the Americans had a good service going with wreckers and tractors towing all vehicles through the fords. They had to pack up and hit the road again, going across mountains to Anyang and beyond, where they found a nice flat area near a river. Some of the locals soon gathered and started going through their swill bins for scraps of food. It was so sad to see a proud people reduced to this; streams of pitiful refugees, crowded trains that weren't going anywhere and, when they did, those that were hanging on to the outside had to be prized from their frozen handholds. There was even the time when an over-weary mother, tired of carrying a baby on her back, dropped the poor ragged bundle into a river.

The LAD however was more fortunate, with a nice area to camp in. The sun had come out, it was comfortable and warm, but soon it was back to reality. Ron saw his first live dog, a rarity in Korea, especially in these troubled times when dog was commonly on the menu. This dog was definitely 'having his day', turning the tables on the human race, growling and chewing on a dismembered forearm from some hapless Chinese volunteer. Ron didn't like the idea of that animal getting the taste for human flesh, so he rescued the limb and threw it in the river. He thought about giving it a decent burial, but was really too busy. The Chinese were now all north of the River Han so, while preparations were made for the crossing, the lads had time to get on with more repairs and get a bucket of hot water for a bath. How they enjoyed those little unexpected luxuries.

On the last day of February, the Padre's 15-cwt truck had broken down in Suwon and they had to go out to tow him in, then take him onto Regimental HQ. They tucked themselves into bed at around 0200 hrs. Then it got cold again at the beginning of March and winter had its last bite. A *GMC* personnel carrier came in with a frozen petrol system, this Ron managed to clear just after midnight, while 'Blondie', one of the LAD fitters, worked on yet another Quad. However, it was not a totally bad day; Chang had brought his washing back - dry, ironed and really clean - to justify his keep.

Being with the artillery meant that they were never in one location long enough to get bored. But now, going into March, the Americans were massing for the crossing of the Han, so they needed good first-class gunnery. Who better than 'The 45th' to supply it? The bombardment started at 0555 hrs on March 7th, some fifteen miles up-stream from Seoul. They had set up camp on a patch of ground that soon became boggy, but the Gunners really 'did their stuff', engaging eighty-four targets over a period of twenty minutes, firing a barrage of 1,300 shells. The Chinese defenders were left either dead or dazed. The crossing was successful and the advance swift; the guns were out of range

General's McArthur and Ridgeway saluting us as they drove by

by nightfall. They moved up to the riverbank where Ron found them, the occasion being to take Taffy their welder to see the MO. Taffy was very much 'under the weather'. They were struck by a bout of leaking Jeep radiators, on which they tried a variety of methods of repair, from mustard to porridge. Oh for some *'Radweld'* (a propriety brand of leak-stopper)! But it gave them the chance to see where Regimental HQ had set up. The Batteries were soon out-ranged again, so what better time to relax and what better than 'messing about on the river' in some borrowed assault boat. They went to view the crossing site but the track up from the pontoon bridge was a sea of mud. As they stood and waited, a Jeep came up from below with both Generals MacArthur and Ridgeway aboard. Ron was too busy with his camera to salute them, but they saluted him as they passed, such was the respect they had for 45 Regt.

A battery of Chinese guns had been captured during that advance and, in a display of appreciation, two of these guns were presented to the Regiment. But due to the Regiment moving west to support 1 ROK Div in the capture of their capital, Seoul, the guns were back-loaded for later recovery. However, they were lost and never seen again by the recipients. Ron has the only known photos ever taken of those guns. At one time, he was able to take a photo of their 25-pdrs in action, which he later showed to Howard, who was surprised to see that Ron had caught a gun at full recoil. When they were together again, up at the guns in action, he asked, *"How do you get a photo of a full recoil?"* To which Ron replied, *"Don't worry, you will"* - and he did! It was a natural reaction to the blast. Sadly, the inevitable 'camera shake' was inclined to spoil the sharp image.

After all that mobility, on March 22nd they crossed the Han River again into Seoul and settled into a school. Not for long though, because the Chinese retreated north of the Imjin River. The guns then moved up the old MSR in support of 1 ROK Div, the familiar road to Kaesong. It is worth mentioning here that, hoping to cut off a lot of the enemy, the American Airborne Div parachuted men in around Munsan, with the Airborne Indian Ambulance, but the Chinese had already left. This gave rise to a fairly quiet period; at least the guns now found time to be calibrated, while supporting the South Koreans, but the road conditions continued to give the LAD plenty of work to keep them mobile. During that quiet spell, Howard and Ron had occasion to go back to Suwon. Young Chang, who had somehow located his father, a wizened little man who looked much older than Ron had expected, came with them. He arranged for them to pick him up on their return journey and take him back to his house in Seoul. This they did, but in Seoul his house was on the high ground in the eastern part of the capital, a very quiet lonely location but in a heavily built-up area that overlooked the Han River. This location had come under heavy bombardment both from the air and from the ground. No doubt 45 Regt had added to the destruction while supporting the SKA. Chang was so grateful for the transport that they left him to sort himself out, which made him happy.

A most welcome break

The bulk of 29 Bde was still in reserve but their time was to come. 45 Fld Regt RA was to join up with them on April 15th 1951, to move up and take up positions south of the Imjin River. They were to be located near Tokchon but, before then, a period of R&R leave was introduced. Howard and Ron were detailed to go to Tokyo on Wednesday 4th April, departure at 0330 hrs. They settled in the back of a QL with others from the Regiment, to de-bus at the Suwon airstrip by 0630 hrs. Served with coffee, they were then sorted into groups for their *'Skymaster'* flights, but not as yet it seemed! They had to wait, while they watched *Sabres*, *Mustangs* and *Twin Mustangs* take off on their various missions. They ate at mid-day, slept and watched the jets take off and land. Later on they had another meal and finally boarded their plane at 1830 hrs, a full twelve hours after arriving. The seating was just a set of foldaway bucket seats down each side of the fuselage, the centre aisle being taken up with two aircraft engines that were going back for overhaul.

As they arrived at Tokyo, they had to circle around, because Tachikawa Airfield was shrouded in fog and, of course, in darkness. After a couple of circular tours, they eventually landed and were bussed to Ibisu, their leave hotel. This is all a bit vague in their memory but they checked in, got rid of their dirty clothes, showered, picked up clean clothes and had supper. Then got into real beds with clean crisp sheets. After breakfast next morning, Ron had new medal ribbons and chevrons sewn onto his battle-dress blouse. The next job was to get his Yen currency and hit the streets of Tokyo on a shopping spree. The contrast, between a busy bustling city, with neon lights everywhere and its shops full of merchandise, and the primitive desolation they had left behind in Korea, was

The Burlesque Show

Learning to use chopsticks!

overwhelming. This was enough to prevent rational thinking. The crowds, the bustle and the traffic were all too much to take in.

Ron's personal purchases were a gold watch, silk pyjamas and a dressing gown for his wife, and a split-cane fishing rod kit, with three top joints, for himself. Then it was taxis back to the hotel, to unload. They returned to the bright lights and found their way to a dance hall. It cost 100 Yen (in those days equivalent to two old shillings or 10p in today's money) for an entrance charge, the same for a beer and for a dance ticket. None too impressed, they mooched around the streets, taking in the sights and fending off the pimps, before finally taking a taxi back to the hotel. Ron packed his purchases for home and posted them, later he learned that the watch had cost his wife £15 in customs duty. So as not to post the fly rod to himself and encourage more customs duty, Ron sent it to his fathers' address. His father was so pleased with it that he didn't have the heart to part with it, so he conveniently 'lost' it. Much, much later, and a little the worse for wear, (sadly) it eventually came back to Ron

.Back to Tokyo. That bit of work done, they decided to try the train into town. They made a few more purchases, walked their feet off again and popped in to see a burlesque show. They only caught the last act, so they just settled for a beer and returned to their hotel. Saturday was not too exciting, but again Ron couldn't help spending, this time on lingerie and nylons, very much appreciated by his wife. This time, they made sure of a good seat for the burlesque show by getting there early and saw the whole show. The highlight for Ron was when one of the Japanese beauties came down in her flimsies and took him up on the stage for an old fashioned waltz. Ron thought she would have enjoyed it more, if he had had time to remove his boots, which came into contact with her dainty toes more than once! Nevertheless, the audience, mainly Americans, was in very good voice with its appreciation and flashing cameras.

Sunday, it was off into the Ginza, again, where they had arranged to meet, with her mother's permission, a young lady named Chiyuka, from one of the street stalls. She was now to be their guide, taking them to see MacArthur's HQ and the Royal Palace. The latter they could only view from the bridge and watch the big kopi carp in the moat. Their next stop, the Zoo, was very pretty, as Japanese as one could imagine, with the cherry blossom in all its glory. But, because it was so crowded, they moved to a restaurant, where Chiyuka sat them on the floor around a low table to dine with chopsticks. This was far too uncomfortable for western rear ends, so they transferred to a proper table and chairs, and had a lesson on the use of chopsticks. They had enjoyed the pleasure of Chiyuka's company, so dutifully returned her to her mother, arranging to meet again on the morrow.

When Ron's parents were in Germany, just after the war, they had bought some very delicate

Dresden china figurines with filigree lace blouses and crinoline skirts. When Ron now saw the almost identical figurines in town, he decided at once to get a pair to send home, along with a pair of metalled vases, much to his wife's pleasure. At a much later date, when they got a bit dusty, the good lady decided to wash them. Alas, the lovely clothes were not of china, but of real lace, coated in something that made them look like china - but melted like butter in the hot water! The vases are still good however and are admired by all who see them.

Monday April 9th soon arrived, their last full day of leave. They made the most of it by meeting Chiyuka by the station and going to the morning showing of *'Wuthering Heights'*. This was followed by a visit to the Kabuki Imperial Theatre for some real Japanese culture, where all the role parts were performed by men. It proved an interesting experience, not to be missed and never forgotten - nor will their willing guide ever be forgotten. And so, dead tired and nearly spent up, they hailed a final taxi back to the hotel. They enjoyed an evening meal then relaxed over snooker with glasses of 'rum and ginger'. They were up early on their last morning, breakfast was at 0600 hrs. While awaiting their transport, they watched the Hotel Commonwealth staff go through their morning fitness routine. Then it was off to Tachikawa airport to await and board their plane. While waiting, they were 'entertained' by a small group of Australians, still under the spell of overnight drinking, tossing coins in their simple gambling game of *'Two up'*. Because it became another long wait, the diversion was welcome before they eventually boarded the *Skymaster* at 1100 hrs. They left the glamour of the city, then had a good view of Mount Fujiyama and a stretch of open sea before they again looked down on the unwelcoming mountains of Korea. Arriving back at Suwon at 1630 hrs, they had a snack of tea and sandwiches. Finally it was back on the old MSR to the LAD, where Ron found two letters from home waiting.

Back with the Brigade

The weather had improved and the Brigade was together again (plus a Belgian Battalion), south of the Imjin River. Contact with the enemy had been lost, there was no way of knowing how far they had retreated. But it gave them time to get on top of the backlog of repairs, which was just as well. A typical day's work consisted of: a *Morris* 15-cwt with an ignition problem; a *Bedford* 15-cwt with a broken front spring; a Jeep from Survey Troop with a worn-out clutch; an Oxford Carrier with steering and combustion problems; and a *Morris* Quad with a damaged gearbox. On April 20th, Brigade sent forward a fighting patrol of tanks, guns and infantry to try and find some opposition. After a distance of eight miles, nothing of note was found and they returned. Patrolling on the

Digging foxholes

The Forgotten Punch in the Army's Fist — Korea 1950-1953

Saturday revealed some low-level activity but Sunday was a different kettle of fish, as the Chinese offensive began in earnest. Because the guns were forward, the LAD had to go forward and set up camp in a pleasant valley. They camouflaged their vehicles as best they could and dug defensive trenches. They settled down for the night and what a noisy night it proved to be!

This was the first time they had come close enough to the 'sharp end' to hear small-arms fire. Come the morning, it was still very noisy up front as an American (they pop up all over the place!) came through their position, took one look at them and exclaimed, *"You Limeys sure dig your foxholes deep"*. At least if the need did arise, they could fire from a standing load. Luckily for them, it did not come to that as they were ordered back to Uijongbu, where they got scrappy information of the battle that was still going on. They do know that at one point the guns were firing over open sights; the Bofors in their defence were doing the same, even firing on the move as they pulled out. So much has been written about that battle, which at the time they themselves had so very little information on. They knew only that, on the 25th, they moved back another six miles or so and slept by their trucks in case they had to pack up in a hurry. The LAD hit the road again on the 26th, re-crossed the Han River and set up in a location in Yongdong-Po. Then on Friday the rain returned, continuing all day and into the night. Three new 'green' officers turned up as reinforcements, urgently needed by the Batteries that had suffered some losses.

It is not difficult to guess who got the job to take these eager young men into the action! What was left of the Brigade had been pulled back to lick its wounds. 45 Fld Regt could not be spared, even though during the battle, all the existing 25-pdr ammunition held in Korea had been fired by the Kiwi gunners and themselves. Col Young arranged for a further supply, which was brought by air from Japan. So here they were, south of the Han River, it was pitch black and raining heavily. Their poor *Bedford* 15-cwt truck was loaded with the three new officers with all their kit - and Chang, who wanted to rescue his father! Ron did not know what hour of the night it was, but they found the RA batteries on a hill in a sea of mud. Amazingly, the Gunners were in a very happy frame of mind. One of the gun commanders explained to Ron that a column of Chinese had been located, marching along the MSR, so a 'box barrage' had been fired. This is where shells are dropped in front of and behind a marching column, gradually getting closer until the shells meet in the middle. In this way, the column had been eliminated.

When the three reinforcements saw the conditions into which they were to be deposited, they were suddenly not so eager. Ron did feel sorry for them, what an unpleasant baptism. The next job on this dreadful night was to go back up that lonely road in east Seoul to find Chang's father – 'Poppa San'. Ron had never felt so uneasy in his life, not knowing whether or not the road was mined or where the Chinese were. He was certainly hoping that none had infiltrated this far south. He tried not to show his anxiety as they found Chang's father and loaded him as comfortably as possible on board the truck, before dropping him south of the river. Ron had no idea what time he got to bed, but the LAD was on the move again in the morning, setting up about half way between Seoul and Inchon, in rather pleasant rolling country. They were to occupy this location until May 23rd. The weather steadily improved, they had plenty of sunshine and were issued with their 'Jungle Greens' and slouch hats, which they immediately christened 'Hats, Horrible'.

By now, the Regiment's vehicles were feeling the strain of all the movements across very difficult terrain. Two days of entries taken from Ron's diary include:

HQ	*Bedford* QL	Gearbox
176 Bty	*Bedford* QL	Transfer box
70 Bty	*Bedford* QL	Rear Axle
116 Bty	Carrier	Oil Leak
	Morris Quad F.A.T.	Rear Spring

The LAD REME, 45ᵗʰ Field Regiment, Royal Artillery

176 Bty	Jeep	Welding
70 Bty	*Bedford* OY	Front Spring
'B' Echelon	*Bedford* QL	Carburettor
116 Bty	*Bedford* QL	Valve Rocker Gear
		Gun Platform's Hand Spike
RUR	*Bedford* OY	Fuel Pipe

During this period the Brigade, or what was left of it, retired to the south bank of the Han River to the west of Yongdong-Po, to protect that front should the Chinese break through. Fortunately for them, the enemy had suffered a severe mauling at the hands of 29 Bde and, over to the east at Kopyong by 27 Bde, along with the Canadians, Australians and NZ 25-pdrs, that they had made a tactical withdrawal. There was also the fact of the strong columns that had been wiped out in box barrages by 45 Fld Regt RA, with help from the mobile American artillery. The Regiment's LAD now had a water point at the southern end of the Han pontoon bridge. From here, while queuing for a fill up, they could watch the *Sabres* putting in air strikes on the hills beyond Seoul. So for them, it was a static period.

They made themselves as comfortable as they could. Their lighting generator was sunk into a hole, to cut down on noise, the vibrations in the ground bringing out quite a few mole-crickets, which disappeared again in daylight. They also saw a few brown snakes that were anything up to a metre long, fortunately they were non-venomous, living on small rodents and frogs, the latter of which were in good supply. Also on the road to Yongdong-Po lived an 'ancient local'. His dwelling remained intact, as did his tall black hat. He would sit under his pergola, smoking a long slender pipe (as was the custom), while climbing up and along the full length of the superstructure was a magnificent blue wisteria plant. The super long racemes of pea-like blooms festooned the whole roof area. In an area of such total desolation, it provided a sight for war-weary eyes. Not such a wonderful sight was provided by a woman who, from her looks, must have been very poor, and held a baby in her arms. Both these unfortunate creatures were covered with sores, like a horrific warning poster for gonorrhea, something to put a randy squaddie off sex forever. They took the sore ravaged woman to a centre where she could hopefully get treatment and they never saw that sad creature again.

One pressing problem they had was to separate the barrel of a 4.2" mortar from its base. This had seen such prolonged heavy action, during the Imjin River battle, that the

Ready to set up shop in the grounds of the Capital Building in Seoul

Page 87

LAD swimming in a local resevoir

heat generated had welded the barrel to the base, putting its repair beyond the reach of their meagre resources. Soon they had another worry, when the Captain QM's Jeep engine required a complete replacement. Because it would take too long to get a new one through the usual channels and the QM would not hear of losing his transport to the Workshop, he and Dolly Gray went on a recce with a crate of beer. Bingo! The new engine came the very next day, with its American escort, who waited for the old engine to take back. The Yanks were astonished at the speed our boys got that Jeep back on the road, without the use of what would have been their fancy tuning instruments. It seems they were easily impressed!

A busy work schedule

The LAD had plenty of work to keep it busy, all the usual troubles caused by the rough conditions - springs, steering drag-links and ball-joints, and now the *Bedford* valve gears were playing up. So 'top overhauls' were becoming a regular practice. Luckily, they had acquired a spare cylinder head, so they could do a quick change, then overhaul the bad one at their leisure, ready for the next change. All they needed was a good supply of exhaust valves, 'felt' valve oil seals and, of course, head gaskets. During the quiet spell, the Regiment had moved into Kimpo Airfield, but had little real work to do. It gave them, and the whole Brigade, a chance to lick their wounds and replace losses. It was also the time to rebuild the Gloucesters back up to strength, from the mere forty or so survivors from Imjin, to practically a new Battalion of green troops. Other units were also brought up to strength, including 45 Fld, who had lost OP parties and signallers, amongst others.

The Chinese had had enough at that stage, and pulled back to regroup, too badly mauled to attempt a Han River crossing. On May 23rd 1951, the Regiment crossed the Han River for the fifth time and set up shop in the grounds of the Capital Building in Seoul, which had once been the seat of the Japanese occupying government. This time, 45 Fld Regt supported 1 American Cavalry, which, strangely enough, was an Infantry Division. When they moved out of Seoul, they moved in to bivouac in the school buildings that they had previously used in November and March. They were not here long, but had time for a game of football - well a kick-about really, but a good way to relax. During this time, Ron's driver remarked that, when they were going south, Ron was quiet and sullen, but would be whistling whenever he went north. The yo-yo was now going back up the string. They then moved up again, just south of Uijongbu, where the Gunners were well and truly in action again. They were on a steady advance once more and moved in just south of Tokchon.

On May 28th, Ron had to go up to the guns once more, back to that *GMC* personnel carrier. He soon got it going again, and then he had to do some more work on a Quad in the wagon lines. On his return journey, he was held up in traffic on a greasy muddy road and eventually arrived back after midnight. The advance was slow but deliberate, behind 1 Cavalry, against stiff resistance. A pattern soon established itself, whereby they would set up camp for a week, then move forward again, usually to the position vacated by their HQ Bty. The weather was getting appreciably warmer, with the occasional downpour. At one location, Chang arranged for them to have a bath, courtesy of a farming couple whose house was still standing. The water was heated in a 2' 6" high square tank by an under-floor fire. They were not allowed to immerse themselves but, from a half scooped-out shell of a gourd, they wet themselves down, then lathered and finally rinsed off, again using the gourd. This method of washing kept the bulk of the water clean for the next bather. By contrast, Howard and Ron, in another location, were able to get a good wash down in a shallow mountain stream.

Later on, they found a reservoir in which the whole LAD had a swim. During the heat, they could 'skinny dip' if ever they got the chance, but always the work came first. At one site, they had a deep stream running alongside the camp and they could sit on the bank, dangling their feet in the water to cool them down. The water must have been inhabited by some sort of baby piranhas, because these diminutive little fish would nibble the loose skin from between their toes. To be honest, it was very delicately done and a pleasant sensation. At another location, one of their boys explored a stream and found a point where it had been dammed, forming a deep pool about fifteen feet in diameter. This provided great fun, until they saw some extra large hornets flying around. With all that bare skin exposed, they were offering such a large landing area for those potential stingers. They hurriedly dressed and vacated the area.

Two concert parties took place, one of them British, with Brian Reece of 'PC 49' (a radio programme of the day) fame leading the troupe. The other was an American unit, entertaining a regiment from 1 Cavalry Div. This was mainly musical, but very colourful, and they thanked the Yanks for their invitation. Ron thought they expected more than just mere thanks, because the next day a couple of them were trying to scrounge or buy some of their beer. They only had a dozen bottles, kept in a crate sunk in the ground (as shown to them by Jack Frost) to keep cool. They just had to refuse the request, the Americans reluctantly departing after a drink, but without the stock. That evening, while catching up on their mail, they heard a suspicious noise outside their tent. It was too late, those intrepid Yanks had arrived in a Jeep and taken off with their beer. Ron shouted to the sentry to *"Stop that Jeep!"* but, by the time he had gathered his wits together, the Yanks were gone, racing down the MSR with their booty.

There is a tale behind the 'requisition' of their tent that goes back a week or so, to when Howard and Ron had to go back to the railhead for their ration of NAAFI supplies, which they duly collected from one of a train of boxcars. As they were driving from the siding, Ron saw another boxcar, its doors wide open, exposing its cargo of Indian pattern tents. They looked around for possible sentries, but all they could see were the railway staff, who were too busy playing football on the other side of the track, facing the closed side of the train. Ron asked the NAAFI chap to stay in his wagon and then backed up their little *Bedford* 15-cwt truck to the boxcar. They quickly transferred the tent and poles and were off before anybody knew they were even there. They explained to the Capt QM that they had found it in the road, apparently fallen 'off the back of a lorry'. The QM knew better than to ask questions.

At the site of the American Regiment where they had watched the concert party, which was located perhaps some half a mile away in a valley, one of the GIs had had a parcel from home. Amongst other goodies, the parcel held a jar of pickled pigs trotters. The GI thought he was safe to offer

25 pdr and limber awaiting recovery

Ron a taste, thinking he might be disgusted with the thought of eating pig's feet. Little did he know that Ron had been brought up on homemade brawn, using pig's trotters and shin of beef. Thus it was that Ron tasted and enjoyed his delicacy. A day or so later, his attention was attracted by a commotion, when a running ball of fire emerged from a tent, only to be smothered by the residents from that tent. Ron thought it must have been a Korean houseboy, who must have suffered terrible burns. That picture is forever burned into his memory.

Sometimes, the opportunity would arise to augment their rations of compo packs with a little local fare, bought with the proceeds from selling empty beer bottles. They never saw any hens all the time they were in Korea, but they did see eggs for sale. These were not sold loose however, but 'by the yard', in long tubes of rice straw, drawn together between each egg, so that each egg was separated from the next. They also bought some green tomatoes, but their cooks didn't wait for them to ripen, foolishly serving them green. The result had them queuing for the four-seat honey box!

After the Chinese pulled back north of the Imjin, 29 Bde moved up from Kimpo, embracing 45 Fld Regt back into the fold. Ron and the LAD welcomed this, it was nice to be back with their own again, never more to stray. Because Comm Div was now in the making and they were right back in the area where they had so reluctantly left a lot of their number, many of which were now prisoners, in April. At the spot where a mule supply-train had been hit by shellfire, part of a mule was found, so that's how 'Half Horse Hill' got its name. The gunners could not find a suitable area where they could go into action, hitting targets across the river without actually moving forward in front of the infantry positions. This would be a possibly precarious situation if the Chinks (Chinese) were to launch another offensive.

Meeting old friends

While 70 Bty was moving up, one of their guns took a sharp corner too fast, either approaching a bridge or too near to the edge, because both gun and limber slipped off the side and down the bank. The *Scammell* crew soon had it back on the road and took it up to the Battery to see it in action, none the worse for its indignity. That was the only time Ron had ever been in front of the infantry. They regularly had errands to run, either back to the OFP for spares, or to the Workshop for anything they couldn't handle. These runs occasionally brought them into contact with other units along the road. When returning on such a trip, extremely hot and dusty, Ron called in, he thought, to the Bde LAD, where he met a SSgt Jack Frost, whom he had last seen at Arborfield in March 1948. (Jack had been

The LAD REME, 45th Field Regiment, Royal Artillery

on the same No.10 Armament Artificer course as himself.) Such a meeting couldn't be celebrated over a mere cup of char, so Jack removed a cover from a hole in the ground and produced two bottles of cold *Guinness* - truly nectar! As Ron was about to leave, the heavens opened and gave them a most welcome drenching. He had seen pictures of people welcoming the rain like it was 'going out of fashion', never thinking that he would one day experience that same pleasure.

On another trip, he came across Maj (or Capt?) Peter Windler, whom he had last seen when they went their separate ways on leaving the Army Technical School in June 1939. He was now a 29 Bde Staff Officer with Brig Brodie. This was quite a cordial meeting, but not as casual as the later one with Jack Frost, whom he met in Isleworth, where they had another drink together. By that time, Jack was a policeman and Ron was a fitter, doing prototype work with the firm *D. Napier* of Acton.

Just south of Tokchon, they started to get nighttime visits from a single-engine, propeller-driven Chinese airplane, which became known as 'Bed Check Charlie' and had a reputation of dropping the odd hand grenade on any unit he located. On one such evening when he was overhead, as luck would have it Ron was Guard Cdr, so he immediately ordered all lights out. Tom Gray, who was enjoying a drink with the Captain QM in their tent, enquired *"Why, what's the matter?"* Ron shouted, *"Don't ask, just put your light out"*. Soon after that, a *Bofors* put paid to his nightly visits, he was only a nuisance really, sad to miss him. Another evening, Ron was having a quiet drink with Howard when he had to go up to the Batteries. He doesn't remember why, but drove as usual in their Jeep. He will admit that he wasn't exactly sober, but he took the mountain road, in total darkness, with a lot more confidence than he would normally have done, and probably a lot quicker too!

In June they were issued with two reversible bell tents. White on one side and camouflaged on the other, these also had a 'floor', so that ground sheets were not needed. The LAD put these to good use, but Ron doesn't remember how, probably because they were too occupied repairing vehicles. Anyway, a portable wooden building, with a pitched roof and all, appeared on site. This became their general recreation mess and bar, where they could enjoy their *Asahi* beer. They had also acquired a wind-up gramophone and two – just two! - records. One was their new favourite, *"China Nights"*, performed by a seductive female Japanese voice; the other was Glen Miller's swinging version of *"American Patrol"*. This location was just off the MSR in a valley, but on a hill just above them was a village, practically unscathed by the war, and indeed inhabited again. The word went around the camp that a couple of 'young ladies' had set up business there. Now they all know, for their protection as well as the girls, physical contact with local ladies was strictly forbidden so they had to patrol the area at night. One night, Ron was again Guard Cdr and he visited the village with the duty sentry. It was a warm, balmy moonlit night. Going by the houses, he saw the pair lying down on their rice straw mats. Beautiful by any standards, the two nubile girls, apparently fast asleep, lay completely uncovered, except for their rather small knickers. None of the men were in evidence so, job done, Ron returned to the camp area, bidding goodbye to the gladsome sight.

His two hours up, that duty sentry was relieved and Ron later took the second man on the patrol round the village. Would you believe it? The sentry he had recently relieved had taken advantage of the ladies' charms! For a single man, the temptation had obviously proved too much, so he was duly escorted back to his tent. Within the week he was reporting sick and had to get his injections. He had learned his lesson the hard way, so got off without being charged, because they were too busy to bother with such details. How do you 'confine a man to barracks' in those conditions? The soldier was soon cured, but what became of those 'ladies' Ron doesn't know. As they moved forward nearer to the Imjin River, he thought of those poor lonely victims of war, desperately trying to earn enough to keep alive.

Ron remembers at one point, though exactly when he does not know, he received a gun with a long wooden pole sticking out from its barrel from one of the Batteries. Apparently a shell had misfired, one that probably had an oversized driving band of copper, which stands slightly proud of the shell profile. This band engages with the rifling of the barrel, to give it the spin to drive it to the target, but with an oversized band, this one had jammed after firing. The tool used by the gunners is a heavy bronze cup that matches the cone of the shell, without actually coming into contact with the percussion cap. Usually a good knock with a sledgehammer would drive the missile back and out of the breech. On this occasion, the extracting tool had locked over the nose of the shell and then spread, the shell being an extra stubborn one. The bronze cup, spreading and jamming in the barrel, had now become a problem of its own. They anchored the gun securely to the ground, then secured the *Scammell* recovery vehicle's winch cable to the pole and started to winch - but nothing budged. The barrel would have got hot while firing and duly expanded, so that once it had cooled down again, it had created a 'shrink fit' with the shell. Ron confesses that the problem was too much for them. No one would be brave enough to apply heat to a gun barrel with a live shell inside, so it was back-loaded to Workshop level. Ron never did learn the outcome.

During this quiet period, when virtually all contact with the Chinese had been lost, one of the Batteries decided to line the path to its Battery HQ with the expended shell cases, pushing the open end into the ground. A Gunner, who was breaking up wooden boxes for firewood, found one piece with a nail in it. Using the casings as a firm base, he attempted to remove the nail, which then hit the percussion cap in the centre of the exposed base-cap of a misfire casing. The resulting explosion forced the shell case out of the earth, hitting the young man in the head and killing him instantly. To go through six months of almost constant action, and then to die like that during a break in the action, is such a tragedy - and all for the sake of a little embellishment.

On July 28th 1951, Comm Div was formed; an inauguration parade took place, comprising British 29 Bde, as well as 28 Bde, with its Australian and British Battalions and their NZ Fld Artillery. The Div was completed with Canada's 25 Inf Bde, with its own supporting tanks and guns. Senior Staff Officers from all countries involved attended the ceremony. Ron is sorry to say the whole event went by without his LAD noticing, so they just carried on, the same as ever. On August 1st, he had occasion to go to 176 Bty, then stayed for dinner, drinks and darts, in their newly built Sergeants' Mess, such an incongruous scene could not be imagined. On August 5th, he had to relieve the duty Guard Cdr, who had been taken ill. The rain had been so heavy that the road up to Regimental HQ and the MO had been washed away. Also, the road back to Div HQ was the same, so they were cut off for the time being, forced to live off emergency rations. It was during this period that the *Bedfords* were suffering from worn cylinder bores and pistons, so that their plugs started oiling up. To get over this, Ron would keep two spark plugs in the filter of the petrol tank filler. Then, when he got a misfiring cylinder, he could quickly change an oily plug with a clean one to motor on merrily.

Looking forward to getting home

Ron was called up on the reserve after two years of his agreed four, so he had two more years to serve. After his years of wartime overseas, he presumed that after those two he would then have an extra year 'For The King', so he signed on for four years. The Korean War was not run on the same lines as WWII, because now they were talking of repatriating reservists. He was thinking what a fool he had been, to commit himself to further regular service, especially when he was scheduled for repatriation on the first boat with Chalky White. However, he must have had a 'guardian angel' looking after him, because the Chief Clerk from Regimental HQ told him that because he was a

The LAD

senior rank, his application for further service required the endorsement of a senior REME officer. Knowing of his superior's sympathies, he destroyed that piece of paper, allowing him to hope to be home early. Ron had his inoculations, so was all keyed up to sail from Pusan on September 15th.

In the meantime, the normal run of repairs kept the LAD very busy. An average day's log from those times gives the detail: *Bedford* QL – engine de-coke; HQ Jeep - rear axle; another Jeep - engine change; *Morris* 15-cwt truck – transmission. Most days were very much the same, with the vehicles feeling the strain as much as the men. On September 8th, Ron was not being repatriated in the first boat, but Chalky White was luckier, he left them today and he will be sailing on the 15th, in HMTS *'Devonshire'*. By way of compensation, Ron was sent on five days Tokyo leave. He flew back to Korea on Tuesday October 9th 1951, at 0345 hrs, but for some reason the plane turned back to Tachikawa, landing at 0600 hrs. After a cup of coffee, it was then back on board to be airborne at 0730 hrs for an easy flight, landing at Kimpo at 1200 hrs. Ron eventually arrived at the LAD at 1800 hrs and handed over his purchases for Margi and the others, having completed his shopping list. Following cups of tea and a turkey sandwich, he caught up with the mail from home, had a cold wash and got into his sleeping bag as early as he could.

On Thursday October 11th, they again crossed the Imjin, almost a year since they last came that way, to get to their new and last campsite, but the picture did not please them. The 8th Hussars had been there before them and their tanks had made a terrible mess of a damp area. They dug their tent into the side of a hill, arranging for any rain to run off round the sides. On October 16th, Ron took delivery of a new engine and steering spares for their *Bedford* 15-cwt, so he was able to get that vehicle, which had faithfully carried them so far, into a fit state to hand over to its new owner, the LAD of 14 Fld Regt. Later, he put two new tyres on the old girl and then had to paint out the name *'Lilly Anne'* that had been on the door since February. The position of their LAD was the nearest it had been to the 'sharp end' since April and the Chinese had decided to call a halt to any further advance by the UN Forces.

They were not so far away, because they could watch the US *Sabres* putting in their air strikes and hear small arms fire. At night, they could see to the west the arcs of tracers searching for targets and were entertained at times by some grand sunsets. Strangely enough, after being home for quite some time, he still occasionally dreamed that those Chinese volunteers had got across the river and cut them off from the south, but that the Navy had come up the Imjin River to take them off. Maybe it was the result of a subconscious fear he had at the time. It was time for Margi to go, a sad parting for them; the Padre took her to an orphanage in Yongdong-Po, after buying more clothes for her in Seoul.

On October 23rd, Tom Gray and the Capt QM left for Hong Kong. The Leicestershire Regt ('The Tigers'), which had relieved the Gloucesters, was heavily attacked in the early hours, giving them another noisy turn on guard, things were really moving now. The advance party of 14 Fld Regt RA arrived on the morning of October 29th and it was Ron who showed them around the site and their equipment. November 3rd, and the Chinese put in another attack on the Canadian troops of the Princess Patricia's, which lasted all night and, in the morning, they regained a last hold with the help of some US *Mustangs*. A Danny Kaye (the famous comedian and film star) concert party visited the area, but Ron was too busy preparing for the hand-over to attend. With the formation of the Comm Div, the three Field Regiments, NZ, Canadian and British came under the direction of Div Cdr RA (CRA), Brig Pike, who had to weld them into a formidable striking force.

When the front was not too busy, the guns could practice the 'combined hit', concentrating all seventy-two guns onto one target. For those in 'B' Echelon, this was purely academic, so they just carried on as before. *Rancid* and *Ringworm* had now become redundant, so were dispatched to Japan, where they were relegated to a training mode. Thus 14 Fld LAD was spared the problems their predecessors had suffered with these vehicles. Chang, their houseboy, had served them with distinction, serving all their meals, including the morning mug of 'Gunfire' tea. He had kept their tent clean, looking after their laundry and clearing up their mess tins and cutlery after meals, without complaint, remaining always cheerful. He was now 'passed on' to 14 Fld LAD, which they later learned, subsequently passed him on to 20 Fld LAD. Apparently, the SKA became suspicious of all the local labour being employed by British troops as porters, carrying supplies to forward units, and as stretcher-bearers to carry the wounded. A lot of these men were arrested, some probably to be absorbed into their Army, but some were shot out of hand as spies. What eventually became of Chang afterwards, nobody knows.

Monday November 5th – and Guy Fawkes Day. It was also the day on which the King's Own Scottish Borderers (KOSB) were attacked and Bill Speakman won his VC. The guns were busy all day and 116 Bty were concerned about some loose rivets, so Ron had to go up to them to see what it was all about and had to wait for three quarters of an hour while they shot off a plan. Then their worries proved unfounded, the attention needed wasn't urgent, and Ron got back to his own area for dinner. There was a definite change in the weather; as the temperature dropped, so did the rain, so the roads became treacherously slippery again. Div REME recovery had positioned a bulldozer on the south side of 'Gloucester Crossing', to give assistance when required to help transport up the steep riverbank.

Handing over the reins

They handed over all the gear to 14 Fld Regt RA on November 7th and left the next day for Britannia Camp. They were all in good voice as they sang their way south in the back of a *Bedford* QL, arriving at 1600 hrs. Allotted their tents, they got fed and settled in. They used up the last of the whisky and it was a case of *"This is where we came in"*, as the first frost took its deadly grip. In the morning, Ron had to break the ice in a stream to get water for a wash and shave, and the razor seemed to pull at his stubble, rather than cut through it. Thank God they were getting out. But there was still a last parade for the CRA to review his Gunners, who had covered themselves in glory. In all they had been involved in twelve months of fighting and, over that period, had fired in excess of 150,000 shells. Those guns were now in the hands of 14 Fld Regt RA.

On November 10th, a Saturday, they breakfasted on scrambled egg (the best use for reconstituted dried eggs) and fried bread, after which they packed up ready to go. They handed in their beds, sat on their kit bags and waited. They bussed out of that camp at 12 noon to board the 1300 hrs train at Uijongbu. It was a passenger train, with seats not bunks, but at least they were not in goods wagons and eventually moved out at 1430 hrs. They had a tea stop at Yongdong-Po, they had crossed the Han River for the last time and it was now 1730 hrs. They fed on 'C7' ration packs and were ready for the long haul to Pusan. They reached that destination at 0900 next morning, it presented a grand sight, but it still stank! They took possession of their kit bags, along with all the non-essential gear they had packed away in Seoul a year ago. They had forgotten all about it and had no idea where it had been stored, but now it had re-surfaced ready for the contents to be explored. Ron's kit bag now resides in the REME Museum at Arborfield, tucked away in the archives and still with its shipping identification marks. How well he remembers carrying it down the gangway, which had been so steep and precarious over twelve months ago. So they were then documented and separated from Regulars; the Reservists had served their purpose and now had to take a back seat.

Monday, November 12th 1951; they were still in Pusan, where they changed their British Armed Forces vouchers (BAFs) for sterling and then assembled ready to move out. The time was 2200 hrs, but they didn't leave until midnight, packed into articulated trucks and transported through that smelly town to the docks, only to unload at 0100 hrs on November 13th, at an empty dockside. So here they were, troops all over the place and apparently no ship to take them home. Feelings were definitely a bit jaded; there was no more singing as they waited in hope. The *'Empire Pride'*, their passage home, docked at 0200 hrs and eventually they boarded at 0345 hrs. Allotted to No.2 stores deck, Ron finally got his weary head down at 0500 hrs. And then, after a breakfast at 0800 hrs, they were finally sailing. No gazing at the grey shoreline as it slipped away into the mist, everybody was just too tired to take much interest in things. They were even excused ship's inspection until the evening, then it was early to their hammocks. But sleep didn't come that easily, Ron guessed he was still too wound up to properly relax.

At mid-day on Friday November 16th, the ship docked at Kowloon, Hong Kong. Ron said his last 'good-byes' to the members of the LAD who, of course, were stopping in Hong Kong to finish their tour. Singapore provided a short stopover, followed by another at Colombo, with enough time to 'see the sights'. On Monday, December 3rd, Aden was not such a good stop, as Ron found himself awarded a spell of shore patrol. By the following Friday, they were dropping anchor at Port Suez, followed by a slow journey through the Canal, stopping to form a convoy in the Bitter Lakes. They got under way at 1630 hrs, arriving at Port Said in the early morning and leaving again after a short three hours or so. These landmarks were going by, as they got nearer home. Malta was left behind at 1700 on December 10th, and then it was through the Straits of Gibraltar and into the Atlantic, to cross the 38th Parallel for the last time. They saw three whales and passed by Cape Finistare, before sighting the Scilly Isles at 2300 hrs on a Saturday night. They sailed across the Irish Sea on the Sunday and finally docked at Liverpool at 0500 hrs, on a Monday morning – start of the working week! But now it was 'hammocks away' at long last. Their first breakfast aboard had been kippers and now the final breakfast, naturally, was kippers again! They said farewell to Liverpool as the train pulled out from Lime Street station around mid-day on October 2nd 1950, as the RA military band played one of the favourite tunes of the day, *'Now is the hour (for me to say Goodbye)'*.

Chapter 12

The Chinese enemy & the second withdrawal southwards

Phase 1: November 27th to December 3rd 1950

The Chinese troops entered the war in the thinly veiled guise of 'volunteers'. The extent of their participation was not long in doubt, however. It was a full-scale effort to bolster the defeated NKA and drive the UN forces out of Korea. The Campaign had only been in progress for five months, although UN troops, still almost entirely American, had won a great victory over the NKA. But they were in no condition to withstand a powerful and well-organized assault by the new enemy. The ROK divisions were still in a crippled state, while US troops were thin on the ground and still in need of reinforcements, more equipment and training. Other UN Army contingents were, at present, in little more than token strength and all had dangerously outdistanced their communications. Confronted with the new threat, withdrawal was inevitable, although in hindsight there are doubts as to whether it need have been so precipitate, or so far, as the withdrawal that followed.

It was not only in the military sphere that difficulties arose. Chinese participation was accompanied by political problems of immense consequence. Were the UN to consider them at war with the People's Republic of China (PRC) 'everywhere', or were they to confine operations to the Chinese in Korea? If this latter policy was adopted, the war would probably remain localized, but at a heavy price. Manchuria would become a 'preserved area' for the Chinese Communist Forces (CCF), where they could assemble troops, equipment and supplies, train their troops and base a large air force. All this in support of the Korean Campaign – but with complete immunity from the air, or any other form of attack. The CCF, with the virtual elimination of the original NKA, were to be the UN's chief opponents for the rest of the campaign.

Like the Russians, the Chinese dispensed with the Corps organisation and placed their Divisions under Armies. A CCF Army usually consisted of three infantry divisions, with a total strength of between 20,000 and 32,000 men - 28,000 being probably a fair average. A division consists of three regiments (Brigades), each of three battalions. A regiment averaged about 2,700 men and battalions – each of three rifle companies and a support weapon company – had an establishment of about 700, practically all of whom were fighting soldiers. In the early days, many Chinese were supported very largely with British and American weapons, including Bren-guns. These had, of course, been captured from the Chinese Nationalists, under Chiang Kai Shek. The standard infantry weapons were the rifle and Chinese stick grenade, with some 7.62mm light machine guns. Most battalions had a proportion of 60mm and 80mm mortars, bazookas, and Soviet anti-tank grenades and, in some cases, 5.7mm. Recoilless rifles. Armoured units were equipped with T34 medium tanks, mounting an 85mm gun. In the latter stages of the Campaign, a number of JS2 Self-propelled equipments, mounting a 122mm gun, were reported.

At the beginning, the Chinese had very little artillery, but this deficiency was soon remedied and, by about the middle of 1951, they were capable of putting down very heavy concentrations. They usually handled their artillery with considerable skill. The artillery battalion in their infantry division was generally equipped with twelve of 75/76mm guns, whilst an army artillery regiment usually deployed twelve each of 75/76mm guns, 122mm howitzers and 37mm AA guns. The largest artillery formation was the artillery division, composed of a varying number of 105mm guns, some horse and some mechanically drawn. In addition, at least one rocket regiment, armed with twenty-four 132mm rocket projectors, is known to have been in action. The enemy was never able to use airfields in Korea extensively, as they were destroyed at the outset by the USAF, then re-destroyed as quickly as they were re-constructed. Throughout the Campaign, enemy air action was thus based mainly on airfields north of the Yalu. This hampered any inclinations they may have had for offensive action but, as the Campaign progressed, the *MIG* fighter - of Russian design and one of the finest machines of its kind in the world - appeared in increasing numbers. These, together with more and better AA guns, gave the enemy's air defence the semblance of a sting, although it was never sufficient to deter, or seriously embarrass, the UN Air Forces.

Although their equipment was not to be despised, it did not bear comparison with British and American equivalents. Consequently, the Chinese relied to a considerable extent on sheer physical numbers. Accurate estimates of the Chinese strength in Korea at any given time are difficult to make. Early in December 1950, the number was said to be 200,000, which is probably reasonably accurate. By June 1952, this strength had greatly increased. Information from the most reliable sources indicates that, at its peak, the CCF numbered between 700,000 and 850,000, practically all-fighting men. The Chinese had never been regarded as a martial race and the view is current that, in this Campaign, UN troops were opposed by a second-rate enemy, whose only merit was its overwhelming numerical strength. Nothing could be farther from the truth. The Chinese in Korea were well-organized, well-trained and well-equipped, and displayed resourcefulness and remarkable courage. They possessed all the qualities and most of the necessary equipment of a modern army, plus the ability to dispense with the 'long administrative tail' that ate up manpower and hampered the manoeuvreability of Western troops. The Chinese were formidable opponents and, from a study of their methods, many valuable lessons should have been learned.

During the last days of November 1950, UN troops were in the first stages of their second withdrawal, which was to be continued to areas more than fifty miles south of the 38th Parallel. By November 28th, the Americans were withdrawing from Pakchon and Tokchon. Rarely in the history of war has such a highly successful pursuit been followed, almost immediately, by such a precipitate retreat. We left 27 Comm Bde moving to Kunu-Ri on the 27th November. Late that night, orders were issued for a move south. On the next day, they set out for Sunchon on foot, as no transport was available. The distance was about twenty-two miles. At this juncture, the Brigade was the only uncommitted body of troops available to form a reserve for the American IX Corps. On November 30th, the Middlesex Btn was ordered to retrace their steps, in order to secure a pass on the Kunu-Ri / Sunchon road and help part of US 2 Div, which was withdrawing from Kunu-Ri and causing considerable anxiety. Attempts to enter the pass were met by very strong opposition. Holding a position south of it, the Battalion became involved in heavy close-quarter fighting. The American column was ambushed in the pass and suffered very heavily, its survivors joining up with the Middlesex. By that evening, the whole party, with vehicles loaded with mostly American wounded, was withdrawing to Chasan. During the move, even more bitter fighting took place, but they got through, while another column of 2 Div got through by another route. In these operations, our casualties numbered about thirty.

During December 2nd and 3rd, 27 Bde, moving from Chasan to Pyongyang, covered the withdrawal of American troops. The situation was extremely obscure, with much confused fighting, moves and counter-moves occurring, in which the ASH were mainly involved. The Brigade had reached the river by the 3rd. It had expected that it might have the task of holding a bridgehead, to cover the passage of the river, by the retreating American and SKA troops. This duty was, however, taken over by the newly arrived 29 British Inf Bde Group, so that 27 Bde was able to continue its withdrawal, passing through 29 Bde positions on the morning of December 4th. They had been among the first to enter Pyongyang during the advance, and had now formed the rearguard up to its northern outskirts during the retreat.

Phase 2: December 4th 1950 to January 6th 1951

By the first week in December, Eighth Army was in full retreat in the face of a steady, but not very swift, advance by the Chinese. The bitter Korean winter was now at its height; snow was falling and, for troops not fully clothed or equipped for the winter conditions, it was a time of great difficulty and extreme hardship. The enemy advance was also hampered by the weather conditions; delays were imposed by the indescribably bad roads, as well as demolitions and bombing carried out by UN forces. Operations at this time centred round Pyongyang, where American and SKA forces, forming 1st and 1X American Corps, were converging on the town. Here, as described in chapter 10, 29 British Bde was holding a bridgehead north of the river Taedong, covering the withdrawal. After passing through 29 Bde north of Pyongyang on December 4th, 27 Bde continued its withdrawal for another 120 miles to just north of the town of Uijongbu, about fifteen miles due north of Seoul. Here, for the time being at least, conditions were peaceful, but the cold was bitter and there was little comfort. 60 Indian Fld Ambulance joined the Brigade at Uijongbu on December14th.

By mid-December, the UN line ran roughly along the 38th Parallel and, as the CCF caught up with the withdrawal, 27 Comm Bde found them, once again in the battle zone. Contact was not close however, and Commonwealth troops spent a quiet Christmas Day with the best of seasonable fare. Dinners were served in the open in a snowstorm, with Army tradition being maintained as the Officers and Senior Ranks acted as waiters to their men. It was expected that the enemy would launch a new offensive about Christmas or the New Year, and arrangements had been made for a withdrawal through Seoul should this become necessary. On the morning of December 23rd, Gen Walker, American Cdr of Eighth Army, had most unfortunately been killed in a motor accident, whilst on his way to present a Korean Presidential citation to 27 Inf Bde. It was subsequently presented by the acting Army Cdr, Lt Gen Milburn, on the following day. A few days later, Gen Walker's successor, American Lt Gen Matthew B Ridgway, assumed command.

The expected Chinese attack began on New Year's Eve. It had been Gen Ridgway's intention to hold the existing line if possible but, by the morning of January 1st 1951, the situation had become precarious. A SKA Division had been roughly handled and was retreating, while some US troops had been forced back nearly three miles. So, on the morning of New Year's Day, 27 Comm Bde was ordered to advance to an area about six miles north of Uijongbu and then to act as rearguard to 6 ROK Div. Throughout the Korean campaign, co-operation with SKA troops was no easy matter, as they were indistinguishable from NKA soldiers. It was often difficult, if not impossible, to tell friend from foe. 3 RAR was given the 'post of honour', farthest north. In due course, the SKA column passed through and, almost immediately, the Australians discovered that the road behind them, linking them with the rest of the Brigade, had been cut by a section of the enemy who had come in from the flank. The road was soon cleared however, and the Australians made their withdrawal, passing through the Middlesex and ASH. The whole Brigade then withdrew to Seoul, where they remained comparatively inactive until the evening of the January 3rd. During that night, they occupied defensive positions in and around the town, to cover the withdrawal of the American 1 Cavalry and 24 Div.

In this task, the Australians had some contact with the enemy. 'C' Coy ASH was detached to protect an important bridge – named the *'Al Jolson Bridge'* - over which the bulk of the American troops were to withdraw. Soon after midnight, the last troops had crossed; the Company then withdrew and the bridge was blown behind them. After the evacuation of the city, the rest of the Brigade crossed the Han River by a bridge farther west. 'D' Coy ASH covered this movement and, when they finally crossed, at about 1000 hrs on January 4th, that bridge was also blown. On the following day, news was received that Maj K Muir, 1 Btn ASH had been posthumously awarded the VC.

Apart from 'A' Coy RAR, which was involved in an ambush near Ichon, the rest of the withdrawal was carried out without incident. 27 Comm Bde moved back to Suwon, then to an area some twenty miles south of Changhowon-Ni, before turning north again to Changhowon-Ni itself (forty-five miles south-east of Seoul), where they arrived on January 6th.

Leaving 27 Comm Bde, attention now turns to 29 Bde. The Brigade had been without the RNF, which had occupied its positions covering Pyongyang by December 3rd 1950. But then, on the 5th, they withdrew under orders to a defensive position at Sinmak, a rail and road junction, some fifty-five miles to the south of Pyongyang. There they remained until December 11th, when they came into the American 1 Corps reserve at Chungdon, about fifty miles farther south and ten miles east of Kaesong. It was here that the RNF rejoined the Brigade. On December 13th, a move to Yangchol Li, north of Seoul, was made, with the role of protecting an important road bridge. Here, on December 23rd, Brig Brodie issued a 'Special Order of the Day' that, in addition to his own Christmas greetings to his men, included messages from the Army Council, Cdr Eighth Army and Cdr 1st American Corps. Whatever the hardships being endured at this time, a lack of traditional food on Christmas Day was not one of them.

By the first days of January 1951, the enemy had caught up with the UN forces and had begun the second phase of its offensive. On the western flank, this was directed against 1st Corps, which was covering Seoul by holding a line north of the Han River, with the 25th American, 1 and 6 ROK Divisions. 29 British Inf Bde, with 21 Thai Inf Regt under its command, was in Corps reserve at Yangchol Li. It was destined to become heavily involved in the fighting of the next few days. Early on January 2nd, the Brigade was ordered into a counter-attack role, but this was later cancelled. Instead, they took up defensive dispositions, which they had themselves prepared for occupation by 1 ROK Div. This position was about ten miles north of Seoul, to the east of the MSR, and ran from just south of Koyang on the left, due east to Chunghung Dong, a distance of about five miles.

The engagement started at about 0400 hrs on January 3rd, when an American patrol was driven in from Koyang. At first light, 'B' Coy RUR was overrun by a surprise attack, in which the enemy were heard shouting in English, *"South Koreans – we surrender"*. Later, a Platoon of 'D' Coy was also overrun but, by 1130 hrs, the situation had been stabilised by a counter-attack. By 1235 hrs, the 2IC – who was in temporary command, owing to the illness of Lt Col RJH Carson – was able to report that the original position had been regained. Meanwhile, the enemy had also attacked on the 5 Fusiliers front and, at about 0930 hrs, had penetrated the position to a considerable depth. The CO asked for tank support, which was given by moving 'C' Sqn 7 RTR forward. By 1730 hrs, the situation on this front had been restored by a counter-attack, delivered by 'W' Coy (which had

Maj Mathews, CO of 11 Inf Wksp REME, giving instructions to drivers on how to drive over the long pontoon bridge.

moved forward from the Han River) and the tanks.

At 1630 hrs, orders were issued for the Brigade to withdraw south of the Han River. This proved a difficult operation in the dark, as the enemy followed up closely and the troops were encumbered by their 'A' Echelon transport, which was difficult to move along the bad tracks and very vulnerable. The withdrawal began at 1830hrs. The Gloucesters (who had not been seriously engaged) and 5 Fusiliers broke contact and got away without undue difficulty, but the RUR became involved in heavy fighting and suffered severely. During the withdrawal, part of the Battalion was ambushed by a force of the enemy that had worked its way unseen around the left flank of the position. The situation was restored by a gallant bayonet charge by the Support Coy, assisted by tanks of 'Cooper Force', a detachment of 8 Hussars Reconnaissance Troop. Desperate hand-to-hand fighting took place, during which some 200 of the enemy were killed. In the final stages of this action, Maj Blake, acting CO of the RUR, and Captain Astley-Cooper were both killed. Contact was broken just before midnight and, before dawn on January 4th, the Brigade had crossed the Han River and the last bridge had been blown. Here, transport was in readiness to take them south to Suwon.

A welcome respite

29 Bde had acquitted itself well in its first serious engagement in Korea. But losses had been heavy – about 230 killed, wounded and missing in the RUR, about fifty in 5 Fusiliers and some twenty, together with the loss of some tanks, in 'Cooper Force'. From Suwon, the Brigade then moved another twenty miles south of Pyongtaek. Thus the withdrawal ended, on January 6th, with 29 Bde on the extreme left of the Eighth Army's new line, near the coast, and 27 Comm Bde some thirty-five miles inland to the east, at Changhowon-Ni. There was now to be a brief period of comparative rest for both Brigades – a welcome respite from the exertions of the past weeks, and a chance to re-group before the severe fighting that was to follow.

The second withdrawal south marked the end of the highly mobilised fighting that had taken place, up and down the main lines of communication, during the first six months of the Campaign. From mid-January until May 1951, it was to become largely an infantryman's battle. Each hill in turn had to be occupied by sheer physical effort, captured in a series of desperate, but local, attacks. The enemy showed himself to be an expert in conducting a skilful withdrawal. Thereafter, fluidity was restored for short periods on parts of the front; but, in general, the Campaign became one of limited set-piece attacks, supported by heavy artillery bombardments; and restricted fighting in which patrolling, field works, barbed wire and the mine were to play a prominent part.

The view from the cab on the drive over the long pontoon bridge.

The conditions of the

The Chinese Enemy - The second withdrawal southwards

retreat made it necessary to destroy immense quantities of stores and equipment, which had previously been brought forward in the wake of the advance. This kind of thing did not unduly depress American troops, backed as they were by immense industrial resources. They obviously took the view that there was *"plenty more where that came from, and plenty of ships, planes and land transport to bring it to us"*. That may have been so in their case but, to the British and Commonwealth troops, it was a grievous matter to lose, or abandon, their precious equipment, which might not be replaced for months. In this connection, it is appropriate to relate the experience of 60 Indian Ambulance at Pyongyang. This fine unit had landed in Korea on November 20th and was accompanied by six months' supply of medical stores. On December 4th, they were at Pyongyang, when the order to evacuate the town was given. They were told that, as there was no transport available, they must burn all their stores and equipment. This was too much for their CO, who was determined to prevent such a disaster if it was humanly possible to do so. Eventually they found a railway engine and a few trucks in a siding. They filled the engine with water, by means of jerrycans and a chain of men, then gathered wood to run the engine on, as no coal was available. In the early hours of December 5th, two Indian soldiers, with some previous railway experience, drove this small train over the last bridge, just before it was demolished. It is difficult to imagine a finer example of initiative and devotion to duty than this.

Those who have never campaigned in really cold weather can hardly realize the difficulties – especially when the arrangements have been hastily made and there is a lack of proper winter clothing and equipment, especially designed for a cold climate. Apart from the discomforts and hardships, the most irksome and difficult measures were necessary for the preparation of food and to maintain equipment in serviceable condition. Hot water, poured into the radiator of a vehicle, froze almost at once. There was a shortage of American anti-freeze mixture and some of Russian manufacture, captured from the NKA, proved useless. Socks had to be frequently changed to prevent frostbite and they could not be removed unless the owner was near a fire or had some other means of warming his feet. On British pattern cookers, water took one and a half-hours to boil. There were difficulties with weapons, owing to lack of a suitable type of lubricating oil, which meant that they had to be kept almost dry. In some units, the problem of maintaining Bren-guns in working order, and of keeping the men warm, was solved by constructing a small 'fireplace' in each slit trench. No accurate meteorological reports were available for the artillery. In the very low temperatures experienced, this made the plotting of defensive fire tasks by night very difficult, as the extreme cold often made a difference of 300 or 400 yards in the flight of the shells.

Whilst that infantry engagement had been proceeding, 29 Bde's Support Wksp had been left at Pyongyang on December 2nd. It remained in this location for two days, until it moved again to Sariwon, caught its breath and moved again on 6th December to Kaesong and, at this location, they opened for work. But December 11th saw them on the move again, steadily moving south. They ended up two miles north of Seoul, located in a large chicken farm, and again opening for work. For ten days the position remained steady, but then it was moving again, to an area some ten miles south of Seoul, to a town called Anyang-Ni. At last, a lengthy stay for work seemed to be on the cards. Christmas Day saw a fire destroy their office truck! Five days into 1951, they moved again, through Suwon and straight on to Chochi-Won, arriving about January 9th. Chochi-Won was near to Sinchon-Ni, seventeen miles south of Taejon. Here, they did not even have time to open for work, but moved on to Yongdong, arriving there on January 11th at about 1230 hrs. No sooner had they stopped, than they were ordered back as far as Taejon, this time to work, for a period of eleven days. By January 22nd - 23rd, they were again packing their trucks and rolling onto Chonan, this time to be located in a school. One more they put up the sign *"Open for work"*, a situation that was to last for another period of eleven days.

Chapter 13

The first withdrawal of 11 Infantry Workshop REME

December 1950

It was obvious by now that, having extended their lines of communication to the limit, UN forces would have to undertake a large-scale withdrawal in order to regroup and fight the new enemy. In their Sinanju location beside the main axis for the left flank, the extent and speed of the withdrawal became apparent. During the night, the complete American 24 Div moved back along this road for a distance of forty miles. 11 Inf Wksp REME stopped with the convoy for an 'English' cup of tea. A photograph taken at the time shows the type of road and terrain they were driving through. Next morning their orders came. In seven moves, with never more than three days in one location, the Workshop moved back over 200 miles to Ichon (not to be confused with Inchon), onto the 9 American Corps axis, arriving there on December 14th. As the Workshop subsequently moved into Ichon on other withdrawals and advances, this first move became known as 'Ichon - First time'. During their move back, while still north of Pyongyang, they met the Battalions of 29 Bde moving up into the battle area for their first time. The advance party of 29 Bde's 10 Inf Wksp was in Pyongyang, looking for a good location – one that they were never to occupy.

On the north bank of the Taedong River, at Pyongyang, 11 Inf Wksp saw a Centurion tank for the first time. It was in serious trouble, a thrown track making it immobile. At that time, the Centurion was in its active service infancy, and this one had eventually to be abandoned and totally destroyed. There were to be many modifications and developments to the tank before this Campaign was over. At Ichon, 11 Inf Wksp settled down to another spell of really hard work, having as many as twenty Carriers, in addition to the normal load of 'B' vehicles, under repair at any one time. By now, the Carriers were in a sorry state; all their spare engines and track had been used; it now became a matter of making up as many serviceable vehicles as possible and abandoning some of the useless ones. They had already been doing this with *Land Rovers* and Jeeps, in spite of the generosity of their friends, the American 24 Ordnance Maintenance Company (OMC), who had provided them with no end of Jeep spares, including a dozen or more engines. During the withdrawal of 11 Inf Wksp, they had picked up Capt Hind and his railhead staff at Munsan and were now working from a new railhead at Suwon. This lay about thirty miles to the left of the American 1 Corps axis. Their friends in 29 Bde, including 10 Inf Wksp, were on

11 Inf Wksp REME stopped for the 'English' cup of tea.

this axis, although contacts with them were few.

The railhead only operated from Suwon for a short time before further withdrawals became necessary, but it was the first time that 11 Inf Wksp had been able to get any NAAFI supplies from a 29 Bde NAAFI train at Suwon. These came just in time for Christmas and were most welcome. The stay at Ichon continued over Christmas, by which time a very generous

Typical type of road and terrain they were driving through

supply of gifts in the way of winter clothing, woollen socks, scarves, balaclavas, gloves, etc had arrived. Everyone in the unit was by now very well off for winter kit; in fact it was a struggle to keep individual hoards down to manageable proportions. The Christmas rations were excellent; Thanksgiving Day all over again, though such delicacies as tinned asparagus never really caught on with the troops! By now, their front was roughly along the line of the Han River through Seoul and running north east to the eastern coast. It was about this time that the Cdr of all UN Forces in Korea, Gen Walton H Walker was killed in a Jeep accident and Gen Matthew B Ridgway, an American paratrooper, took over in his place.

27 Bde had been strengthened by the arrival of 2 Btn PPCLI and 60 Indian Fld Ambulance. Later, they were to be joined by part of 57 Coy RASC, so the Brigade, which since the arrival of the first Commonwealth unit had been called 27 British Comm Bde, eventually comprised:

HQ, including Signal Troop LAD and Anti-Tank Troop RA
1 Btn ASH (UK)
1 Btn Middlesex Regt (UK)
3 RAR (Australia)
2 Btn PPCLI (Canada)
16 New Zealand Fld Regiment (NZ)
60 Indian Fld Ambulance (India)
57 Coy RASC (Part) (UK)
27 OFP RAOC (UK)
11 Inf Wksp REME (UK)

Thus it was a truly Commonwealth Brigade, which from time to time had additional support from a Squadron of American tanks and a Chemical Mortar Battalion.

Christmas activities included the production of a souvenir foolscap-sized menu by the Chief Clerk. On the reverse of the menu was a map of Korea, with all of the Workshop moves and dates. This became something of a collector's item, appearing in several UK local newspapers, and extra copies were still being run off well after Christmas. By the end of 1950, it was apparent that a further withdrawal was to take place. But the new Cdr had made it clear that this was a limited one only, to stretch the enemy lines of communications and to allow for new UN troops to be assimilated into the line. This also applied to new SKA Divisions being made up.

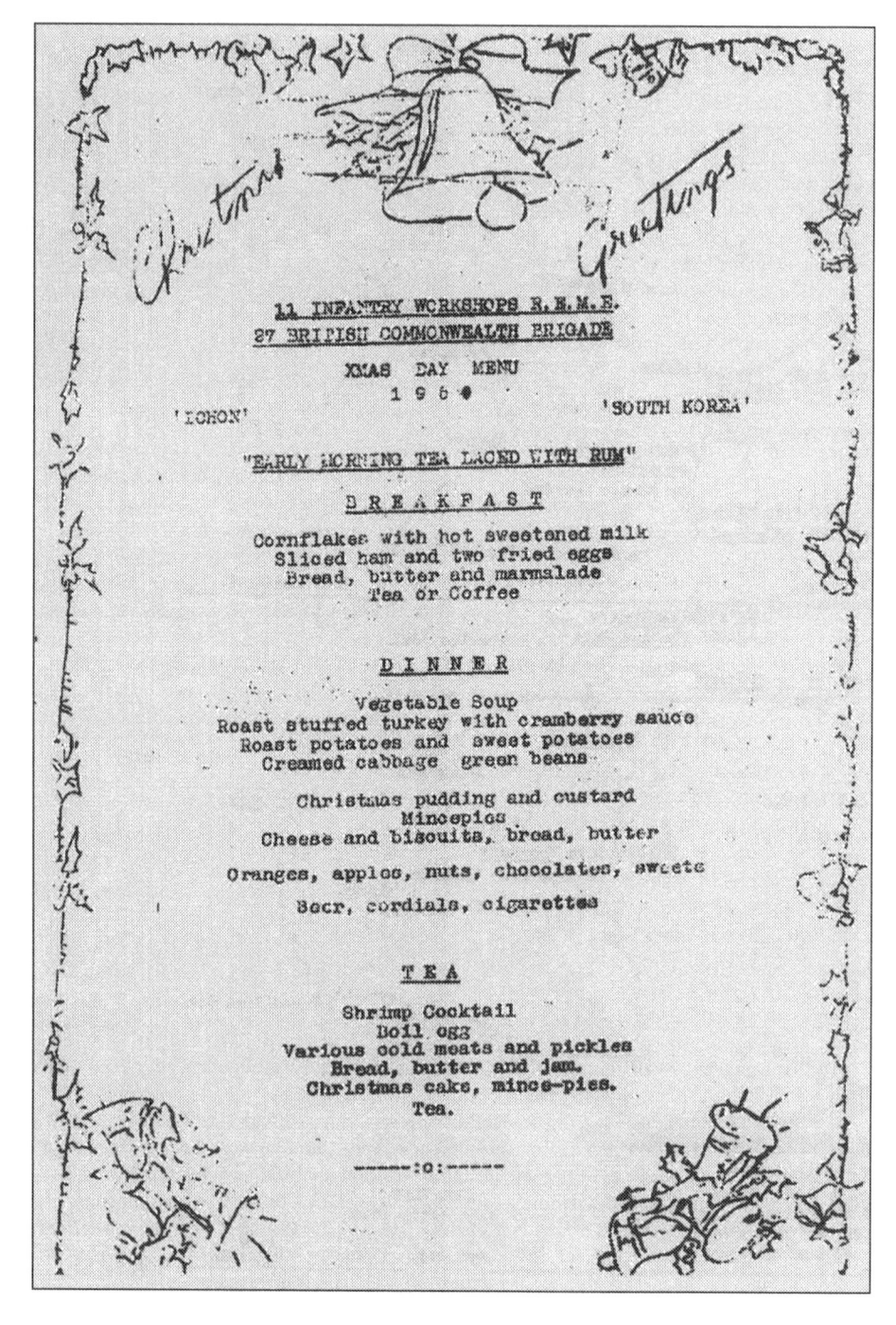

11 INFANTRY WORKSHOPS R.E.M.E.
27 BRITISH COMMONWEALTH BRIGADE

XMAS DAY MENU
1960

'ICHON'   'SOUTH KOREA'

"EARLY MORNING TEA LACED WITH RUM"

BREAKFAST

Cornflakes with hot sweetened milk
Sliced ham and two fried eggs
Bread, butter and marmalade
Tea or Coffee

DINNER

Vegetable Soup
Roast stuffed turkey with cranberry sauce
Roast potatoes and sweet potatoes
Creamed cabbage   green beans

Christmas pudding and custard
Mincepies
Cheese and biscuits, bread, butter

Oranges, apples, nuts, chocolates, sweets

Beer, cordials, cigarettes

TEA

Shrimp Cocktail
Boil egg
Various cold meats and pickles
Bread, butter and jam.
Christmas cake, mince-pies.
Tea.

------:o:------

January 1951 - The withdrawal continues

It was now the New Year of 1951, but it was to start in much the same way as before, with one rapid move after another. On January 2nd, there were frantic efforts made to reduce the vehicle repair load, or at least to make them capable of being towed to the next location. By the 3rd they were in Chongju, but only overnight, the next day moving on to Umsong. This move took until the 6th, just an overnight stay again, followed by a further move next day to Hamchang. But still no respite, as on the 8th they pulled in at Kumchon. During these seemingly endless moves, the CO has been away in Pusan, trying to find some spares, as by now practically all their 'bread and butter' items had been used up. He was successful and they picked up many necessary items upon their arrival in Kumchon. Those moves required practically every man in the unit to either drive or steer a vehicle under tow. The driver-training programme in Hong Kong had certainly paid dividends. During this interrupted withdrawal, there was one particular range of mountains that stretched the poor old tired *Fordson* machinery lorries to the full. Nothing was lost, but there were some unhappy moments when the cooks truck, which always went off in advance, was found broken down with no empty truck available to off-load its precious contents. A couple of VMs dropped off the convoy and brought it safely home. It is worth mentioning at this point that the unit had moved to Korea about 130 strong, some forty men under strength, with practically no General Duties (GD) men and several load carriers short. There were therefore none of the niceties of Officers' or Sergeants' Mess trucks, all cooking was done centrally at the one kitchen with the four ACC cooks. *(N.B. This was reduced to three after Harwood went absent at Kaesong, during the advance.)*

While the Workshop was at Ichon, a small detachment of RAEME (the Australian REME) joined them. Up until then, they had been operating with their own RAR Battalion but, for a number of reasons, it was decided to attach them to the Workshop. The detachment was from their static workshop in Kure, Japan, and its personnel changed over every three months. The location in Kumchon was, as usual a riverbed, a long wide one, with plenty of room for the whole of Bde 'B' echelon. The stay here, for a little over three weeks, once again gave the opportunity to catch-up with some work and to obtain spares. This was a welcome respite and, although very cold, it was a fine arrangement. Kumchon was only forty miles north of their very first location, Taegu, so it was 'back to square one', well almost. It was at this location that a R & R leave scheme to Japan started. The Workshop leave allocation was naturally very small, but a 'points' system was drawn up, so that the outdoor trades such as VMs, cooks, etc had a good chance of getting away first. As it happened, the first man to go was one of the ACC cooks.

By now, they had picked up four South Korean permanent helpers who they fed and clothed and who, in return, did some of the chores. There was a barber, two kitchen hands and a shoe repairer. These helpers travelled up and down the country with them. Unkind critics said it was to dodge the local call-up, but they certainly 'earned their keep' with the Workshop. By the end of January 1951 the front was stable. New Korean Divisions had been formed; French, Greek and Philippine troops had arrived and there were some seven American Divisions, including 2 Marines and some specialist airborne units. The American Combat Engineer effort had also been considerably stepped up. Bridges were now beginning to bear several claims by these units, such as 'built by', 'destroyed by' and 'rebuilt by', as the process of advance and withdrawal continued unabated.

Chapter 14

The second advance north January to April 1951

By mid-January 1951, the UN retreat had reached its limit. The line now ran from the coast near Pyongtaek (about the 37th Parallel), near Wonju in central Korea, and thence to the eastern coast at Kangnung, some twenty miles south of the 38th Parallel. In the west, there was no contact with the enemy in the Wonju area, but the Chinese continued to attack the Americans, but were repulsed. 29 British Bde was on the extreme left of the line about Pyongtaek, with 3 American Div on its right. 27 Comm Bde was at Changhowon-Ni. On January 22nd, 16 Fld Regt Royal NZ Artillery (RNZA) joined this Brigade as its supporting Artillery Regiment. The Kiwis were all volunteers and, apart from some senior officers, very few had been gunners before. They had only three months training as artillerymen, but what they lacked in experience they more than made up for in enthusiasm. They did not take long to become accustomed to Korean conditions and, a week after their arrival, they were attached to the American 24 Div.

It would be idle to pretend that the retreat had not had a negative effect on the Eighth Army. In the two British and Commonwealth Brigades morale was high, but the men were somewhat puzzled by the poor military situation. They felt that Western troops, with the wealth of military experience garnered in WWII, and equipped with fairly modern weapons, should have been able to stand their ground in the face of the Chinese enemy, however great their numbers. In particular, there was a feeling that the SKA was not fighting well in defence of its mother country. It is true that they were often unable to withstand the Chinese onslaughts, but this was often due to shortages of guns and other heavy equipment. There was also the fact that they had not fully recovered from the strenuous fighting of the early days. There was no lack of determination and, in the circumstances, the SKA troops fought well.

The new Army Cdr, Gen Ridgway, was not satisfied with the positions taken up by the Eighth Army at the end of its withdrawal and, soon after he assumed command, he planned a limited advance to approximately the 38th Parallel. By the end of January 1951, by a series of methodical attacks, the line in the west had advanced some twenty miles to Suwon, Ichon and near Yoju, and was moving slowly towards Seoul and the Han River. During this advance, very fierce fighting continued on the IX Corps front in the Wonju area, the town having changed hands several times. The next three months, mid-January to mid-April, were to witness a somewhat different type of fighting to that previously experienced in Korea. It was primarily an infantryman's war. No large-scale set-piece battles occurred but, almost daily, there were engagements on either a Company, Battalion or, sometimes, a Brigade scale. These were usually in attack, sometimes on the defensive, but always in difficult, precipitous country, devoid of roads. The motor vehicle gave way to the porter as a means of supply. Mules would have been invaluable but unfortunately there were none. The recipe for victory was to be found in minor tactics and the initiative of junior leaders, rather than high-level decisions and complicated fire plans. By their training, Commonwealth troops were well suited to this type of fighting and, compared with other UN troops in similar conditions, kept their casualties to a remarkably low figure.

The activities of 27 Brigade

On January 7th, 27 Bde took up defensive positions about Changhowon-Ni, about forty-five miles southeast of Seoul and fifteen miles southeast of Ichon. Contact with the enemy was not close and, although constant vigilance was necessary, the main activities were long-range patrols,

The Second Advance North - 7th January to 22nd April 1951

mostly to Ichon. 6 ROK Div was on the left and 5 RCT of American 24 Div on the right. There was a gap of some 2,000 yards between the Brigade left and the South Koreans. A few days later, a patrol of that South Korean Division visited Ichon, but did not meet the enemy. This was a bitterly cold day, the temperature being 19 degrees below zero. On the 15th a patrol of 3 Btn RAR also went to Ichon, but again drew a blank. However, two days later, an Australian patrol passed through the town and met some Chinese about a mile to the north, inflicting some casualties, without loss to the patrol. On January 19th, Brig Coad went on leave to Hong Kong. On the following

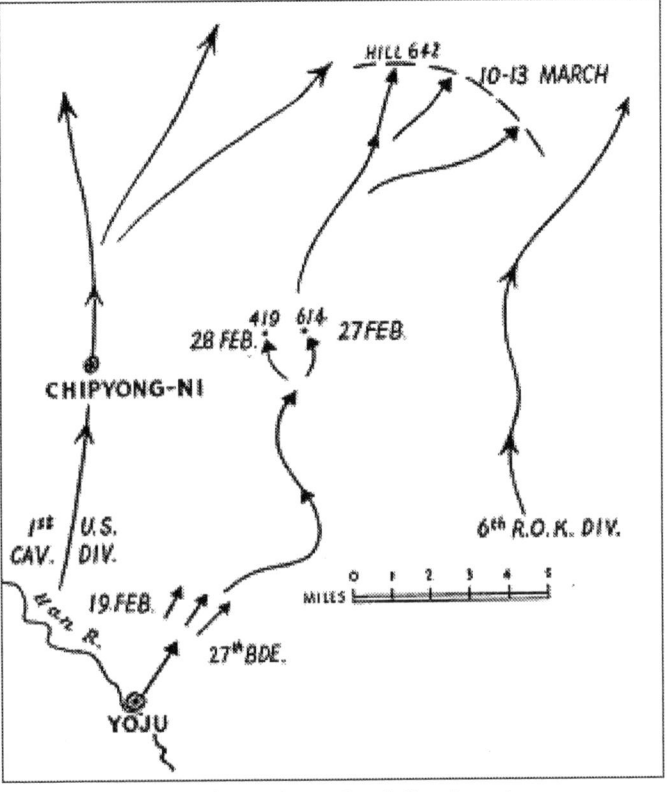

Tactical sketch map of Australian & Canadian advances

day, an Australian Company, on patrol near Ichon, had a sharp engagement with a party of Chinese. Enemy casualties were estimated at ten killed and fifteen wounded. The Australians had one man killed and two wounded, while one officer and four ORs were captured.

January proved a memorable month, however, as a system of leave began; five days in Tokyo, with an air passage both ways. Arrangements were also made for married men with wives in Hong Kong to spend a few days' leave there. On the 25th, an Eighth Army offensive began, but 27 Bde did not participate in the initial stages. On the 30th, the Brigade came directly under the American IX Corps. It vacated its positions and concentrated at Changhowon-Ni, with the Australians guarding Corps HQ. The enemy counter-attacked the American 24 Div, north of Ichon, on February 4th. This attack met with some success and, as a precautionary measure, the ASH were moved forward that morning to Yoju, twelve miles east of Ichon, while 27 Bde HQ opened at Chongan-Ni. On the following day, the RNZA Gunners returned to the Brigade and took up positions south of Yoju. By then, however, the situation for the American 24 Div's front had greatly improved. On the 10th, a very surprising incident occurred. The enemy released the Australian officer and men who had been captured near Ichon. They reported that they had been fairly well treated, but subjected to a very thorough course of Communist indoctrination. It can only be supposed that the Chinese thought that this process had been so effective that the officer and his men would immediately make many converts among their comrades!

On February 11th, the CO of 2 Btn PPCLI arrived, as his Battalion was shortly to join the Brigade. On the 14th, 27 Bde came under the command of the American 2 Div and received orders to immediately cross the Han River at Yoju and advance north. They were to relieve the American 23 RCT and its accompanying French Battalion, who had been cut off in the Chipyong-Ni area, some ten miles north of Yoju. It is a matter of interest that 23 RCT had under its command the French Battalion, which earned a very high reputation in Korea. Many stories are told of them, one of which is typical of their spirit and general attitude. It was a rule that, after dark, no fires should be left burning, but this was an order that had never appealed to the French. On one occasion, an American duty officer telephoned the Battalion and remonstrated, *"Get those fires out at once, or you'll have all the Chinese in Korea round you",* he said. *"But monsieur",* replied the French officer, *"that is magnificent. As you say, the Chinese will see our fires. They attack us - we kill them".*

27 Bde was directed on Chipyong-Ni. The intervening country was rugged and inhospitable, without definable roads or any normal amenities of life. During subsequent operations, the Brigade was continuously on the move for a month, pressing forward against a stubborn enemy that was adept at rearguard fighting. On the night of February 13th, about six miles south of the Han River, Hill 112 was occupied by part of the Reconnaissance Coy of American 2 Div, who had just withdrawn there. On the morning of the 14th, they were heavily attacked and suffered serious casualties. They withdrew through the ASH, who were occupying positions around Yoju. The Chinese followed the retiring Americans down the road very closely, to within a few hundred yards of the ASH, who were waiting for them with their machine guns. It was, however, difficult to distinguish friend from foe and the Highlanders were forced to hold their fire. By 1730 hrs that evening, the Middlesex, who had led the advance, captured Hill 112. The Australians moved up to another feature on their left, while the ASH took up positions on the right. At about 0530 hrs next morning, the Middlesex were counter-attacked. For a short time, there was some confused fighting, but the situation was quickly restored. The RNZA Gunners played a conspicuous part in repelling this attack and, soon after first light, the advance was continued.

February 18th was a day of continual blizzard, but a notable one apart from that. On this day, 2 Btn PPCLI arrived. It is doubtful if those soldiers, deployed on their windswept hills, realized that this was a red-letter day in the annals of our Commonwealth Forces. 27 Comm Bde now consisted of Australian, Canadian, English and Scottish Battalions, a NZ Fld Regt and an Indian Fld Ambulance. It was commanded by an Englishman, Brig Coad, who returned from leave on this day. There is no record of any other Brigade, or force of a similar size, being composed of so many contingents of different

Moving through typical terrain

The Second Advance North - 7th January to 22nd April 1951

Commonwealth countries. It seems unlikely that there is a parallel in the history of any Army. Mention must also be made of the American 2 Mortar Btn, which had been with the Brigade since December 1950 (and remained with it until April 1951). This fine unit, organized in three Companies of 12 x 4.2" mortars each, became firm friends of the Brigade, and gave them magnificent support on many occasions.

The forward move continued on the 19th, with the Middlesex to the left, the Canadians in the centre, and the ASH on the right. Little opposition was encountered and it transpired that the enemy had in fact retreated. The

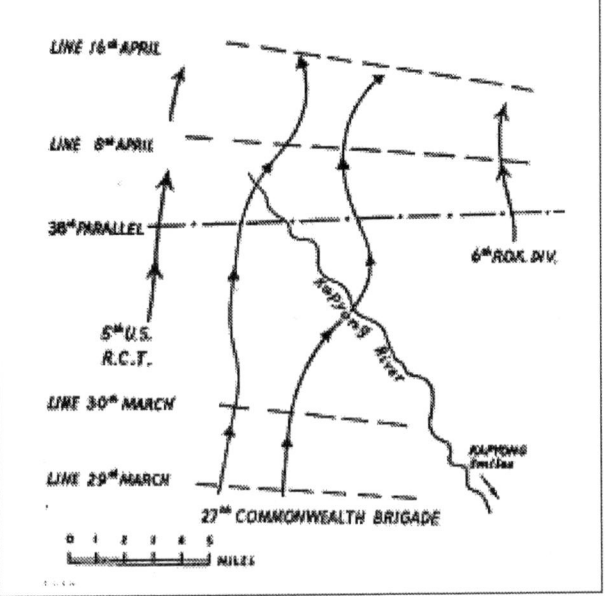

2nd Advance of the 27th Commonwealth Brigade

Chinese intention had been to seize the Han bridges, east of Yoju. Heavy losses inflicted by the Americans in the Chipyong-Ni area, and the steady advance of 27 Comm Bde, caused the Chinese to abandon the attempt and withdraw. On this same day, Gen Mark Clark, the American General of WWII fame, visited the Brigade. Led by the Australians and Canadians, the advance continued day by day until February 27th 1951. At first, opposition was slight, but it increased considerably as the leading troops approached Hills 419 and 614, two prominent features on a good defensive position about four miles south of Chipyong-Ni. On the right, after severe fighting, the Aussies captured Hill 614 on the 27th and, next day, the Canadians made a successful attack on Hill 419 on the left. On the afternoon of the 28th, the Aussies repelled a counter-attack and the methodical advance continued. On March 1st, some additional South Korean porters joined the Brigade, bringing the total up to about 100 per Battalion. These porters were a great help in solving the problem of moving supplies to forward troops. With kindly treatment and good food, the Korean porters were cheerful and efficient men. They were to become a feature of most British and Commonwealth units.

On March 8th, the enemy withdrew on all fronts, leaving behind a good deal of equipment. Their losses had been very heavy and it was characteristic of Chinese policy that they withdrew out of contact, once it became apparent that the attack was unlikely to produce worthwhile results. On the 13th, the Brigade was relieved by the American 5 Cavalry Regt and concentrated in the riverbed near Nolbunyo-Ni, about fifteen miles north of Yoju. This ended the very strenuous operations that had lasted for twenty-six days, conducted in bitterly cold weather, against an enemy that merited respect as tough and skilful fighters. The Brigade's casualties had not been heavy, amounting to twenty-one killed and seventy wounded. 27 Bde remained at Nolbunyo-Ni until March 24th, in IX Corps reserve, resting and refitting.

On the 25th, the Brigade moved fifty miles by mechanical transport to Hyon-Ni, where they came under the command of the American 24 Div. A few days later, they took over from the American

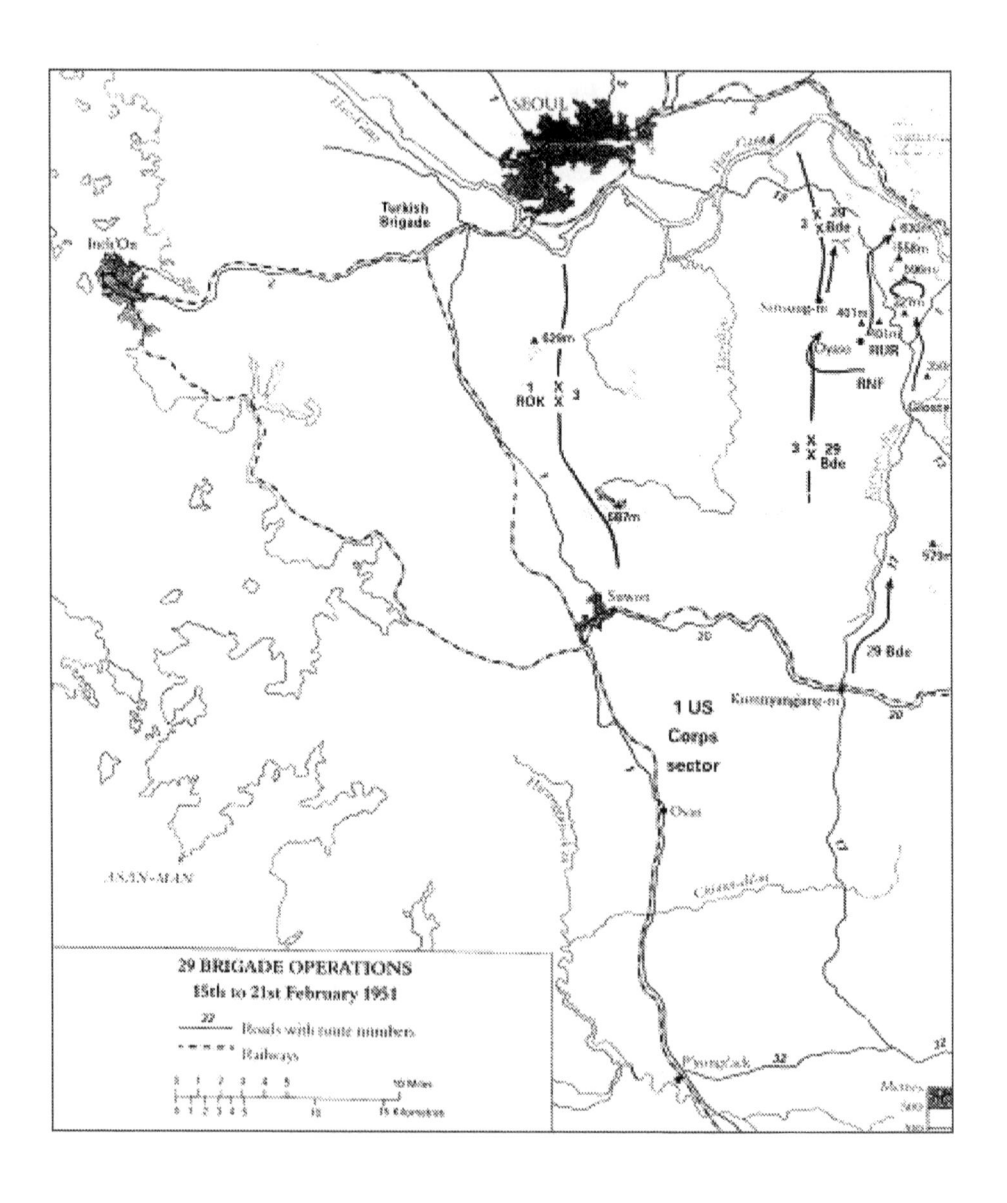

29 BRIGADE OPERATIONS
15th to 21st February 1951

The Second Advance North - 7th January to 22nd April 1951

19 RCT, in the front line just north of Hyon-Ni. The advance was to be continued until April 16th. The last week up the Kopyong road was a very strenuous period for the whole Brigade. The ASH lost two officers killed and some men wounded in their last engagement. Finally, the Australians and Canadians captured the last objective in this phase of operations. It is interesting to note that, on March 31st, artificial light, by means of which an extensive area can be lit up, was used in Korea for the first time in the Brigade area. On April 19th, 27 Bde was relieved by 19 Regt of 6 ROK Div and returned to the Kopyong area in IX Corps reserves. The RNZA Gunners, however, remained behind in support of the South Koreans.

Policy governing the relief of Commonwealth units and individuals, which the continuance of the Korean War made necessary as far as British units were concerned, fixed a tour of duty of approximately one year in Korea for fighting units. About the same period for formation commanders, staff and administrative officers was decided on. Most Commonwealth countries adopted a similar policy. There were, of course, many exceptions to the rule, particularly in administrative units. In accordance with this decision, arrangements were made for the relief of HQ 27 Bde, 1Btn Middlesex Regt and 1Btn ASH. The relief of 27 Bde by 28 Bde was a special one, as the relief of headquarters higher than unit level was not repeated. Brig G Taylor DSO (28 Bde) had arrived on 14th April 1951.

The activities of 29 Brigade

Turning back to the period beginning on January 6th 1951, 29 Bde had arrived in the Pyongtaek-Songhwan area, on the left of the Eighth Army line near the coast and about forty miles south of Seoul. On February 1st, they moved to Osan-Ni, about twelve miles to the north on the Seoul road. At the same time, 45 Fld Regt and 'C' Sqn 7 RTR were detached from the Brigade in support of 1 ROK Div and the American 25 Div respectively. On February 11th, a somewhat hurried move north to Pablamak was made. It was here, on the next day, that they relieved 5 Cavalry Regt of the American 1Cavalry Div. For the next ten days, they were engaged in hill fighting in conjunction with the American 24 RCT, a coloured formation of the American 25 Div. The Gloucesters, 'C' Sqn of 8 Hussars and the RUR were the units mainly engaged in these operations. On the 23rd, the Brigade was withdrawn to Suwon, where it came into Corps Reserve. This was a quiet period for the British Brigade, which moved to Ichon on March 7th and then later to Yongdong-Po on the 21st.

On the last day of March 1951, 29 Bde came under the command of the American 3 Inf Div and, on the following day, took over the line of the Imjin River. This was to be the scene of 29 Bde's epic stand during the famous 'Battle of Imjin River' between the 23rd and 25th April. This position, extending from Choksong on the left to the junction of the Imjin and Hantan Rivers on the right, was held with three Battalions forward. 1 Btn RNF were on the left; 10 Battalion Combat Team (BCT - Philippine), which was attached to the Brigade, in the centre; and 1 Btn RUR on the right.

The next three weeks was a period of intensive patrolling and preparation for a continuation of the methodical advance, which had been going on along practically the whole front since the end of January. On April 4th, the Belgian Battalion relieved 10 BCT, which then left the Brigade. Frequent reliefs were carried out within the Brigade and some slight adjustments of boundaries made. On April 22nd, the front was held with the Gloucesters to the left, 5 Fusiliers in the centre and the Belgians to the right, with the RUR being held in reserve. The Chinese were about to deliver a blow, designed not only to halt Eighth Army's advance, but also to break the front and lead to big results. Both 29 British Bde and 27 Comm Bde were to play a leading part in defeating the forthcoming enemy offensive.

Chapter 15

11 Infantry Workshop REME February 1951

On February 4th, the Workshop moved forward again to Umsong for the second time, in the area of Hungju, this time for a period of three weeks. With very little action to report, this at least brought them much nearer to the Brigade, and they were able to give closer support to the unit fitters and get some of the minor jobs put right as well. Then it was on to Ichon for the second time, stopping in a riverbed for nearly a month, a mile or so west or south west of Ichon, on the Ichon-Suwon lateral route.

They were able to make some contact with 10 Inf Wksp REME and were also back in contact with the re-established railhead and NAAFI. From Ichon, on March 24th, they moved northeast to Ipo-Ni, then on the 26th they swung back again, first crossing the Han River and then its largest tributary, the Pukhan River. Arriving at Punwen-Ni about the 29th, it was the very next day that they were told to move yet again. They found themselves on the Seoul – Chunchon axis, about twenty-five miles northeast of Seoul, at a location by the name of Masogu Ni. These three moves gave the Workshop a few hair-raising experiences, negotiating their way across some rather shaky pontoon bridges, precariously located over very fast flowing rivers. Some of the worst road conditions were also experienced at this time. Nearly a month was eventually spent in this location, during which time the temperatures again started to rise.

11 Infantry Wksp in a river bed

Crossing the Han River

Chapter 16

The Chinese spring offensive

The battles of the Imjin and Kapyong Rivers April 1951

During the early days of April 1951, Eighth Army continued its methodical advance northwards, with the object of securing a line of commanding ground north of the 38th Parallel. The advance was directed towards a triangle formed by three towns, Pyongyang being the northern apex, with Kumhwa to the east and Chorwon to the west. This area was located in central Korea, the middle of the triangle being about twenty miles north of the 38th Parallel and about sixty miles northeast of Seoul. It had been known for some time that the Chinese were preparing another large-scale offensive, designed to check the UN advance. In order to interrupt the enemy preparations for attack, on April 9th the American 1 and IX Corps launched an offensive south of 'the triangle'. Resistance was stiff and progress slow but, by the 21st, American troops had secured an intermediate line and arrangements were then made to push forward along practically the whole UN front. These offensive moves may have hindered the Chinese, and possibly delayed them; but they did not prevent the launching of their attack, which began on April 22nd.

Meanwhile, as a background to any immediate action, certain happenings of a political nature were taking place. On April 11th 1951, US President Harry Truman dismissed Gen MacArthur and relieved him of all his commands. He was succeeded in Supreme Command by Eighth Army Cdr, Lt Gen Matthew B Ridgway. Then, on April 14th, Lt Gen James A Van Fleet took over command of the Eighth Army. On the day that the Chinese attack started, the two Commonwealth Brigades were located as follows:

29 British Inf Bde - under American 1 Corps in front line, holding the line of the Imjin River, about thirty-five miles due north of Seoul.

27 Comm Inf Bde - under American IX Corps, in support to 6 ROK Div, in the area just north of Chongchon-Ni on the Kapyong River, some thirty-five miles north east of Seoul.

29 Brigade, with the Belgian Btn under its command, was holding the line of the Imjin River, from Choksong on the left to the junction of the Imjin and Hantan Rivers on the right, a frontage of more than 12,000 yards. This was regarded as a 'check position' in the Eighth Army's forward movement and, in consequence, it was neither wired nor mined. Except on the right flank, where the Belgians and 'B' Troop, 170 Mortar Bty RA were north of the river, the defences lay along the south bank, but were in places as far as 1,000 yards from the river. Contact was not close, indeed, patrols were able to penetrate several thousand yards to the north without meeting the enemy. In this area, and at this season of the year, the Imjin was fordable to infantry almost anywhere, while most types of vehicles could negotiate recognised fords. The hills were steep, but not generally precipitous; there were few trees but much scrub. At the time of the battle, the greenery of spring had not yet made its appearance. Some four miles south of the river and about 2,000 feet high, Kamak-San was the highest point but, in the vicinity of the river itself, the country was, in many places, flat.

On April 22nd, the Brigade had its usual patrols across the river and contact was made with the enemy, much further south than usual. By 0600 hrs, a patrol of the Gloucesters was withdrawing in the face of the enemy. 1000 hrs. A 5 Fusiliers patrol had also made contact and, later in the evening at about 1800 hrs, the Belgian Btn reported that one of their patrols was also in contact. It

Page 113

was thus clear that considerable parties of Chinese were on the move, with reports from prisoners indicating that an attack was imminent. Air reconnaissance in the late afternoon reported that the roads leading south, from Pyong and Chorwon, were crowded with marching troops and vehicles. By last light, enemy patrols had reached the river and some guns of 45 Fld Regt were engaging targets to the north of the ford on the Gloucesters' front. At about 2100 hrs, the three front line Battalions (Gloucesters, 5 Fusiliers and Belgians) were all in contact with the enemy. By 2130 hrs, the Gloucesters' fighting patrol, covering the ford on their front, was hotly engaged and, on withdrawal, was very closely pressed by the enemy.

The Chinese followed a technique at which they had become most adept. There was no appreciable pause in their advance and the attack came in strength before midnight, under the eerie light of a full moon. At midnight, 'A' Coy of the Gloucesters, immediately west of Choksong, was being very heavily attacked by Chinese who, despite their being under heavy artillery fire, had crossed the ford some two miles to the south of the nearby villages. Some penetration into the Company's position was made. An hour later, the fighting had spread to other companies, 'D' and 'B' of the Gloucesters, 'X and 'Y' of the Fusiliers, and 'A' and 'C' of the Belgians. Some Chinese had established themselves south of the Belgian Btn and crossed the river in this area. This now being St George's Day, 5 Fusiliers were wearing the traditional red and white roses in their hats, a custom that each Battalion had previously succeeded in carrying out every year during WWII. By dawn on that day, the enemy, estimated at battalion strength, was established in Choksong, and 'A' and 'D' Companies of the Gloucesters were being heavily attacked. During the morning, 'A', 'D' and 'B' Companies withdrew, under orders, to the vicinity of Btn HQ, their withdrawal being covered by artillery fire. 'A' Coy was sadly depleted; its Coy Cdr had been killed and there was only one officer left.

On the Fusiliers' front, 'X' Coy had withdrawn, again under orders, before first light. At 0610 hrs, the Chinese, in great force, attacked a Platoon of 'Z' Coy. They must have infiltrated through the thinly-held front of the Belgians and also by-passed 'Y' Coy. So, by sheer weight of numbers,

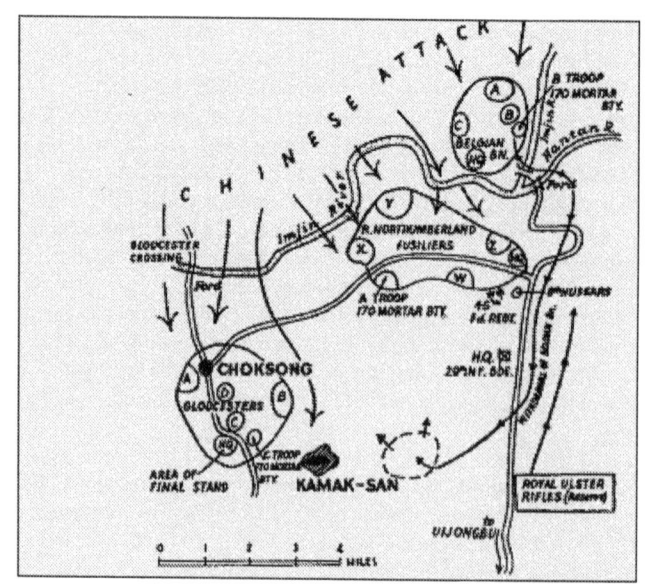

Battle of the Imjin River
22nd to 25th April 1951

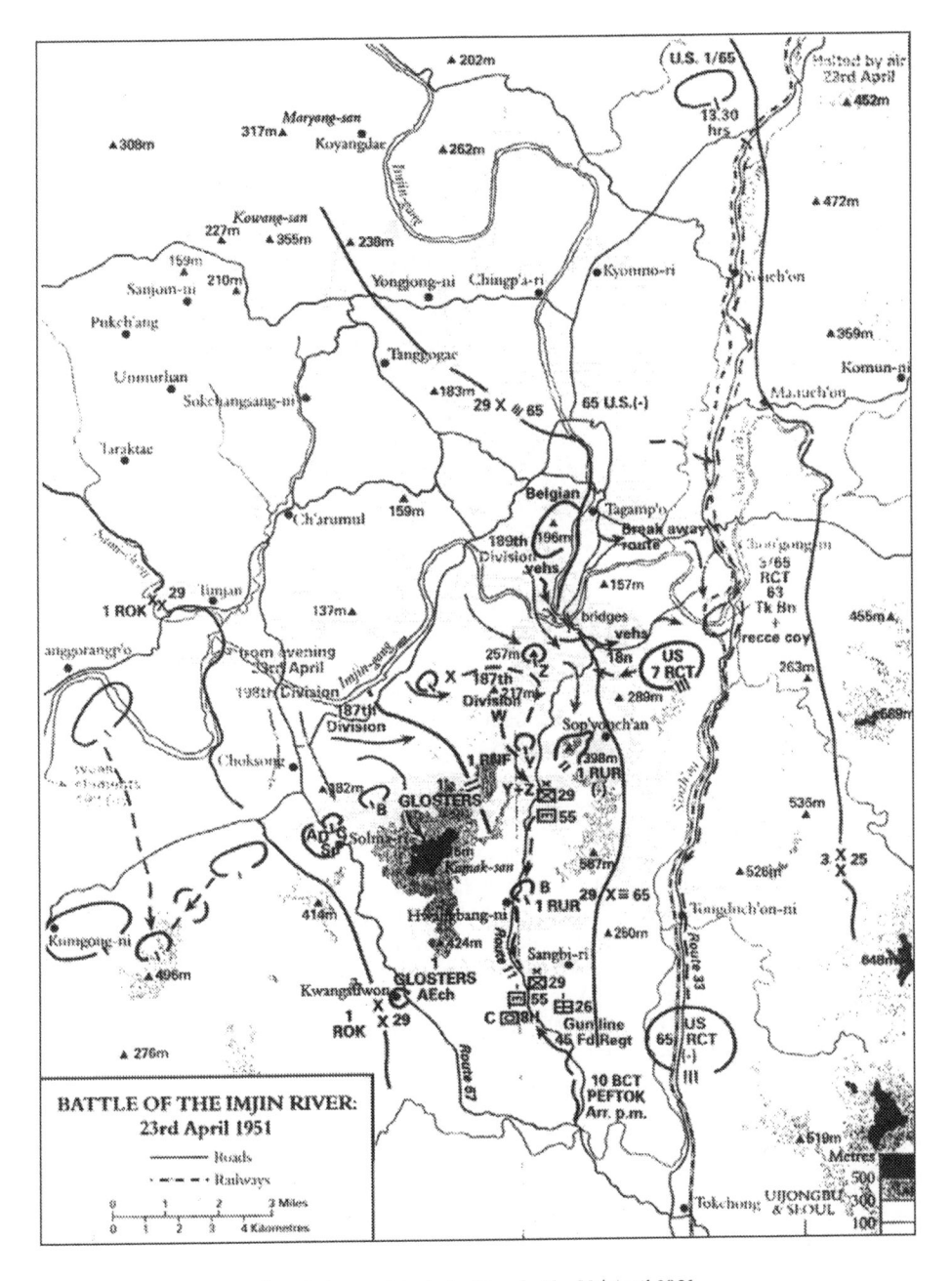

THE CHINESE SPRING OFFENSIVE THE BATTLES OF THE IMJIN AND KAPYONG RIVERS APRIL 1951

Detailed map of the Imjin River battle, 23rd April 1951

The Forgotten Punch in the Army's Fist — Korea 1950-1953

A view of 'Gloucester' Hill, taken after the battle, it is amazing how the Chinese could scale that hill face?

this position was captured and, as it was a commanding feature of some importance, in the angle of the road junction and only about a mile from some of the gun positions of 45 Fld Regt, its loss was a serious matter. The Belgian Btn and 'Y' Company of the Fusiliers were now placed in a very precarious position. By about 1245 hrs, a counter-attack by 'Z' Coy, supported by tanks, reached the position after severe hand-to-hand fighting, but was later driven back, again by sheer weight of numbers. Another attempt by some Americans, desperate to retake the position, also failed.

By this time, it was apparent that this was no local attack with a limited objective, but a full-scale attempt to break the Eighth Army front at the point where it turned north. If successful, it would be expected to produce far-reaching results by cutting off the UN troops to the east. 29 Bde was bearing the brunt of a well-prepared attack in strength. The situation was not improved by the fact that 1 ROK Div, on the left, had been driven back several thousand yards, which exposed the Brigade's left flank. A glance at the sketch map will show that the original forward positions of five Companies had held a front of over 12,000 yards, an average frontage of 2,500 yards per Company. Under these conditions, it was clearly impossible to prevent penetration by a strong, well organized and skilfully executed attack, carried out during the darkest hours of night.

Confused fighting continued throughout April 23rd and, soon after last light, the position was as described below. The Gloucesters, with 'C' Troop, 170 Mortar Bty, were now more concentrated, although their front was still nearly 2,000 yards. The RUR had advanced from their reserve positions on the road some six miles to the south and had taken up defensive dispositions, with one Company left of the road and three on the right. 'Y' and 'Z' Companies 5th Fusiliers had been withdrawn and the Battalion occupied a position with 'Y' Coy left, 'X' Coy centre and 'Z' Coy right. 'W' Coy was in support, linking up with the RUR. Furious fighting continued throughout the night on this front and 'Y' Coy was driven back. But 'W' Coy, whose position was echeloned back to the rear of 'Y' Coy, managed to hold the left flank of the Battalion's position. On the right, the Belgian Btn, assisted by some American tanks, had successfully withdrawn to the east from its isolated position north of the river. The enemy continued to press his attack in great strength, particularly on the Gloucesters' front. The first attack had been made by the 187th Chinese Div, of which it was estimated that not less than one whole Regiment had been directed against the Gloucesters. Later, on the 24th, a second enemy Division was committed.

The stubborn resistance of the Brigade had blunted the enemy's attack and, despite a gap of some four miles between the Gloucesters and 5th Fusiliers, the enemy was slow to exploit it. This enabled Brig Brodie to move the Belgian Btn, which had been successfully extricated from its position across the Imjin, to fill the gap. They arrived and took up their new dispositions by the late afternoon of April 24th. During the early hours of that day, survivors of 'B' Coy of the Gloucesters, together with elements of their Anti-Tank and Mortar Platoons, withdrew to Pt 235, which was to be the scene of the Gloucesters' final stand. By this time, 'B' Coy was only fifteen strong, some of whom were wounded. The Battalion was now surrounded and under constant attack, so it became clear that the survivors could only be extricated by a successful counter-attack. Early in the afternoon, a detachment of Philippine tanks advanced up the road, in an attempt to relieve the Gloucesters. But about two miles short of the position, the leading tank was disabled in a very narrow gorge with precipitous cliffs on either side. Further progress was impossible and, fired at from both flanks; the column was forced to retire. Later in the evening, Centurion tanks of 'C' Sqn 8 Hussars, along with American, Puerto Rican and Belgian infantry, made another attempt to force a way through, but were also forced to withdraw.

Several attempts were made to drop supplies and ammunition by air; but they were not successful, most of the containers falling out of reach. An American helicopter hovered overhead with the intention of evacuating seriously wounded men; but coming under fire, and finding no suitable place to land, it was forced to withdraw without fulfilling its mission. The 25-pdrs of 45 Fld Regt supported the hard-pressed infantry throughout the day, and the USAF operated continuously against enemy avenues of approach and against his rear areas. These measures no doubt relieved the pressure; but still the Chinese infantry continued to press forward. Just before dusk on April 24th, the CO, Lt Col Fred Carne, ordered the withdrawal from all outlying features and for the whole Battalion to concentrate in a small area on Pt 235, subsequently to be known as 'Gloucester Hill'.

While these events were taking place on the left flank, other parts of the front were being subjected to almost continuous attack. 'Y' and 'Z' Companies of 5th Fusiliers and 'A' Coy of RUR bore the brunt of these assaults. In the centre, now held by the Belgian Btn, strong Chinese forces, based on the dominating feature Kamak-San, pressed eastwards across the front with the apparent intention of cutting the road behind 5 Fusiliers and RUR in the vicinity of Uijongbu. Moving 'C' Sqn 8 Hussars to the west of the road, early on April 25th, eased the position. During the night of the 24th / 25th, orders to withdraw to a position just north of Seoul were issued and, at 0800 hrs, the leading troops began to disengage. The withdrawal was very closely pressed by the enemy and proved a most difficult, confused and costly operation. 'B' Coy RUR, supported by 55 Sqn RE, acting as infantry, held a vital defile on the road and, in the initial stages, succeeded in keeping the withdrawal route open. Throughout the movement, 'C' Sqn 8 Hussars covered the withdrawal in an exemplary manner.

5 Fusiliers got away without undue difficulty, but their CO was killed while the withdrawal was in progress. RUR and the Belgians had a more difficult task and parties of both units had to fight desperately. Some took to the hills and others became casualties; the last survivors were not clear until after midday. 45 Fld Regt fired an immense quantity of ammunition even though, on occasions, their gun positions came under small-arms fire. The unhappy Gloucesters were not

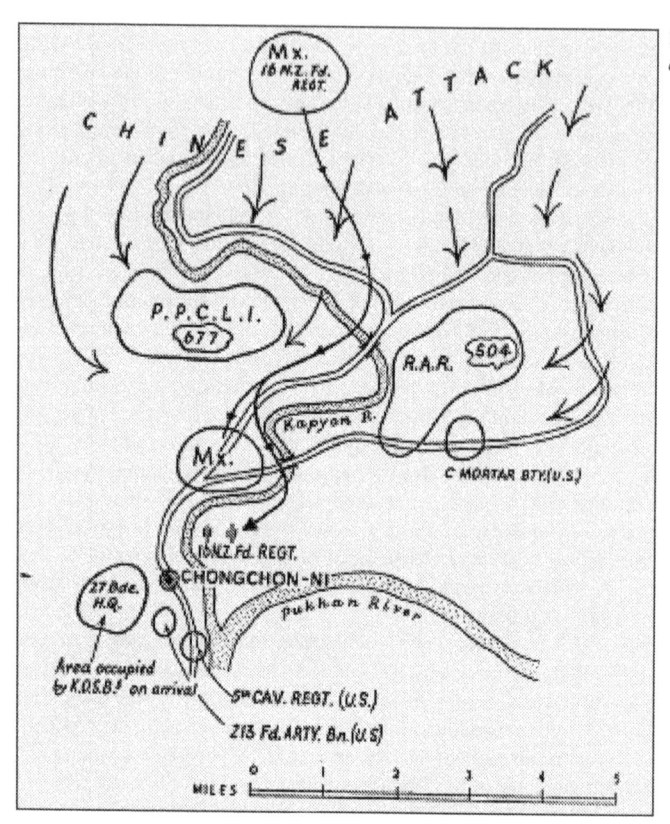

The battle of Chongchon-Ni and the Pukhan River

destined to take part in the withdrawal. All attempts to relieve them, or to replenish their supplies and ammunition, had failed. Five miles away to the west they were completely isolated, with ever diminishing numbers and a diminishing perimeter on Gloucester Hill. The men must by this time have realized their hopeless position, but were in the customary good spirits of British soldiers in adversity. A cheer rang out as *Reveille* was blown about dawn. Soon after this, 'A' Coy was attacked and lost some ground, but promptly retook it with a fierce counter-attack.

At 0600 hrs on April 26th, the Battalion was finally informed that all attempts at relief had failed. Some time later, the CO received a message from Brig Brody, leaving the fateful decision to him. Either the Battalion should endeavour to rejoin the rest of the Brigade or, if this was impossible and further resistance useless, it would surrender. It was the message that ended with the *words "Only the Gloucesters could have done it"*. The USAF carried out three air strikes in an attempt to give the Battalion some relief. But, soon after 0930 hrs, the CO received news that no further artillery support would be available after 1030 hrs. He then gave his Coy Commanders permission to fight their way out independently. The Chaplain, the MO and some of the medical staff, both Regimental and RAMC, remained with the wounded; it was this group that was captured.

Throughout the battle, Lt Col Carne had been an inspiration to his men, moving from place to place wherever the fighting was hottest and encouraging his troops. During the breakout attempt, he and three others defied capture for twenty-four hours. The remnants of 'A', 'B' and 'C' Companies moved south, but their attempt to join up with other troops failed and all were either captured or killed. 'D' Coy took a different route. Coy Cdr, Capt M G Harvey, led his men northwards for a short distance, then west and then south. During the first three miles they only met a few Chinese, who were promptly killed. All seemed to be going well when they suddenly came under heavy fire from hills on either side of their route. Nevertheless, the movement continued along a small ditch, which afforded them some cover. On reaching more open ground, they sighted some American tanks and it seemed that their troubles were over. Then occurred one of those unfortunate incidents of mistaken identity that had already occurred too often in Korea. The tanks mistook these gallant survivors for Chinese and opened fire. Some men were hit, before the Americans perceived their mistake and soon afforded the Gloucesters protection. Eventually, the thirty-nine men of 'D' Coy, the sole survivors of the Battalion who had taken part in the battle, were carried to safety on the tanks.

At 1235 hrs on the 25th, 29 Bde HQ arrived at Uijongbu, fifteen miles north of Seoul and the Brigade then continued its withdrawal towards the Han River. By the 27th, they had reached the Yongdongpo area, where they came into 1st Corps reserve, with the operational task of defending Kimpo peninsula to the west of Seoul. 29 Bde had suffered very heavily. More than a quarter of its fighting men had become casualties, with one Battalion, the Gloucesters, having been practically wiped out. Much of its equipment, including some tanks, had also been lost. Bu that stand by the Brigade had, in short, completely frustrated the Chinese plan to break the Eighth Army front. For three days, it had blocked all attempts to cut the road to Seoul. Numerous casualties had been inflicted on the enemy, which brought his offensive to a halt and resulted in his withdrawal. All of 29 Bde had fought bravely and well, while the stand of the Gloucesters was worthy of the highest traditions of British Infantry. On May 8th 1951, Gen Van Fleet, Eighth Army Cdr, presented 1 Btn the Gloucestershire Regiment and 'C' Troop, 170 Independent Mortar Bty RA with an American Presidential Citation, as a tribute to their exceptional services during the Imjin River battle.

At the same time as 29 Bde had been fighting the Chinese on the Imjin, 27 Bde, some thirty miles to the east, had also come under heavy attack. During the night of April 22nd / 23rd, the Chinese attacked the South Koreans. The attack met with considerable success and the Koreans were soon in full retreat. With some difficulty, 16 NZ Fld Regt disengaged and came into action just south of the important road junction, about four miles north of Chongchon-Ni. This was in the early morning of the 23rd but, a little later, an order was received from HQ IX Corps that the New Zealanders were to move again, in support of the Koreans. Brig Burke obtained permission to send 1 Middlesex with them for protection and both units then advanced some seven miles up a subsidiary valley, to the northwest. Here, the guns were brought into action and the infantry took up defensive dispositions. It soon became clear, however, that 6 ROK Div was continuing its retreat and that 16 NZ Fld Regt and 1 Middlesex were in a precarious position. Both units were then ordered back.

Meanwhile, the rest of the Brigade had taken up defensive dispositions astride the bend in the River Kapyong, north of Chongchon-Ni and north of a big east-to-west loop in the Pukhan River. The forward Battalions were 2 Btn PPCLI, to the left on Hill 677, and 3 Btn RAR to the right on Hill 504. These positions were about three and a half miles north of Chongchon-Ni, where Bde HQ was located. Some little time before midnight, 1 Middlesex and 16 NZ Fld Regt commenced withdrawing inside the Brigade area. Later, the Middlesex took up positions in support about two miles north of Chongchon-Ni, while the Kiwi (NZ) Gunners came into action about a mile behind them. 1 Btn ASH, which had just been relieved by 1 Btn KOSB, remained in the assembly area and moved to Inchon on April 24th, for embarkation to Hong Kong. During that same day, the KOSB moved forward to positions near Bde HQ. The surrounding countryside was typical of Korea, with steep-sided, scrub-covered hills. Only in the immediate vicinity of the rivers was the ground flat.

During most of the battle, it was raining hard.

On April 23rd, by 2200 hrs, SKA resistance to the front had crumbled and the Chinese were probing the defences of 27 Bde, mostly on the Australians' front. An hour or so after midnight, the Australians were being heavily attacked from the north and northwest; their Battalion was already supported by tanks of the American 72 Tank Btn. At about 0400 hrs on the 24th, a reinforcement of tanks and a Company of the Middlesex were sent to their assistance. A dangerous situation had arisen, as some Chinese had penetrated to the vicinity of Btn HQ but, as dawn was breaking, the situation began to ease. The next day, the enemy continued to attack the Australians throughout the day. They lost heavily, but still came on. As it seemed unlikely that the Battalion would be able to sustain another night of attack, it was ordered to begin a withdrawal at 1730 hrs. The enemy closely followed it, but artillery fire, plus that of American tanks, relieved pressure considerably. By about 2245 hrs, the Aussies had passed through the Middlesex ranks and had taken up new positions near Bde HQ, bringing thirty-two Chinese prisoners with them. While all this was taking place on the right flank, the Canadians on the left had been in continuous contact with the enemy. But, on this part of the front, the attacks were not pressed; here, the enemy seemed to prefer the policy of working round the flanks. Shortly after midnight on the 24th, however, heavy attacks came in on both flanks. Some severe close-quarter fighting took place, especially on the left flank held by 'D' Coy.

Just before first light next morning, 'A' Coy, American 72 Tank Btn, was ordered to move to an area behind the Canadians' positions, in an attempt to ease the situation. At dawn, the Canadians' positions were still intact, but the Battalion was surrounded. Just before midday, supplies of food, water and ammunition were successfully dropped by aircraft on the Battalion and, by the evening, communications to the south had been re-opened. Two helicopters were also able to evacuate some seriously wounded men. Unexpectedly, the battle came to an abrupt end. In the late afternoon, little activity was seen to the northeast, on the Australians' old position, and by 1630 hrs, all was quiet on the Brigade front. The enemy had withdrawn as quickly as he had arrived. Throughout this engagement, great difficulties were experienced in distinguishing friend from foe, especially in the early stages of the Chinese attack, when parties of defeated SKA troops were making their way south.

27 Comm Bde fought its last battle in the same manner as it had fought throughout its eight months of campaigning in Korea - with great skill, courage and resourcefulness. At midnight on April 25th 1951, 27 Comm Inf Bde changed both its Commander and its designation. It now became 28 Comm Bde, with Brig G Taylor DSO taking over command from Brig B A Burke DSO. The composition of the Brigade remained the same. The flag of the old 27 Comm Bde was presented to Lt Col IB Ferguson DSO, MC, commanding 3 Btn RAR, described by a senior officer of one of the original British Battalions as, *"The finest fighting infantry battalion I have ever seen"*. On the 26th, the Brigade withdrew south, on relief by 5 US Cavalry Regt. For their gallant service in the battle of Kapyong River, the following units received an American Presidential Citation:

    2 Btn PPCLI
    3 Btn RAR
    'A' Coy of the American 72 Heavy Tank Btn

Thus the two British and Commonwealth Brigades had played a notable part in defeating the CCF spring offensive of 1951.

Chapter 17

29th Brigade Group

10 Infantry and 5 Medium Workshops REME

February to May 1951

10 Inf Wksp REME had been left located in an old school at a town called Chonan. A stay of eleven days gave them time to gather their wits once more and to reshuffle the loads on their trucks. But before they knew what was happening, it was once again time to pack up and move. The date was February 7th, and a short sharp drive to Pyongtaek brought them another week when they could get on with some work. On February 15th, the Workshop moved again, this time to Suwon. Here they managed a reasonably long stay, with plenty of work, before moving again. This time to Yongdong-Po, to be housed in what was an old and nearly demolished shoe factory. April 4th brought a visit from the Assistant Director Electrical & Mechanical Engineering (ADEME), Lt Col Good, remained in the area until the 12th. By the following day they had been static for quite a time, so the 'powers-that-be' decided to start some recreational training. A unit football league, consisting of eight teams, was formed but, by April 29th, they were on the move yet again. They ended up at Osan and were located in a riverbed, a favourite location, as the ground was usually firm and level, with easy access and exit. Since arriving in Korea and starting to move with the Brigade, they had lost the equivalent of fifty-four days in production time, due to the numerous moves between November 22nd 1950 and April 30th 1951.

On May 3rd, a new member of staff arrived, in the shape of Capt Victor S Moore, posted in from 5 Med Wksp, to take up the post of AO. Another higher-ranking visitor was Brig Heath, DEME Far East Land Forces (FARELF). He inspected the unit and discussed the tactical situation with the CO and his staff. Towards the end of May they were moving again, very slowly forwards, this time to within two miles of Yongdong-Po. The Commonwealth Base Camp at Pusan was situated outside the main town and its accommodation was mainly in tents. It was reasonably comfortable and was commanded by a much-respected officer, Col Mann of the Middlesex Regt. 5 Med Wksp Detachment REME had found themselves at the base camp after the withdrawal. But it was evident that they could not stay there, they did not fit, and there was no suitable accommodation for their detachment.

They were sent off to 'recce' for a possible site on the other side of Pusan, near to the sea, where there were a couple of roofless factory buildings. This would at least give them a working space with some hard standing. This was quite good considering the circumstances, so they duly drove through Pusan, around the headland, to their new Workshop location. They made themselves comfortable and announced that they were 'ready for work'. As Pusan was the main port of entry into Korea, there were quite a few Commonwealth troops and vehicles with equipment in the area and they were soon as busy as they could be, repairing whatever they could. But there was no stores backing for them and it was a hand-to-mouth existence. They did carry a reasonable selection of spares with them, but no major assemblies, and 'cannibalisation' was very much a necessity. One irreparable vehicle provided a wealth of spares and they were thus able to complete the majority of work that came to them. There was an American Motor Maintenance Company (MMC) close by, which proved most helpful by giving them 'bits and pieces' of equipment, if they suited their needs.

Amongst their tradesmen they had an excellent sheet metal worker and he was invaluable. He could straighten out the bent bits and work wonders with his welding torch and electric plant. He even made one of the best shower units they ever did see in Korea! It consisted of a diesel burner, heating the water in a fifty-gallon drum. The water rose to a header tank by convection and then fed out to showerheads complete with controllers. The whole contraption was tied together with iron tubing and was almost portable. It worked a treat and, naturally, was in constant use. Meanwhile, transport was still a constant problem. Unlike the Americans, they had very few small vehicles such as Jeeps and they were thus forced to use something like a 3-ton QL to undertake the smallest journey. One bottle of the finest Scotch export solved that problem for them and their Jeep was soon painted with a new number, *"5MEDWKSPREME"*

.On the beach near their establishment, there were a number of large mono-wheeled armoured trailers. They happened to know what they were but Col Mann was apparently not so sure. When they told him they were some of the napalm trailers, for the Churchill Flame-thrower tanks that were up with the Brigade, he was none too happy. A few days later, he instructed them to inspect these trailers, to see if they were empty and, if not, could they empty them and dispose of the contents? This was a new one for them but, having looked at them, they did appear to have something in them. They had pressure cylinders and it was a small task to open some cocks and to blow out onto the beach a considerable quantity of 'thick black goo'. This they promptly ignited with a trail of petrol, having first retired to a safe distance. They had never seen napalm burn before and the resulting roar and dense black smoke was somewhat of a shock. It was also a shock to the Americans based in the port, not too distant! There was an almighty flap until the cause of this conflagration was discovered. Col Mann was highly amused but felt it right to tick them off, for having upset Pusan Garrison. It was again a case of 'live and learn'.

One last task

Although they were quite busy, it was a situation that was not totally satisfactory. The detachment was not surprised when, within the month, they were instructed to pack up and ship out, to rejoin the main Workshop in Kure, Japan. But before doing this, they were given one last task. Maj Turp, who was a military attaché with the British High Commission, sent for them. It seemed that the British Government wanted some 'captured enemy weapons' for display in London. This provided some difficulty with their American friends, in allowing them to take the weapons out of Korea. In particular, a Russian tank was required and - could they get one? Well, this was something else. But it so happened that there was a number of Russian tanks further north, lying in the fields alongside the roads, which could possibly be obtained. The main difficulty would be getting a tank through Pusan, and then onto one of their Tank Landing Ships, without the Americans knowing and stopping it. If Maj Turp could get a suitable tank down to Pusan, they would tow it into the port at night and load it for him. They don't know how the tank was duly recovered and sent back to Pusan, but it arrived outside the town a few days later. It wasn't that heavy and they soon had it connected at the back of their Diamond-T Tractor. Then, in the dead of night, it was towed through the streets of Pusan and safely delivered to the dockside in the main port. Here, it was loaded for (presumably) transit to Japan and then to the UK. Thus, having completed their last task, the detachment of 5 Med Wksp REME said goodbye to Korea and embarked for Kure in Japan.

The Kiwis ran a very important air-shuttle service between Japan and Korea. From Japan, they would fly to Pusan and then 'bus-stop' at any airfield they could get into, as far north as they could go. Then they would turn around and fly back the same way. The pilots and crew were great chaps, flying in any weather, and doing a magnificent job for the Brigades. They flew those wonderful old *Dakota* aircraft that carried anything and everyone that they could reasonably get on board. If you

29TH BRIGADE GROUP 10 INFANTRY AND 5 MEDIUM WKSP'S REME. APRIL TO MAY 1951

Ichon – Pukhan River, The Dam that the Americans opened, Dec 14th 1950 to Jan 2nd 1951

turned up at your 'local airstrip' and waited, you could usually persuade the pilot to cram you in with the stores and other persons. Sometimes there wasn't really enough room, but you got on anyway! On one such occasion, Capt Vic Moore was able to get a flight from Pusan to Iwakuni in Japan and was met by a Japanese driver in a very small car. They trundled off through the countryside and, in due course, came to a very strange and very large city. Victor said it was strange, because every building looked temporary and all were just one storey high. With some difficulty, the driver made him understand that this was Hiroshima. Then he realised why the city had such an odd appearance and such an uncomfortable atmosphere.

Some days later, he returned to that fatal city, to see for himself in more detail the place where the first atomic bomb had been dropped. He was there on April 17th 1951 and visited what is now the memorial site. Only one building was still standing in that area, directly under where the bomb had exploded. An enterprising Japanese priest was selling tiles from the roof of the building, which clearly showed the effect of the heat from the explosion. Victor bought a tile and the priest painted his name, date etc on it. He still has it as a souvenir of a day he will always remember, in view of the terrible thing that happened there just a few years before.

Victor was made welcome in 5 Med Wksp, at the barracks in Kure. After a rest and change of clothing, he took the comfortable sleeper train, up the scenic Japanese coast to Tokyo. Here, he booked into the Maranuchi Hotel, which was reserved for British and Commonwealth Officers. From there, he had a most welcome, pleasant and interesting week of R & R leave. On his return to Kure, he was not in the least bit surprised to be told that he was off to Korea again, with instructions to join 10 Inf Wksp with 29 Bde as its AO. Although Japan was a tremendous place to be in, he did not want to stay and duly booked himself a flight with the worthy NZ air boys. Capt Moore later arrived back in Pusan, refreshed and ready for the next phase of his time in Korea.

Chapter 18

11 Infantry Workshop REME forward to the Pukhan River then back to Ichon for the third time May 1951

Nearly a month was spent in this location, during which time the temperature started to rise. As the Workshop was located in the dry riverbed area of the Pukhan River, some hardy creatures even decided to take a swim. It was a good spot, with wide gradually sloping banks, a feature most important when the rainy season is in the offing. In fact, of all their riverbed sites, not one location was selected unless it had good 'escape routes'. Some of the rivers were up to a mile wide but only filled for probably one month of the year. Their stay here was highlighted by the controlled opening of the dam gates further up river, without being fully notified by their friendly allies, the American Engineers. This was carried out to reduce the water level above the dams, so that the Chinese could not flood that part of the country by turning the taps full on. This led to some amusing incidents as the water level rose at their location. As it rose, there was a reluctance to move vehicles until it was really necessary, with most of the Workshop vehicles located well up the river's sloping banks. Their ASM, Mr Carrington, having just crawled out of his tent, found the water a few feet from his canvas home. Some light recovery was already going on, there was a fitter's workbench just about to float away, so a rope was hastily being attached to allow its subsequent recovery. Drivers were detailed to wade out to their vehicles, start them up and pull back to dry land.

Fitters Bench being saved, Dec 14th 1950

11 INFANTRY WORKSHOP REME - FORWARD TO THE PUKHAN RIVER

11 Inf Wksp carrying out self-recovery after the Americans flooded them out

It was at this precise time that they had a visit from Lt Col Good, the ADEME from Japan, who was later to become CREME of the Comm Div. He was impressed by the Workshop's apparent indifference to water. During this incident, the river level rose by about twenty feet and widened from 300 yards to 1,000 yards. But it was a false front that they had presented to their visitor, they were very concerned indeed that they had got their feet wet! By April 25th, the battle had taken a turn for the worse again, entailing a short move to the rear, in order to get back on the south side of the two main rivers, the Han and the Pukhan. So it was back to that place called Ichon for the third time, this time in a riverbed about a mile south of the town. This was another good location, with a good lead into the bed from the main axis. Although it was sandy, it was also quite firm. It had a mobile American Bath Unit already located, which was handy and of which full use was made. Everyone was soon sporting new American underclothing, which was an automatic issue on such occasions. The weather was now quite warm and it was good to shake off all the heavy clothing and get the sun on their backs. Everyone was now working in the minimum of clothing and enjoying the sunshine.

Brig Heath, DEME FARELF, paid them a visit in this spot and what impressed him most were the two big US ovens in the kitchen which were producing an excellent roast. Another visitor was Col Faulkner from Scales Branch, but he had rather a rough time and they were probably a little hard on him. They had left Hong Kong with a scale of spares to cover the vehicles used in Hong Kong. But with the Australians having many American vehicles, the Kiwis a mixture (but mostly Canadian *Chevrolets*) and the Indians owning all sorts of WWII vehicles, the scaling proved nowhere near sufficient to cover this assortment.

Page 125

Chapter 19

The Commonwealth Force Gather Strength and the first withdrawal continues 1951

In reading the narrative that follows, it is necessary to appreciate that, at the end of April 1951, when it came into existence, 28 Comm Brigade was in reality the old 27 Comm Brigade. It had changed its designation and its Commander. 1 Btn King's Own Scottish Borderers had relieved 1 Btn Argyll and Sutherland Highlanders, but otherwise the troops were the same.

Both the British and Commonwealth Brigades, especially 29 Bde, had a gruelling time during the three days April 23rd to 25th, engaged in defence against the Chinese spring offensive. Periods of inactivity were rare in Korea but, as far as battle fighting was concerned, the three months between the Imjin and Kapyong River battles and the formation of the Comm Div at the end of July, were comparatively quiet. However, 25 Canadian Inf Bde was to experience some sharp fighting. The Chinese had received what another commander, in an earlier campaign, would have called a *'bloody nose'*. In accordance with their practice after an unsuccessful attack, the Chinks had withdrawn for some miles out of contact. No doubt this was done in order to avoid the now considerable artillery fire of the UN forces, which at this time was so much heavier than the Chinese could themselves administer. This period of comparative tranquillity was certainly welcome to British Commonwealth forces. It enabled 28 and 29 Brigades to re-organize, carry out some much needed training and settle down, after their battles at the end of April. It must not be supposed, however, that this period was entirely free from incident. There was much activity, which merits a brief description.

It will be as well to first explain the general situation. With the halting of the Chinese offensive at the end of April 1951, the Eighth Army line ran from west to just north of Seoul, then due east to about Kapyong, thence north-east to the east coast about Yangyang, just north of the 38th Parallel. The month of May then saw big additions to the Canadian contingent in Korea. 2 Btn PPCLI had already distinguished itself under 27 Bde at the battle of the Kapyong River. During the first week of May, the following Canadian HQ and units arrived in Korea:

HQ 25 Canadian Inf Bde
2 Btn Royal Canadian Regt (RCR)
2 Btn Royal 22' Regt
'C' Sqn, Lord Strathcona's Horse
2 Fld Regt, Royal Canadian Horse Artillery (RCHA)
57 Independent Fld Sqn Royal Canadian Engineers (RCE)

These units - together with 2 Btn PPCLI, which had been withdrawn from 28 Comm Bde – made up 25 Canadian Inf Bde Group. The Brigade Group (less the Princess Patricia's, already in Korea) left Seattle on three consecutive days, the 19th, 20th and 21st April 1951, in three troopships – namely the *'Marine Adder'*, the *'General Patrick'* and the *'President Jackson'*. Disembarkation in Japan took place on 4th, 5th and 6th May and subsequently the Brigade Group moved to Korea.

The Commonwealth Force Gather Strength May to July 1951

On May 14th, 1 Btn King's Shropshire Light Infantry (KSLI) relieved 1 Btn the Middlesex Regiment, thus completing the relief of the original units of 27 Bde. The 'Die Hards' had fought in the manner expected of them during the early, and most difficult, months of the campaign, before a well-earned return to Hong Kong.

Early May 1951 found 28 Comm Bde to the east of Seoul, on the left flank of the American 24 Div and under the Americans' command. On May 21st, IX Corps assumed the offensive, in which the Brigade participated. Led by the Australians and KOSB, little opposition was encountered although the KOSB met with some minor resistance. There followed a week of steady advance and several minor engagements, in which all Battalions were involved. On the 29th, the Brigade came under the command of the American 1 Cavalry Div and took up positions on the line of the Imjin River. It had advanced north some thirty miles since the 21st. 29 Bde, with the Belgian Btn and 5 ROK Marine Btn under its command and after its heavy losses in the Imjin battle, spent the next month on the Kimpo peninsula, west of Seoul. Conditions here were quiet and the Brigade spent its time patrolling, absorbing reinforcements, reorganizing and training. In a very short time, units were again battle-worthy. The Gloucesters, whose fighting personnel had nearly all become casualties at the Imjin, were brought up to strength and, under their new CO, Lt Col D B Grist OBE, became operationally fit in a few days.

At the end of May, the Brigade moved to the left sector of its old positions on the Imjin River, where it set about the task of digging, wiring and mining the defences. Meanwhile, 25 Canadian Bde made some important changes in its equipment, which included the conversion of the Armoured Sqn from self-propelled anti-tank guns to Sherman tanks. May 15th saw a forward move to a concentration area near Kumnyangjang-Ni (ten miles east of Suwon) begin. On May 24th, the Brigade had reached an assembly area northeast of Uijongbu. Here, 10 BCT, Philippine Expeditionary Force, was placed under command of the Brigade. The role of 25 Div was to advance to the 38th Parallel as part of 'Operation Initiate'. By May 27th, the Brigade had advanced further and, on the 29th, it took part in 'Operation Follow-up', a move on the Uijongbu-Kumhwa road towards the former 'Iron Triangle', over which the Chinese April offensive had been launched. By the evening, Unchon had been reached and it was here that some opposition was encountered.

On June 1st, the bulk of the Brigade was under the command of 3 Inf Div, which had relieved 25 Div on this axis. 2 RCHA Regt continued in support of the formation, while the rest of the Brigade moved into reserve covering Seoul. After a difficult move forward from its reserve area, south of the Imjin, the Brigade was in position by noon on June 19th. The front was 7,500 yards long, the right flank based on the western outskirts of Chorwon. 2 Btn held the forward areas; PPCLI the left; and 2 RCR the right; with 2 Btn. 22' Regt in reserve.

On July 16th, the Brigade came under the orders of the American 25 Div and, on the 18th, was relieved by the Turkish Bde. It was not destined for a period of rest, however, as it went straight up to another front-line position, to the west and immediately north of the junction of the Imjin and Hantan Rivers. The new position was astride the Imjin River, where it runs due north and south. Here, 28 Comm Bde was on the left of the Canadians and 27 Inf Regt of the American 25 Div on the right.

The front was about 5,000 yards long. This very important, but somewhat precarious, position was held with 2 RCR forming a bridgehead west of the river and the rest of the Bde Group on the eastern bank. In carrying out this role, Brig Rockingham experienced many difficulties and irritations. Higher authority ordered frequent changes in dispositions. The footbridge and ferries, by which the troops on the western bank were supplied, were constantly going out of action owing to the seasonal rise in the river.

On July 26th, 25 Canadian Bde moved to an assembly area in the rear of 28 Comm and 29 British Brigades. The three Commonwealth Brigades were now located together, holding the line of the Imjin River, between Choksong on the left and the junctions of the Imjin and Hantan on the right. 29 British Bde held the left flank; 28 Comm Bde held the right flank; and in reserve, dispersed to the rear of the leading Brigades, was 25 Canadian Bde. Armour, Artillery, Engineers and administrative units, substantially equivalent to those that are normal in a Division, supported the three Infantry Brigades and they were deployed on a divisional basis. The stage was thus set for the formation of 1 (and the first) Comm Div. Maj Gen A .J H Cassels C.B, CBE, DSO, the Div Cdr designate, and most of his staff, had been in the theatre of operations for some weeks. All arrangements had been made for the integration of the three Brigade Groups under his command.

It is customary for the fighting troops to receive most of the historian's attention. The object of any war is the destruction of enemy forces and it is the fighting soldier who does this. He prevents the enemy from destroying him, or perishes in the attempt, thus the preponderance of publicity he receives seems only logical. Nevertheless, under modern conditions, the actual fighters in a Western Army are dependent upon a staff and administrative organization of great complexity, and whose numbers often far exceed the front-line combatants. Every big road move or air strike involves a substantial amount of staff work, in the form of orders, instructions or messages. These are sent out over a complicated system of communications, manned by many highly technical personnel, using very elaborate and costly equipment. The routine process of delivering daily large quantities of constant supplies, such as food and mail, and arranging for fluctuating requirements in petrol, ammunition and the like, requires an immense organization and thousands of men, using large numbers of railway wagons, motor vehicles and other equipment. The evacuation of the wounded and sick and their efficient treatment, the forward movement of reinforcements, arrangements for leave and the relief of personnel, plus recreational requirements – these are only some of the problems which faced this army administrative staff in the field.

To the rear of the fighting troops, and even further to the rear in the case of the Korean Campaign (mostly in Japan and about the base port of Pusan), other essential activities go on. Numerous establishments are maintained, many of which are unknown, even by name, to the average fighting soldier. Transit camps, leave centres, dock facilities, hospitals, establishments for the repair of equipment, stores of food, equipment, ammunition, spare parts, petrol, etc, to mention only a few! On top of all this has to be added spiritual welfare, the press, arrangements for VIPs, the initial care of refugees and many other functions. Due to previous experience, mainly of two World Wars, the degree of co-operation and standardisation between the armed forces of Commonwealth countries was high, but it was hardly complete. There were minor differences in equipment, rations, etc, among the various contingents, which added to the complexities. However, backed by the C-in-C BCFK, Lt Gen Sir Horace Robertson and directed by Maj Gen Cassels, the Divisional Administrative Staff, led by Lt Col AWL Vickers, the AA and Quarter Master General (QMG), overcame all difficulties and the Comm Div started its existence on a thoroughly sound administrative basis.

Chapter 20

11 Infantry Workshop REME

Forward again & a change to their unit title

May to July 1951

Towards the end of May, 11 Inf Wksp moved forward again, to its original location on the Pukhan River, the scene of their aquatic exploits. While in Ichon, the Hong Kong based elements of 29 Bde, that is to say its HQ, Signal Troop, Anti-Tank Troop and the two Battalions, had gradually moved back to Hong Kong on a 'one for one' swap with 28 Bde. The Comm Bde was renumbered to 28 Comm Bde and now had its two British Battalions, the KOSB and KSLI. It is believed that Capt J D Kelly was the 28 Bde BEME at that time. Information came in that 11 Inf Wksp REME would soon move back to Hong Kong, ten men at a time, changing over with 16 Inf Wksp REME. This was to avoid disruption of the repair effort at either end and meant that the normal Royal Australian Air Force (RAAF) flights, from Japan to Hong Kong, could cope with the load. A few days later, Maj Germain, OC 16 Inf Wksp, arrived in Korea with the first party of ten and joined them at the Pukhan location. A few days afterwards, they moved forward to a very good location, a few miles south of Uijongbu, to the northeast of Seoul. This was to be the last Korean location of 11 Inf Wksp REME.

The change-over personnel continued every two or three days until, finally, on July 1st 1951, the last ten, including the AO, left Uijongbu for Kimpo air field near Seoul, and flew to Japan. Even the trip of the last party was not without incident! From Seoul, they flew with the RAAF, landing at Okinawa and bursting a tyre in the process. After taking off and getting within striking distance of Hong Kong, the plane was diverted due to fog and had to make for the Philippines. According to the pilot, although he could have been milking it a bit, they landed there with just a thimbleful of fuel in their tank. This was on the most northerly airstrip and the date was 'The 4th of July', which just happened to be Independence Day for the Filipinos, as well as the Americans. The Workshop party finally arrived in Hong Kong on July 5th, ten months after leaving for Korea.

During the time that 11 Inf Wksp REME was in Korea, 27 Bde (later 28 Bde) was under command of either American 1 Cavalry or 24 Inf Div. These Divisions were both in IX Corps. The Workshop had always found the OMC of the American 24 Div most helpful in the matter of spares, they were a very efficient unit and always eager to help. The only way they could find to repay them was the gift of the occasional bottle of whisky, whenever they themselves could lay their hands on some. Looking back, two of the Workshop's Craftsmen were on leave in Japan, at the time the unit had left for Korea. They had been attached to another unit in Hong Kong, on their return from leave. But they made themselves such a nuisance, in their desire to join 'their own unit', that they were put on an RAAF aircraft going to Japan and told to find their own way across to Korea. This they did and duly appeared at one of the unit's most northerly locations.

At some time during 27 Bde's fighting in the south, the unit was awarded the President of Korea's citation but, due to the fact that the British had no similar method of honouring a Korean unit, this had to be turned down. Though later, as previously mentioned, citations from the American President were accepted.

Page 129

Chapter 21

North again to join 10 Infantry Workshop REME

April to October 1951

With Capt Moore's prior knowledge of Korea, the journey back to Pusan was uneventful and he had soon found his way to the old 5 Med Wksp site, where he was reunited with his kit and driver, who was to go to 10 Inf Wksp with him. They hitched up their 5-cwt trailer to their 'liberated' Jeep and persuaded a friendly American Ordnance Unit to repaint the identity numbers on the Jeep to read *"10INFWKSPREME"* and to include the Brigade sign on the rear. Their only advice was to follow the MSR again until he found the Workshop. Pretty vague instructions, but this time it came as no surprise, so they set off north knowing that, in truth, they could hardly get lost.

The road as far as Taegu was familiar to him and they drove in convoy with the mass of American vehicles, laden with stores and personnel. The road was dry and the dust was a solid entity, which enveloped them so completely that they could see little but the back of the vehicle ahead. They were forced to wear goggles and wrap scarves around their faces, as the dust penetrated into every inch of their clothing, making life most uncomfortable. The refugees were still fighting their way against this flow, but their ranks were thinning. They reached Taegu that same day and stayed the night in their old school building. They were self-sufficient for food and water and it did not take long to break out some tins of Compo and have a warm meal, with the aid of their small solid fuel 'Tommy' cooker. They slept in their sleeping bags and woke early next morning, opened a tin of bacon, brewed the inevitable tea, shaved and washed, and were soon on their way again.

Victor had ascertained that 29 Bde was south of the Imjin and Seoul, so they knew they still had a good way to go. There was no question of a quick drive, because the road was still busy and the old bottlenecks of river crossings and heavy traffic were still with them. The MSR was simply one road, with one line of traffic each way. It had a gravel surface that was in the main very heavily corrugated and always in need of maintenance. The corrugations rattled their teeth until it became a constant misery. The only way to smooth out the ride was to drive at something over thirty miles an hour, which one did whenever one was able, but was not that often. The access areas to river crossings were congested, very cut up, and vehicles constantly bogged down and had to be winched out, making for further delay. The Americans had done a great job in building pontoon bridges to replace the permanent bridges, but they were of necessity very long and usually one way only.

The second day was another long slow drive in convoy, with the all-pervading dust, passing through the barely recognisable ruins of small towns. Kumchon and Taejon had both suffered, to the extent that there was virtually nothing of use left standing. The night was spent in a bivouac area; they awoke early and, after a quick breakfast, they were on their way again. They were obviously getting near the active area, as there were now more American MPs directing traffic and the occasional vehicle with a gun in tow. Small convoys of infantry with weapons were also much in evidence. If a vehicle broke down, it was a major disaster and the paddy fields on either side of the MSR were littered with vehicles that had been pushed over the edge, in order to clear the way and to keep the majority moving.

Nothing as yet indicated that they were in 29 Bde area. Through Chochiwon they drove, then Chonan and towards Pyongtaek, watching for any sign of the marker for 10 Inf Wksp REME. And then there it appeared, a small sign with the familiar REME colours, pointing off the MSR to the right, straight into a riverbed surrounded by low hills. Not exactly the sort of Workshop site Victor

North again to join 10 Infantry Workshop REME

Officers of 10 Inf Wksp in May 1951.
Maj Smith, Capts Tinkham, Husband, Moore & Lt Cribb

had expected, but then, he had never seen a Field Workshop, let alone one in an active war zone. He was directed by a sentry to an office vehicle, the HQ vehicle, and he was soon introducing himself to the Chief Clerk and, in turn, being led off to meet the CO, one Maj JC Smith. The office truck at 10 Inf Wksp was a good place to work and made life bearable for the office staff to work in. They had three such vehicles, one for Administration, another for a Workshop office and a third for the RAOC stores section. As far as he can recall, the Workshop was only bivouacked at the time that he arrived and was about to move north. He seems to remember that he took over from Capt Charles Tinkham, who went off soon afterwards to Japan, to join 5 Med Wksp.

There was a tremendous character in the unit called 'Nick' Nicholson, who was the Ordnance Stores officer. He lived in his own truck, always managed to appear in an immaculate uniform, whatever it was at the time, and kept them amused with a fund of stories. Their Tels officer was Tony Cribb, a very likeable young man with a shock of curly blond hair. He could play the piano and produced a series of very witty songs and verse about their life in Korea. What a great pity they were never written down at the time. The 2IC and Wksp Officer was Capt Gordon Ewing. He may not have arrived from Bde Troops LAD at the time but, if not, then he arrived very soon afterwards. Vic still wonders why a qualified engineer was used for this appointment, and why the appointment was not reserved for a non-engineer. But his was not to reason why and so he got on with the job, such as it was. His WOII Chief Clerk was a splendid chap by the name of Heath and he likes to remember that they got on well.

The day he joined 10 Inf Wksp in the riverbed it had begun to rain, so they posted guards on the dry riverbed, to warn them of the first sign of water. Flash floods in the mountains were a great danger and they soon recognised the need to treat wet weather with the greatest of respect. They did not stay long in that location; within a couple of days they were gathering themselves and moving out onto the MSR and travelling north, with their motley collection of somewhat ancient vehicles and equipment.

(N.B. He and many others often wondered just what the Americans thought of them, with their pre-war (1939-45) worn-out trucks of every make and description, particularly the old Diesel 6x4 Scammell, which really did look like something out of the past. What a poor run-down army they were in those years. Old vehicles, old equipment, inadequate clothing for the climate and hidebound by the systems of the war in Europe, which had little relevance to a war in this country. The best things they had were the men. To the Brits, adversity was a challenge, and they invariably rose to that challenge with an ability and cheerfulness that never failed to amaze. It made him feel particularly good to be there with them. As the author of these words, I can only say that situations have not improved with the march of time.)

A much-admired equipment

There was one piece of equipment that *was* good. Capt Moore thought it was the best in Korea and probably the best of its sort anywhere at that time. That was the British Centurion Tank, so ably crewed and deployed by 8 Hussars. With its electrically stabilised gun and its electric kettle, it was much admired by the Americans.

Capt Tinkham had already been forward and selected a site, a few miles north of this riverbed, and they soon found themselves struggling through a sea of mud, onto an open site on a low hill. This turned out to be nothing less than a Korean cemetery. The weather had turned cold and rainy and altogether it was a cheerless situation; but this was the best they could have found in the area near Osan and they were literally stuck with it. In quick time, the vehicles had sorted themselves out into suitable places to work and he was seeing a Field Workshop ready itself to work, for the first time. Vic's office truck was soon in operation and the CSM was off sighting the cookhouse and latrines. Their mess staffs were erecting the officer's tent, as they had now done many times before. The signs were out on the road and repair work soon began to flood in to them. The Workshop site was surrounded by paddy fields, which were flooded at that time, and the nights were filled with the hideous croaking of what seemed like millions of bullfrogs. It was impossible to sleep at times and it was very trying for everyone.

Vic had been to Bde HQ and reported himself as 'arrived'. He was delighted to hear that they were to be hosts for some entertainers for a few days and that they would be responsible for seeing them conducted to other Brigade units. He guessed it was ENSA, he does not recall, but there was great excitement when it was disclosed that the entertainment was to consist of a female opera singer from England and a Korean male opera singer, with two musicians. What on earth would they do with a female in their camp area? It raised all sorts of problems. They solved them of course, mainly by Vic giving up his tent for her and digging a separate ladies loo nearby. The party arrived and settled in without trouble. The lady's name was Elaine, but the Korean's name he never did know. She was young and wore a dress and the boys loved it. The couple sang beautifully and gave a great concert, after which they were provided with Major JC's *Humber* staff car, in which they toured the units in the Brigade. It was a pleasant episode for everyone and much appreciated.

Gordon Ewing was now definitely with them and he had time to see how the working side of the workshop was conducted. His recollection of this time is that the Workshop was fairly busy and they were changing many worn out engines on their old trucks. The *Bedford* QL 3-ton 4x4 was a good vehicle and would go almost anywhere, given time. But it was a grossly underpowered vehicle and the engines soon indicated their age and short life. The *Willy's* Jeeps were the same. Engines just did not last the pace, due to the grinding damage of the dust. Spares were difficult to come by, 'make do again' was the order of the day. But the vehicles were kept going and they did the job, after a fashion.

Oh how they envied the Americans with their big powerful *GMCs*, their modern Jeep with its side screens and heaters; and, in particular, the super tents with heaters and the excellent cooking facilities

Capt Gordon Ewing 2i/c 10 Inf Wksp

North again to join 10 Infantry Workshop REME

with which they were equipped. He had the opportunity to visit their MMCs from time to time. These were the Yanks' equivalent of the Workshop and, for them, life was so very different. They had plenty of well-designed vehicles, good working conditions, usually under cover, and excellent repair and recovery equipment. Their *Ward de le France* recovery truck was a light year ahead of our venerable *Scammell*, which everyone reckoned should have been in a museum. April neared its end, the weather was getting hot now and the work continued to come in.

Capt Moore made frequent trips to attend 'O' Groups at Bde HQ and he was now able to see that HQ at work and to see what was happening at the front. 29 Bde was astride the MSR and thus facing the enemy's main line of advance. This advance had in fact by now been stopped, while plans were in hand to reverse the process and cross the Imjin River, thirty miles north of Seoul.

They were put on notice to move again soon, and recces were made as far forward as possible. It was important for the Workshop to keep up close behind the Brigade if it was to be effective, but space was at a premium. The hills and paddy fields offered very few suitable locations for them and they did not want to stray too far from either the centre line or the comfort and protection of the other units. They had no trouble from the air so, camouflage was not normally necessary. They had their guards out around the area of the Workshop, but there was virtually no infiltration by the enemy and they never had reason to stand to.

The capital, Seoul had been fought over again and again and was in a terrible condition with almost total destruction everywhere. The Americans had declared the city closed to all but a few units and all civilians had fled. The Workshop wanted to cross the Han River into the city, and further north if possible, to shorten the lines of communication which had by now become too extended. This was out of the question and so an alternative site, just south of the river, was selected in an abandoned biscuit factory in the 'town' of Yongdongpo. The site was a mess of mud and with little to offer, but there was nowhere else and here they camped, uncomfortable and able to do very little work. Inchon was less than twenty miles away to their west, so they took the opportunity to visit the port, of which very little remained. Not long before that, the Americans had achieved a major success with their amphibious landing and, in so doing, had turned the course of the war in their favour. Tragically, the Workshop lost one of its Craftsmen while at the biscuit factory location. He died from a gunshot wound to the head, the reason for which they never ascertained.

Their stay in Yongdongpo dragged on through May 1951. The weather had improved steadily and they had all made themselves reasonably comfortable. Most of the office buildings were intact, as were a couple of typical English-style bungalows, which they assumed had been the residences of the factory manager and his assistant. They were overjoyed to find that, for the first and only time in Korea, they had a normal toilet that worked. Such are the small pleasures in life! During this time and previously, at the end of April, great things were happening just to the north of them, but they knew little or nothing of the Battle of the Imjin until it was over. The Chinese had attacked in great force over the Imjin, commencing on April 22nd, and had been repulsed with very heavy casualties by 27 and 29 Brigades. *(This proved to be one of the great battles of the war and is recounted in detail and most vividly in "The Korean War", by Max Hastings.)* Had the enemy attack proved successful, it is quite likely that the retreat south would again have been swift and disastrous. As history has recorded, the Chinese were repulsed, and they never again mounted an all-out assault that had any chance of a strategic success. The front was stabilised on the Imjin and, towards the end of June or into July, they were at last permitted by the Americans to move up over the Han River into Seoul.

The move into Seoul was a short day's drive up to and over the only permanent girder bridge left standing. The city showed every sign of having been fought over at least three times and hardly a building had escaped damage of some sort. As they neared the centre of the city, they saw the main avenue leading to the large government offices and the President's Palace. To their surprise, there was in this area a large tram depot with hundreds of trams lined up, looking for all the world as if ready to drive off. Not that this would have been of any value, as there were no people to use trams. The city was deserted - partly because the population had fled ahead of the war - but subsequently because the American Army discouraged any attempt by the civilian population to return. One or two Army units were allowed to stay, which included 10 Inf Wksp and its American counterpart, a MMC. They found themselves next to each other in the same ex-Japanese Army Barracks. Although somewhat damaged, the big brick three-storey buildings provided good accommodation and the huge parade ground was ideal for the Workshop sites, probably the best they would ever have in Korea. The work soon found them and they were all kept busy. Maj JC Smith had left around this time and his replacement, Maj Rogers, had arrived and taken over command.

It was interesting to see the Americans close by and, again, the British lads envied them their vastly superior equipment and supply services. Every morning, they paraded in clean fatigues and white T-shirts, drilling enthusiastically to their rendition of *"Hop, two, three, four"* etc. Much to their and our amusement, Victor Moore must confess. The Workshop also managed to set the barrack block on fire one night, which provided them with some anxious moments. Fortunately no one was hurt and the loss of the building proved of little consequence. It was very strange living in a deserted major city and they took the opportunity to explore many of the government buildings and offices, including the central hospital and the music academy. Little remained in these buildings, as everything of any value had gone. But, here and there were signs of the previous occupants, such as desks and pianos. Vic recalls wandering through the huge hospital. Long echoing corridors had empty wards on either side, with empty beds, empty staff rooms and empty store-rooms. Then the operating theatres, still with much of their equipment still standing or strewn around the floor. He thought that seeing this once quite modern city, so stripped of life, brought home the futility and tragedy of the war as much as anything else.

Driving up to Bde HQ was now quite an experience in itself. There were very few civilians, as they had all gone south. The MSR ran north, straight out of Seoul to Uijongbu and on to Tokchon, a distance of some fifteen miles. To reach the 29 Bde area, their route branched off to the left over a very bad road, which does not to this day appear on most maps. There was one very wide and difficult river crossing to navigate. The rail and road bridges had been destroyed, while the American Engineers were busy rebuilding them. There was a pontoon bridge, but many trucks forded this wide river to get past the congestion. Some made it, many did not, and a recovery bulldozer was in constant demand to pull the failures over to dry land - one took one's choice. Vic opted to wait and cross on the pontoon bridge, which frequently meant a long wait, but was the safest way in the long run. The road also ran through a high range of hills and these, together with the river crossing, made the back-loading of vehicles to Seoul a long and difficult task for the LADs at the forward area.

Protracted peace talks

Everywhere were pockets of soldiers, vehicles and equipment, the unit signs of many nations, and now the faint sound of heavy guns. This was definitely the 'sharp end' of the Army. Bde HQ Rear was, as always, well dug in on the reverse side of a slope and camouflaged, but there was no real indication that the war was just a short way ahead. The Deputy QM, Maj Hugh Beech, was always interested in the Workshop's situation and found valuable time to brief them of the current situation in the Brigade area. On July 10th 1951, the Communist and UN armistice delegations met for the first time, in a little village called Kaesong, a few miles over the Imjin river, west of Panmunjon. It is a very sobering thought to know that, forty-seven years later in this year of 1999,

North again to join 10 Infantry Workshop REME

the two antagonists are still facing each other across the tables in the neutral zone at Panmunjon, still arguing and with no peace treaty signed.

Although the two sides had started discussions, there was no end in sight at that time to the war, as fighting continued. Because the Chinese were now in no position to break through, the front had stabilised in the west along the line of the Imjin, but this did not mean that the intensity of the war had diminished in any way. It was no surprise, therefore, that in August 1951 the Workshop was ordered to move up once again. This in order to reduce lines of communication with Brigade, particularly in view of the approaching winter and the difficulties of movement which would come with it. And so they vacated their Japanese Barracks in their deserted city and trundled off north again, to an open area alongside the MSR at Tokchong, not too far from the branch road up to Brigade.

It was during this time in Korea that Vic Moore met a number of American officers from an American Engineer unit. One night, the sentry came to his tent and said there were two American officers here and that they wished to speak with one of the English officers. He asked them to come to his tent and they introduced themselves. They said they were bridge builders, who were working up on the MSR. They asked whether the Workshop could help with some brackets they needed. It was no problem and Vic said they would make them. They made the brackets that were wanted and, a few days later, after delivering the same, Vic was asked to go and meet the other officers and have some 'chow' with them. Of course he went, and took along 'a bottle' to help cement the relationship. The two they met initially were Lt Ray Reynolds, a big slow spoken man from Iowa, and Lt Bell. The other officers were all nice people, well educated and very professional. Capt Moore was made welcome in their Mess and a strong relationship developed. The unit was 'B' and 'C' Companies, 84 Engineer Construction Btn, 2 Engineer Construction Group, while the OC was a Capt Hauser. They had a small mahogany table in their Mess, which they had liberated from somewhere and, on one occasion, Vic remarked upon it. Whereupon Ray Reynolds said, in his slow southern drawl, *"We are going to build a bridge up the way, one thousand feet long and fifty feet high for you guys, and it will be all mahogany"*.

This was thought to be a bit of typical American 'bull-shine', but it proved nothing of the sort. They were going to build Teal Bridge, the main crossing over the Imjin, in front of Gloucester Hill. There were going to be three bridges on their sector front, 'Widgeon', 'Teal' and 'Pintail'. All were trestle bridges, and certainly, Teal was a 60-ton bridge, capable of carrying their Centurions. Vic was to watch this bridge being built and have the opportunity to attend the opening ceremony. This friendship with the Engineers was to their mutual advantage, the Workshop had the hard drinks and the Yanks had fresh food. The Workshop had 'Compo' rations and the Yanks loved that. It was great to meet these men from America, especially as, fifty years ago, it was not that easy to go to each other's country. The American boys showed a genuine interest in the British way of life and it was fascinating to hear how they lived. Moreover, what a difference there was in those days. Rationing and austerity in the UK, while the Americans seemed to have everything.

The Workshop site at Tokchon was a good open, reasonably flat area of dry ground and they were able to disperse into a classic layout for work. There was no threat from the air and there was no need to camouflage. There was good access to Seoul and, although the road up to Brigade was difficult, it was open at all times and the LADs were now able to get to them for repairs and spares. It was said that there was no air threat, but they later recalled that there was some mysterious old biplane that appeared now and again, flying at high level and reportedly dropping the odd grenade by hand. This caused much alarm and confusion for a while, but their attacker eventually became known as 'Bed Check Charlie' and was looked upon as a minor diversion. They never did know who or what it was.

Quite close to them, on one of the opposite hillsides, was an American MASH, since made famous in a film and follow-up TV series. They were pleased to have them near to the unit and to be able to observe the comings and goings. The Korean War was the first time that helicopters had been used extensively and they became used to seeing these 'flying skeletons' tracking low above the road, carrying a pannier on each side for the wounded. Capt Moore has watched the TV series many, many times and marvels at how accurate the settings were, with the scenes of the 'choppers' arriving and leaving. It took his memories straight back to that time and place. Names came back too, and Vic recalls that they had a 'Captain MC Dix' in the Workshop at one time. He got a 'ticking off' for writing his name as 'Capt Dix MC'. Then there was a new arrival from UK, Lt Rose, while another recollection, although with a little uncertainty, was of two brothers, ASM Jack Sinton and Capt Jim Sinton.

There seemed to be plenty of work in 10 Inf Wksp, including once a Churchill ARV that required an engine change. The weather was hot and the days were passing by with no further sign of a move. The Brigade LAD, as far as HQ was aware, did not have an officer in command, so Capt Moore was told by Brigade to have some leave and, on his return, report to Bde HQ and take over the LAD. That delighted him as it was going to be his first unit and his first command. He also looked forward to being a bit closer to the action. There was still plenty of that, despite the meetings now taking place to try to stop that crazy war. And so Vic Moore took himself off to the local air-strip at Uijongbu and waited for the friendly *Dakota*, with its Kiwi crew, to arrive. He was told that there was room for him and another Captain, also waiting to go back to Japan. This turned out to be the Provost Marshal, Ted Williams, and they were both soon packed into the Dakota, alongside a stack of stores. Having arrived in Tokyo, they booked in to the Maranuchi Hotel, had a bath and haircut and a good meal, then planned to spend some time in each others company. It proved to be a splendid week. They found Japan a fascinating place and the people very friendly. It was very hard to reconcile this with their record during the last war, only four years previously. But they were out to enjoy themselves, not to be too concerned with the past. They had the use of the American Officers' Club in Tokyo, and there they made the acquaintance of an Engineer Colonel. It was he who suggested that, instead of flying back to Korea, they could go with him via Sasebo by sea to Pusan, and then on the American Troop Train, which was now running as far as Seoul. They happily accepted and set off by car to Sasebo, which was the main American embarkation port on the inland sea.

Here, they were accommodated on a small troop ship that took twenty-four hours to get to Pusan, sailing the length of the inland sea before the short crossing. The train from Pusan was an overnight journey and they had sleeper-cars, with two rows of bunks on either side of a central corridor. Off they rattled into the night and soon settled down in their respective bunks. In the early hours of the morning, somewhere in the mountains, the train stopped and MPs rushed through the train, checking that everyone was all right. Apparently, an unfriendly party in the hills had set up a machine gun to attack the train. It had simply driven through a stream of bullets, which had stitched a neat row of holes through three carriages. No one was hit, although one could see the next morning that it was a good thing everyone had been lying down!

There was no problem getting a lift from 10 Inf Wksp and, the next morning, Capt Vic Moore was up early, packed and ready to get on the road to 29 Bde HQ LAD - his very first, albeit humble, command. It had been a good association with the Workshop and Vic was sorry to be moving on in some respects; but then he was not going far and fully expected to be back from time to time. In fact that proved to be the case, because he took the opportunity to visit with 10 Inf Wksp from time to time, to collect much needed spare parts for the LAD, and to have a good meal, a shower and an evening with his many REME and RAOC friends.

Chapter 22

29 Brigade Group, 10 Infantry Workshop REME and the formation of 1st Commonwealth Division

28th July to 15th October 1951

To summarise the events as related by Capt Vic Moore, whilst with 10 Inf Wksp, on June 4th 1951, Capt Gordon Ewing did arrive from 29 Support Troops LAD, to become the Workshop Officer. On June 11th, a complaint was received by the Workshop that their standard of work left much to be desired, this complaint coming from 45 Fld Regt RA. Their actual point was that the Workshop had been carrying out 'makeshift' repairs. This was immediately explained, that in order to keep their guns in action, the so called makeshift repairs were absolutely necessary, owing to the lack of new spares in the theatre.

June 21st saw them move forward to the Japanese Barracks in Seoul, where nothing additional happened but, on July 22nd, 82nd American Ordnance Coy was to assume the Defence Command for the area and this included 10 Inf Wksp. On July 26th, the ADME conference took place, which eventually affected a considerable number of tradesmen in the theatre as it was 'The Phase II' REME conference, to deal with those tradesmen still operating within the Regiments and Battalions. Those attending this conference were:

Lt Col Good	DADME, BCFK, CREME Designate 1 Comm Div
Maj Pogmore	DADME 29 Independent Inf Bde.
Maj Lewis	DADME 25 Canadian Bde (2IC CREME Designate)
Maj Rogers	2IC CREME, 1 Comm Div (OC 10 Inf Wksp Designate)
Maj Christie-Smith	OC 10 Inf Wksp (DADME, BCFK Designate)
Maj Germain	OC 16 Inf Wksp

Up to this stage in the story of REME in Korea, Commonwealth troops had operated independently, virtually as part of the US ground forces. It is true that, since early May 1951, there had been three Independent Brigade Groups and that common sentiment and 'a feeling of union' had existed for some time. Nevertheless, the preponderance of American strength had denied our contingents the status that their now considerable total numbers and high standard of operational efficiency warranted. Now they were to be integrated in a Commonwealth Division, with consequent elevation in prestige and increased participation in the planning and conduct of major operations.

The Staff of Div HQ started to assemble from all parts of the world, to organise early in June 1951. Maj Gen AJH Cassels, CB CBE DSO, the Div Cdr designate, who had visited Korea for ten days in May, reached Japan from Australia. There, he had been Chief Liaison Officer, UK Services Liaison Staff, and it was there, on June 11th, that he met most of his senior Staff Officers and Heads of Services. Soon after this, Gen Cassels and his staff moved to Korea, where they visited Commonwealth troops and got to know those American commanders and staffs, with whom they would serve and co-operate. The main body of Div HQ arrived at Pusan towards the end of June and, on July 26th, moved from Suwon (whence it had moved by stages from Pusan) to the following locations:

Main Div HQ - located north of Tokchong, in a valley with good cover from the air
Rear Div HQ - to an area south of Uijongbu.
2 Regt RCHA (Lt Col AJB Bailey, DSO MBE ED)

Page 137

Near Tokchong, at midday on July 28th, a short ceremony was held – attended by Gen James A Van Fleet, Cdr Eighth Army, Lt Gen Sir Horace Robertson, C-in-C British Commonwealth Forces in Japan and other senior Commonwealth and American officers – to mark the formation of 1 Comm Div. Here, for the first time, a Comm Div flag was flown – alongside the flags of Commonwealth countries and that of the UNO.

The following outline order of battle gives the names of senior officers, in the HQ:

Cdr	Maj Gen AJH Cassels, CB CBE DSO (UK)
GSO1	Lt Col ED Danby, DSO (Canada)
AA & QMG	Lt Col AWNL Vickers, OBE (UK)
CRA	Brig WGH Pike, DSO (UK)
CRE	Col ECW Myers, CBE DSO (UK)
CRSigs	Lt Col AL Atkinson (UK)
CRASC	Lt Col MGM Crosby, MC (UK)
ADMS	Col G Anderton, OBE (UK)
CRAOC	Lt Col MF MacLean (UK)
CRÈME	Lt Col HG Good, MBE (UK)

Divisional Troops:

8 KRIH   (Lt Col Sir WG Lowther, Bt) (equipped with Centurion tanks)
'C' Sqn, Lord Strathcona's Horse (Canada) (Maj JW Quinn) (equipped with the new Sherman battle tank)
16 Fld Regt RNZA (Lt Col JW Moodie, DSO ED)
45 Fld Regt RA (Lt Col MT Young, DSO)
170 Light Bty RA (Maj TV Fisher-Hoch) (Mortars).
11 (Sphinx) Light A-A Bty RA (Maj LVF Fawkes, DSO MC)
28 Fld Engineer Regt RE (Lt Col PNM Moore, DSO MC)
57 Independent Fld Sqn Royal Canadian Engineers (Maj DH. Rochester)
4 Fld Park Sqn RE (Maj JA Keer)
25 Canadian Fld Ambulance RCAMC (Lt Col BLP Brosseau, MC)
26 Fld Ambulance RAMC (Lt Col A Maclennan, OBE)
60 Indian (Para.) Fld Ambulance IMC (Lt Col AG Rangaraj, MVC)
25 Canadian Inf Bde: Cdr – Brig JM Rockingham, CBE DSO ED
2 Btn Royal Canadian Regt (Lt Col RA Keane, DSO)
2 Btn PPCLI (Lt Col JR Stone, DSO MC)
2 Btn Royal 22 Regt (Lt Col JA Dextraze, DSO)
28 British Comm Inf Bde: Cdr – Brig G Taylor, DSO
1 Btn KOSB (Lt Col JFM Macdonald, OBE)
1 Btn KSLI (Lt Col VW Barlow, DSO OBE)
3 Btn RAR (Lt Col FG Hassett, OBE)
29 British Inf Bde: Cdr – Brig T Brodie, CBE DSO
1 Btn RNF (Lt Col MC Speer)
1 Btn Gloucestershire Regt (Lt Col DB Grist).
1 Btn RUR (Lt Col RJH Carson)

29 Brigade Group, 10 Infantry Workshop REME 28th July – 15th October 1951

The additional units required to form the Division were provided from the UK and by various Commonwealth countries. Some units were composite ones, consisting of components from more than one Commonwealth country. The Belgian Btn was also attached to the Division.

In addition to the units and contingents provided by Australia, Canada, India, NZ and the UK, many individuals from these and other Commonwealth countries were to be found in the Division. Later, a team of officers from South Africa joined. As an example of its integrated character, it may be mentioned that the General Staff Branch of Div HQ consisted of a Canadian GSO1, a British GSO2 and 3, and Liaison Officers from Australia, NZ, Canada and India.

In the course of the next two years, many changes were made among unit personnel, but the Division's truly Commonwealth character was not altered and the Commonwealth spirit was maintained throughout. Men from many countries, races and creeds were to support each other in battle. They were to deliver each other's rations, ammunition and stores and tend each other's wounded – all part of the armed forces of this great association of nations, which had been built up over the centuries with so much toil and good will – and occasional disappointment. 1 Comm Div was part of the American 1 Corps, commanded by Lt Gen JW O'Daniel. This stout hearted American commander – affectionately known to the troops as 'Iron Mike' – was to become a good friend to the Division and one under whom all ranks were proud to serve.

Superimposed on this operational chain of command was the C-in-C BCFK, Lt Gen Sir Horace Robertson, with his HQ in Japan. He was also responsible for the administration and domestic arrangements of Commonwealth troops in Korea and for the administrative units and installations – in Korea and Japan – which succoured the Comm Div but were not part of it. The only two branches persistently under strain, in what was essentially a static battle zone, were those providing ordnance services – the RAOC – and the Electrical and Mechanical Engineers – the REME.

The former had to supply weapons, vehicles, equipment (including spare parts) and clothing, derived from many sources for a Division using items of British, US, Australian and Indian origin. The latter recovered and repaired items of these diverse origins, swollen by increments provided to meet the special circumstances, such as weather and the remoteness of some localities in Korea. In theory, the RAOC and REME should have broken under the load of their work. That they did not was partly due to rationalisation of their functions, but as much because their officers and men often worked for twelve and more hours a day throughout the year of their service in Korea, during which they engaged themselves at all levels in remarkable feats of improvisation.

Only a very brief description of the administrative arrangements is possible, in general as follows: 1 Comm Div was under operational command of 1 US Corps but was NOT under its administrative command. The whole administrative support for the Division was supplied from Commonwealth sources, controlled by Main Administrative HQ BCFK, except for petrol and a proportion of rations, ammunition and engineer stores, which were supplied by the US Army. There was no normal Corps or Army administrative backing for the Division. The base installations were in Japan, forward base units in Pusan, and a forward maintenance area in Seoul, immediately behind the Division. All personnel and stores came from Japan to the base port of Pusan, about 350 miles from Seoul. By rail, the journey sometimes took five days and there was always a shortage of rolling stock. At this stage of the Campaign, the roads were in a shocking condition and there was no road delivery between Pusan and Seoul. Vehicle movement on the roads was often difficult, owing to precipitous hills or flooded rice-fields. Important operational stores were often flown direct from Seoul. There was a daily courier service from Japan to Seoul for personnel and mail, with some 18,000 to 30,000 pounds airfreight moved daily, operated by RAAF, RCAF and USAF. Another service was provided by Landing Craft Tank (LST), American or Commonwealth, from Japan or Pusan to Inchon. There were, on average, three deliveries per month, used for vehicles and heavy stores. The line of communication (L of C) however was by no means certain and delays were frequent. Due to bad roads, there was no road delivery over the L of C between Pusan and Seoul. The railway served the whole of the UN Forces and there was keen competition for freight priority. Thus the lack of normal Corps installations behind the Division, coupled with the long and difficult L of C, had thrown great strain on the Div administrative services. The appalling roads of Korea, plus the mountains and very wide temperature range, all had major administrative implications. The wear and tear on equipment was very heavy. A Jeep or *Bedford* truck required a major overhaul every 5,000 miles.

Equipment losses by the Infantry were high, due to the wild country. Clothing and equipment, for use in tropical heat and extreme cold or rain, had to be progressively issued and withdrawn over the year. There were virtually no buildings and most accommodation was either tented or a combination of sandbags and local resources. It was most difficult to get off the roads, due to wet rice paddy or hills. This made it impossible to establish a normal Administrative Area and led to a wide dispersion of administrative units. Due to the distances involved, and the lack of facilities, the rearward signal communications, provided for administrative staff and services, proved inadequate. For instance, it was impossible to talk from the Division to Main Administrative HQ BCFK, which was the equivalent of the AA and QMG of a Division in Europe being unable to talk to his Brigadier AQ at Corps. Also, the need to conserve dollars led to strict accounting for the issue or receipt of stores between members of the Korean operations pool account, Australian, UK, NZ and Canadian or Indian units and all other members of the UN Forces.

CRASC assumed command of all ST activities at 1200 hrs on July 28th 1951. The three Brigade Companies were amalgamated, to form 1 Comm Div Transport Column:

HQ RASC   - an integrated HQ with a Canadian 2IC
Amn   - 54 Coy RCASC - 3 Plns, 2.5-ton trucks
Sups, POL - 57 Coy RASC - 4 Plns, 3-ton GS
Gen duties - 78 Coy RASC - one UK Pln and one RNZASC Pln.

Casualties due to battle exhaustion were low, probably due to the lack of enemy shelling. Such casualties showed a marked increase when hostile shelling has increased. All but slight casualties were evacuated through MASHs to US Army Casualties Evacuation Hospitals and thence by air to the BCOF General Hospital at Kure, in Japan. The Norwegian MASH, which proved to be a most efficient medical organization, also supported the Division. The health of the Division was generally good. The major causes of sickness have been gastro-intestinal diseases and venereal disease. Statistics for the period July 28th to October 15th 1951 showed the following:

Daily admittance rate per 1,000........................ 2.65
Daily returned rate to unit per 100.....................1
Battle casualties...389
Total non-battle casualties, admissions..........3,864
Total evacuated from Korea........................1,358

29 Brigade Group, 10 Infantry Workshop REME 28th July – 15th October 1951

Due to the numerous channels of supply of stores and equipment for the various Commonwealth contingents, it was not practicable for CRAOC to assume command until August 10th 1951. On this date, 25 Canadian Ordnance Company, 28 Inf Bde OFP and 29 Independent Inf Bde Group OFP were amalgamated and formed into the 1 Comm Div OFP, 1 Comm Div Stores Distribution Detachment (SDD). The major ordnance problem was the lack of Corps and Army Support. The nearest adequate ordnance installation was 350 miles behind the Division. This fact, coupled with the delays on the L of C, resulted in:

CRAOC and Div ordnance units being forced to undertake tasks for which they were not designed.

SDD being forced to hold a large stock of general stores that it could not move.

Continual demands on the Base to fly in urgently needed stores and an everlasting search of all movement agencies to find out where stores had got to.

Procurement of US stores presented many problems. Stores for Canadian units were requisitioned in the forward area but, due to stringent financial control, all requisition of US stores for other contingents was done by BCFK in Pusan. An operational reserve of warlike stores was established at Suwon (twenty-five miles south of Seoul). This reserve amounted to approximately the equipment for one rifle-company and was directly controlled by Division.

It also contained some heavy weapons for support companies, a few vehicles and some signal equipment. It proved to be of the greatest value and, to a very minor degree, off set the lack of Corps support.

CREME assumed command of all Mechanical Engineering (ME) units at 1200 hrs August 4th 1951. The ME order of battle was:

HQ REME - an integrated HQ with a Canadian 2IC.

10 Inf Wksp REME (29 Bde)

16 Inf Wksp REME (28 Bde)

191 Inf Wksp RCEME (25 Canadian Bde)

An immediate reorganisation took place and, by withdrawing the Recovery (Recy) and Telecommunications (Tels) elements from the three Workshops, the following additional units were formed: Comm Div Recy Coy and Comm Div Tels Wksp. The Div Recy Coy was most successful, the reorganisation providing much more flexibility. It was centrally controlled by HQ REME and allowed the full weight of all Recovery resources to be deployed as required.

The Div Tels Wksp worked in conjunction with 'M' Troop 1 Comm Div Signal Regt. It reduced the backlog of Tels repairs to practically nil and allowed an 'over the counter' service. 8 Hussars HAD was established in their 'B' Echelon area, thus making it possible to effect major repairs to Centurions 'in situ', without recourse to back-loading to Infantry Workshops.

The whole ME problem had been aggravated by the severe climatic and terrain conditions in Korea. Because of such conditions, the general wear and tear on equipment and vehicles was about double for the equivalent usage or mileage under European conditions. As a result, the work loading of all ME units was much higher than normal. The major problem experienced by ME had been the lack of major assemblies and expendable stores for UK equipments. Spare parts for UK equipments remained in reasonably good supply, but there was a serious shortage of all spare parts from US Army sources for US equipments and those vehicles operated by Canadian units.

During the period covered by this report, the work handled by ME units, which was originally on the secret list, is shown at Fig 1. The figures cover only a period of 79 days and will, it is hoped, give some idea of the workload placed on the members of the EME branches within Korea during the period July 28th to October 15th 1951.

Type of Equip	Received	Repaired
Tanks	130	108
Vehicles of various types	1659	1030
Armaments	73	57
Small Arms & Machine Guns	390	241
Instruments	819	613
Miscellaneous	1790	1355

At this time, at the end of July 1951, the UN line ran, in general terms, from a point on the west coast about twenty miles south of the 38th Parallel, roughly north-east to the east coast, approximately twenty miles north of the 38th Parallel. It cut the Parallel some forty miles northeast of Seoul. On most parts of the front, contact with the enemy was not close. 1 Corps sectors consisted of defensive positions some thirty miles north of Seoul. The portion of 1 Corps line held by 1 Comm Div was about 11,000 yards long, protected by the river Imjin. Positions were as follows:

Left: 29 British Inf Bde.
Right: 28 Comm Inf Bde
Reserve: 25 Canadian Inf Bde
Belgian Inf Btn (Attached)

On the left flank was 1 ROK Div and, on the right, the American 1 Cavalry Div. The enemy line was, on average, some 7,000 yards north of the Imjin. Contact was only possible by crossing the river by improvised ferry or raft, as no bridges existed. Also, at this season, the river was too deep for fording, being in flood after heavy monsoon rain. The role of the Division was to maintain its defensive positions and to harass the enemy by vigorous patrolling and raids. As all guns were, of necessity, located south of the Imjin, it proved difficult to provide artillery support for ventures of this kind, as the range was usually too long. Gen Cassels had expected some teething troubles in the early stages but, in the event, these were surprisingly few. Initial difficulties were experienced, owing to differences in British and American Staff procedures and methods of command. These took some time to iron out and might have caused friction, had it not been for the good will, which always characterized American and British relations.

The principle enemy of the Division at this time, and during ensuing operations, was the 64th Chinese Communist Army, consisting of the 190th, 191st and 192nd Divs. When the Comm Div was formed on July 28th, it was actually faced on its front by the 192nd Chinese Div, with two Regiments in the front line, each consisting of about 2,000 men. At that time, the enemy held a very light outpost screen some 2,000 to 3,000 yards north of the Imjin River, with well-prepared defensive positions from 6,000 to 8,000 yards in the rear. The enemy did not patrol extensively and generally avoided battle in front of his main position. Until the Division advanced to a line north of the river, as described later, enemy artillery fire was almost unknown.

29 Brigade Group, 10 Infantry Workshop REME 28th July – 15th October 1951

The period from the formation of the Division until October 3rd was a comparatively quiet one, but included a practically unopposed advance of the Divisional line to the north of the Imjin River, plus a number of minor enterprises. These activities were admirably suited to the purpose of settling down into a Divisional organization. Troops, staffs and services got to know each other, a Divisional 'drill' was evolved, and the Div Cdr was able to see for himself the high quality of his new and diverse command. The Division's first task was participation in 'Operation Slam'. For this purpose, 25 Canadian Inf Bde was placed under the command of American 1 Cavalry Div on August 3rd, with the role of holding defensive positions in order to free the Cavalry Div for mobile operations north of the river. The task of the rest of Comm Div was to advance with, and to protect the flank of, the Cavalry Div in a combined crossing of the Imjin and an advance north of some four miles. Commonwealth troops taking part were:

    Left: 29 British Inf Bde - 1 RUR and the Belgian Btn
    Right: 28 Comm Inf Bde - 1 KSLI and 3 RAR.

The leading troops crossed the river early on August 4th and reached their objectives, about 6,500 yards distant, by 1600 hrs. No contact was made with the enemy. It had been planned that both Brigades would withdraw on the following day, but torrential rain, which caused the Imjin to rise to a depth of twenty feet, dislocated this arrangement. Consequently, the troops remained cut off north of the river. Battalions withdrew successfully just before dark on the 6th, but nine Carriers remained on the north side of the river during the night of August 6th, guarded by one Company of the Gloucesters, and were brought back the next day. Only very slight contact with the enemy took place, and there were no outstanding incidents. On August 8th, 25 Canadian Inf Bde reverted to Divisional command and returned to its reserve position.

A brief description of the more important operations will be given, as these indirectly produced work for the Battalion fitters, LADs and Infantry Workshops. On August 14th and 15th, 'Operation Dirk' took place. This consisted of a raid on an enemy objective about 7,000 yards north of the river, carried out by 2 RCR. Contact was made and some casualties inflicted on the enemy. The raiding Battalion withdrew to the south bank of the Imjin at dusk on the second day. On the 21st, the Belgian Btn was withdrawn from Gen Cassels's command, which was a matter for deep regret throughout the Division. All ranks had been on very friendly terms with the Belgians and greatly respected their soldierly qualities. During the next three days, the Canadians carried out a more ambitious raid – 'Operation Claymore'. The Brigade, less 2 RCR, crossed the river and advanced on two objectives, 6,000 and 10,000 yards to the north respectively. Two air strikes carried out by American aircraft were estimated to have killed more than fifty of the enemy, while some interesting and useful documents were captured. On September 2nd, first reports of enemy tanks on the Divisional front were confirmed. Normal patrol activities across the river continued, in which small parties of the enemy were engaged by infantry and by artillery fire. Between September 3rd and 6th, 25 Canadian Inf Bde relieved 28 Comm Bde in the right sector of the line, the latter coming into reserve.

On September 6th, following some activity on the American 1 Cavalry Div's front on the right, 3 RAR crossed the Imjin on rafts and established a firm base, preparatory to carrying out a raid code-named 'Boomerang'.

It was intended to advance to the objective on the 7th but, early that day, orders were received for a major Divisional operation and the Australians were ordered to maintain their base north of the river, as a screen to cover the crossing of the remainder of the Division. September 8th saw the development of the new 'Operation Minden'. 1 KSLI and 1 KOSB of 28 Comm Bde crossed the river and established further bases. Thus, the whole of 28 Bde was now north of the river. The enemy did not interfere with these crossings; but some minor fighting occurred on the Australians' front and the Battalion suffered a few casualties. Three prisoners were captured. On this day, the Engineers constructed a Class 50 bridge over the Imjin River. The object of 'Operation Minden' (see sketch map) was for 1 Comm Div to establish a new line 5,000 yards north of the river, which would be an extension of 1 Corps forward line. By the evening of September 12th, this line had been established, with 29 British Inf Bde on the left and 25 Canadian Inf Bde on the right. 28 Comm Inf Bde was in reserve, guarding both the original bridge and a second one that had by now been constructed. The forward troops were subjected to some artillery fire and twelve men were killed on this day.

Conditions in the new position were very different from the previous ones. The forward troops were close to the enemy outposts and patrol clashes were frequent, casualties being inflicted on the enemy by ground troops, artillery and air strikes. Numerous prisoners were taken, some of who reported that an enemy offensive was imminent; but it did not materialise. During the period September 13th to 20th, over 1,500 Korean civilians were evacuated to the rear from the Divisional forward area.

On September 21st 1951, orders were received for 1 Comm Div to take part in a full-scale Corps offensive, with the object of advancing some 6,000 to 10,000 yards along the whole Corps front, in order to establish a new one. This line, which was to be the scene of the Comm Div's activities for the next twenty-two months, will be referred to as 'the Divisional line'. This advance was to be carried out with 1 ROK Div on the left, 1 Comm Div in the centre and the American 1 Cavalry Div on the right. Orders for the Comm Div to carry out a preliminary raid, 'Operation Brodie', was later cancelled. The Corps operation was given the code-name 'Cudgel' but, on September 27th, this was changed to 'Operation Commando', with 'D' Day being fixed for October 3rd. On September 28th, some preliminary skirmishes took place.

Comm Div side-stepped approximately 3,000 yards to the right, to establish new boundaries as follows:

    Left - The River Samichon
    Right - The River Imjin (in area where river runs due north)

On October 2nd, 28 Comm Inf Bde, which was to carry out the first phase of the attack on the right, moved to its assembly area behind 25 Canadian Inf Bde. By the evening of that day, the stage was set for Comm Div's first major attack against a defended position.

The relatively quiet period of semi-position warfare since the Division's formation had enabled the settling-down process to be carried out in almost ideal conditions. The only aggravating factor was the weather, which provided the usual heavy monsoon rain, customary at this season of the year. However, a good deal of useful training had been carried out, including the instruction of some personnel in the use of searchlights in a ground role, for employment on the Divisional front. Another useful thing was a demonstration by 1 KSLI of 'The Platoon in defence at night', attended by the Corps Cdr and representatives from most formations and units in 1 Corps.

Chapter 23

The Divisional Commonwealth Telecommunications Workshop

With the formation of 1 Comm Div, which was 'a first', came other firsts. The Div Tels Wksp was one of them, combining the telecommunications sections from the three Infantry Workshops in Korea that formed it. The new formation located itself a few hundred yards south of the 'Pintail' pontoon bridge across the Imjin River. It was a joint British / Canadian unit of thirty-five personnel, with a British CO. At its concept, that was Lt Tony Cribb, ex-10 Inf Wksp, then for most of 1952, it was Capt Jake Toombs. The Canadians had two up-to-date purpose-built Tels Workshop wagons. The British 'Z' wagons were built onto a *'Dennis'* chassis, which carried a brass label engraved 'Renovated in 1927' (the birth year of the author). The wagon used by the Mobile Inspection Team dated from the pre-windscreen era, probably of WWI vintage, with a top speed of 15 mph via two gearboxes. At that speed, in a normal European climate, windscreens were not necessary, but here they most definitely were! On one occasion, as an American convoy passed them on the road, the whole lot ground to a halt, open-mouthed, as the Yanks took in with disbelief the vehicle's unique features.

A few days before they were due to take this wagon across the Imjin River, to continue servicing the front-line units, the river rose overnight by fifty feet, almost up to the underside of the newly built steel bridge. The Chinese troops upstream of the bridges pushed tree trunks and large floatable items into the river, with the express purpose of trying to damage the bridges and lines of communication. The American Engineers were rightly concerned, but damage was not caused. They kept a close check on the bridge, with theodolites trained on the super-structure to monitor any movement. If the team did not take its chance, it might be weeks before it could cross the river again. So, setting the speed to walking pace by the use of the hand-throttle, and steering to the centre line of the roadway, the truck was left to make its own way across. Meanwhile they, the team, equipped with life-jackets, very gingerly followed along behind it to the other side. In the event, the bridge survived the monsoon floods that, within a few days, fell as rapidly as they had risen.

One of the units visited was 3 RAR and, after completing the servicing of all their radio and phone equipment, the communications officer asked if the team could look at some 'other' equipment. This turned out to be a marquee, stacked with US Army communications gear that the original owners had somehow mislaid! (Or so the Aussies said!) Unfortunately however, they had no spares for

1st Commonwealth Division Telecommunications Workshop

American equipment. At another location, the only flat area that 2 Btn Royal Vingt-Deuxieme Regt could find to locate their Sergeants' Mess tent was over a small stream, which ran down the middle and under the table. After an incredible four-course dinner, the chef appeared, to be congratulated in true Gallic fashion. That was quite a visit! The other Canadian unit that they visited was 2 Btn RCR, remembered for their breakfasts of waffles and maple syrup alongside the bacon.

"Pintail" pontoon bridge

The Div Tels Wksp depended for its power on a diesel engine-driven generator on a trailer. During the winter of 1951, because it was too cold during the night to be outside for more than an hour or so, everyone, including the CO, took their turn of one hour's guard duty. At the end of that the, generator's engine had to be started up, to avoid the diesel freezing. Even for two people, swinging the starter handle was quite a tussle, especially for those of smaller build. Each workshop truck was fed by its own cable from the generator but, due to the volt-drop, the metal bodies of the trucks floated above ground potential. They soon learned not to hold the door handle before jumping onto the back step! Even local earth-spikes failed to cure this problem. Earth currents were a special problem in wet weather and, on one occasion, two people were carrying a heavy steel-cased communications receiver between them, when the difference in potential at the two ends of the set caused them to dump it in haste. The generator tent also housed the battery-charging unit. One afternoon, there was a loud explosion from this area and the Craftsman who ran the unit staggered from the tent with his face covered in pitch and acid, having connected a battery up in the wrong direction. Fortunately, he wore glasses and, after first-aid, was none the worse, except that thereafter one lens of his glasses was star-crazed and always reminded one of the famous shot from the early film *'Battleship Potemkin'*.

The *'Daughters of the American Republic'* (who must have been an early feminist group) had successfully lobbied for a prohibition on alcohol

Div Tels Wksp trucks, L-R, Jimmy Collins, Brian Norman and NK

The Divisional Commonwealth Telecommunications Workshop

The Mobile Inspection Team on the road. Note, the fully ventilated cab, circa 1930

for the US forces in Korea, but the NAAFI had no such problems. The team was delighted to exchange a case of Scotch for a Jeep trailer, when a very tall negro GI came knocking at our door one night. How the Jeep itself was obtained is not known! Although there was supposedly a US dump in Seoul, where one could simply walk in and pick the vehicle of your choice. Speaking of barter, another useful item was the chocolate *'Hershey'* bar. This was part of the American Emergency 'C' rations pack and, since it was quite inedible, was only ever used as a form of currency. How the *'Hershey'* company built a business on it is beyond comprehension, unless of course they only ever sold it to the American Military!

One day, a Divisional Order was posted, to the effect that it had been noticed that many units appeared to have more vehicles than they had been issued with and that, in two days time, a special inspection would be made. By the following morning, scores of vehicles of all shapes and sizes had been deposited at the roadside throughout the Div area. The REME LADs spent a busy two or three days bringing them in.

Four Korean 'house-boys' had attached themselves to the unit. 'Johnny' had been a student at Seoul University when the war began. Kim and Lee were probably fifteen year-olds and 'Papa-san' was around fifty. One of Papa-san's jobs was to collect up all the rubbish and burn it in a large pit that the house-boys had dug. Having done this for a day or two, Papa-san decided things needed speeding up a bit and poured a whole jerry can of petrol over the rubbish before throwing a match in. As the column of flame leapt twenty feet into the air, the accompanying roar brought everybody all out of their wagons to see Papa-san in full retreat, unhurt except for losing both his eyebrows.

Although the USAF *'Starfighters'* had total command of the air, a Chinese light spotter plane would occasionally fly over under cover of darkness. One evening, to the amusement of the whole Division, it dropped a hand-grenade into the bonfire kept burning all night at the nearby Press Camp, causing considerable alarm and confusion, but no injury. As a small and somewhat isolated unit, the Workshop was responsible for its own security. Since the wagons backed onto a hillside, they were dug in part way and their fronts covered with camouflage netting. This merged their outline into the hill, when seen from the air. A short while later, the HQ unit of the Royal Corps of Signals moved in right beside us. As the larger unit, they took over responsibility for local security and soon mounted an inspection of our lines. They were not pleased with our sloppy camouflage nets and insisted that they must be re-erected on poles, so that they were all dead square and in line with one another. Their next move was to lay lines of stones, painted white, between all their own tents! It was clear that, as 'mere engineers', we had not grasped the true purpose of camouflage!

Chapter 24

'Operation Commando' October 2nd to 15th 1951

'Operation Commando' was conducted by American 1 Corps and involved an advance on the whole Corps front to secure a new line. 1 Comm Div was required to advance from 6,000 to 8,000 yards along the whole Divisional front. Gen Cassels planned the advance to take place in three phases, as follows:

Phase 1; 'D' Day.
An attack on the right, by 28 Comm Inf Bde, to secure a dominating feature, Pt 355

Phase 2.
An advance by 25 Canadian Inf Bde on the left on 'D' plus 1, to secure a line of high ground about 3,000 yards from their present position.

Phase 3.
Phases 1 and 2 were planned for two successive days, in order to permit each Brigade in turn to have the support of the whole Divisional Artillery, plus some 8" and 155mm Batteries of 1 Corps Artillery. But a complication had arisen. One Battalion, 1 Btn RUR of 29 British Inf Bde was due to be relieved by a Battalion from the UK, 1 Btn Royal Norfolk Regiment (RNR), commanded by Lt Col JHR Orlebar, in a few days' time. All the necessary rail and shipping arrangements for the outgoing Battalion had been made some time before. It was, therefore, arranged to employ individual Battalions of this Brigade to support other brigades, rather than use the Brigade as a whole.

By the evening of 2nd October, 28 Brigade had moved up to its assembly area behind the front, and all other preparations were complete. The leading troops were in contact with the Chinese and, with every indication that stiff fighting lay ahead, this indeed proved to be the case. The attack by 28 Comm Bde was launched at first light on October 3rd, with 1 KSLI on the left, 1 KOSB in the centre and 3 RAR on the right. Initially, all Battalions made good progress, especially the Australians who, by taking advantage of a morning ground mist, made a rapid advance.

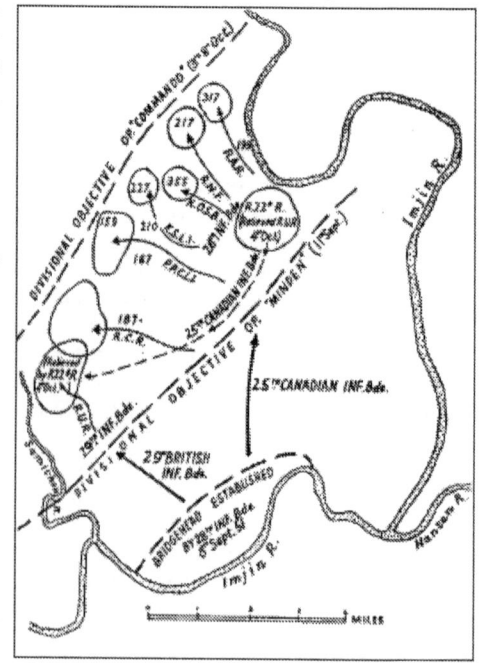

Sketch map showing 'Op Commando'

But, by 1000 hrs, the other two Battalions were meeting strong opposition and, for the rest of the day, their progress was slow. By dark, KSLI were about 1,000 yards short of the feature Pt 210, KOSB were about the same distance from their final objective, Pt 355, while the Aussies had reached Pt 199. During the day, 1 RNF had been deployed to an assembly area behind 28 Bde front and put under its command. Before the initial assault, and throughout the day, the enemy had been subjected to a heavy bombardment, some 27,000 rounds being fired by the Divisional Artillery. Casualties for the day were ten killed and forty-one wounded. The tanks took an active part, but found the going very heavy and several became bogged down. Twelve enemy prisoners were taken, including one officer.

The night of October 3rd was a quiet one and no contact was made with the enemy. At first light on the 4th, KSLI attacked and, by 1000 hrs, had captured Pt 210. By 1300 hrs, KOSB had secured their Pt 355, but only after fierce fighting. At 1100 hrs, 25 Canadian Bde attacked on the left where, except at Pt 187, little opposition was encountered. 2 Btn PPCLI eventually captured this feature, on the right of the Brigade front, after two hours of desperate fighting. On the left, the RUR of 29 Bde, conforming to the advance of the Canadians, also made rapid progress. From Pt 187, the advance continued and, by late afternoon, 2 Btn RCR had seized the high ground, some 500 yards northeast of Humurhan. During this operation, the Battalion was very heavily shelled. At the same time, 'B' Coy of the same unit advanced towards the high ground northwest of Ochon. This Company came under very heavy fire and had difficulty in extricating its leading elements. Meanwhile, PPCLI had also advanced to some high ground, 800 yards to the west of Pt 187. As the day was drawing to a close, the advance was finally suspended and the front adjusted for night defence. Enemy resistance seemed to be weakening and it was clear that the heavy artillery fire to which he had been subjected was beginning to tell. By last light on this day, 25 Canadian Bde was just short of its final objective but, on the right with 28 Comm Bde, Pt 217 and Pt 317 still defied capture. The former was to be the scene of bitter and almost continuous fighting for four days before it was finally occupied.

The third day of the attack, October 5th, was one of severe fighting on 28 Comm Bde's front. This Brigade had attached to it 5 Fusiliers from 29 Bde; they and the Australians set about the task of capturing both Pt 217 and Pt 317. At about 1500 hrs, the Fusiliers actually took Pt 217 but, just before dusk, they were heavily counter-attacked and forced to withdraw – due mainly to a shortage of ammunition. At 1700 hrs, the Aussies, after a successful air strike and a very heavy artillery bombardment, succeeded in capturing Pt 317. On the rest of the front, the Battalions consolidated the positions that had been gained on the previous day. The Ulsters of 29 Bde, who were withdrawn from the line owing to their impending relief and move to Hong Kong, were replaced by Royal 22' Canadian Regt. 25 Canadian Bde met with less opposition and, by late afternoon of this day, had captured all their objectives and were in touch with troops of 12 ROK Regt on their left. Casualties in the Division on October 5th amounted to five killed and forty-four wounded. Over 100 enemy casualties were counted and thirty-six prisoners taken. On the right, 1 Cavalry Div was meeting very strong opposition and had not yet reached its final objective.

On October 6th, 5 Fusiliers made vigorous attempts with the Australians to capture the only part of the Divisional objective not yet reached – Pt 217. After capturing it, they were again forced back by heavy fire, while the remainder of the front was quiet. The Division suffered ninety-five casualties, including ten killed, on this day - nearly all from 5 Fusiliers. The Australians made yet more strenuous efforts to capture Pt 217 on October 7th, but were again unable to make progress. Heavy shelling of the Aussies and Fusiliers positions continued all day. Several air strikes on enemy gun positions were made, culminating in the dropping of four 500 lb bombs by American

THE FORGOTTEN PUNCH IN THE ARMY'S FIST — KOREA 1950-1953

B29 aircraft, during the night of October 7th / 8th. During that night, the Aussies beat off several counter-attacks. On the next evening, following three successive air strikes, RNF occupied Pt 217 unopposed, thus finally completing the capture of the Divisional objective. On the 9th, Canadian and Comm Brigades worked hard on consolidating their positions. Enemy shelling was considerably less than before. On this day, Brig AHG Ricketts, DSO OBE, took over command of 29 British Inf Bde from Brig T Brodie, CBE DSO. 29 Bde had seen much hard fighting, including the stubborn defensive 'Battle of the River Imjin' in April 1951. Its successes were due, in no small measure, to Brig Brodie's outstanding leadership.

On October 10th, 1 Btn RUR left for Hong Kong and the relieving Battalion, 1 Btn RNR became operational. The Norfolks had landed at Pusan on October 1st and, a week later, their leading Company, 'A' Coy, had taken over part of the KOSB position on Pt 355, just south of Kowang San. On the 11th, they relieved 5 Fusiliers in the area just east of Pt 355 and came under command of 28 Bde. Pt 355 was a commanding feature, some 355 metres high and located at the head of a valley that lead straight to Seoul, the southern capital. The shape of Pt 355 was of an advantage if in a defensive position, as its forward face had a near vertical slope, such that it did not need too much in the way of wire defences. But the rear slope was also very steep, making it extremely difficult to carry ammunition to the defence positions on the upper areas. It has been said that it took four hours to reach the top with a full case of small arms ammunition.

REME was approached with a request for assistance in solving this problem. 10 Inf Wksp put its collective thinking cap on and came up with a solution, a powered skid that could haul the munitions up the slope. The manufacture was achieved by using an old quarter-ton *Chevrolet* truck, with its rear body shell removed. Swinging jacks were made and fitted to the rear axle, from which had been removed the rear wheels and their tyres. Welded metal strips across the wheel rims, to simulate a capstan effect, replaced these rims on the axle. Now a heavy structured wooden pallet type platform with steel skids and a towing eye was produced, braced between these skids. A large snatch block was obtained and a suitable length of steel hawser. With 'eyes' fitted into both end of this hawser, a length of heavy-duty chain and shackles were used to join this 'DIY' effort together.

The Author, Staff Sergeant John Dutton as he was in 1952, sitting on the rim of a 61mm mortar pit, just below the crest of hill Pt 355. The 1st Bn Kings Own Scottish Borderers and The Welch Regt, 29th Brigade held this feature.

Page 150

On the rear face of Pt 355, near the top, a snatch block was anchored, using ground anchor pins and recovery ground plates. A cable was fed through the block and both ends brought to the base of the hill. One end was attached to the pallet eye and the other end to the *Chevvie* rear wheels, which were now raised from the ground on the swinging jacks. The front of the truck, facing away from the hill, was also secured using recovery ground anchors and plates. The slack of the cable was wound onto the capstan type wheel rim, so that when the engine was started and reverse gear engaged, the cable wound onto the rims and pulled the skidded pallet up the hillside. The chain fitted between the pallet and the cable allowed for uneven surface movement of the pallet. It worked satisfactorily but did cause one or two heart failures when the chain broke and the wire rope under strain whipped across the hillside, making the defenders dive for cover.

1 Comm Div had now been in existence for nearly three months. It had experienced a period of very active defence, followed by a major offensive against stiff opposition. These operations had all been very successful. It is, however, useful to take stock of the position, and to quote some interesting statistics. The quality of troops was first class and their training satisfactory; most were now seasoned fighters. Generally speaking, the equipment had stood the test of operations well, although there were a few exceptions. The Universal Carrier had not been a success in Korea. It had poor cross-country performance and often slipped its tracks. On the other hand, the Oxford Carrier proved very satisfactory. Consequently, many units were put on a 'Jeep and trailer' basis. The Oxford Carriers were retained and also a few Universal Carriers, for load carrying on the good roads. The 4.2" mortars of 170 Bty RA, which had operated with 29 Bde, had been an outstanding success. There was some diversity of method regarding supplies. All Canadian units subsisted on American rations and most of the remaining troops on UK rations, plus some fresh rations from American sources. Special rations were issued to 60 Indian Fld Ambulance. The Americans supplied petrol and oil for Comm Div. During periods of active operations, such as 'Operation Commando', it was found that transport units were allotted approximately as follows:

    Supplies, petrol and oil ... ... 22 per cent
    Troop carrying, engineer stores and miscellaneous stores ... ... 28 per cent
    Ammunition ... ... 50 per cent

Most of the transport was provided from Commonwealth sources but occasionally assistance was obtained from the Americans. The daily average mileage was about thirty miles per vehicle and the total mileage, from 28th to 15th October 1951, was 725,000. In the same period, the LAD/HAD REME handled some 130 tanks, about 1,650 vehicles, and a quantity of other equipment that were repaired by either unit fitters, LADs and/or Brigade Support Workshops.

The method of evacuating casualties has been summarised in earlier chapters and it proved satisfactory. Considering the scope of operations, battle casualties had been surprisingly light – 389 killed, wounded and missing, from the time of the formation of the Division until October 15th. The health of the troops had been good. During the same period, 3,864 officers and ORs were admitted sick to medical establishments, of whom 1,358 were evacuated from Korea.

On July 1st, the Peking Government had broadcast a message from the NKA and CCF commanders in Korea, informing the Supreme Allied Cdr, Gen Ridgway, that they were authorised to agree to a meeting of representatives, concerning the cessation of hostilities and the eventual establishment of peace. As a result, what were euphemistically known as the 'Cease fire' talks began on July 10th 1951, at Kaesong.

Chapter 25

29 Brigade & 10 Infantry Workshop REME

Aug 5th to Dec 1951

The OC, Maj Christie-Smith, handed over his command to Maj Rogers who assumed that post on August 5th 1951. August 9th was a day to remember, as the event taking place set a precedent within the Corps. The Tels repair sections that had left UK with 29 Bde were withdrawn from 10 Inf Wksp. A similar event took place in 28 Bde, with 16 Inf Wksp's Tels repair section being withdrawn, to combine with 10 Inf Wksp's to form a totally new concept, to be known as Div Tels repair section.

It was located alongside HQ Div Signals at Div Main. The Tels officer from 10 Inf Wksp, Lt Cribb, moved to command this new section.

September 12th saw the Workshop moving forward again, leaving the quiet of the Seoul location and trundling up the MSR to a village called Tokchon. Their new location was on the left of the MSR, in a re-entrant in the hillside, with a stream running through the centre of the work areas, acting as a boundary between the vehicle repair and A&G areas. On October 1st, the Workshop had some good news. In a competition that had been entered, referring to the design of heaters for tents, vehicles etc, theirs had turned out to be the winning design. The proud welder responsible for this design now awaited his award of five days R&R in Tokyo, Japan. November turned out to be a month of work, more work, then even more work! On December 15th, the unit had to supply manpower to assist in a 'sweep' of the area, looking for any Koreans that had no right to be in this area. In essence it was an anti-guerrilla hunt, as Koreans supplied half of the Workshop strength. The remainder of the month was a repeat of November, the work ethic being fully tested!

The Workshop Officers in post at this time were as follows:

OC	Maj Rogers
AO	Capt G Ewing
Wksp Officer	Capt MC Dix
A/Wksp Officer	Lt Spittle
A/Wksp Officer	2Lt Morgan
Teles	Lt Cribb
MTO	Lt Rose
RAOC Stores Officer	Capt CW Nicholson RAOC

Chapter 26

29 Brigade HQ LAD, Officer Commanding Capt Vic Moore

September 1951 to February 1952

The journey from Tokchon to the Imjin was only about fifteen miles, but it took time and there were still long delays on the way. Capt Moore and his driver found the LAD tucked into a small valley in the hills near Munsan-ni that, as far as he could see, no longer existed other than as a name on a map - not that they had a map in any event! He did not take a handover from another officer. He didn't think the LAD had 'owned' a previous OC, but had been looked after by the BEME, Maj Vic Snow. Vic had never met BEME, but assumed he had been with HQ most of the time. Having checked in with HQ, he sorted himself out a tent and a spot for his kit, then settled in with his new minor command. He found that he had a WOII (AQMS), a Sergeant, and about twenty-four tradesmen, capable of doing most repairs required to the HQ vehicles. He had a Wireless truck and was in contact with other REME units, his own cooks, and a diminutive Korean boy called 'Number One', who had been with the LAD for a long time and was an orphan. He was a great chap, spoke quite good English and Vic determined to look after him, which he did very well. Before he eventually left Korea, he arranged for Number One to go into one of the very few orphanages in the country. Sgt Woodward knew of this orphan's home, so he collected some money, packed clothes and food, and took him in a Jeep, with his parcels of clothes and food, to this new home. Number One gave him a farewell present in the form of a pair of brass chopsticks, which he still has. Vic often wonders what happened to him, thinking that he probably became a 'captain of industry' or a politician.

He was surprised to find the LAD very busy, not only with HQ vehicles, but with many 'waifs and strays', which came in off the MSR. In the hills around the location, he now found the rear echelons of Brigade units and soon had many callers. A short way off was their Field Ambulance unit, which had three doctors and a dentist, who was commonly known as 'Snatcher' Ronnie Baines. They were all of

Capt Moore with the diminutive Korean boy called "Number One

vivid personality, full of fun and 'very English' versions of the American characters featured in the TV series 'MASH'. But they were also very experienced at their job, as Vic was to see at a later date. His other close neighbour was 'B' Echelon of the Welsh Regiment and their QM became a frequent visitor, until he became extremely ill and was evacuated. Being Welsh, the men sang a lot could often be heard in fine voice. They sang superbly and to hear them at night, in the middle of this unfriendly country, was quite an experience.

The water-point was nearby, as well as elements of many other units, including their tank Regiment, 8 Hussars, whom he had seen only once since arriving in Korea after their trip together on the *'Fowey'*. The Kiwi Gunners were here, with their 25-pdrs, also a Regiment of Americans with self-propelled 105mm Howitzers. The Americans were pretty close and used to fire all night long, at random intervals, in what they called 'H and I'. They learned that this stood for 'Harassment and Interdiction' and consisted of firing shells all over the enemy area, in order to cause random damage and maximum confusion. They fired right over the top of the LAD; the noise was alarming and Vic's tent roof flapped every time. One night, he paid them a visit and found that the personnel of the Regiment were all black. They were delighted to have Capt Moore visit them and he was soon invited to climb up on a gun and join the crew. As it turned out, he never did fire his own revolver in anger, but at least he had now fired a few 105mm rounds at the Chinese and, in his own mind, this justified his being there!

To his pleasure, he found the American Engineer Btn, with Capt Hauser and Ray Reynolds, up on the river, just about to build the 'big bridge', just as they said they would. The three men soon became frequent visitors with each other. Their meals improved and they were delighted to be able to have the odd whisky or gin for special occasions. One day, Vic sent Sgt Woodward to scrounge some fresh food and he returned with a block of frozen steaks, which must have weighed forty pounds, plus a crate of fresh eggs. They lived 'like lords' for days. Capt Moore was not very comfortable in his spacious tent. It was difficult to put up and was rather a waste just for him, so he again visited an American stores unit that he knew, coming away with a wonderful Bell-tent of green nylon, with a white liner and plastic floor. There was also a petrol fired heating stove unit, which would prove invaluable in the coming winter. He kept a 4-gallon jerry can filled with water on the little stove and thus had a constant supply of hot water.

Tuning in to Tokyo Rose

At night, he usually had one or more of his NCOs stop by his tent and they enjoyed powdered eggs and fried bacon, as a nightcap, cooked in a couple of mess tins. His men also made themselves comfortable. One had acquired a gramophone, on which he would play Japanese records well into the night until, in desperation, he would yell, *"Casey! Turn that ****** thing off and get to sleep"*, whereupon there would be a rousing cheer. He was presented with one of the records on leaving and he still has that too - *"Tokyo Rose"* - it was a great favourite at the time. During the summer of 1951, the two Brigades had been formed into the Comm Div and included in the Div HQ was a CREME, at the rank of Lt Col. This had no impact on them at Brigade, but he called in from time to time. CREME was more concerned with the Field Workshops, whereas he (Vic) was responsible to his Bde Cdr. Although he was a member of Bde HQ mess, for practical reasons he lived with the LAD a short distance away. The HQ mess was a tent, tucked into a hillside and heavily camouflaged. Inside it was quite comfortable, with easy chairs made from sandbags. Vic would eat there from time to time and the food was always good. The Bde Cdr, Brig Brodie, was quite a character and he usually found time to talk and ask about REME and how things were going, which was much appreciated.

Winter was now creeping up and it looked like being another hard one. Teal Bridge was taking shape and they stopped by there on every occasion to watch progress. The Imjin River was very wide here (1000 ft) and, during dry periods, there was little or no water, so that crossings could be made on the firm riverbed. The river banks were some fifty feet high, so getting down to, and out of, the river could be difficult, if not nearly impossible, after rain. The *Scammell* recovery vehicle was thus frequently in demand.

Too cold for the poor old "Knocker"! The diesel would not flow so a friendly Centurion helps out once again.

Building the bridge was a big task. It had to be strong enough to take the Centurions, which were believed to be the heaviest tanks deployed in Korea by the UN, and robust enough to stand the tremendous wall of flood water that roared down the river course after every storm. They saw the river go from empty to full on one occasion in a matter of minutes, preceded by a surge of water that spilled over the banks, passing at the speed of a train - and sounding like one too!

Vic happened to be on the bridge one day, during its construction, when a cable snapped on a crane lifting a span into place, causing three Americans to be badly injured. Utilising his Jeep and two more from the Engineers, they carried the casualties down the road on stretchers to the Bde Fld Ambulance Unit. Here, he saw the doctors go into action to provide first aid, until a helicopter was summoned and the men were taken off to their own MASH. When the bridge was completed, the American 1 Corps Cdr cut the tape, and the LAD was privileged to be there and to attend a celebratory lunch, for which Capt Moore himself provided the suitable celebratory drink.

Inevitably, winter closed in and it was a cold one. The ground froze and it was difficult to keep water flowing. The water-point was always having problems and the queue of water trucks and trailers, waiting to fill up, was always a long one. Their water-trailer usually arrived back with the taps frozen solid and with ice on the surface in the tank. This entailed either heating the tank with burners under it, or thawing the taps with their precious acetylene welder. They eventually found that one of the American petrol-fired immersion heaters, which they used for heating and cooking, just fitted nicely into the top of the water trailer, keeping things warm enough to stop the water freezing on the way back to camp. The sight of this weird contraption caused some amusement, but it worked and they were all the better for it. Somewhere on their travels, Vic had won a welfare wireless set, which he discovered to his amazement would receive the BBC from London on 1500 metres long wave, if conditions were favourable during the night. He got into the habit of getting into bed and fiddling with the tuning dial to find the BBC news, before going to sleep each evening. He was dismayed to hear the announcer, in February 1952, tell the world that King George VI had died. Vic imagined that he was probably the first person in the Brigade to know about the sad event.

As predicted, the winter came with bitter cold and snow. Life became infinitely more difficult and repairing vehicles in the open was a protracted and miserable operation for everyone. The snowfalls were unusually heavy and this reduced movement to a minimum, as the roads became ice slicks with vehicles sliding off into the ditches on either side. Christmas arrived and, although they made an attempt to celebrate this occasion, it proved

Teal Bridge opened by 1st Corps Commander 23rd Dec 1951.
Statistics: 1,050 Ft long, 50 Ft High, 80 Ton Imp capacity
In flood the Imjin River could fill the valley to Bridge height in minutes

particularly difficult due to the weather and the lack of cover other than their individual tents. Soon afterwards, they moved a short distance forward and set up to work again. But although the new site was a bit more convenient, it was very exposed and, with strong winds blowing, work was almost impossible.

Closer to Teal Bridge, Vic had seen the remains of a small village, which was tucked well in to the lee of a hill and would make a good Workshop site. With HQ's blessing they moved yet again but, by this time, it was very cold and the ground frozen solid. The Engineers sent a bulldozer to level and clear the site, which it did only with the greatest of difficulty. The blade would lift great sheets of frozen mud, which had to be broken down before levelling. Digging the latrines was like trying to dig concrete and the solution was to explode a four-pound gun cotton charge on the ground to break up the frozen soil beneath. It worked well, but was not too popular too cold for

with their neighbours, who wondered what was going on. The site, however, proved to be a good one and they were able to get things done in a much more efficient manner and be more comfortable at the same time.

The 'peace talks' were now getting under way, although the fighting continued much as before, with little respite. Vic desperately wanted to see what was going on around him and to take advantage, as a young officer, of this wartime experience. He had the Brigade Armourer in the LAD, who spent much of his time forward with the Battalions, looking after their weapons; so Vic went with him a couple of times. There was a troop of Centurions in their area, dug in and overlooking the front. Their troop commander was pleased to see them and they had their first good look at the tank and saw how the crew lived. Through the big high-powered binoculars mounted on the tank, Vic was able to see his first Chinese enemy at one place, improving their trenches.

Their American engineer friends were now working on the north side of the Imjin River, improving a road and starting construction of what was to be called the 'Peace Camp', in Panmunjon. They were taken there one day, but there was not much to see. Vic drove across the Imjin on the ice, where some Canadians had lit huge fires and were playing ice hockey. There can be no doubt however, that the soldiers in the fighting units had a very tough time. Not just dealing with the enemy, but fighting the country and the weather as well. It was an education and a tremendous experience just to be there; it set standards for them for the rest of their Army service.

Thoughts turn to home

And so the days went by. January became February and Vic began to think that it was time he went home to UK and his family. Many of the people he had come out with in 1950 had gone long ago and yet there was no indication that his posting was imminent. Finally he spoke to Brigade about it and they agreed that seventeen months was a fair spell and that he was due for a home posting. Young Lt Rose was summoned from 10 Inf Wksp and Vic duly took him around and indoctrinated him into responsibilities of his new job. He gave him the rather nice little tent, complete with heater, and made his farewells. Then he drove down to 10 Inf Wksp, for the last night with them, before once again scrounging a lift on the *'Dakota run'* to Kure and on to 5 Med Wksp.

On arrival there, he found he had some time to wait for the departure of the next boat for home, which was to be the *'Devonshire'*. So he granted himself leave and took the night sleeper back to Tokyo for a few days of R and R. He thinks that it was on this occasion that he met up with Maj Bob Birch and that they took the local train up into the mountains to Nikko. They had a night in a beautiful hotel there, overlooking a lake, and the next day travelled back in great style and at great speed on a 'bullet train' to Tokyo.

Finally, back in Kure, and his final packing done, Vic said his final goodbyes all round and set off to the docks to board the *'Devonshire'*. His kit was hoisted on board and he was called forward to make his way up the gangway, which he duly did. Reaching the top of the gangway, he gave his name to the boarding officer who, after searching through his list of names, told him that his name was not there and therefore he could not board. That was the last straw for him; he refused point blank to leave and asked to see the ship's CO. In fact it was the ship's Captain himself who sent for him and Vic explained the situation. He had orders to go home and he was going! The 'skipper' agreed and Vic was escorted to a suite of rooms just below the bridge, which he was told was his until they arrived in Singapore, at which time there would be room elsewhere. So all was well after all and as March came in, they sailed for home, while he enjoyed the best billet on the boat all the way to Singapore.

AQMS Peter Hills and Sgt Dave Kaye in the 'Fall Back' area of 29 Bde LAD.

Chapter 27

1 Commonwealth Division   1 Infantry Troops Recovery Unit

August to December 1951

Whilst in location at Inchon in early August, the unit had been running some recovery training courses. But things were about to change, such that they would again take on their designated task and fulfil their proper function, which was back-loading from Field Workshops to the docks area in Inchon and then onwards to base at Kure, Japan. Another aspect that was to have long-term effects on the unit was that, within a week, a Canadian element was to be attached, making up the unit strength as near as possible to its War establishment of eighty-four. In fact, their combined strength was to total only sixty-six.

But now, with a few more hands aboard, it was time to 'up the tempo'. By August 8th, a LST had berthed at Inchon, and the unit's job was to unload - not normally a difficult task, as these vehicles were 'runners'. By August 11th, the LST had been reloaded with three Churchill tanks, all BLR, five serviceable Cromwell tanks, ten assorted but serviceable Carriers and some forty-one assorted BLR vehicles. The rest of that month was a series of repeats, it was only the individual items that varied. September arrived and, on the 4th, there was a surprise detail for them, not their normal 'run of the mill' recovery. The RAAF was back-loading one of their fighter aircraft, a *'Meteor'*, its destination as far as can be recalled, was Iwakuni in Japan. The lads were very gentle and managed not bend it.

A Scammell Recovery vehicle about to pull a 15 cwt Bedford casualty back to the road it left, the other casualty will be left as beyond help.

1 Commonwealth Division 1 Infantry Troops Recovery Unit

The 7th saw the arrival in the unit of a Korean Police Detective. He had been requested to assist the unit in reducing the pilfering being carried out by young children. At the time, one had to all but nail down most items, otherwise they 'grew legs and walked'. It was not always practical to remove loose items such as seats, but somehow they managed to loosen themselves! On the morning of September 8th, there was another increase in staff, by the arrival of 2/Lt JC Rose. 10 Inf Wksp had lost another of its officers and his post was to be the 2IC of the recovery unit. Orders were then received to move up most of their recovery vehicles, in support of 'Operation Minden'. That kept everyone busy, making sure that all was well before they set off for the fighting area. Orders such as *"Move forward"* tended to arrive out of the blue, but the unit was well trained by now and able to quickly respond. All the kit that they could manage was packed into what vehicles they had left; what they couldn't pack, as the move was an advance, they would come back and collect, leaving a guard to look after it. This particular move was up through Seoul to Uijongbu, about 15 miles due north of the Southern capital. Once the move was completed, they settled down and carried on working.

These signposts were common in many theatres of war!

On September 20th, came an inspection by the Brigadier, who was most interested in their new location. The same day, but one hour later, another inspecting officer arrived, this time the ADEME. After his visit, their advance detachment was ordered back to Seoul. So, the locations for the second half of September show both forward detachments at Uijongbu and Inchon. On October 2nd, one forward detachment moved to a new location, four miles south of Tokchong. Time to settle in once more, but what happens? Almost inevitably, on October 4th, that forward detachment was detailed to move back to Seoul.

So the two new locations were now at Seoul and Inchon. October 12th – 15th saw the arrival of yet another officer, this person was Lt G Wilson, to replace 2/Lt Rose, who was to return to 10 Inf Wksp. Work had been heavy and steady, slowly building up a backlog of vehicles awaiting onward transmission to Japan. By October 29th, the situation had become acute and signals were sent, informing staff that more shipping was required. The backlog at Inchon was now over 100 vehicles at Inchon and a further twenty in the BLR park at Seoul. Heavy flows of vehicles continued to be loaded and unloaded during November, so the area was scoured to find a more suitable vehicle park. This pattern of work was repeated during December 1951.

Chapter 28

16 Infantry Workshop REME June to December 1951

27 Bde had been relieved by 28 Bde and had now moved back to Hong Kong. 27 Bde's support Workshop was still in the process of moving back to Hong Kong, to be replaced in Korea by 16 Inf Wksp. 11 Inf Wksp was warned that they would move back to Hong Kong, but on a slightly different basis. Ten men at a time would arrive from 16 Inf Wksp, while the same number would return from 11 Inf Wksp. Thus, by July 1st 1951, the changeover was complete without disruption to either Workshop. Uijongbu was to be 11 Inf Wksp's last station. Whilst those changes were in motion, other personnel changes were taking place from other sources; these were completed by the end of June. T/Maj HG Germain assumed command of 16 Inf Wksp on June 24th, his new Workshop taking on strength twenty-six *'Acanthus'* personnel from 11 Inf, with a further twenty-five arriving directly from the UK. The management team supporting Maj Germain, CO, was made up as follows:

2IC & Adjutant	Capt R Swift
MTO	Capt J Sinton
RAOC Stores Section	Capt GR Hill

Joe Adey's arrival

The establishment for the Workshop was 159, while its actual strength was 113. It is difficult to piece together a story without first-hand knowledge to start with, but let us try! 16 Inf Wksp was a Commonwealth Workshop, with Craftsmen from NZ, Australia and UK. It has already been stated that 11 and 16 Inf Wksps exchanged places, both in Hong Kong and Korea. Encounters in both areas were, to say the least, surprising! Those arriving back in Hong Kong wore a strange mixture of British and American Army clothing, their sole possessions seeming to be what they were wearing at the time. They had returned by various methods, seemed quiet and looked very tired. Transit in the opposite direction, to Korea, was in small parties of ten by air, initially to Japan and then on to Kimpo Airfield via RAAF *Dakotas*. SSgt Joe Adey (Weapons) and SSgt Johnny Doig (Armourer) came via a luxury trip, flying in an USAF *Globemaster*, via Okinawa and then Iwakuni.

Some gilt was rubbed off the gingerbread of their trip, however, because they were accompanied by a large load of essential spares. But one other passenger put a smile back on their faces, she was dressed in a Red Cross uniform and had to enter the plane in the same manner as all others - by climbing a twelve-foot steel ladder. There was much comment as she first entered. too bad though, as it emerged she was the wife of a Captain in one of the Infantry Battalions already fighting in Korea. A couple of hours later, they were disembarking at Kimpo Main Airport near Seoul and could see a stream of transport waiting, like taxis at a station. At the bottom of the ladder, an American Top Sergeant was handing out metal chains on which to hang their identity discs on. Each chain was accompanied with the greeting, *"Welcome to the Asshole of the World"*! How little did they realise just how apt that description was at the time!

One of the last parties travelled in the luxury of a large BOAC airliner, creating a few lifted eyebrows as they clattered up the steps, with minimal kit, weapons and ammunition. Jack Warner ('Dixon of Dock Green') and his concert party were on board, so there was a queue for autographs. After a good evening with the Kiwi and Aussie troops in Japan, the *Dakota* came as something of a shock. It was loaded to the limit with all sorts of boxes and weapons, presumably on some sort of 'milk run', as it landed a couple of times before they reached Kimpo, with various personnel getting off and freight being unloaded at each stage. They were met by a unit driver, with a battered old *Bedford* QL, and they bumped their way over and along the MSR, the journey seemed to take forever. Huge sighs of relief greeted their reaching of the unit location, seeing familiar faces and weighing up their new surroundings of heat and dust, with the various types of tent used for accommodation. These varied from American two-man pup tents to the four-man British pattern that had been used in Hong Kong. Johnny Doig's 'home' was to be in a pup tent, with a blood-stained but well-scrubbed stretcher as a bed, supported at each end by a small wooden crate, to keep it raised above the sandy ground. This was to remain his bed until his departure for the UK some twelve months later. The other occupant, Sgt Bill Jackson, had a folding, wooden framework military canvas bed.

A meeting of old friends

Joe Adey was fortunate in that, when he pulled off the road some thirty miles north of Seoul, into what was now 16 Inf Wksp, he was welcomed by Ian (Jock) Main. They had formerly slept in adjacent beds at Arborfield, when on boys' service in room E4, then again at Blackdown, whilst attending their 'Tiffy' Course. A mutual acquaintance, WOII Alec Alexander had heard that Joe was coming up from Hong Kong and let Jock know of this. As Jock's original tent mate had left, he kept the space clear for him. This was a lucky break for Joe, as Jock had obtained an American tent, some 8ft x 6ft, with 3ft walls, an absolute luxury suite! Most Workshop personnel at that time slept in pup tents, with a few bedding down in their own vehicles. Next day, as Jock showed him around the 'estate' that they were located in, Joe discovered that they were in the middle of a Korean cemetery and near to a village called Uijongbu. A clear stream ran through the middle of the site, bringing water down from the surrounding mountains. In two places, the stream dropped over waterfalls, each about eight feet high, which were used as showers.

The location was in a largely sandy area, a dried up riverbed, with an American repair unit alongside. Most of their personnel sported a generous growth of stubble. Meals were eaten in the open air, as there were no mess tents or dining areas; this was not a problem, as it was high summer at the time. Days were long and there was some illumination, courtesy of a large vehicle battery and 12-volt bulb, and enough current to produce some crackling reception on the civilian radio brought in from Hong Kong. The only place to gather for an evening drink was in the tents. The Adjutant used to collect beer and spirits from the British rail-head and they were all allowed as much Japanese *Asahi* beer as they wanted. In addition, officers and senior ranks were allowed as much spirits as they wanted, except Scotch Whisky, which was rationed to one bottle per month. With most of the senior ranks, crates of gin were kept under the bed, or even acted as supports for their beds - a useful item for bartering with the Americans. There was a thriving black market between the Yanks and the Commonwealth forces.

The senior NCOs of 10 Inf Wksp in 29 Inf Bde, who were mostly reservists called up for the Korean War, were said to have made well in excess of

Mk II Sten Gun

The Forgotten Punch in the Army's Fist — Korea 1950-1953

£1,000 each in an eighteen-month tour. The first instructions issued to new arrivals were to carry a weapon at all times or have it close to hand, including visits to the field latrine. A Sten-gun and six magazines of ammunition was the standard issue, it was regarded at the time as only slightly better than useless! This weapon was very primitive, its magazine springs used to jam after a few hours of compression, allowing the ammunition to rattle about inside them. Fortunately, there seemed to be an abundance of 'spare' weapons and a .303 rifle with two hundred rounds of ammunition was soon acquired. A neat American semi-automatic carbine and a *Colt* 45 automatic pistol soon followed.

The newly arrived 'Tiffy' Weapons soon found that his prime job was the 25-pdr field guns of 16 NZ Fld Regt, which were in an unbelievable state. No modifications had been carried out to them since they were returned to NZ from the Middle East at the end of WWII. They had so many cracks in the trails and saddles that had been welded and re-welded, in fact they looked ready for the scrap heap! However, these guns would still fire and were very accurate if the sights were in good order. That was soon discovered to be a main problem, and Joe would spend some 90% of his time stripping and re-building these sights while he was in Korea.

He took the job because he was the only Weapons Tiffy in the Workshop, apart from Alec, and he had the whole of A&G Section to run. Joe realised that, once the 25-pdr sighting gear was beyond the limits of adjustment, the only thing that could be done with it was to carry out a 'Base Repair' job, as replacement sights were not available. This, of course, was not a Fld Wksp job, but the spares were indeed available to carry out the Base Overhaul. So, as a gun came in for repair, Joe was able to 'base overhaul' the sighting gear. He soon became very expert at carrying out this overhaul and built himself quite a reputation with the Kiwi Gunners. They reckoned that, when an infantry patrol called for covering fire, they could drop HE rounds to within twenty-five yards of the patrol.

The heart of the Workshop was the big trailer-mounted *Lister* generator, which powered all the equipment in the machinery vehicles and also the lights in the American 'Squad' tents, a later issue. In the depths of winter, the generator was running non-stop because of the severe cold. It was a little too close for comfort at the time, with its exhaust note being in full cry for about fourteen hours a day. Keeping body and clothes clean was not too easy but, fortunately, a short distance away, there was a stream and pool which was used as a bath. It was also close to some Korean dwellings, the women there being willing to wash clothes in return for bars of soap, any form of food, chocolate, etc. At the first location, after heavy rain, a skeleton was washed up, presumably from a casualty of the action that had taken place earlier in the war. The GD soldier on the QM staff reburied it, having to do a repeat but more efficient job after the next heavy storm.

It seemed that any vehicles brought in by the Australian infantry had to be thoroughly searched before repairs were contemplated, as they were usually awash with ammunition, explosive and primed hand grenades, rolling about under the seats and anywhere else it was possible to store items. Their own attached Aussies had a celebratory New Year booze up, the end result being demolition of one of the officers' latrines by a hand grenade rolled in from outside. Fortunately it was not occupied at the time! One item of Admin interest was a directive from CRAOC in relation to 'missing vehicles'. This was to the effect that, after a long accounting check, there were a large number of vehicles that had disappeared and were not accounted for. A return of all vehicles in possession was to be carried out and arrangements would be made, on the date given, for a physical check. It was an open secret they had more vehicles than they were supposed to have on strength. It was not sure if any of them were bequests from 11 Inf Wksp, but they had 'found' a few, no doubt to enable more spares to be carried and speed up repairs. It could be assumed that 'extra spares' had been liberated from badly damaged vehicles, before they were sent back for base repairs. The appropriate Warrant Officer was summoned to the Admin truck and asked how many extra vehicles they had. *"Fourteen"*, was the firm reply. There was a long pause, followed by an instruction to send those vehicles out with their drivers, who were to 'practice the art of concealment' during the day of the inspection visit.

When vehicles beyond Field Repair capability had to be sent to the rear for Base Repair, or even repair in Japan, as many as possible were towed by one of the *Scammell* recovery vehicles. They went stacked up. The bottom layer was usually three 3-tonners; in the back of these there would be a stripped-out 15-cwt truck; and, if possible, a crunched Jeep or any smaller items would be loaded in the back of these. It was quite a sight to see as it progressed very slowly on its way towards the railhead. Other non-standard issue items in the Workshop were several small electrical generators. Driven by a Jeep engine and trailer mounted, they were very useful to have, easing the power burden on the massive *Lister* generator unit.

'Bootlegging' seemed to be a lucrative pastime from reports given by 11 Inf Wksp, who quoted up to $50 for a bottle of whisky to the Americans. As the supply seemed to be more plentiful, or the Americans got wise to it all, this price fell to about $40 a bottle and gin plummeted to $20. Not being in receipt of a spirit ration, Joe accepted the chance to go on a 'bootleg' run with one of the attached Aussies and two more of their own personnel. They seemed to be going north for quite a while through the few remains of Uijongbu and as far as the signboard, which proclaimed *"You are now under enemy observation"*. This did not seem to make much difference to the scheme of things, except that the Yanks seemed to have now moved. Eventually, a sentry outpost came in view along the track and their Aussie friend made a suitable negotiation. By this time, the day was closing in and it was necessary to get on with the return trip before daylight ended. This experience had been quite educational.

At the rear of the location there were some steep hills, covered in a dense growth of coniferous type trees. Exploring this area, and climbing to the top of the ridge, was quite good exercise. From the debris of the foxholes, cartridge cases and ration tins, there had obviously been some form of fighting there in the past. There was a young Orderly Room junior NCO, who worked in the *Bedford* QL office truck, shared by the Adjutant, Chief Clerk and Joe Adey. This youngster had assumed that active service would see a drop in the volume of paper normally generated, but was surprised to find that there seemed to be as much, if not more, than before, if only of a different variety. Surprisingly, most of the lower ranks had no idea of their true location, they never saw a large scale map at all, assuming that the CO and other officers had them. They could only say they were 'near to somewhere'. Uijongbu seemed to be one of those places.

As mentioned earlier, they had minimal kit, just two sets of 'jungle green' jackets and long trousers, accompanied by PT vests and shorts, underclothes, socks, one pair of boots, jungle hat and beret, two shirts and the normal issue pullover. Everything else - steel helmet, greatcoat, battledress, large pack and one of their two kit-bags, had been handed in prior to leaving Hong Kong. A 'Chinese dragon' shoulder patch was still sported, which must have been somewhat confusing. As it was July, the weather was hot, somewhat warmer than Hong Kong for a short period. Days merged one in to the other and the repair work went on for as long as necessary to finish jobs. Sunday was a privilege day, with a free afternoon, enabling letters to be written, kit to be checked over and any 'do it oneself' repairs. Drinking water was available from the water trailer, being reminiscent of a swimming pool, very blue in colour and with an awful taste of chlorine.

The RAEME personnel attached to the Workshop were a law unto themselves, living and eating separately, and seemingly with a ready availability of beer and spirits. During the hot weather, it was not unusual to see them clad only in Aussie Felt hat, cigarettes and lighter secure in the folded-in top of the hat, jungle green issue underpants, suitably modified, and local flip flop foot wear. But it all seemed to work very well and they were really hard workers. The period before dusk produced plenty of 'heavy-duty flying nasties', in the shape of beetles, mosquitoes and other unidentified insects. These were reminiscent of the New Territories in Hong Kong, but on a larger scale. One exaggeration told at the time was to the effect that one of these really large insects had landed on a forward air-strip and that the ground crew had put twenty gallons of fuel in to it before realising it was not an aircraft!

CREME takes control

On the first day of August 1951, CREME 1 Comm Div assumed full control of all REME units within the Div. In making this formation, unique smaller formations and moves took place within the Div area. 10 Inf Wksp moved its Armourers, along with their vehicle, to 16 Inf Wksp. All Tels repairs were to be carried out in a new central unit alongside HQ Div Main, to be known as Div Tels Wksp, (a joint British / Canadian unit). Equipments and personnel were withdrawn from the three Divisional Field Workshops. One other Div formation came into being. By the withdrawal of a percentage of Fld Wksp recovery vehicles and personnel, Div Recy was formed, under Capt Jim Sinton of 16 Inf Wksp.

CREME had obviously heard of the good work being carried out by Joe Adey on the gun sights, so he loaded him with another task. The Field Bakery bread production had slowed almost to a standstill, due to worn bearings in the piece of machinery called 'The Thrower Upper'. The bakery was located on the outskirts of Seoul, so Joe was given a time limit from midnight on Friday to midnight on Saturday. During that period, the machine was to be repaired, in order that the Div Cdr could have fresh rolls on Monday morning! Arriving at the bakery with a fitter, promptly at midnight, Joe found the building was still like a hothouse and reeking of hot vegetable oil. The job amounted to having to drill out a three-inch long taper pin from the shaft, plug and re-drill the shaft and manufacture and fit a new bronze bush. These machines had been made as long ago as 1900 and the metal was extremely hard. It took several hours, stripped to the waist and stinking of vegetable oil, to drill out the offending pin and remove the shaft and bush. Then they drove back to the Workshop, manufactured a new bush on the lathe, filled and re-drilled the shaft and made a new taper pin. The Div Cdr got his fresh rolls all right, but they were accompanied by the suggestion that the ancient equipment be exchanged for something a bit more up-to-date!

As time moved on, personnel changes took place, tours ended and fresh faces arrived. From around May 1951, a high percentage of the senior NCOs were all ex-boys from Arborfield and 'E' Company, among them being Mick Graham and 'Jumbo' Rainer. At one stage, counting Joe Adey, there were about eight in the one unit. In September 1951, came the arrival of the last Hong Kong personnel, a Capt HWG Way and a Staff Sergeant. The month started to pass quietly, with plenty of work to keep them happy. But a movement warning order, received at 1700 hrs on the 25th, put paid to that, with a move to occur in four days time. The Workshop officer went forward on September 26th, to locate and inspect the designated new area, which happened to be adjacent to a hill known as Solam-Ri. It was a well-known location, as it had been the area of the Gloucesters' famous battle and last stand. It was reported that the area would be quite suitable and, on the 27th, a party was sent to secure the new site. The operational order from CREME, detailing the unit to move, was received on September 30th for the move to take place on October 3rd. During the latter end of September, two more officers who joined the Workshop were Capt CH Hedworth-Young and 2/Lt SJ Hetherington. The forecast move meant that they would 'leap-frog' 10 Inf Wksp and this situation would remain so for quite a few months.

Joe's extra-large Condemnation Certificate!
Just before the forward move, the guns of 16 NZ Fld Regt had to be inspected and Joe Adey got the job. Driving through Gloucester Valley, he passed the two Centurion tanks that had become bogged down in the mud during the Chinese action against the Gloucesters; they were still there, because the Chinese had nothing heavy enough to recover them. Joe based himself at the LAD and got started on the examination of the twenty-four guns. It was slow work, owing to the guns constantly being called into action; it then required the barrels to cool, so that accurate measurements could be taken. When it was quiet, from the top of the ridge in front of the guns Joe could see the Chinese moving about. This gives some idea of the proximity of one to the other. On the third day of the inspection, a barrel was found with a dangerous crack in the chamber and SSgt Adey ordered it to be taken out of action. A message, received that same evening, ordered him back to the Workshop, to be told that the OC of the Kiwis' LAD had reported him for 'drinking excessively'. This was denied and the fact explained that eleven guns had been examined in two-and-a-half days. The OC LAD was requested to go in front of CREME and repeat the charge. The condemned barrel arrived back in the Workshop within two days and CREME arrived to inspect it for himself. The size of the crack was demonstrated by inserting a 0.004" feeler-gauge into the crack and, at the same time, Joe informed CREME of the terrible general state of the whole Regiment's guns. CREME asked if the whole lot should be replaced, to which the only answer was *"Yes"*. Thus, Joe had condemned a complete Regiment of twenty-four guns as 'BLR' and he was told to forget about the charges!

On the very evening of the day that Joe Adey left the Kiwi Gunners to return to the Workshop, the Chinese launched an attack on the positions held by the KOSB, the action in which Private Bill Speakman won his VC. It was also the first time that the Chinese artillery had dropped rounds on the NZ Gunners. A few weeks later, twelve replacement guns arrived from Singapore, having sometime in the past been overhauled by 40 Base Wksp. They still had to be stripped, their buffers and recuperator systems repacked and many of their sights overhauled. They later heard that the remaining twelve guns had been on a ship that had run aground on a reef somewhere in the Pacific.

One thing about 'moves forward', although all the packing has to be done, at least if there was an item or too big a load of BLR vehicles to be moved in one go, they at least could be returned to and collected. It certainly didn't work the other way round! On October 4th, the unit reported to CREME that it was operational. Next door to them, which was handy, was 60 Indian Fld Ambulance, although not for long. That unit had received orders to move north of the Imjin, so they soon packed up and left the Workshop on its own. On the 12th, instructions were received for the commemoration of the ninth Corps Birthday, better late than never. There was a parade on the 14th, with everyone dressed in best 'bib and tucker' ready for Lt Col Good to take the salute. All went well but, and this was anyone's guess, CREME must have noticed the area vacated by the Indians. This must have obviously impressed either him or his 2/IC because, the very next day, they were moved 500 yards north of their present location, destined to remain here for a long period. The location could have been an agricultural area, with an orchard of sweet chestnut trees on site.

Although the beginning of October was reasonably comfortable, climatically, thoughts began to turn towards the prospect of an issue of clothing suitable for the cold weather. The lads remembered the stories told by personnel of 11 Inf Wksp, who would probably have died from the cold had it not been for the provision of clothing by the American Army. It was therefore with some relief that they received battle-dress (BD), the first pattern heavy-duty khaki brown pullover, camouflaged 'Para' heavy-duty jackets and the new style boots with moulded soles. More tents had also appeared, including three large marquees; one for the Officers' Mess, one for the Sergeants' Mess and one for the ORs dining hall. The next problem was how to produce heat for them. Jerry cans appeared as if by magic, complete with a brass tap at the base and lengths of petrol-proof hose-pipe, terminating in another brass tap. Brass shell cases had been liberated from the local dump and three rows of holes drilled in the case's side, close to the base – just the right size for the second brass tap. Corrugated iron sheets were discovered and rolled flat, courtesy of their *Scammell* or Diamond-T recovery trucks. Suitable asbestos (no health and safety worries then!) was available to wrap around the chimney, where it went through the top of the tent. Petrol was put in to the jerry cans, taps adjusted for flow and there was super heat in a very short time. They must have got it right, as there were no tent fires as far as they could remember. The bravest man in each tent was the one who got up first on a winter's morning to light the fire!

A sectional wooden building was made available, with authority, so there was somewhere for the cooks to work, under better conditions. Meals could be now eaten inside, as each housed a small unit canteen and films could be shown inside too. The final luxury was the manufacture of hot water heaters, to enable a decent wash and shave at the start of day. Forty-five gallon petrol barrels were acquired and one end cut out. Support legs were made out of metal bar and welded on. The bottom end had a hole cut in it, to take a brass shell case with chimney, suitably welded to be watertight, and a jerry can, complete with support, to provide fuel. These water heaters were placed a safe distance from the tents, being 'fired up' by the last pair of sentries from the guard at about 0500 hrs, ready for *Reveille* at 0600 hrs. No excuse for not shaving or washing now!

This is perhaps a good point at which to recall some of the names that mattered in the day-to-day running of the Workshop:

CO	Maj HG Germain
2/IC and Adjutant	Capt R Swift
MTO	Capt J Sinton
CSM	WOII H Vernon
Chief Clerk	WOII N Harper
Electrician	SSgt Petrie
Clerk, Technical	SSgt Attwood
Armourer	SSgt J Doig
Armourer	L/Cpl Blackwell
Welder	Sgt Hillier
Sheet Metal Worker	Cpl Pirnie
Armament Artificer	SSgt Graham
Armament Artificer	SSgt Joe Adey
Vehicle Artificer	SSgt Ian (Jock) Main
Vehicle Mechanic	Sgt (later Capt) W Jackson
Electrician	Cpl R Binnie
RD	L/Cpl R Mitchell
Recovery Mechanic	Cpl Dangerfield

The situation was improving. Having been issued with the full winter kit, from string vest and long johns to combat jacket, trousers, parka and three layers of gloves, plus heavy-duty socks and the luxury of two sleeping bags, the low temperatures were now bearable. There was a choice of parka, either British or Canadian. The majority chose the Canadian version, which did not have the long 'shirttail' appearance of the British garment. It was dark green, well insulated, with a hood.

16 Infantry Workshop REME June to December 1951

The peaked khaki ski-cap style headgear was classified as a 'Rommel hat' and was universally disliked. The woollen 'cap, comforter' proved much better for warmth and comfort, although the standard issue beret remained in use by most throughout the winter. One unusual item of kit, issued in the early days, was a pair of brown plain-fronted boots, with strange type studs, and whose leather was really hard. Nobody can remember seeing anyone actually wearing them, other than just to try on. There was a theory they were South African pattern, but the actual source remained a mystery.

After the first experiences tender flesh sticking to bare metal, hand tools were suitably warmed before the start of the working day. One useful bit of kit, for keeping draughts out of trousers and the tops of boots, was the short cloth puttee. The worst of the winter slowly passed and with the thaw arrived the problems of mud and slush, making life a little more difficult. American style over-boots, calf high, were issued to go over the Cold Weather Waterproof (CWW) boot, making everyone's feet appear exceptionally large. Things gradually improved with the arrival of spring, with warmer temperatures and the withdrawal of winter kit. Then it was back to summer, being careful to walk with caution in the compound area after dark, as the summer nasties emerged. Joe had a close encounter with one such 'nasty'. The access steps to the Admin truck had been removed for a minor repair, so it was a case of heaving oneself up, through the door aperture. As Joe did this, with his hands on the floor of the truck, a short but very brightly coloured snake went over the back of his hand, but did not bite. He enlisted some help to locate it and three of them moved gingerly, with bayonets on the end of their rifles, having a good search of all the odd places a snake could be in. Nothing was found, but Joe made sure that, for the next few days, there was a thorough inspection of their working area. It was possible that the intruder had made its way in via the vehicle camouflage net, then through a small open window, as the truck was dug in to the riverbank. One of the Armourers was on a routine visit of inspection and repairs to one of the forward Infantry Battalions. He had been away considerably longer than expected and, on his return, explained that he had chosen a bad time. Enemy action had started, with plenty of mortar fire from the opposition ranks, and it had been impossible to do anything except take cover.

Section locations were laid out with a specific entrance area for vehicles and equipment, with Cpl R Buck dealing with the necessary paper work and records. There was a parking area for 'vehicles awaiting repair'. The two ancient *Leyland* machinery vehicles comprised one fitted out with lathe, pillar drill, grinder and workbenches, while the other was equipped for electrical repairs. There were various lean-to affairs of corrugated iron for the welders, tinsmiths, and general fitting. The smaller vehicles, such as Jeeps and 15-cwt trucks were tipped on to their sides to give suitable access to undersides, this being no problem in the relatively smooth sandy areas of the locations. The Armourers had a place on their own, suitable for testing weapons after repair. The Instrument Mechanics had their own individual repair truck. The Admin truck, QM Stores, living area and cookhouse were separated from the main Workshop operations, but the MT and Recovery sections were both contained within the Workshop area.

Everyone in the unit worked six days a week, or seven if the urgency was required. They did not all have the same days off, so that all Sections were suitably manned at all times. The only way they could tell the day of the week was by flying the REME flag upside down on Sundays! Trenches were dug for use in the event of a guerrilla attack or the attention of the ancient aircraft, known as 'Bed Check Charlie'. This nuisance was eventually shot down by ground fire from the American sector. With the formation of the Div Tels Wksp and a Recy Coy, this meant there were less people to go round for the nightly duties of guard and Standby Pln. The latter had to be fully dressed at all times, ready for immediate duty, with personal weapons and several Bren-guns. They were kept in tents, but guard duty was different, from 1800 to 0600 hrs, six personnel and Guard Cdr, with sentries patrolling in pairs. This was not too bad in the spring, summer and most of autumn, when one could enjoy the spectacular sunrise and fleetingly appreciate the 'Land of the Morning Calm'. Winter was rather different. The sentries had to do their patrols clad in the maximum amount of clothing because of the low winter temperatures. It was necessary to have only one-hour periods of duty, each man of the pair keeping a watchful eye on his companion for any signs of frostbite. The only cheerful part of guard duty was the supply of tea, suitably fortified with the thick red issue rum, poured from a large glass carboy by the QM staff. Even when the tea had gone cold, there was still a kick in it! Cooks were roused by the guard at 0500 hrs, hot water heaters were fired up, then it was back to the luxury of one's own tent at 0600 hrs, to get ready for another day. Not much of anything seemed to happen for most of the time, except an irritating frog chorus through the hours of darkness in summer.

One amusing incident that comes to mind was the receipt of an American MP version of a charge sheet, addressed in flamboyant language to the Commanding General the British Comm Div. This had taken some time to progress through the various levels of Admin to the Workshop. It related to 'Diamond-T motive unit, with sixty-four wheeled tank trailer and a Centurion tank aboard, exceeding the speed limit of 15 mph in Seoul'. This was considered to be a figment of someone's imagination, as it was difficult enough to achieve that sort of speed with just the motive unit on its own. The 'offending' driver was brought in just to keep the procedure correct, confirming that it was not possible to achieve that sort of speed and that was that. The usual drill, when being stopped by an American MP, who always moved to the left-hand side of the vehicle to question the driver, was to send him round to the right-hand side. As they were somewhat puzzled by the multiplicity of cap badges and types of headgear, imaginations ran riot in stating the name of one's unit. The announcement that one belonged to the 'King's Own Engineering Dragoons' or similar, plus the fact that one was not running on an authorised 'trip ticket', was just too much for those Yankee cops, who would wave one on without further ado.

The end of a tour

The weather returned to summer heat and people started to disappear, as their three-year tour of overseas duty was completed. The majority of personnel were Regulars, with some National Servicemen. This brought about some change, as the newcomers had a different attitude in many ways, trying to alter well-used and successful methods of unit operation, with their non-flexible UK attitude. July 1952 arrived at last, Joe's turn for the journey south, his Korean tour was over. A wait of two weeks and then *"HMTS Devonshire, here he comes"*. SSgt Joe Adey's impression of the country, 'Chosen' to the natives, but commonly known as Korea, was that it was a pretty barren and desolate place in those days, having been fought over from end to end a couple of times. It was a land of paddy fields and harsh grey granite hills, covered with low scrub. Outside of the cities, the roads were dirt and, in dry weather, the dust kicked up by traffic was terrible. The war had become a pretty static business, with both sides well dug in, roughly along the line of the original border between North and South Korea. Thus, Joe was not too unhappy when, late in November, Jock Doherty arrived from Kure as his replacement and he said farewell to all his mates. But there was no way round that uncomfortable, slow, train ride to Pusan - which is another story.

Chapter 29

Consolidation and counter-attack on the Divisional Line

16th October to 26th November 1951

On the conclusion of 'Operation Commando', Comm Div continued to hold and consolidate the positions that it had captured. On its left was 1 ROK Div and on its right the American 1 Cavalry Div. Originally this front was some 20,000 yards long. The country was exceptionally wild, consisting of a mass of hills and valleys running in every direction. This made it necessary to have seven Battalions in the front line, with one in support on the left flank and one in reserve, a most unsatisfactory state of affairs. It provided no depth to the position and the importance of 'depth in defence' had been one of the main lessons of the Campaign. Gen Cassels was of the opinion that, if the Chinese had launched a full-scale offensive, it would have been very difficult to hold the position. He continually represented that the front was too long for the troops available, but it was not found possible to shorten it until towards the end of November.

This is a convenient place to mention the Korean Service Corps (KSC), now serving with Comm Div. For some time it had been the custom for American and Commonwealth units to employ South Korean labour as porters, commonly known as 'Chiggies'. Now the system was on a more regular basis. KSC Regiments were part of the SKA and that one in support of Comm Div – 120 KSC Regt – consisted of three Battalions, each of four Companies. They were employed as porters, on road repairs, loading and unloading vehicles and digging. Very often, they carried up ammunition and supplies to forward posts – frequently under shellfire. They worked under the executive command of their own officers and NCOs but, for security reasons, were always closely supervised by Commonwealth personnel. Originally it was intended that they should be armed with Japanese weapons, but this was never carried out and they remained unarmed. This organization should not be confused with South Korean fighting soldiers, some of whom were later attached to the Division and known as 'Katcoms' (Korean attached to Comm Div). More will be said about these later. It should also be mentioned that most units had small 'private armies' of South Koreans, who had been with them for a long time. These were fine men, who showed extraordinary loyalty to their parent units and invariably wore their cap badges. There were many instances of gallantry by these men, the original 'Old Contemptibles', before the days of either the KSC or 'Katcoms'.

The period October 16th to 31st was a comparatively quiet one, although there was some shelling. The enemy concentrated on the construction of a new line, which the capture of his old positions had made necessary. Comm Div was similarly engaged in consolidating the Divisional Line. 25 Canadian Bde carried out only one important operation in the latter half of October – on the 23rd. 'Operation Pepper-pot' consisted of a raid on a prominent feature, Pt 166, about 1,000 yards inside enemy-held territory. The aim of the operation was to seize the feature, destroy the enemy defences with explosives and then withdraw. The attack was carried out by one Company of the Royal 22'Regt, with other attacks at Company strength farther north – one from the RCR and the other from the PPCLI. These two Companies had little difficulty in reaching their objectives, but the main assault on Pt 166 met with very stiff opposition, and the attacking troops were held up about 200 yards from the feature. Two attempts were made by the Company of the Canadian 22 Regt to cover this intervening ground, but they were unsuccessful. All Companies were then ordered to withdraw. The Canadians lost five killed and twenty-one wounded, while enemy casualties counted were sixty-one killed and twenty wounded.

THE FORGOTTEN PUNCH IN THE ARMY'S FIST — KOREA 1950-1953

On October 19th, 1 Btn RNF was relieved by 1 Btn, Royal Leicestershire Regiment (RLR – Lt Col GEP Hutchins), who were placed under the command of 29 Bde. The RNF left Korea for Hong Kong. On the 25th of that month, Lt Col (later Brigadier) JFM Macdonald OBE who up to then had commanded 1 Btn KOSB, assumed command of 28 Comm Bde in succession to Brig G Taylor DSO. On the night of October 31st, a small attack by Chinese troops against the PPCLI was caught in the glare of Divisional searchlights and at least four of the enemy were killed. A heavier attack, in approximately Battalion strength, was launched against 'A' Coy RCR on the night of November 2nd, but was beaten off with heavy losses to the enemy. Over the next few days, up to the 8th, there were a series of local but determined attacks against 28 Comm Bde, holding the right sector flanked by the Imjin River. These attacks were notable for the greatly increased enemy artillery fire, which was heavier than anything experienced before. On November 4th for instance, it was estimated that 10,000 shells fell in the Div area and that 28 Bde was receiving ninety to 100 rounds per minute, heavy shelling by any standards.

On that same day, the relief of 2nd Btn by 1 Btn PPCLI was completed. This was the first of a series of theatre reliefs by Canadian Infantry, in which the 1 Battalions from Canada relieved the 2 Battalions in Korea. With the departure of 2 PPCLI however, Comm Div had lost one of its toughest and most efficient units. Heavy shelling continued along the whole front that day and, from about 1300 hrs, it was most intense against 28 Bde. Soon after noon, enemy tanks were reported to be advancing in a very forward position. These may have been self-propelled guns but, whatever they were, 'friendly' aircraft engaged them and are believed to have destroyed four of them. At about 1645 hrs, the enemy launched a heavy attack from the north against the KOSB, now commanded by Lt Col DH Tadman OBE and on the left of the Australians. This was followed by an assault on the KSLI. The battle raged until midnight, with the main effort against the KOSB, which Battalion was eventually forced back from two dominating features, Pts 217 and 317. Both had been the scenes of bitter fighting, and had been so hardly won, on 'Operation Commando'. In this phase of the action, KOSB lost very heavily, their effective strength being reduced to the equivalent of about two Companies

It was on this day that Private (Pte) Bill Speakman, 1 Btn KOSB, late of the Black Watch, so greatly distinguished himself. Pte Speakman, a member of 'B' Coy HQ, collected a party of six men armed with grenades. He led some ten charges and, after being twice wounded, continued to resist several enemy assaults. For this almost incredible feat of arms, he was awarded the VC and passed into the folklore of the British Army. Soon after midnight, increased shelling and other activities indicated that the second phase of the attack would soon begin, but this did not materialize. It was thought that the concentration of troops was broken up by two bombing attacks and heavy artillery fire by Commonwealth gunners. The RLR was now placed under command of 28 Bde and moved into the Brigade area. By dawn, all was quiet. At first light on November 5th, it was discovered that the enemy had withdrawn to his original positions, except on Pts 217 and 317, which the enemy now held in strength. At about midday, RLR attacked Pt 217 and the Australians made a diversionary attack towards Pt 317. The 'Tigers' of RLR fought hard all day, but were unable to reach their objective.

On this morning, the American 2 Btn 65 RCT had been placed under 29 Bde and took up those positions vacated by RLR. During the night of the 5th, PPCLI were attacked twice in about Battalion strength, but successfully beat off both. The Division had been supported by thirteen air strikes against located bodies of enemy during that day, then on the 6th, the 'Tigers' relieved the KOSB, who now moved back into 28 Bde reserve. Heavy rain now set in and all aircraft were grounded. The battlefield became a quagmire on the flat, an area of running streams on the hills, with cloud and mist above. During the preceding thirty-six-hour period, ending at 1800 hrs on November 5th, it is estimated that Div Artillery fired 30,829 rounds. On the 7th, the troops were able to enjoy a fairly quiet day. Since the end of October, Div had been under the temporary command of the CRA, Brig WGH Pike but, on this quiet day, Maj Gen Cassels returned from duty and leave in Japan and resumed command.

Information was received that the 'Commonwealth' character of the Division was to be expanded shortly, by the posting-in of two South African officers to Div HQ and three others to the Artillery. There was to be one more day of fighting before there was a break in the assault on 28 Bde. During the night of the 7th, strong attacks developed against the Australian Btn, which lasted for three hours. These attacks were made by a force estimated to be at regimental strength, supported by artillery and a few tanks. Eventually, the enemy attacks broke down, as their casualties had been exceedingly heavy. There followed a week of comparative quiet, in which the only major incident was a raid by 'C' Coy and the Scout Pln of 2 Btn 22 Regt on Pt 166 on November 9th. Part of this force reached the summit of the hill, after which there was much confused fighting for some four hours and in which the Canadians suffered seven casualties – all wounded.

Several theatre reliefs took place during November 1951. On the 7th, 14 Fld Regt RA relieved 45 Fld Regt RA and 120 Mortar Bty relieved 170 Mortar Bty. On the 11th, 1 Btn the Welch Regt relieved the Gloucestershire Regt in 29 Bde – the latter thence returning to the UK. On the evening of the 17th, the enemy suddenly launched a powerful attack against KSLI, holding Pt 227 on the left of the 28 Bde sector. A little later, an attack from Pt 217 (still held by the enemy) developed against the RLR, as well as a light probing attack against PPCLI. It looked at first like a full-scale attack against both Brigades – the 25 Canadian and 28 Commonwealth – but in the event, only that against KSLI was pressed home. After very fierce fighting, the forward Company of KSLI was forced from Pt 227, although one Platoon, with a MG section to the east of the feature, hung on and was never dislodged. During the attack, a Platoon of RLR had also been overrun. A counter-attack on Pt 227, by 'D' Coy KSLI, started shortly after midnight, but was halted and postponed when the Company came under very heavy enemy small-arms fire. At dawn on the following day, this Company, supported by two troops of tanks from 8th Hussars, renewed the attack and occupied Pt 227 against light opposition.

RLR also reoccupied the position on which its Platoon had been overrun on the previous day. By noon on this day, all of the ground lost during the night had been regained. During this fighting, KSLI and RLR had some forty casualties each. Further fierce fighting continued on both of their fronts during the early part of the night on the 18th, but at about midnight enemy pressure slackened and the KSLI, who had again been driven off Pt 227, reoccupied the feature. During that same day, a Battalion of 15 Regt, American 3 Div, was placed under command of 28 Bde and took up a position close behind the front, on Pt 238. This ended the enemy's series of autumn attacks against Comm Div, although they continued for a short time on other parts of the front. It had been a time of some anxiety; any deep penetration, followed by resolute exploitation, would have led to a nasty situation, owing to the lack of depth in the defences. It had been a comfort to have the support of the American 2 Btn 65 RCT of the American 15 Regt holding blocking positions in the rear, but the battle had been a fairly close-run affair.

The Division had learned a great deal from the actions of the first three weeks of November. It was evident that the Chinese now had a great amount of artillery, which they could use efficiently and which was well supplied with ammunition. Against bombardments of the kind experienced, barbed wire was of little use unless it was in considerable depth, and this also applied to mines. Bunkers and dugouts had to be very strongly constructed. Telephone lines were cut at an early stage and reliance could not be placed on wireless, unless the sets were positioned in bunkers with thick overhead cover. The operations emphasised the importance of early warning of an enemy offensive; when this was obtained it was often possible to break up an attack with artillery fire, before it got under way. It was found that the enemy followed up his artillery concentrations very closely and, on occasion, actually reached the objective before his artillery fire had ceased or lifted.

Enemy casualties were difficult to accurately assess, as the Chinese always made the most strenuous of efforts to remove their dead and wounded, under cover of darkness, at the first opportunity. During these operations, however, they must have suffered very heavily. During the night of November 20th, 119 enemy dead were counted on the front of 28 Bde and, at about the same time, a 'heap' of dead bodies, estimated at between five and six hundred, was found. It was also around this time that reports were received of several Chinese attacks being led by *"a woman in black"*, but these were never confirmed. As a result of the recent fighting, which had revealed the over-extension of Comm Div's front, plus General Cassels's repeated representations for a shorter one, on November 20th, it was decided that the American 3 Div, which was relieving the American 1 Cavalry Div on the right, should take over part of the right sector of the Div, held by 28 Bde.

The original orders catered only for a partial relief of 28 Bde but, early on the 21st, the order was changed so that the whole of the front held by 28 Bde was taken over. The junction point was not, however, very satisfactory, as the new deployment gave Pt 355 to the Americans, while the western slopes of this feature, including a small ridge south-west of it, facing Pt 227, were left to Comm Div. This meant that, at the right of the line that Brigade at this time, 25 Canadian Bde had to push a Company across the valley to hold this part of the front. On the left flank, Comm Div was to take over a small portion of the line held by 1 ROK Div, west of the Samichon River. On balance, this gave the Division a slightly shorter front and permitted some defence in depth. Two Brigades could now hold the new front, leaving a complete Brigade in reserve.

The reliefs took place on November 22nd 1951 and, in general terms, the new dispositions were as follows:

Left – West of the river Samichon:
    29 British Inf Bde:
        1 Btn RNR
        1 Btn RLR
        1 Btn the Welch Regt
Right – From the Samichon River to a junction point with American 3 Inf Div, near Kigong-Ni:
    25 RCR:
        2 Btn RCR
        1 Btn PPCLI
        2 Btn Royal 22 Regt
    Reserve
    28 Comm Inf Brigade:
        1 Btn KOSB
        1 Btn KSLI
        3 Btn RAR

The enemy formations opposing the Division at this time were the 190th and 191st Divs of the CCF. On November 23rd, various moves were in progress all day long to complete the redeployment of 1 Comm Div. In the evening, the enemy made a strong attack against 7 American Cavalry Regt on the right and captured the important feature Pt 355, which Comm Div had captured on 'Operation Commando'. This was a serious matter, as the feature dominated most of the Divisional front.

Sgt Bob Westbrook, Armourer with 1st Leicester's Regt.

Its recapture was a matter of some urgency and vital to the security of the Division. During that night, 2 Btn Royal 22 Regt, on the extreme right of the Division, was attacked several times after heavy shelling, but no ground was lost. This was a very creditable performance, as their position was dominated by Pt 355, now held by the enemy only about 100 yards away.

The 24th was a day of desperate fighting for 7 American Regt, in their efforts to recapture Pt 355. Comm Div gave the full weight of its artillery support and, eventually, the Americans were successful in reoccupying the position. 2 Btn Royal 22 Regt, now holding the features immediately east of Pt 227, was also heavily attacked again on this night. One Platoon position was overrun, but it was recaptured soon after midnight. On the following day, 7 American Regt consolidated on Pt 355 and linked up with the Canadians.

Due probably to the snow, which had just started, the front then became very quiet and was to remain so for some time. One satisfactory feature of the recent heavy fighting had been the fine air support given by the 5th USAF. During the period October 31st to November 26th 1951, the figures for air strikes were as follows:

Number of strikes in the twenty days in which flying was possible:
    105 aircraft used.. ….. ….. ….. ….. ….. ….. 438
    Most strikes in one day, 6th November.. ….. ….. ….. 13
    Average number of strikes each day.. ….. ….. … . 5

By now the Korean winter had begun. The first fall of snow occurred on the night of November 23rd and by the following night there were sixteen degrees of frost. Snow fell heavily all day on the 25th. The provision of what was termed 'Wet / Cold weather clothing' to wear during the winter caused much unfavourable comment in the press and elsewhere. It was alleged that there was a serious shortage, but this was not so. The total quantities available were more than enough, but it was the sizes that did not match requirements in all cases. Australian troops were found to require larger boots than the British - one man said he wanted size 14 and in fact, he did! Some delay was also experienced in obtaining tents, stoves and other winter equipment that, by arrangement, were to be provided from American sources; but this was quickly put right. These matters caused inconvenience, but not the serious hardship that was alleged in some quarters at the time.

Chapter 30

The winter of November 1951 to April 1952

On November 27th 1951, the armistice delegates at Panmunjon arranged for a 'Demarcation Line', from which both sides were to withdraw, two kilometres at a time, to be specified in the Armistice Agreement. By this time, the Campaign had assumed some unusual features, apart from the prolonged 'cease-fire' talks. From a military point of view, it seemed that neither side was capable of sustaining an offensive that would bring final victory in Korea. Even if the UN succeeded in doing so, and occupied the whole country, they would still have large Chinese forces threatening them from Manchuria, which would immediately advance south again if UN troops withdrew or were seriously reduced in numbers. Moreover, such a situation might extend the area of hostilities and even bring about a third World War. For the Koreans, from both north and south of the 38th Parallel, the war offered little comfort. Death, destruction, disease and starvation were their only lot. The sole object of the Campaign now appeared to be to uphold the prestige of the UN and to show the Communist nations that aggression did not pay an easy dividend. This was a stand that the simple Commonwealth soldier, holed up in his bunker or slit trench, with the temperature some degrees below zero, was hardly likely to appreciate. It seemed to many that the war was purposeless. Probably the most important factor in maintaining morale was the system of reliefs, which at least made it rare for an individual to spend more than one year in Korea.

The period that followed to the end of the year was a quiet one. There was some shelling and a few minor incidents. But activities were mainly confined to strengthening the defences, improving communications and training, receiving distinguished visitors and preparing for eventualities that rarely occurred. On December 4th – in the presence of Lt Gen W Bridgeford CB CBE MC, who had succeeded Lt Gen Sir Horace Robertson as C-in-C Comm Forces in Japan and Korea, along with the Corps Cdr, Lt Gen JW O'Daniel, and Maj Gen Cassels – Gen Van Fleet presented a Presidential Citation to 3 Btn RAR. On December 6th, 5 Royal Inniskilling Dragoon Guards (5 RIDG), who had disembarked at Pusan on December 1st, relieved 8 Hussars, who then embarked for the UK on the MV *'Georgic'*.

Periods of inactivity in war are usually accompanied by insatiable demands, on the part of the higher level Intelligence Staff, for prisoners in order to help their attempts to keep pace with changes in the enemy order of battle. This led to much patrolling in which the Division suffered a few casualties almost every night. In these activities, 2 Btn RCR and 1 Btn Welch each captured a prisoner, and one deserter was apprehended. On the whole, the results were meagre and hardly commensurate with the efforts made and the losses being incurred. On the night of December 10th, a party of the enemy ambushed a vehicle some distance behind the front line. As a result, 'Operation Skunk Hunt' took place on the 15th. This consisted of a sweep of the whole Div area, with the object of discovering enemy guerrillas, agents and unauthorised civilians. Otherwise, the 'booty' was not large – one skeleton, two deer killed by mines, a little ammunition and one bag of rice! After this, 'Skunk Hunts' became a regular practice in the Div area.

On the night of December 10th, PPCLI carried out a Company raid on Pt 227. Some sharp fighting followed, in which the Canadians had one man killed and twenty-four wounded. The Division received many Christmas messages, including greetings from Generals Ridgway and Van Fleet, as well as from the Secretary General of the UN. Some tokens from the Chinese were also

THE WINTER OF NOVEMBER 1951 TO APRIL 1952

received. On the 19th, some men of the Division had apprehended a small boy carrying a sack containing propaganda Christmas cards and 'gifts' from the enemy! Cards from the enemy were also found in various places in the Div area. During the Christmas period, the battlefront remained quiet; the fare was good and, as far as food was concerned, there was no cause for complaint. Owing to operational requirements, the Christmas dinners of many units had, however, to be staggered over a period of several days.

The Korean winter was now well and truly installed. It was extremely cold and snow was falling. This is, therefore, an appropriate place to turn to matters of a domestic nature. Military history is too often confined to strategic and tactical affairs, moves and counter-moves, to the

Map showing the Demarcation Line

exclusion of the more intimate subjects affecting the daily lives of the troops. A short digression into the manner in which the men lived during the Korean winter will not be out of place. During the first winter, of 1950 - 51, operations had been generally fluid and the troops frequently on the move. Accommodation, in the normal meaning of the word, was unknown. For the fighting troops, buildings and tents were very rare luxuries, even during periods of inactivity out of contact with the enemy. In the front line, the men occupied slit trenches or bunkers, with some overhead cover as protection against the elements. More often than not, these were still incomplete when the next move took place. As explained earlier, some units managed to keep warm in the trenches, using small fires, maintained by collecting wood locally. In rear areas, bonfires were lit, when the tactical situation permitted, around which the men crowded. Otherwise, bivouacs of a very crude type were constructed.

During the first Christmas period, tents on a scale of about one per Company, with one stove per tent, were issued as a special luxury. It was towards the end of the winter that what were known as pup tents became available for some troops, these being small American tents of the bivouac type. Each held two men and, on the move, were a two-man load, one man carrying the poles and the other the fabric. They provided protection from rain, but were cold, as it was not possible to light any form of fire in them. Most men preferred a slit trench, using the tent fabric as part of the overhead cover. It cannot be said that these conditions had very greatly improved by the second winter of 1951 - 52. Accommodations remained on an improvised basis, with bare earth the chief means of insulation against the bitter cold. The war was, however, now semi-static and more elaborate protection was possible, as troops remained in the same localities for a considerable time. Undamaged houses were rare and, in any case, they were invariably infested with rats and lice. For health reasons, they were avoided by Commonwealth troops.

The infantry in forward areas lived in slit trenches, bunkers and dugouts, with overhead cover constructed of timber, sandbags and sometimes tent fabric. The artillery, and others located around the gun area, had a few tents, which were usually dug in. Empty ammunition boxes, filled with earth, were often used to construct walls. REME did not stay idly in the rear; they too felt the cold, so a simply designed heater was produced to try and improve ones lot. The construction of these has already been told elsewhere. Smaller than those used in the Workshops, a considerable heat could be generated, without any smoke to indicate ones position. A considerable number of this type of heater was produced, for the comfort of forward troops in slit trenches and dugouts.

At the HQs of Brigades and Divisions, the accommodation was by no means on the scale that the troops usually associated with these establishments. Dugouts, office lorries and tents, partially dug in, were the rule. A little more luxurious than elsewhere perhaps but, nevertheless, primitive for the considerable amount of 'office' work that was necessary, even in Korea. Summarised, it may be said that no accommodation existed that was not either provided by the Army or self-constructed by the troops. Practically all shelter was improvised and the tendency was to get below ground level. Lorries and other vehicles were found to be too cold to sleep in. Commonwealth troops had considerable warfare experience in tropical and temperate climes, but very little in intense cold, in a country without permanent shelter in the form of buildings or huts. Not since the Crimea had they experienced a campaign of this kind, and there the hardships were due to mismanagement rather than the climate. In most of the campaigns of the two World Wars the fighting was fierce, but the troops could usually look forward to reasonably good conditions. At least they were then mainly in a recognised form of accommodation, when not actually engaged in combat. Not so in Korea, except for the infrequent short periods of leave in Japan, or when one's time came to go home.

The winter of November 1951 to April 1952

Nevertheless, as already indicated, the health and spirits of the troops remained good. Undoubtedly, a contributing influence was that there was a general feeling that everything possible was being done to mitigate hardships and that, whatever perils and discomforts existed, they were unavoidable. In this large UN Army, the men in the Commonwealth forces felt that they were the select representatives of a group of countries, with a high reputation to maintain. This, too, was an important factor in maintaining a high morale and a grim cheerfulness.

January was a comparatively quiet month. The whole of the Div Artillery fired a series of heavy concentrations on the enemy, welcoming in 'The New Year'. During the night of January 5th 1952, another ambush took place behind the front, in the same area as the previous one, during which one man was killed. On the 19th, 28 Comm Bde completed the relief of 25 Canadian Bde on the right sector of the front. The Canadians had been in the line continuously since September 4th of the previous year. On relief, they moved back to the Imjin River in reserve, where they then engaged in planning a reserve position in the vicinity of the river. Yet another ambush had occurred on the night of 15th, when a Canadian vehicle was attacked and one soldier killed and two wounded. Towards the middle of the month, considerable digging by the enemy was noticed close to Comm Div's forward positions. At about the same time, HQ 1 American Corps issued a warning that the Chinese were liable to become very bold and carry out 'desperate missions' after their somewhat lengthy New Year celebrations.

On the night of the 26th, 3 Btn RAR made an attempt to occupy and dig in on that disputed feature, Pt 227, in 'No Man's Land' in front of the right Brigade sector. The attack was made by two Platoons at last light and, by 2100 hrs, the feature had been captured in the face of light opposition. The Chinese reacted very strongly to this move, putting down very heavy artillery and mortar concentrations, followed around midnight by a two-Company counter-attack. Eventually, the Australians were forced back, with the loss of seven men killed and eight wounded.

On January 29th, Brig AHG Ricketts (Cdr 29 British Bde) was wounded in the arm by a mine and evacuated to hospital. Temporary command of the Brigade devolved on Lt Col VW Barlow of 1 KSLI. On February 6th, all ranks in Comm Div were shocked to hear of the sudden death of His Majesty King George VI. The Div Artillery first fired a salute against the enemy, followed by a salute for the new monarch, Her Majesty Queen Elizabeth II. On February 10th, on the orders of 1 American Corps, 'Operation Snare' began. This was a somewhat novel operation, whereby the whole of Eighth Army maintained its existing positions for a period of seven days, without engaging the enemy with any form of fire, except for small-arms fire in the event of an actual attack. It was thought that this would mystify the enemy and cause him to patrol actively in order to find out what was happening. This would give UN troops the opportunity to capture prisoners – or so it was hoped. Gen Cassels was by no means convinced of the wisdom of this plan and, as far as Comm Div's front was concerned, it did not work. The Chinese did indeed send out a few small patrols but, when they discovered that the positions were still occupied, they returned to carry on the digging that, as stated earlier, they had recently started. By this means, the enemy was able to continue work on strong and deep bunkers on the forward slopes, near the Commonwealth troop positions, without interference. Previous efforts to prevent this happening were completely nullified.

The fourth ambush in the Div rear area occurred on the night of the February 12th, when a vehicle was blown up, one man wounded and another reported missing. No major operational incidents took place during the next two months, with the action confined to a few minor clashes that occurred. On February 16th, the day when 'Operation Snare' ended, RIDG carried out two small armoured raids on either flank of the Div front. That by a Troop on the left was held up by bad going and failed to reach its objective, but the enemy was not encountered. On the right, two Troops reached their objectives and made contact with the Chinese. A mine damaged one tank and an officer of the RE was killed. On the 18th, another sweep of the Div area – 'Operation Polecat' – took place, essentially to round up guerrillas and suspected persons, but only a few civilians were apprehended. On the same day, five South African officers joined the Division for service in Korea. On the 20th, in the presence of the C-in-C, 16 NZ Fld Regt was presented with a South Korean Presidential Citation.

During the period from February 24th to 29th, the enemy made two small attacks. The first, by night against the KOSB, was preceded by a heavy artillery and mortar bombardment, but was easily repulsed. The second, a few days later against a forward post of the RLR, was also beaten off, but with the loss of two men killed and a further two wounded. Vigorous patrolling continued throughout March. On the 7th of that month, a patrol of RIDG in 'No Man's Land' had one Centurion tank bogged down, and it had to be blown up. On the 10th, 25 Canadian Bde, in the left sector west of the Samichon River, relieved 29 British Bde. Towards the end of March, the weather became much warmer. This was very welcome, but nevertheless produced some difficulties. The thaw made road conditions extremely bad and drastic orders had to be issued to curtail traffic. At this time of year, road surfaces were apt to break up completely

On March 24th, Brig Ricketts resumed command of 29 Bde, having recovered from the wound he received at the end of January. During the night of March 26th, the enemy launched another attack, at about Company strength, against a Platoon of the Canadian 1 PPCLI, which was holding a spur south-west of Umdalmal, some 1,200 yards west of the River Samichon, which later became known as 'The Hook'. This attack lasted from 0130 to 0330 hrs. There was no withdrawal and, for a time, the Platoon was surrounded, but eventually the Chinese were beaten off. A further attack against 2 RCR's outpost, on Hill 163, followed this attack. This group was again forced to withdraw. PPCLI had four men killed and ten wounded, while 2 RCR lost two killed and had six wounded – mostly from heavy artillery concentrations put down along the whole Canadian Brigade's front. Thirty-one enemy dead were later counted in front of the Platoon's position, while one prisoner was captured. A number of leaflets and letters from Commonwealth POWs were also found.

During the first week in April, the weather became still warmer. However, the roads remained very rough, but passable, with difficulty in places. On the night of April 6th, 'A' Coy KOSB was very heavily shelled. This started at 1700 hrs and continued until 2200 hrs, when the enemy put in two sharp attacks, both of which were beaten off. These attacks had been thrown into confusion by the heavy defensive fire of more than 7,000 rounds put down by Div Artillery. Exhortations over the wireless, to press home the assault, were heard from among the attackers. The KOSB had two men killed and a further five wounded, while twenty-eight enemy bodies were later counted in front of the positions.

The second week of April brought the Division a most welcome reinforcement, when 1 Btn RAR completed its concentration in the Div area and immediately began a six-week period of intensive training. On June 1st, it was to take its place with its sister Battalion, 3 RAR, in 28 Comm Bde. One feature of life during that winter of 1951 - 52 was the large number of distinguished visitors who came to see the Division. With its many Commonwealth components, Comm Div probably attracted more than any other formation in Korea. Politicians, church dignitaries, senior officers and others came from far and wide. Most were from Commonwealth countries, but there were representatives from other countries as well. It is not possible to give the names of all this multitude of visitors, nor details of their visits.

Chapter 31

10 Infantry Workshop REME November 1951 to June 1953

The author's own experiences

Back in the UK, in about September or October of 1951, SSgt John Dutton was drafted and told to report to the Depot REME at Arborfield. At that time he was a member of the permanent staff in Instrument Wing, No.4 Training Btn REME, stationed at Blackdown, Hampshire. Living in married quarters with his wife and two daughters, it was an awkward time to have to leave the family, because the Battalion was about to move to Bordon with the intention of amalgamating with No.6 Trg Btn, to form a new training school. *(N.B. The formation of the School of Electrical and Mechanical Engineering – SEME – did not in fact take place until 1961.)*

Arriving at the Depot, in Poperinghe Barracks, John took the long walk to the far end of the camp, to a group of buildings that formed Drafting Coy. Reporting in, he was reacquainted with a CSM Scott, a well-known member of the Corps. He was then allocated to a barrack room full of Senior NCOs, all on draft and going to distant places, known only as 'Port B' and 'Port A' (very few were going to the latter). As was the norm, he immediately got to know his 'barrack room buddies', who they were and what trade they were, whether married or single, etc. It was soon established that in this one barrack room there were three Instrument Tiffies, all with the rank of Staff Sergeant. Putting their heads together, they tried to determine, *"Why three Instrument guys?"* They had sort of guessed by now that it was either Japan or Korea that they were bound for. Knowing that there were only two Field Workshops in Korea, and that they only had one Instrument Tiffy each, they decided that perhaps the theatre was about to set up a new advanced base; thus the reason for three of them. But, as they later found out, it was a case of 'wrong again'!

The days moved on and they were issued with peculiar kit - string vests, long johns, brown boots covered in white dried-up wax (these looked as though they had come out of the Ark), and many sizes bigger than their fitted size. Explanations were to come later. Each was given a rifle and steel helmet; the rifle was to be thoroughly degreased and cleaned, but other items of kit cannot be recalled. Then came a visit to the Medical Centre for the normal 'cough' and check up. All was well, time dragged on for a bit, but eventually the call came to pick up their kit, get down to the train, and start their journey. Memory may let John down here, but he thinks Southampton was the embarkation port that they eventually arrived at. This was not his first troopship, so John reckoned they were fortunate that the ship was the MV *'Georgic'*. She was a 27,000-ton diesel, with two main engines each of ten cylinders and each cylinder developing 1,000 HP. This allowed her to cruise at twenty-two knots. The boat had a history, but more on that later.

Aboard the *'Georgic'*

Berths were allocated and John found himself on 'A' deck starboard, in a four-berth cabin, about amidships. The next chore was to hand in to the Armoury, that rifle that had been cleaned and polished, hating to think of the effect that the salt air, at sea for four weeks, would have on the ungreased weapon! Back to the cabin they went to stow their kit, then it was quickly to the second-class lounge for all the senior NCOs. It has been said before but a ship is like a barracks, it runs on rules and regulations, and with those go duties. The ship's Regimental Sergeant Major (RSM), who was chairing this meeting, was calling for volunteers to carry out the respective ship's duties. The ship had on board the 5 RIDG and a complete Armoured (Armd) Regt. Then there were the likes of John and his companions, some twenty-eight REME senior NCOs, plus an unknown quantity of RE, R Sigs, RA, ACC, RMP and many more ORs. That outward journey, during November/December 1951, was to last for thirty-four days.

The allocation of duties went ahead, with the REME lads keeping quiet at the back of the lounge, until it seemed that there was only one more duty to be allocated, that of 'Ship's Police'. What the attraction was, nobody knew, but they all as one said a hearty *"Yes"*. With all duties allocated, they then dispersed, the 'ship's police' being told to report to one of the Master at Arms (MA), these guys were like Warrant Officers, only in merchant marine uniform. An explanation of their duties followed. From 2300 hrs to 0600 hrs every night, they would take it in turn and walk every nook and cranny that the ship possessed, alongside a MA, who carried a 'Tell Tale' clock. This was 'punch' recorded at various stations during the tour throughout the decks as their walk progressed. It took one hour to walk the route from below the bridge to the chain locker, down through the engine decks to the bilge, then finally back to the Bridge. The rest of the day was their own, except when in port, then there were gangway police duties.

Came the day when the ship had passed through the Straits of Gibraltar during the previous night and, as far as they knew, had not stopped. Even so, as they came off duty and went to breakfast, it was noticeable that a considerable number of extra passengers had appeared, mainly female. The steward at breakfast was asked why and how had they suddenly appeared? The answer was simple - they had been 'sea sick' in their cabins. They were mainly wives and children, *en route* to join their husbands and fathers in the Far East, Singapore and Hong Kong. The families' cabins were located on 'A' Deck port side; officers were on 'A' Deck starboard, forward end, and all senior ranks on 'A' Deck starboard, mid-ships to aft. In a nutshell, the males were on one side and the females were on the other, which was interesting from the point of night police duties. The MV *'Georgic'* was of interesting construction; it did not have multiple bulkheads throughout its length, thus one could stand either at the stern, or in the bows, and look from one end to the other. Any movement on 'A' Deck could be seen without any effort!

As their journey progressed through the Mediterranean, the RI DG thought it was time to get some firing-practice in with their machine-guns. The MAs were not amused, as the soldiers wished to fire from the poop deck at the stern, which was the MAs' home. Being up all night, it was natural that they wished to sleep during the day. A compromise had to be reached. Suddenly, it was resolved, without a problem. The ammunition that had been loaded on board did not match the calibre of the machine-guns, so it all had to wait till it could be changed at Port Said.

The first meal of the day seemed to herald interest for the day ahead. Having stood down from the night duty, a walk on the main deck from one's cabin, after a wash and brush up, was the morning ritual. Over the stern, could be seen the upper structures of a ship on the horizon, but it was too far away to identify. So breakfast called, there would be plenty of time for that ship after the meal. Back up on deck, they were only just in time to see what had been 'a distant smudge' now alongside them and really moving at speed. The *Georgic* was cruising at a good twenty knots and the aircraft carrier, as it had turned out to be, was leaving it standing. The carrier had a full deck cargo of trucks, buses, Jeeps, ambulances and some aircraft. HMS *'Warrior'* passed by quite close, its crew and passengers lined the deck and, along with ours, shouted across the water to one another. Then she was gone; the next sighting was in the harbour of Port Said. Our ship came alongside, but there was no shore leave; ammunition was changed, any mail picked up, then she moved out and started to form the convoy to go through the Canal. *'Warrior'* was to lead and the *'Georgic'* brought up on its stern, with many more merchant ships to follow.

10 Infantry Workshop REME November 1951 to June 1953

Through the Suez Canal

The Suez Canal administration was on strike and the British Navy was in charge. The convoy moved into the Canal but, before long, we were left well behind. The speeds being used were far in excess of the set limits. On reaching Suez, at the lower end of the Canal where it joins the Red Sea, *'Warrior'* was nowhere to be seen. Stops were made at the ports of Aden, then Colombo in Ceylon (now named Sri Lanka), both with a few hours of welcome shore leave. John was on gangplank duty at Aden and was put on his back by a right cross to the jaw, from one of the lads returning from shore leave. Needless to say, they were drunk! The culprit was grabbed and into 'the brig' he went, pending a court marshal, to be held in Singapore, for striking a Senior Rank. This was later cancelled, as the accused was on his way to Korea as well. Colombo was interesting! Having returned to the ship, a roll call of the ship's company counted 'one missing'. RAF shore police found him in a Mosque, well over the drink limit. This time, John was not on duty but watched from the head of the gangplank. The police launch came alongside, with the drunk being held by two of the shore patrol. What happened next was in a flash. The prisoner stepped forward for the gangplank, but missed it. The police let go, but grabbed him as the water reached his chin. They heaved him up, put him on the gangway, and he walked up those steps as sober as a judge.

The next port of call was to be Singapore but, on the way, the weather got very rough. All storm hatches forward had to be closed, waves were breaking over the bow and the spray reached eighty feet up, to just under the bridge. Furniture that had been secured as fixtures on the forward deck was smashed to bits and washed over the side. Singapore was reached quite safely however and, two days of shore leave followed. On one of those days, 'duty called'. During the evening, while stretching his legs, John had walked down onto the jetty and was now well clear of the ships bows when he turned, and could not help but notice the ship's hull. It looked as though a giant had been hammering on it, and showed severe signs of buckling. Back on board, he asked one of the MAs what had happened. The answer was that the ship had been bombed during the last war, with one bomb dropping down one of the funnels, blowing it off. The ship had later been beached somewhere off Egypt and that was the reason for the 'wavy' sides. She had been eventually re-floated, repaired and hundreds of tons of concrete poured into the hull to reinforce the keel. She had latterly been used on the emigration/immigration runs to Australia etc. Whilst ashore, the soldiers also had the pleasure of the brand new *'Britannia Club'* that had been built in Singapore. It was understood that it was funded, or at least partially funded, by the famous Billy Butlin, of holiday

The Britannia Club in Singapore

camp fame. It was built opposite the *'Raffles Hotel'*, on the seaward side of the East Coast road. They were on the last leg now, with the families getting excited, but there were still four to five days of sailing ahead.

After travelling halfway around the world, they had arrived. A Regimental band was on the jetty to greet them, with husbands looking anxiously for their wives and children, who were now disembarking. The remainder, going on to Japan and Korea, were allowed a few hours shore leave before the very last leg of their journey started. The ship now felt as though it had gone into mourning, the 'social' side had completely gone. The ship sailed again, but now with an escort for Korea. On approaching the island of Formosa, a NZ frigate placed itself between the ship and the mainland to act as a shield. The ship was ordered to 'black out' and drop all lights in the cabins etc, but the journey happily remained quite peaceful. On approaching the southern tip of Korea, a pilot was taken on board to steer the ship into the harbour at Pusan. A reception party, consisting of the President of South Korea, Syngman Rhee, and many of the Army Commanders, was supported by an American brass band, doing its party piece.

On to Japan

5 RIDG, together with their own REME support, left the ship, so only the tail end support troops were left on board. Little did they know, but it was to take a further twenty-four hours at sea before they would reach Kure, in Japan. The draught of the ship was too deep to cross the Japanese inland sea, so it had to sail right round the southern tip of Japan instead. But at last land came into view and the ship started to lose way, eventually picking up a pilot to take it into Kure harbour. Instead of maintaining a steady speed, it actually started to pick up speed. For those who have never sailed into Kure, to give some idea of the waterway width that the ship was sailing through, a person could hit the shore, on either side of the ship, with a good cricket ball throw. The channels were narrow and dotted with many small islands, through which this pilot seemed to negotiate without bothering to slow down. Sitting in the ship's lounge, watching the shore pass by, one minute John was looking at the shoreline, then the boat would heel over and he was looking at the top of the surrounding hills. You could say that they were all glad to reach the safety of the very large harbour at Kure.

The boat hove to at one of the massive floating buoys in mid-harbour. Using steel cables to secure itself to the buoy, the ship's engines were stopped, and they had arrived. Within minutes of the engines stopping and the silence descending, there was an almighty crack. The steel cables securing the boat to the buoys had parted and the ship was drifting away at a rapid rate. Although the water surface appeared as smooth as the proverbial millpond, they were told later that there was an extremely strong under current. The engines were quickly restarted and the ship was brought back to the buoy. This time, the anchor chain was used, fore and aft, to secure this 27, 000-ton monster.

Whilst waiting patiently to disembark, John and his companions leant on the side rails, watching two giant barges being manoeuvred alongside. Then, just like one of those 'Jack-in-the-box' toys, the covers were thrown back and literally hundreds of Japanese women poured out, armed with buckets, cloths, brushes etc. Before the remaining passengers had left the decks, these women were furiously at work, washing the ship from top to bottom. (This was prior to a repaint, before it eventually left on the return journey to UK.) The date was December 3rd 1951. One could not help but notice the shoreline of Kure, totally demolished. The buildings seemed mainly of metal sheeting, but were bent, twisted and totally wrecked. It was just one large rust patch, with debris wherever one looked. But it was in amongst this scene of dereliction that a group of vehicles was being drawn up. These were to take the remaining passengers on their first leg, to a small village

10 Infantry Workshop REME November 1951 to June 1953

outside Kure called Hiro, a camp called the Joint Reinforcement Base Depot (JRBD). Some of the draft had to be re-equipped, then sent on their way to Korea, while others, including a certain SSgt John Dutton, would stay at JRBD a few days more.

Slowly but surely, the draft numbers diminished, as postings were made. Some went across the road, to a very large Workshop called 3 Advance Base Workshop (ABW), which had a large increment of Japanese labour. During the waiting time for posting, there was a visit to 3 ABW, to see for themselves what went on there and to find some of their associates who had accompanied them from UK. John cannot remember their names now, but recalls one particular Sergeant who was a fitter. He now had his own section, with a number of Japanese civilian fitters who John could already recognise as being very good at their jobs. These civilians were working 'on the floor', their working positions one could only describe as 'a three point suspension'. Just as John was about to leave, the Sergeant made a remark that John has never forgotten - *"I will get them a decent place to work, I can not have people working on the floor".*

And back to Pusan

The days had passed and it was soon December 23rd. By this time, those of the draft who had not yet been posted thought it was unlikely to happen now, at this time of year. Wrong again! John was soon to be on his way to 10 Inf Wksp REME, the supporting Workshop to 29 Inf Bde. On arrival at the JRBD, they had handed in their weapons and steel helmets, and John cannot remember being re-issued with anything of importance. There followed that ride again, back to Kure harbour, and then onto a very, very old ship, whose engine was a single-piston steam-driven, of very questionable state. The vessel's name was either *'Wosang'* or *'Esang'*, and it had been built in the UK back in the 1920s. It took them through the Japanese inland sea, back to Pusan, but, as this ship was only very small, they were able to come in alongside the jetty, after a journey of twenty-four hours. The next day saw them all get onto a train, what vintage that was, they had no idea. The journey was rough, very rough, and cold, very cold. And so, their introduction to the next eighteen months had begun.

The end of that journey has vanished from John's memory, all he can remember is that it had taken a full twenty-four miserable hours. Off the train they clambered, with their full kit, just glad to move about a bit. A *Bedford* QL, 3-ton truck, was drawn up for the remainder of their journey, the party splitting up at this juncture, going to various units in the Brigade. To get to 10 Inf Wksp, if memory serves John right, entailed going through a cutting in the hillside and then taking a sharp turn to the left. To the driver, this must have been a blind corner but, having manoeuvred around it, they saw a sign similar to a UK pub sign, which proclaimed that this was in fact *"10 Infantry Workshop REME".*

It was not a good day to arrive anywhere, being Boxing Day 1951, and it was very clear that the Workshop personnel must have had a good Xmas Day and had not yet surfaced. The guard directed SSgt Dutton to the Sergeants' Mess, a quite large marquee. He put his kit down outside and went through the flap entrance. No one was about, so he went back outside and brought his kit into the Mess tent. The noise he made must have been sufficient to disturb the bar steward, who had been resting behind the bar. John cannot remember that Sergeant's name, but they introduced themselves and the man gave him a run down on aspects of the unit. As for a bed, bunk, tent etc, there were none. Later in the day, others appeared and, as they all got to know each other a bit more, he remade the acquaintance of SSgt Jock Lamont, who had been on his draft, but had come directly from the *'Georgic'* into Korea. John Dutton was very shortly to relieve Jock Lamont, as he to leave for home. It was unknown at the time why Jock had only been there for two months but, years later, they met again and it transpired that Jock had been invalided out of the services.

That first day in his new unit was very cold and very casual, to the point where one might say no one seemed to have much interest in any new arrival. Boxing Day evening, John spent totally in the Mess and had to wait for the stragglers to leave before he could retire for the night. His first bed was going to be a six-foot GS fold-flat table top in the Sgts' Mess. It was positioned under the marquee's top ridgepole, which had been bedecked with fairy lights for Xmas so, before the bar steward and himself settled down for the night, all the lights had to be switched off. John couldn't say why, but he woke from a reasonably good sleep, tucked up inside his double sleeping bag, on his back. The first thing that struck him was that the fairy lights had been switched on! He lay there, he supposed for what may have been several minutes, watching the 'lights' flicker, before realisation struck. They were not lights at all, they were flames, running right along the ridge-pole. The marquee was on fire and the barman and he were in it!

John shouted to the Sergeant behind the bar who, like himself, had been in a deep sleep. With some difficulty, he struggled to wake, then both hurried to get some clothes on as, at this time of the night or year, one couldn't go anywhere without being fully dressed in warm clothing. By this time, the roof was well alight and decisions had to be made quickly. The water in buckets, any sand buckets and all fire extinguishers were all frozen solid and he could not reach the height where the flames were anyway, even if things hadn't been frozen. The Sergeant made the first move by jumping onto the bar top, taking out his jack-knife and slashing the burning sections of the roof away from those not yet alight. He pulled the flaming sections away from the bar end and, as they fell flaming to the ground, John pulled them away into a clearing. By the time dawn broke, the marquee was reduced to two uprights and a ridgepole, all severely scorched, and the end section that contained the bar and bar stock. Plus, of course, two very tired dirty, cold and homeless Mess members. Slowly, other members arrived for breakfast and in nearly every case their jaws dropped, with the same repeated question, *"What's happened?"* By this time, those in authority had been appraised of the situation. ASM Jack Sinton, CSM Jock Mullhern and AQMS Bill Saunders, these three seemed to be the 'kingpins' in the Workshop. That afternoon, the burnt sections had been replaced and the marquee was back in one piece. At least John and the barman had a bedroom for another night, and a peaceful one they hoped!

On December 28th 1951, his first full day in the Workshop, John went down after breakfast to the A&G section, where the Instrument vehicles were parked. These were to be his responsibility for the foreseeable future. He met Jock Lamont, who suggested a tour of the other sections and to meet some of the 'inmates'. These were Maj Rogers, OC, Capt G Ewing, AO, Capt MC Dix, Wksp Officer, Capt CW Nicholson RAOC, OC Stores section, Lt Rose, MTO, Lt

Instrument shop group: S/Sgt Jock Lamont, Nobby Clarkson, Cpl "Kit", Jordy & Jock Imray. All were ex-boys except Jock Imray

10 Infantry Workshop REME November 1951 to June 1953

On the hillside behind Admin, looking across the workshop Vehicle Compound, towards A & G section. The Instrument section on the far hillside behind the long shed. Blacksmith's section is on the left, tucked in behind the middle distance trees.

Spittle, Asst Wksp Officer, ASM Jack Sinton, AQMS Sam Dixon, AQMS Bill Saunders, CSM Jock Mullhern and SSgt Fred Bishop, CQMS. He met a lot more, but can not recall all of their names. The initial crowd that he had met were all 'Z' reservists and, in most cases, were about to leave, as the new arrivals from the 'Georgic' were the first Regular replacements, to allow the 'Z' reservists to return home. The Instrument shop that he was about to take over had SSgt Jock Lamont in charge.

Two more incidents were to stick in his memory, both having an association with fire or heat. The first was serious but, at the time, appeared slightly comical. The Admin truck burned out, with the reason for the fire, as far as John knows, never established. But, of course, being the Admin truck it contained paper work of significant importance. Of the many items lost, the payrolls were to cause the most hilarity and/or consternation, depending upon one's outlook. Because, when the fire had been put out and the extent of the damage ascertained, the CSM was then seen hurriedly going around the unit, from one man to the next, pleading with each that they re-sign for their pay. One or two tried to plead that they'd never had it in the first place, but one didn't try that successfully with CSM Mullhern!

After finding his way around the Workshop area, John had started to think of his own welfare and comfort - items that were sadly neglected and certainly not supplied. Whilst he was still kicking that about in his mind, a message was brought to him, to report to the Workshop officer, Capt Dix. After the customary handshake, he asked John what he knew about electrical work? *"Sufficient"*, was the firm reply. After which he was told, *"OK then, assume control of the Electricians' shop! And good luck".*

It was now New Year's Eve 1951 going into 1952, a time for a bit of merry making. The officers had been invited to the Sgts' Mess, for an evening of the ancient tradition of 'elbow bending'. In the Mess, and thankfully saved from the burn out, was a piano. Now amongst the Mess members was a very talented pianist, an AQMS (Guns), whose name was Phil Rawlings (although John is not certain of the spelling) and who could play anything you named. Certainly he had a talent to be envied, even more so, playing along without recourse to written music. So everyone had a good singsong, which rather made them thirsty. Drinks were free and it was realised that too much profit was being made on the bar!

The Forgotten Punch in the Army's Fist — Korea 1950-1953

The CO had decreed that it must be reduced, so he and John tried hard by drinking the brandy, but they seemed to be the only ones doing so. John's turn came round to go to the bar, but it was a case of *"What? No more brandy?"* There was now only 'Cherry Brandy', so they both changed to that, but never again! The tale was later told that he had wandered off to his bed, which by now was luxury, a tent over a dugout, with its own space heater. He had turned the heater up, as it was about four o'clock in the morning, then dropped onto the bed, fully clothed. Another Mess member had stuck his head into the tent, to check on him, and all that could be seen was a large glowing red object through the smoke, so he turned the heater off and went on his way. John eventually came to, frozen stiff at some ungodly hour, climbed

Ssgts Chippy Lupson, Jock Lamont, Nutton (RAOC) & Jack Drennon sitting on Korea grave!

into his sleeping bags and did not surface till five o'clock that afternoon! New Year's Day 1952 was as good as over and John had missed it.

It was time to look at his new job. No time like the present to learn, and that was what John did in the course of the next few months. The Workshop was equipped with DC generators 110 Volt, three rated at 9KW and two at 5KW. This certainly was a trade field that was about to stretch his knowledge during every day, that of supplying all the Workshop lighting and power to heavy machinery, light machinery, instrument repair, the Electricians' shop and Carpenters' lorry. At night, the DC power was diverted to the lads' tents, the Sergeants' and Officers' Mess tents, the Guardroom tent, and whatever else was thought to require lighting. This was all right but, for that time of the year, there was the ever-present problem with snow. The only cable available to carry the power was highly inadequate, it was supposedly used by the Signallers for telephones etc. John recalls that it was referred to as 'Don 8', and it was certainly not meant to carry any real power. The DC voltage loss was high by the time it got to the end of its journey, this state of affairs requiring constant attention by the duty electricians, as the snow got into the poor cable joints and caused short circuits. At least one didn't need to search for the cables in the snow; the power loading on the cables was such that the cables were always hot, causing the overlying snow to melt – a dead giveaway!

This situation continued until, one day, CREME visited the unit and John was told to report to him. CREME first asked him about the Electrical section and then proceeded to tell him that the Workshop had been asked by CRAOC to carry out 'Initial Charging' of all new vehicle and signals batteries. RAOC reported that they could not deliver sufficient supply of 'ready to use' batteries to meet the Division's demands. John stated that, with the present generator capacity, it would be impossible, due to the age of the generators and the Workshop's existing demand. The electrical requirements for 'initial charging' meant that the generators would be providing power for days on end and for a full twenty-four hours each day. CREME answered, *"Let me look at the equipment you have"*. When he had finished his tour of inspection, with no hesitation, he stated, *"Demand*

10 INFANTRY WORKSHOP REME NOVEMBER 1951 TO JUNE 1953

a new generator, Red Star, top priority". A huge *Meadows* 27.5 KVA, trailer mounted generator arrived within a matter of weeks.

The batteries awaiting their 'initial charge' had been arriving in the Workshop's RAOC Stores Section, all brand new, still in their packing. As John had admitted to the CO, he had a slight knowledge of the electrician's normal routine but they were now about to go well outside that parameter. It was very fortunate that the electricians' section had at least one tradesman up to speed in this field of 'initial charging'. Electrical and Mechanical Engineering Regulations (EMERs) were publications covering all aspects of the REME technical side, including initial charging. It must be remembered, however, that they were still well in the Korean winter and the sub-zero temperatures were going to play a large part in the project for the next few days, until they were 'up and running'.

There were no covered areas in which the battery electrolyte could be mixed, so in the open air it had to be. Water was already known to freeze in the prevailing temperatures, so things had to be completed fairly quickly, hopefully a routine set up. A large rubber lined tank had been obtained, in which to mix the electrolyte. It was all a bit daunting! The (distilled) water, which was provided in large bottles, was first poured into this large rubber lined container. It was decided to mix a large quantity and hope that the water did not freeze before they could pour the sulphuric acid into it. Unfortunately, the basic guidelines failed to apply, and the Specific Gravity (SG) density of 1.215 at 60 degrees Fahrenheit was somewhat out, as they were mixing at a temperature of minus 80 to 90 degrees! The first mix failed, as it almost instantly froze, until more acid was gently poured into it. This was repeated until a mix that could be poured was obtained. John's memory fails on the final density figure, but it was in the region of 1.750 plus. Not to prolong this part of the story, the batteries were eventually charged, but not without a lot of sleepless nights, watching over their brood, so that they did not boil over or freeze. Eventually it became a routine, like most things.

Whilst they had waited for the new generator, there had been 'a flap', in the shape of a directive from HQ Div Main, saying, *"Fully disperse the vehicles in the A&G Section, there is a possibility of air raids"*. John was becoming embarrassed with some of the negative situations that prevailed. For instance, the technical vehicles should all have had 100 feet of 80-Amp cable, to 'jump' power from one vehicle to the next, if required. Over the years, these cables had either been stolen or used for other reasons. The CO's directive was to, *"Work out what you want and demand on Red Star"*. Within a matter of weeks, a low loader vehicle

Carrying out T & A on No 9 Dial Sight. Note the locally manufactured heating system adjacent to rear wheel from a 25 Pdr shell carrying case and a spent shell casing, top tubing for chimney, angle iron for legs, wiper motor, modified to act as blower. Petrol fired and heat feed over the rear wheel through the wheel arch. A very effective system. The truck was known as the "Tomato house" although they were not grown though.

Page 187

arrived in the compound with a large 'Henley' reel of cable, capable of carrying 80 Amps at 110 Volts DC, but by this time 'the flap' was over. So the cable was then used to supply the living quarters with better lighting, and to reduce the requirement for duty electricians. The section, of course, had all the normal electrical duties to perform, working in the open on the vehicles, changing starter motors, alternators, generators and a hundred and more minor items. John Dutton thinks that, under the circumstances, they did very well, thanks to the lads.

In time, a replacement SSgt arrived, by the name of Jack Drennan. He was electrical by trade and this brought that part of the establishment up to full strength. Jack did not complete a full tour, as he was waiting to be called for a commission. His replacement was SSgt Cyril Luger; he was an Electrician, Control Equipment (ECE) by trade. Perhaps 'someone up there' knew that the HAD would fold up and their tanks would then come back to 10 Inf Wksp. Jack Drennan, whilst with the Workshop, was always 'broke' – or so he said. Someone in the Workshop, on Jack's 'behalf', contacted the American local radio station that played requests for the troops. The song requested was *"If you 'se so clever, why ain't you 'se so rich?"* It came over the radio at breakfast time and our Jack was not amused, but they never did find the culprit!

The vehicle repair area was another world, or at least that is how it felt. On the other side of the stream or hill that divided the compound, they were having their own problems, could it be that they were seeing cases of 'sabotage' originating in the Base repair areas? It has already been stated that the running life of an engine in Korea was short, so it follows that a considerable number of engines were always in the process of being changed; this time of the year was most appropriate for this type of sabotage. A Scammell recovery vehicle had come into the Workshop for an engine change, so the old engine was removed and the replacement unpacked and fitted. The vehicle fitters were trying to turn it over manually, but found it impossible. All the normal checks were carried out, but it did not make any sense, it still would not turn over by hand. It was decided to remove the engine and strip down the sump and the valve gear, to investigate the problem. The removal of the sump revealed nothing but, when the cylinder head was removed, the Workshop officer was sent for, because the headspaces in the cylinders had been filled with water. Naturally, in these temperatures, this had frozen solid; there was no way that this could have happened naturally, it was clearly sabotage. The Special Investigations Branch (SIB) was brought in and tracked the dastardly deed all the way back to Singapore. That was not the only occasion, as nuts and bolts were later found in other engine heads. The problem to the Workshop was the increased workload, as engines had to be stripped and checked, prior to fitting.

Winter had moved on and, even though it was still cold enough to wear heavy woollies, life had recently been routine and reasonably pleasant. Whilst working outside the Instrument truck, carrying out tests and adjustments on a No.7 Director, out of the corner of his eye John noticed an officer moving across the compound in his direction. He stopped what he was doing and turned towards the officer. The officer was the first to speak, knowing John's name. It was Capt Armstrong, BEME to 29 Bde, and the last time they had spoken to each other had been at 4 Trg Btn REME Blackdown, where the officer had been the 2IC of the Instrument Wing. He explained that he had come on behalf of the RA, then asked who tested and set the Directors and how exactly was this done? In reply, it was explained that the head of section normally 'out inspected' and proceeded to show him how and what was done, including the sub-standard compass that was used in the tests and adjustments. Capt Armstrong explained that, when the RA was asked to give close infantry support to a patrol or such like, the shells were dropping short and had caused casualties to our own troops. This was of great concern to 10 Inf Wksp, and especially its Instrument Section, but having satisfied himself that the Workshop seemed not to be at fault, the Captain said his farewell and no further reports were made. It was some weeks later, actually on the banks of the Imjin River, whilst John Dutton was going for a swim, that Capt Armstrong also happened to be there. Chatting to him later, John asked if that RA problem had been resolved – and, if so, what had been the problem? The short answer was *"Yes"*, it had been resolved; the Americans had issued the local magnetic map corrections, thus giving the British and Commonwealth Brigades a one-degree error. That was a great relief for the Workshop, to say the least.

Peter Hills looks back

Both of the Brigades had senior Armourers, known as Bde Armourers. They were usually WOII in rank, and one of these was Peter 'Pinnel' Hills. He used to pop into the unit lines when he was in the area and, on the first such meeting, he appeared as tall, well built and a happy go lucky type. He had arrived in Korea as Armourer to 1 Btn Welch Regt and told John that, like others in November of 1951, the Battalion made their way past a shantytown of cardboard hovels and squalid looking tin shacks to the railhead. He could still picture the scene; they were all aboard the train, except for the Regimental officers, who were promenading the platform, near a Women's Voluntary Service (WVS) lady who had been dispensing tea or whatever. The time for departure having been set, a short whistle emitted from the train and, within seconds, the train was moving at a running pace, with the officers belting along the platform, attempting to scramble aboard. It turned out that the US Army Master Sergeant engine driver was 'in charge'!

One soon noticed an absence of trees in this war-torn land, for when the North Koreans decided to take over South Korea, they very nearly succeeded and came within a whisker of doing so. The American Ninth Air Force rained down their bombs, thus stopping the NKA forces just short of Pusan, but blowing the countryside to pieces as they did so. Peter's train took him through this bleak-looking terrain to Seoul, the capital of South Korea. The unit transferred to lorries and went northwards, then took up positions to relieve the remnants of 1 Gloucesters, just north of the area in which they had come to grief. As Peter has said a 'Speleologist' he was not, but he had done his share of digging in Europe, India, Burma and now, once again, it was out with the pick and shovel or entrenching tool and get digging. On 'schemes' (peace-time practice runs) he used to begrudge every inch that he had to turf up, but now that it was for real, he 'set to' with a different spirit. In his case, he had to dig a deep and large enough hole in which to work, leaving a solid bench of earth at a convenient working height. As previously mentioned, a precarious heating contraption of 'Heath-Robinson' style had been 'invented' - a 40-gallon drum of petrol, some thin copper tubing and a shell casing. Provided that the tubing was squeezed sufficiently to permit a drip feed, then a reasonable source of heat could be gained. American and Canadian troops had commercially-made 'Space Heaters' and some of these were later 'acquired' by the British lads! The forward Companies had no such luxury and, after a very severe year and winter in which they had lived in holes in the ground, the Battalion finally left Korea for Hong Kong. Those killed were buried in Pusan Military Cemetery.

However, Peter was moved sideways and remained in Korea for a further spell with HQ 29 Bde LAD REME as the Bde Armourer. He re-called the mud that they had encountered when pitching camp at 'B' Echelon, 1 Welch Regt. The ground had thawed out, then torrential rain turned the flat area into virtually a rice paddy field, with mud one foot deep. In this setting, they had to erect a marquee, probably not Peter's favourite 'cup of tea'. But it did make it easier to appreciate the latest 'Flanders and Swann' hit tune, *"Mud, mud, glorious mud"*. As Bde Armourer, Peter had the opportunity to move around the Div area, visiting the various Battalions. On one such occasion, dropping in on 1 Black Watch, he took one of their attached REME, a Cfn Watkins, with him to help in checking the Battalion's mortars. They received some 'incoming mail' and Watkins did not duck quickly enough and suffered a head wound. On the 'outgoing' side, the Mortar Pln reckoned they could get ten bombs in the air before the first one exploded! In one instance, Peter was not too popular, because he condemned a mortar barrel for excessive wear. Their CO was reluctant to let it go so, being a good sort, Peter went back to 10 Inf Wksp 'had a chat' with SSgt Johnny Doig. He got a new barrel, then took it back to 1 Black Watch and, by the next day, after a battle on the 'Hook', he fitted it. He was then asked to re-measure, as the Platoon had fired so many bombs.

Christmas Day 1951 saw the height of Chinese nerve. They crept up on 1 Welch and planted a banner with the following inscription, *"Whatever the colour or creed, all plain folks are brothers indeed. Both you and we want life and peace. If you go home, then war will cease"*. These sentiments were echoed on the UN side, they were all keen to leave of course, but what a nerve! An example of 'unexpected jobs' took place about January 1952. Peter was called forward to the MG Pln, who had been so heavily engaged that they had fired their *Vickers* (water cooled) guns so continuously, that the water evaporated and the heat melted the end cap to the gun. In peacetime, this would of course have been a 'factory repair', but Peter just had to get on with it, in such dire circumstances where every gun counts. A lot of trenches and gun positions were on the forward slopes of the hills, so those REME lads who had to get there were exposed and often attracted a few shells as a welcome!

One day, during the spring of 1952, rumours came down the line that 'Pinnel' had been struck down with a very serious illness, called 'Haemorrhagic Fever' or, as it was more commonly known, 'Manchurian Fever'. US troops had suffered very badly from this fever. Their isolation hospital was not too far from 10 Inf Wksp, whose personnel were able to see the helicopters continuously flying patients in. It can now be confirmed that the rumour was true and had come about when 1 Welch Regt left Korea and Peter Hills was side moved to HQ 29 Bde LAD. Here, he took over from an AQMS Ted Cooper, even inheriting his spacious hole, dug in the hillside, in which there was a roughly-made wooden bed. After a good night's sleep, a dead rat was found in the place. It had been killed but not disposed of so, when 'Pinnel' had used his new accommodation and slept, mites from the rat must have jumped onto the nice warm flesh of Peter Hills and, in no time, down he went. Having collapsed, he was showing the effects of haemorrhage under his skin. But he was still conscious and able to answer questions, as to where he had been and doing. Within days, Peter was first taken to Seoul, then evacuated on a stretcher lashed to the outside struts of a helicopter. He was taken to an American field hospital, where it was confirmed he had this haemorrhagic fever. Thanks to expert American medical help he survived the spell and eventually got back to HQ 29 Bde LAD.

Whatever he was able to tell the American doctors enabled them to start looking for an antidote against this haemorrhagic fever. A long time afterwards, Pinnel returned to the Mess, a shadow of the man that he had originally been, but alive. He would not hear a thing against 'the Yanks' after that as, in his eyes, they had saved his life. *(N.B. It was only whilst researching this book that confirmation of the above details was possible. Peter Hills' address was obtained and he confirmed the story - it had only taken about forty-six years!)*

After his return to duty, a task of inspecting 'C' Coy 1 Btn RNR was his due reward! After crawling all over their positions, he reported to the Coy Cdr with the results of his examination of their weapons. To his surprise and delight, Maj Martin (for it was he) instantly remembered that the last time they had met was back in 1938. He had then been a PT Instructor to both Peter and AQMS Ted Cooper, when these two 'youngsters' were on boys' service - what a small world!

One other detail of this 'Forgotten War' has come to light. When the Welch Regt left for Hong

10 INFANTRY WORKSHOP REME NOVEMBER 1951 TO JUNE 1953

Kong, they presented Peter Hills, their Armourer, with a vehicle. This was a Jeep, which he kept going throughout the rest of his time in Korea. When it started to burn oil, he even bought a new engine, courtesy of the Canadian Workshop. Peter presumes that his successor inherited it, unless someone else snaffled it.

Back with John Dutton – and 10 Infantry Workshop

The time came when most of the 'Z' reservists had left for their homes in UK, much happier and, in some cases, much wealthier - but more on that subject later. They had left the unit 'the makings' of many useful items and it was up to the Regular lads to finish what they had started. The Workshop had come by an American 2.5-ton *GMC*, six-wheel drive vehicle and, sitting in its rear load area, was a 5,000-gallon water tank, which had the makings of a fine bath unit. The Fitter section, headed by SSgt 'Nick' Nicholson (or was it Nickerson?), first secured the water tank in position at the rear of the vehicle. Then Nick visited the RE yard 'on the scrounge'. He came back with a long length of copper pipe, about an inch and a half in diameter, several shower heads, some lengths of standard copper half-inch pipe and, most importantly, a water mixer unit. He set to work and made a bath unit with six showers, which fed into a 'squad tent', an American type marquee. The carpenters made duckboards and seats for the clothes to be placed on, it worked very well.

Some peculiar modifications

It must have been about this time, the spring of 1952, when the CO, Maj Rogers, sent for John Dutton again. On his arrival, John discovered that the CO had CREME with him. CREME explained that he had been approached by the CRA, with a request to provide lighting sets for the 25-pdr Field Gun Dial Sights and their carriers. John knew that these items were not provisioned for, but this job was to be 'top priority'. It was such an unusual request that exact confirmation was sought from the RA Branch at HQ Div Main itself. The exact detailing of light quantity required, and on which positions, needed to be stated. It turned out that a light was required on the Graticule in the Dial Sight, the Cross-level bubble, the Range-scale cone, the Sight Clinometer and the cone reader arm, a total of five lights. In response, a request was made to have on loan a complete Dial Sight and carrier, to take back to the Workshop, together with a Clino. This was quickly granted. A lot of midnight oil was burnt on this project. The only other time in John's service that a similar system had been mentioned, was during his instruction on the Dial Sight theory at a Training Battalion. But nothing on this scale was ever written about or taught, it was entirely up to him, with REME agreement, as to what was finally produced. The rifles in the Division had a few of the their brass oil-bottles suitably modified to hold a bulb, to illuminate the Graticule in the Dial sight. The machinists in the Workshop's light machinery truck were kept busy making bulb-holders, of varying shapes and sizes, until one day the Wksp Officer, Capt Dix, was called for to *"Okay"* the Mark1 kit.

John then took this to 45 Fld Regt RA, where he requested their permission to fit the kit to an active gun, which he found very interesting. The 'Number1' on the selected gun asked for permission from the Troop Commander for 'Gun out of Action', then told John, *"Take your time Tiffy, we could do with a rest"*. Well, it was certainly not a 'rush' job, taking some time to be completed, not forgetting this was a prototype fitting. With the kit being powered by a battery, this had been placed in the spare parts case bracket, on the rear of the gun shield. The Troop Commander came over to check the fitting, then cleared the gun to fire, which it duly did, throwing the batteries, with their lead wires still attached, many yards to the rear of the gun pit! This was obviously a 'design fault', as no securing straps had been fitted, so it was back to the drawing board. John soon corrected that error and a further round was fired, to prove that the second fitting was OK. He then left the lighting set fitted to the gun, for the RA to trial.

Very quickly, the trial was over. The gunners liked the lighting concept, except for one small thing - could we make the lighting brilliance variable? It was too bright when the batteries were new, while different gunners saw the light in varying strengths. Oh! And could they quickly have sufficient lighting kits to equip the complete Div Artillery? That would mean 'seventy plus' weapons! That came as a complete surprise to John. The prototype, yes, but to manufacture for the whole Division! Firstly there was the additional modification to allow a variable powered lighting, not too bad if one was in the UK, but damn difficult in the middle of a 'paddy field'! Not too far away was an American QM unit, so John thought he would try there first - why not? They offered their help, having first listened to a theoretical description of the requirement. And, guess what, they turned up the ideal item, a cylindrical steel container to hold the batteries, which had a rheostat fitted into one end cap. This meant a different type of battery than that used initially, and John can't remember if they issued it or gave it freely, but they would be 'advised', if it worked. John told them that a further requirement of some seventy to eighty would be needed, but got a casual shrug of the shoulders and a simple statement - just let them know, it was no problem!

The Sighting Gear discussed is to the left of the breechblock slightly above the breech of this 25 Pounder.

The cylinder fitted perfectly in the Telescope Holder, within the Dial Sight carrier, while permission was obtained from CREME and CRA to drill and fit a clamping screw, through the holder casing. Then it was back to the RA Battery where the trial had taken place, to fit the modification and leave them to notify the result. Two days later, the CO received a message that it was what they required, and the request *"Could the Workshop now go ahead and supply the Division?"* They were duly manufactured, with valuable assistance from the QM of 10 Inf Wksp, who obtained the entire requirement of brass oil bottles. The light machinery lads did the entire turning and threading to take the bulbs, the tinsmiths soldered all the necessary bits together, and the Instrument lads assembled the complete kits. John Dutton went forward to the RA Troop/Battery locations and fitted the lighting sets, a very 'enlightening' job that turned out to be! One problem raised its head in that NZRA Regt were fitted with an old pattern No.7 Dial Sight, but this was soon remedied when they were issued with the later No.9 Dial Sight as a matter of urgency.

A small episode that came out of these trips concerned a young National Service driver, with a very nervous disposition, who was detailed to drive the Jeep. All was well until crossing the Imjin River and approaching the area of the RA gun locations. As has been well recorded, they never stopped firing - and the driver never stopped jumping and going all over the place! After the first stop, John took over the driving. When they stopped for meals, the young driver would not leave the Jeep so, on their way back, with the driver's nerves by now very ragged, he sat holding on tightly while John drove. As luck would have it, the MTO passed them on the MSR just outside the Workshop. After parking the vehicle and the driver departed for his billet, the MTO stopped John and informed him that he was charging him with unlawful driving. This he duly did, but the Admin Officer showed some common sense and ticked off the MTO for wasting his time, while dismissing the case out of hand.

The Staff at Div HQ had been thinking along the line that routine inspections, of all types of equipment, should now take place. The Workshop was given a calendar of inspections to be carried out, the first being in the central section of the Div front. The unit was the Welch Regt, both 'A' and 'B' echelons. 'A' echelon at that time was on top of Pt 355 and its rear slopes. This time the driving was done 'officially', unit accompanied by the Welch's relief Armourer, by name Sgt Charlie Hepworth. *(N.B. Since starting on this book, I have at last contacted Peter Hills, who was the Armourer to the Welch Regiment when it landed in Korea. So, when Charlie Hepworth relieved him, it must have been at the same time that Peter went to 29 Bde LAD.)* It was a pleasant drive up towards the front. Stopping at 'B' Echelon, Charlie took a look at the Battalion's reserve weapons, while SSgt Dutton checked their Instruments. These included Telescopes Sighting for the Anti-Tank guns held in this location, reserve instruments, Binoculars, Compasses, Watches, Sights Mortar, an odd pair of Binocular-Telescopic and much routine office equipment, with typewriters, duplicators etc. That little job done, they both pressed on to 'A' Echelon, Charlie to present himself as the Welch Btn replacement Armourer and John Dutton to inspect all their instruments. Well, they first found the location, then the Coy HQ, which was a sand-bagged dugout. They proceeded to go in to announce their arrival to the Coy Cdr. It was very quiet and dark on entering, in fact they ended up disturbing some six to eight officers who were asleep! One dropped down from a top bunk and introduced himself as the Coy Cdr and, in the next breath, apologised for being asleep. The remainder then all arose, explaining why they had been asleep. It seems that they had gone out the previous evening, forward of their position, on a patrol and got lost. So they had sat out the night till dawn broke, then made their way back and fell into bed tired out.

Whatever happened to Betsy?

It was lunchtime by now and the officers invited both the inspectors to join them, as it was their fresh ration day. But both visitors declined the fresh rations and asked for 'C10 packs', an acquired taste. All requests were met and they started to enjoy their lunch when, all of a sudden, the Coy Cdr jumped up and loudly exclaimed, *"Has anyone seen my 'Betsy'?"* Charlie and John looked at each other, then at the others in the dugout. They obviously knew what he was talking about, but the visitors didn't have a clue. When they quietly asked one of the junior officers what it was about, he told them that 'Betsy' was a pickaxe handle! They said no more and joined in the hunt. Thank goodness it was soon found, down behind one of the bunks. They were not certain, but perhaps their faces showed a look of bewilderment, because the Coy Cdr started to explain that he always led his patrols and never went out armed, but always carried this pickaxe handle. If they got into close quarter fighting, then a bash on the head with Betsy soon put people out of action. Also, it was handy when climbing out of a slit trench to pull people up from the trench quietly. *"Plausible"*, thought John, who found out later that day that this Coy Cdr had transferred from Battalion to Battalion, so he was currently on his third tour!

Lunch over, they said their farewells and thanks for lunch. Charlie went one way and John another, climbing up Pt 355 to find the CSM, who eventually poked his head out of a cave, three quarters of the way up the hill side. From there, he spotted the climber and shouted to attract John's attention. They introduced themselves and the CSM explained that he had gathered together all the instruments that were not in immediate use. These could be seen laid out on the top blanket of his bunk, the equipment looked to be in a fairly good state and John informed him so. Having completed this part, John was about to leave, when the CSM suddenly said, *"Ah! You are just the chap I need"*, telling John to follow him up the hillside. Without thinking, John did so, and when they stopped just below the rim of the hill, they were actually standing in a 61mm mortar pit. Without further ado, the CSM fired three mortar bombs, then dashed out of the pit, dragging John behind him. Stopping at the top of the hill, against the forward barbed wire, he pointed across the Samichon valley, indicating an old paddy field with a wrecked tank stuck in its top right corner. *"See that tank? Watch for the bombs"*.

They were all three dead on target and, with that, they walked back to his mortar pit. That is exactly what it was, **his** 61mm mortar pit, no-one else was allowed near it, and he now started to explain what his problem was. This type of weapon, American mass-produced, was not a repairable item. The sights had worn and were now loose, but were never meant to be repaired, they were die-castings. Explaining this to John, the CSM said that there was not a mortar that could beat him onto target, especially when close support was called for, so he would just make allowances for this problem and keep firing. John suggested that he ask the Yanks for a new mortar sight!

Steel helmet time

Towards the end of summer 1952, a similar inspection was to take place, but this time with 1 Btn King's Liverpool Regt. Arriving as before, John made his presence known to the Coy Cdr and explained that the OP forward of their location was to be inspected. From John's memory again, it was OP 35, and the OC explained how to get there. Thanking him and just about to leave, John was halted by the OC calling out, *"Staff, where is your steel helmet? You cannot go forward without one"*. John explained that he had never been issued with one, and heard the command, *" Sergeant Major, lend him yours"*. The route that had to be taken was down the forward slopes of the hill that they occupied. One went down a virtual 'goat-track', more like a cutting that had camouflage netting stretched over it, to conceal one's movements. At the time it seemed very eerie indeed but, at the bottom of this cutting was a sign that said, *"The next 300 yards is open ground and you are in view from the Chinese positions, if you value your life, RUN"*. At this point one stopped, looked, gathered one's wits, took a deep breath, then RAN! Once behind the hill, on whose summit the OP was located, John stopped and again caught his breath. Looking around, he now realised that it was some considerable distance into the Samichon Valley, well in front of the positions that he had just passed through.

OP 35 was located in front of the King's Regt, on a promontory, which allowed one to look forward to the Chinese side of the Samichon Valley. It also look back at the 29 Bde positions, those John had just left. As the accompanying picture shows, bombing, shelling and mortaring had decimated the area in front of their positions. The Chinese had burrowed very deep into their hillsides. Following the track up the back of this hill, concealed from the Chinese, John came to the OP. Pulling the netting aside, he scrambled into a slit-trench, which had been covered with timbers and sand-bags, leaving an observation slit at the front. The two residents, officers, from the RA, listened to John's reason for being there and then allowed him to start on the items not immediately in use. This visit had only been of a couple of minutes' duration, when the shriek of shells and mortar bombs passing overhead made John jump. The telephone rang at that same instance, requesting if they could see where the firing was coming from. The two officers looked as hard as they could, but answered in the negative. They explained that most of the firing was done

10 Infantry Workshop REME November 1951 to June 1953

from below ground, which could not be seen at all in daylight but, if one was lucky at night, you may see a small glow.

The opposing sides of the Samichon Valley could not help but be noticed, through the observation slit of the OP. Looking across at the Chinese side, the ground looked like sand dunes, with not the slightest sign of vegetation, but through the back of the OP, towards their own positions, these hill sides were completely covered in growth. Having finished the inspection, John thanked the two gunners and crept to the beginning of the mad 300 yards dash! He took a deep breath and sprinted back to safety. Three days later he leaned that the OP had taken a direct hit!

For a Field Workshop, a lot of experimental manufacture was undertaken. Trench warmers, Jeep ambulance heaters, side-shelter heaters - most of this work was done in the Fitter's Section, under the auspices of SSgt Nickerson, a man who deserved an award for his toil. The carpenter, 'Chippy' Ron Lupson, who lived in the side-shelter attached to the Instrument truck, was also a Staff Sergeant, and he was constantly manufacturing. Three *Bedford* TCV type vehicles were brought to the Workshop, and first made fully roadworthy. Then they were taken down to the Carpenter's Shop for conversion to Div and Bde Cdr's caravans. A fine job was made of these, all vehicles being fitted with a bed, a writing desk, a wash-stand, a fitted heater and armchair - and all this inside a panelled structure, very nice too. To top it off, when the tailboard was lowered, it exposed a door to the caravan and also acted as a veranda, with a folding awning that could be pulled out from the rear of the vehicle, to allow one to sit out and get some fresh air!

Ron, was also asked to make a farewell present, for CREME, Lt Col Good, on his posting from the Division, Ron produced two book ends and the fitter Sgt made an "A" frame for each of these book ends, out of brass, then got them plated in Seoul, Col HG Good has indicated that they are still in his possession and in use.

Because such a good job was made of the bookends, another farewell present, this time for the Div Cdr, Lt Gen Cassels. It was to be a lump of Korean hillside rock, mounted on a shield, easier said than done. In the end, it was let into the shield from the rear, a time-consuming job. Then the back of the shield had a fitted cover to hold the rock in place. It was not the Workshop's choice of a present, but it was well received and well made by 'Chippy'.

John can't remember how many wooden floors the Workshop helped to fit in unit messes, when requested and timber was available, but it all went to help the comfort and moral of the service. During the summer of 1952, came a move for the second Instrument Shop location, onto a hillside that had a convenient flat space big enough for the vehicle and side-shelter etc. Still within the Workshop compound, this enabled a better field of view for the optical repairs, while the move gave the new location a slightly elevated level over

The farewell present, made by Ssgts Chippy Lupson and Nickerson to be presented to CREME on his return to the UK

the other vehicles.

Whilst in this location, bits and pieces were obtained to provide a power source to drive an AR88 radio receiver, which was 110V AC, as opposed to the normal 110V DC power in the Workshop. Once this was accomplished, from then on, with the two big 12" speakers placed on the *Leyland* Instrument repair vehicle roof, broadcasting the BBC overseas service and the American local 'canned' radio stations to the Workshop was much easier.

Canoeing and other assorted sports

The summer of 1952 was slowly making its mark and a mention of an amusing incident about the CO, Maj Rogers, will not go amiss. Now running through the camp area at Tokchon, which was situated in a re-entrant, was a stream that, in the wet season, became quite a formidable torrent down the incline. Whether he just felt like it, or just wanted to let off steam, on this particular day the CO decided to go canoeing! The Officers' Mess was situated higher up in the re-entrant than the Sgts' Mess, and therefore the force of water was greater at that point. The CO had half a napalm bomb-case, which is very similar in shape to a canoe. He launched this, jumped in and, with a great shout, sped past his senior ranks. They just looked on in amazement, as he eventually ran out of water deep enough to carry his craft, just before he reached the lads' lines.

As that summer arrived, there were lots of cases of sunburn and the inevitable clouds of dust. At this time, the unit was still located at Tokchon, just off 'MSR3'. One particular day started out as routine. The few members of the Instrument crew were in their wagon on the hillside, with the side-windows fully extended to allow some air to move through. A loud rumble of thunder occurred, or that is what it sounded like. In the next few seconds, the flaps of the canvas shelter containing the Blacksmiths' shop, which was located just below the Instrument truck, flew open and Cpl 'Paddy' Cronin came out at the speed of a 100-yard sprinter. He didn't stop until he was clear of the Workshop compound. While he was still in the process of disappearing, a large explosion and a sheet of flame blew the Blacksmiths' shop to pieces. What made it even more of a spectacle was the MTO/Fire Officer, who had thrown fire-extinguishers into the back of a 15-cwt *Bedford* and bounced round to the incident. By this time, the acid foam had reacted and everything was covered in the stuff. The officer grabbed one extinguisher and dashed into what remained of the shelter, only to fall down a hole made by the explosion. Picking himself up, he came out to see everyone standing around with cameras in their hands and broad grins on their faces - he was not amused! It turned out that a previous unit

Outside the Blacksmiths shop the Armament and General section with Cfn Finlayson on the right.

10 INFANTRY WORKSHOP REME NOVEMBER 1951 TO JUNE 1953

Engines and assemblies waiting to be fitted

had buried cordite blocks in the very spot where Paddy had placed his shelter. Thank goodness no one was hurt.

Time passed by as though everyone was locked in a sealed box; very little theatre information from the Brigade actions was released to Workshop personnel. The only time one received some 'outside information' was from new arrivals. One of them was a SSgt Gibbings, Art Vehicle. He was allocated the 15-cwt line, RA Quads and Field Generators. A couple of months after he had settled in, a Workshop move forward was rumoured - CREME had decided it was time to exercise one of his Brigade Workshops. The 2IC to CREME, a Canadian Major, had carried out a recce and we were to move forward of the other Bde Wksp, 16 Inf Wksp, in the old leapfrog method. Our new location was to be on the southern side of the Imjin River, adjacent to the Canadian Bde, which was in reserve and resting.

No, it's not just a rumour!

The war going on up country had seemed like only a rumour, but this time they were all going to move forward. The standard practice applied – *"All packed and ready to move, in convoy order"*. This order had been previously issued, so the Workshop moved out onto the MSR, heading for the 'sharp end', with regulation convoy distance and speed being maintained. Only about twenty miles distant, they turned into a large green area and drove around its perimeter, so that the lead vehicle was in a position to move off the next morning. The area was large enough to contain all the vehicles except 'the heavies', Diamond-T Recovery and *Coles* Crane, they stayed in an adjacent field. However, it was not a working move, only an exercise 'Bug Out', to use the local lingo. Looking around the temporary location, the older and wiser of the Workshop staff, who happened to be senior NCOs, looked at the ground and very quickly recognised an old dried up paddy field that had gone to grass. During their next mealtime, this observation was discussed and they all prayed that it would not rain. It turned out that they did not pray hard enough because, as dusk fell, so did the rain. It came down with the buckets still attached! Orders were quickly passed that no one was to sleep under their vehicles that night; it was so wet and cold that the CO ordered 'inclement rations' to be issued, very much appreciated - a tot of rum each to warm them up.

Morning arrived and a very wet and sad looking lot started to get the vehicles ready for the drive back to Tokchon. Orders were given and the lead vehicle moved some forty-sixty feet and promptly sank up to its axles in mud. This was repeated as they all tried to get out of the field. It was thought that the very old *Leyland*, which had six wheels, would make it, but no - down it went like the rest. The recovery vehicle they had with them just could not cope, so Div Recy was sent for. Slowly they hauled everyone out onto firm ground, and they made their own way back until only 'the heavies' remained. They were in the process of pulling them out when a shell exploded, right in the area that they had just vacated, followed quickly by a further nineteen. Fortunately, they suffered only one

Page 197

casualty, when the vehicle AQMS received a piece of shrapnel. The Canadian Bde was, to put it mildly, 'not amused', as it so happened that the shells had arrived in the area next to them. By this time, all sorts of signals had flashed around the Div area. As the location was south of the Imjin, not exactly in the front line, from where had the shells been fired?

Later in the day, it was discovered that the RIDG had brought a troop of their Centurions to the northern bank of the Imjin. Their intention was to fire HE rounds only, in depression, at the rubbish that was caught on a drag line, which protected Pintail Bridge from the debris thrown into the Imjin, up stream by the Chinese. The heavy debris had caught on the flood currents and acted as a battering-ram against the legs of the bridge. Subsequently, it had been decided that the wire had to be cleared by high explosives. But in such a unique situation, the positioning of the tanks had turned out to be the critical angle for a ricochet of the 20-pdr HE shells. The Commander of the RIDG duly apologised to our CO.

Having got back to Tokchon lines with no more mishaps, the MTO decided to have some work done on the old *Scammell* 'Knocker' 6x4. The front axle and brakes were to be overhauled. When the fitter in the MT section told the MTO that he had no experience on this vehicle, the MTO replied, *"Not to worry, you are to work under my supervision"*. Duly the old brake drums were removed and sent to A&G for skimming, in the 'Mary X' heavy machinery lorry. They were completed and returned and, under instructions from the MTO, refitted to the vehicle. Now for the road test and bedding the brake linings in. The *Scammell* moved out onto the MSR and turned left, which meant it would go over the small hump-back bridge that spanned our stream. It got that far, but suddenly the front end dropped, as the front wheels left their stub axles and rolled to a stop. Recovery had to lift the old *Scammell* and return it to the Workshop, where questions were asked of the MTO. *"Why had advice not been sought from the vehicle sections?"* The fitter was cleared of all responsibility and the brake drums re-spun, but they only just made it within tolerance, as the stub axle thread had really chewed up the braking surface. The *Scammell* was back on the road in no time; this time the wheel nuts were correctly fitted, using that 'small' 4-foot spanner and the sledge hammer to tighten them!

The only other occasion that comes readily to mind concerns the Vehicle section. The *Coles* Crane was to pick up a Ferret Scout Car, which it was quite capable of doing. But on this occasion, things didn't quite 'gel' and, before it could be stopped, the Crane had pulled itself down onto the Ferret, rolling the whole vehicle on its side. Luckily, no damage was done. The Crane's jib angle had been far too low for the lift. The error was soon corrected and some polite instructions given to the operator! Summer had well and truly arrived, the ground was baked hard, dry and dusty. A flash rumour spread that the Workshop was on the move again. The rumour was slightly amended in that they were about to move forward, but this time to a location adjacent to 16 Inf Wksp on 'Route 2Y', just outside Gloucester Valley. It all went without a hitch. Vehicles and personnel all located themselves in the designated areas and the lads started to put up their tents and shelters. Then came the order that they must dig the vehicles in to the hillside. That proved to be great fun as shovels bounced off the ground! Small holes were soon bored into the ground and explosives used, but that didn't last long, there was no way that A&G section was going to get its vehicles dug in. It was eventually decided that it wouldn't matter anyway, as the Chinese had no air power, so there was no risk of bombing.

SSgt Gibbings, having now found his bearings, was on duty as Guard Cdr, a large guard having been mounted in this new location, owing to the extensive area it was spread over. The relief had gone out and the remaining guards were trying to get some sleep, when one jumped up, screaming, *"It's going to hit us!"* He then ran, still screaming, out of the guard tent. He was stopped by the gate guard and calmed down. He had been asleep and was woken by a fly in his ear and thought it was a plane crashing on them. He really was disturbed and took a lot of convincing. The fly was later removed with a drop of oil! One of the field generator mechanics, a Scotsman, one day said he was tired of his present employment and wanted a change. It so happened that a call was received from Air Co-Op Unit, stating that they wanted a fitter. Disregarding comments made to him, he volunteered for the post. He left 10 Inf Wksp about mid-day and, later that same day, the unit was informed that he had been taken prisoner. Apparently he had been offered a trip in a plane, which was subsequently shot down behind the enemy lines. To John Dutton's knowledge, that lad was the only REME soldier taken as a POW.

A nice little earner!

The unit watchmaker, Cfn 'Jock' Imray, had developed a small sideline. It started by his pointing out to SSgt Dutton that, although a considerable amount of Army issue watches were made 'BER', due to enemy action in those forward units that had come under enemy fire, and had what was called the QM's 24-hour write-off, the Workshop could always tell. But it still gave the impression that everyone up there in the front line would occasionally turn out his kit-bag and bring all the 'junk' into the Workshop for repair or condemnation. Well, sometimes this was quite genuine; watches had perhaps been in a fire or similar disasters and could be 'written off'. Jock would carefully shuffle the movements and cases, so that he ended up with workable watches that he would overhaul in due course. Then he would spin (turn the markings off) the watchcase backs in the lathe to remove ID numbers, and spin the dials off, ready for re-enamelling. He would go round the Workshop personnel and find out who would like a watch and what type of dial they would like i.e. *"Black with white figures"* or *"White with black figures"* and the type of finish. When this was established, he would package the dials, suitably labelled in a matchbox, and post them to Glasgow. They would be duly returned, nicely finished to order. Jock would then re-assemble the movement and the case, *"£5 to you Sir"*!

During the spring of 1953, permission was obtained to take the *Leyland* Instrument 6x4 for a run-out. In fact it went all the way to Seoul, where some of the locals washed it down in exchange for a bar of chocolate. Then it was turned round and headed for home, driving along the MSR towards Tokchon. Some Yanks overtook the crew, then flagged the truck down. The driver pulled over as far as he dared and stopped, while the Jeep driver, an American Top Sergeant, got out of his vehicle and came back towards the *Leyland*. Looking amazed and bewildered, he asked, *"What is this truck?"* Having been told, he then asked, *"How many cylinders has it got?"* He got the reply of *"Four"*, to which was added their size. It was obvious that he just could not take it in, but he told them, *"By the way, your back axle is falling off!"* With that remark, he re-mounted his own Jeep and drove off. Having inspected the rear axles, the crew thought they looked OK. They started up and drove back to camp, with no further incident. That evening in the Mess, John mentioned the incident, of the rear axles 'falling off', to the vehicle AQMS. He did not hesitate in his reply. *"Your two rear axles float, to allow for the cross-country aspects of the Leyland"*. Then, going on, he explained that, from the rear, the two axles would certainly appear to move left and right against each other, due to the floating action. So a little more is learned every day!

A fond farewell

The spring of 1953 moved on into early summer. The months had not been too eventful and time was now getting near for John Dutton to say *"Goodbye"* to Korea, which he hadn't once left since December 1951, except on duty. That long and tedious journey beckoned, twenty-four hours

The Forgotten Punch in the Army's Fist — Korea 1950-1953

from Tokchon to Pusan by rail, then another full day from Pusan to Kure, Japan, by boat - if that can be considered as an apt description of that old tub! For John and his companions, the trouble started at the quayside. It was the day of Queen Elizabeth's Coronation. Now let no one forget, these guys had just come back directly from the war in Korea. Admittedly they were in scruff order, but so what? They were only going to get into a truck and go directly to the JRBD for a bath and kit-change etc. But, oh no! The staff on the quayside had better ideas. These 'scruffs' had to remain on board until the 'Big Coronation Parade' was over and the crowds had dispersed. Then they were ushered quickly onto the trucks that had been waiting for them, the canvas back was secured and then, like the wind, they drove to the JRBD.

Bathed, re-kitted and all nice and shiny, that little party of 'time served' personnel decided to go to Kure, to the WOs' & Sgts' Mess, only to find it totally deserted! They enquired where everyone was and the bar steward, a local Japanese employee, told them, *"Everyone has gone home"*! Looking at each other in amazement, they asked, *"Home, what do you mean, gone home?"* The steward explained that most of the Mess members lived out in Japanese houses with local girls. That explained the reason for the 'Shop' they had noticed when they arrived in the Mess, with the title of 'Dry Goods'. There wasn't much to do, so off they went looking for 'Q' Rawlins, that pianist who had rotated back to Japan. Taking a taxi to the Gun Park, a security guard on the gate told them *"He's at home"*. So the party obtained his address and got the local driver to take them there. Well! It turned out to be on a street of typical Japanese bungalows, all paper and timber. They knocked on the door and stood back. The door slid aside and they confronted a young girl in traditional kimono. In quite good English, she asked for their names. A voice from behind her said, *"Let them in"*. It was Phil Rawlins and he explained that this was standard practice in Kure. He signed for the Gun Park on the hand over/take over and this was the last item, it cost about 11/6p a week! Those that sailed had a very pleasant trip home on the 'Orwell', calling in at all the same ports that had been visited on the way out.

Cyril Luger looks back

SSgt Cyril Luger arrived at 10 Inf Wksp as a replacement ECE for Jack Drennan, which was towards the end of John Dutton's time. Cyril recalls going out to visit 'the tankies' of 1 RTR on several occasions. On one such occasion he was sat inside the turret of one of the Centurions when an overflying USAF jet fighter strafed the tank park with machine-gun fire. Cyril recalls hearing the bullets ricocheting off the turret and thanked his lucky starts that he wasn't doing any external checks! The tank gunner popped his head out of the turret and remarked, *"It's okay Staff, he's one of ours!"* Cyril later heard that the CO had been none too pleased by this 'friendly fire' incident.

Cyril also recalls the occasion when someone came dashing into the guard tent one night, shouting, *"A Yank has just shot his mate. Come quickly Staff, he's still got his gun!"* Cyril hitched up his Colt-45, kindly donated by the departed Jack Drennan, and made his way swiftly to the canteen. The tent was full of British lads and the lighting was terribly dim, as the canteen tent was at the far end of the supply cable. Cyril thought it was like a scene from a Western movie. The GI still held his gun and Cyril envisaged having to face him down in a shoot-out! But the young soldier handed over the weapon, muttering *"Ah'm sure sorry I shot my buddy"*. The wounded guy, Cyril thinks was called Gomez, was sent off to the nearest MASH in the back of a 15-cwt Morris – the worst possible vehicle, as the springs were useless. By the time poor Gomez got to the hospital he had expired and Cyril reckons he'd probably been shaken to death. The offended was subsequently taken to a court martial and given ten years for manslaughter. Cyril has fond memories of being treated like a Lord, staying in the Americans' Officers' Mess during the trial.

Chapter 32

Late summer and winter July to October 1952

By this stage, operations in the Campaign had become almost completely static. Both sides had constructed strong and deep defensive works, protected by mines and wire, and had perfected their defensive fire arrangements to an extent that made patrols and raids very hazardous undertakings. There seemed little prospect of the resumption of a more mobile form of warfare. The truce talks continued their leisurely and quarrelsome trend. At least their continuance had some influence on confining operations to minor enterprises, without much thought by either side of bold plans to produce decisive results. Moreover, from a purely military point of view, it appeared unlikely that either side could achieve a resounding victory. The seemingly unlimited manpower of the CCF was fairly evenly balanced by the superior ground equipment and air power of the UN forces. Both Armies were operating at the end of long and difficult lines of communication and were, to a considerable extent, the prisoners of logistics. In the tactical sphere, operations had undergone a considerable change since the autumn of 1951. When Comm Div was consolidating its positions after 'Operation Commando', its patrols dominated 'No-Man's Land' and raids and other minor enterprises always had a good chance of success. The CCF had been thrown off balance by the loss of their positions and their artillery, although greatly improved, was not then very numerous and technically not very efficient.

But by July of 1952, all this had changed. The Chinese now deployed a great weight of artillery and mortars and had evolved a very efficient system of defensive fire by both day and night. The period of easy successes were over. The weather had now become very hot and sultry, combined with spasmodic heavy rain and occasional gales. As a result of the rain, the Imjin River rose sharply and, on July 1st, there was some anxiety for the safety of the bridges over the river, by which the troops of Comm Div and other formations were supplied. In the event, the river subsided and the bridges remained intact. On July 2nd, 1 Btn RAR carried out its first operation. This was a raid, at Company strength, against Pt 227 with the object of capturing prisoners. The operation began at 0900 hrs and, within half an hour, the objective had been reached. But then the Australians came under heavy fire from artillery, mortars and machine guns. By 1030 hrs, enemy fire had become intense and the order to withdraw was given. Many enemy troops were trapped in their bunkers and disposed of with bombs. Four bunkers had been destroyed and an unknown, but probably considerable, number of the enemy killed. The Aussie casualties were heavy – three killed and twenty-eight wounded. But, in view of the damage inflicted on the enemy, the action was certainly not a failure, but it failed to achieve its main purpose, which was the capture of a prisoner.

On the night of July 13th, 3 Btn RAR carried out a similar type raid, again at Company strength, and again with the object of capturing a prisoner. But their previous experience was repeated and they were forced to withdraw, without reaching the objective. They again suffered casualties, with one killed, fourteen wounded and one 'missing in action'.

From the experience of enterprises of this kind, in the past few weeks, it was apparent that the Chinese had developed a very efficient defensive fire technique. In the half-dozen raids on this scale, since the middle of June, more than 120 casualties had been suffered, mostly among Canadian and Australian units. It seemed that operations of this sort, which never met with Gen Cassels's approval and had been carried out on direct orders from higher authority, were proving much too costly. This, even when the importance of obtaining prisoners for identification purposes was taken into account. As a result, Gen Cassels ordered the frequency of this type of raid to be reduced and reported his intentions of trying to obtain prisoners by other methods.

The remaining days of July passed without any major incidents. There was much patrolling, a few casualties and one or two probing attacks on a small scale by the Chinese. These activities were of intimate concern to those involved, but the historian must, of necessity, pass by. The last four days of the month was a period of continuous heavy rain. The Imjin River rose thirty-nine feet during the peak period and the high-level bridge known as 'Teal' collapsed and a gap of 280 feet developed. In an effort to save it, tanks were employed on the banks to shoot at the debris that rushed down the swollen river. Another bridge, 'Pintail', narrowly escaped a similar fate. In the Infantry positions, many trenches collapsed and, for a period, the KOSB (28 Bde) were completely cut off by floodwater in the Samichon Valley.

During the night of August 2nd, the Norfolks (29 Bde) fought a successful action. The enemy were tricked into moving onto a small feature, where they were heavily shelled and then rushed by two Platoons of RNR, who had been lying up about 400 yards to the east. A third Platoon had a sharp engagement elsewhere. Six wounded prisoners were captured, but they all died later and, in addition, the bodies of fourteen enemy dead were counted. It is an interesting fact that at least one of these prisoners was only slightly wounded. He received treatment at the RAP, but died later on his way back in an ambulance. There are good reasons for believing that Chinese prisoners sometimes committed suicide. The RNR had three men killed and eighteen wounded, mostly only slightly. The heavy rains ceased on August 1st and the Imjin fell rapidly to normal level. The month was one of routine static warfare, with no very outstanding incidents. On the 9th, the KSLI captured two enemy agents in our minefield. On the night of the 13th, 3 Btn RAR carried out a Company raid, but ran into heavy fire and suffered twenty-five casualties, one man killed, twenty-three wounded and another posted as 'missing'.

On August 4th, 1 Btn KOSB (28 Comm Bde) left for the UK, being relieved by 1 Btn Royal Fusiliers, under Lt Col GR Stevens OBE. During the period August 8th to 10th, 25 Canadian Bde relieved 29 British Bde in the right sector. A patrol of 1 RAR was badly ambushed on the night of the 23rd, with one man killed, nine wounded and two missing. Rain started again on the 24th and continued for three days, causing the Imjin to rise forty-one feet. 'Pintail' high-level bridge was slightly damaged and traffic over it had to be restricted. The bad weather caused many other difficulties and, on the 26th, a small patrol of 3 RAR got into difficulties on the River Samichon and the men were nearly drowned. By the 27th, the rain had ceased once more and both the Imjin and Samichon became nearly normal.

There's nothing like a spot of leave

Many factors combined to make this phase of the Korean war a very difficult one: its now static character with little hope of reviving mobility; the primitive life without proper accommodation; and the Korean weather which, although good at its best, was one of extremes. Extreme cold and snow, excessive rain and flood, heat and high winds, all took their toll. In times of activity and crisis, Commonwealth soldiers are normally at their best but, in the conditions to which the Korean Campaign had degenerated by the summer of 1952, special measures were necessary to maintain spirits and prevent boredom. As has already been mentioned, every man was entitled to at least one period of five full days leave in Japan, during his tour in Korea. To John Dutton's knowledge, those that did not take this leave in Japan said it was a pure case of finance. Some of the troops in Korea were married and their money was left mainly in the UK, for the wives to manage on. Money in a soldier's pay packet was nothing like it is today, even taking other things into comparison. In

Late Summer and Winter July to October 1952

Professional artists including Ted Ray, Carole Carr, Larry Adler, Eve Boswell and Frankie Howard gave many concerts for the entertainment of the troops.

Tokyo, for their R&R, they received free accommodation and services in a rest camp, which was run on the lines of a good hotel. It was said in the Comm Div that, on return from five days in Japan, another twenty-four hours of a different kind of R&R was necessary - *"Rest and Recovery"*!

During the period from the start of July until the end of October 1952, 514 men went on R&R leave. In addition, the Division had its own Rest Centre at a small village by the sea, near Inchon. Men were sent there every few months and it became a very popular relaxation. At this centre, men could sleep in a proper bed, have unlimited baths and bathe or play games, according to the season. The centre was fully winterised. It was run with the minimum of rules by a permanent staff, which included two ladies of the WVS, who acted as hostesses. These two WVS members worked unceasingly in the interests of the centre and their efforts were greatly appreciated by all who went on leave there. The capacity of the camp was up to eight officers and 200 men. *(N.B. It just goes to show that, as earlier mentioned, communication was not the best that it could have been. Until I came to put pen to paper to compile this book, I did not know of that leave camp at Inchon, I had never heard a whisper!)* September opened with a brush by 3 RAR against an enemy party about thirty strong, twenty-one of whom were estimated to have been killed, against one Australian killed and nine wounded. Chinese infantry, supported by a heavy artillery bombardment, attacked a standing patrol of the Canadian 22 Regt. The Canadian patrol withdrew under orders and later, when another patrol went out to investigate, it too came under heavy artillery and mortar fire, suffering eight casualties, of whom four were killed. The Div front was heavily shelled on the afternoon of the 5th and one Centurion tank received a direct hit. Although the tank was not badly damaged, the crew of four was killed. On September 4th, Gen Van Fleet, with the US Legion of Merit, had decorated Maj Gen Cassels and, on September 7th, he relinquished command of the Division. His period of command had been a memorable one. His had been the responsibility for welding the first fully integrated Division in the history of the Commonwealth into a fighting machine. A senior officer from one of the Dominions said, *"If you had searched the whole world over, you could not have found a better man than Jim Cassels"*. Maj Gen West CB DSO succeeded him in command

.The period September 8th to 14th was one of slightly more activity than usual, although on a minor scale. On the afternoon of the 11th, two Sherman tanks of 'B' Sqn, Lord Strathcona's Horse, were hit by enemy artillery. There were no casualties, but one tank was destroyed. On the 12th, a party of one officer and four ORs of the RCR set out to lay up behind enemy lines. They returned sixty hours later with very valuable information. During the night of the 13th, the Div area was heavily shelled, mainly in the left forward sector, held by 28 Comm Bde, and in the rear areas. The Norfolks' RAP, which was in reserve, was hit and a number of shells fell near 60 Indian Fld

Ambulance, as well as in one RA gun area. Casualties were not heavy, however, with one man killed and seven wounded. Later that night, a patrol of 1 RAR ambushed an enemy patrol and captured two prisoners. In the middle of the month, the new Div Cdr held a conference, from which it was decided that troops in the forward areas would always wear steel helmets, and not only during periods of shelling and mortaring. Enemy-held features were to be given code-names and Infantry Brigades would do eight weeks in the line and four in reserve.

On the 11th, 1 Btn Durham Light Infantry (DLI) arrived in the area and started training to relieve 1 Btn KSLI in 28th Comm Bde and, on the 21st, 1 Btn King's Liverpool Regt arrived in relief of 1 Btn RNR in 29th British Bde. On the night of September 23rd, 1 Btn RCR made a very fine 'snatch' of a prisoner from behind the enemy lines. The party went to the same area in which they had concealed themselves a week before. They captured a prisoner at first light and returned with him, although under fire during part of the journey. On the 29th, a patrol of 3 RAR made contact with some forty or fifty of the enemy. Enemy casualties were believed to be heavy, while the Aussies had two men killed and three wounded. It was about this time that the enemy became more aggressive along the whole Eighth Army front, although at first there was no noticeable increase in activity on the front of Comm Div. Attacks at Battalion strength were made in several sectors and resulted in heavy fighting. Among these was an attack against 3 US Div (on the immediate right of Comm Div), in which the Chinese captured a position known as 'Kelly' and also an adjoining outpost called 'Big Nori'.

October 2nd October was a notable date for the Div Artillery, when they fired their millionth round against the enemy since the formation of the Div on July 28th July 1951.

During the night of October 4th, 29 British Bde relieved 28 Comm Bde in the left sector. Another adjustment of the Div front now took place. On October 23rd, the Div received orders to take over the sector of the right Battalion of 1 US Marine Div, west of the River Samichon and to hand over the Battalion sector on the extreme right of the front to ROK Div. These adjustments began on the October 27th, with the sector on the left taken over from the Marines. This position included the vital 'Hook' location, which was to be the scene of much bitter fighting by Commonwealth troops some months later. During the afternoon of the 23rd, 1 RCR, in the area of Pt 355, was heavily shelled and, just before dark, the bombardment became intense. A successful air strike had been directed against a party of about fifty enemies but, at about 1900 hrs, 'B' Coy of the Canadians was heavily attacked. The positions had been almost entirely destroyed by the shelling and the Company was overrun. The reserve Company was immediately ordered to stage a counter-attack and a Company of the Royal Fusiliers, from the reserve Bde, was ordered forward to take the place of the Canadian counter-attack troops. This attack began at 0120 hrs and, by 0330 hrs, the enemy had been driven off and the position reoccupied. The Chinese attack had been at Battalion strength and it was estimated that some 4,000 shells had fallen on the Canadians within twelve hours. Our own Artillery had not been idle, with some 8,000 shells and 4,000 mortar bombs expended in support of the Battalion. Canadian casualties were heavy in this engagement, with fifteen men killed and eighty-two either wounded or missing. This was the fiercest single engagement that had taken place on the Div front for some time.

For the Comm Div, the rest of the month was fairly quiet but, on the night of the 26th, 1 US Marine Div was attacked in strength out on the left. The enemy captured two outpost positions and, for twelve hours, occupied part of the main line of resistance. However, after much heavy fighting, the situation was restored, despite the Marines having heavy casualties. Comm Div's Artillery was able to assist the Marines with a considerable amount of fire. On the 27th, 3 RAR, from 28 Bde in reserve, relieved 1 Welch of 29 Bde in the line. The latter departed for Hong Kong, being relieved by 1 Btn Duke of Wellington's Regt (DWR), who arrived in the area on October 31st. Many changes in the staff appointments had taken place, one of which was the relief of Lt Col HG Good MBE, during the month of September, by Lt Col PG Palmer, in the post of CREME.

The composition of the Brigades forming Comm Div was then:

    25 Canadian Bde:
    1 Btn RCR
    1 Btn PPCLI
    1 Btn Royal 22 Regt
    28 Comm Inf Bde:
    1 Btn Royal Fusiliers
    1 Btn DLI
    1 Btn RAR
    3 Btn RAR
    29 British Infantry Brigade –
    1 Btn King's Regt (Liverpool)
    1 Btn DWR
    1 Btn Black Watch

Summarised, it may be said that the late summer and autumn of 1952 had been a quiet period for the Comm Div.

Something of a stalemate

As has been made clear elsewhere in this narrative, the outstanding development in the Chinese armies in the latter part of 1951 and in 1952 was both the quantity and quality of their artillery. They had many guns, with plenty of ammunition, and their shooting was good. Moreover, they had a very good warning system, which ensured the prompt opening of fire, and they were not afraid to bring down fire close to, or even on, their own troops. In the first months of Comm Div's existence, their patrols dominated 'No Man's Land' and their artillery was overwhelmingly superior to that of the Chinese in quantity and technique, as well as in the amount of ammunition available. But this was no longer the case by the end of 1951, with the result that the operations had to be very cunningly contrived, and well supported, if they were to be successful. The number of unsuccessful, or only partially successful, raids carried out by Commonwealth troops, and the considerable casualties suffered, are the measure of the toughness and skill of the Chinese soldiers in Korea in 1952. The enemy also used mortars in considerable numbers. Indeed much of the fire, which was loosely termed 'shell fire', came from mortars.

The enemy did not use wireless or line communications to the same extent as UN troops. Their control of artillery and mortar fire, particularly defensive fire, was normally by signal, in the form of coloured flares, tracer ammunition, and noise signals. This somewhat crude system was, however, very effective. The other main characteristic of the enemy, which has been mentioned earlier, was his remarkable capacity for digging. All their position had deep and well-made bunkers. When his positions were overrun, he preferred to remain in these and risk being killed underground by bomb or explosive, rather than come out and surrender. POWs were very difficult to take. Between July 1st and October 31st 1952, Comm Div captured only twelve, despite the many raids, patrols and ambushes carried out. Desertion was amongst the CCF was very rare. During the last few days of October, there were the inevitable signs of the approaching winter and the temperature fell to 25 degrees by night.

Chapter 33

The winter of November 1952 to March 1953

Before continuing the story of the Commonwealth Division, it will be as well to remind the reader of the support that the Land Forces received, throughout the Campaign, from Commonwealth Naval and Air Forces and from those of other UN allies.

During the winter of 1951 - 52 and until the end of hostilities, operations conducted by Commonwealth Navies included measures for the security of the many islands fringing the west coast and in the river estuaries. The air support given to the Division was, of course, more intimate than that of the naval type and the soldiers had less difficulty in appreciating the part played by airmen, both in the general pattern of operations and on their own front in particular. Comm Div had its own airstrip, while Commonwealth and American airmen on the ground, as well as planes in the air, were seen very frequently.

The air support given to the Army consisted of:

(a) The bombing of enemy rear areas
(b) The engagement of enemy aircraft
(c) Close support in the form of air strikes
(d) Reconnaissance

All these tasks were carried out by the American Fifth Air Force, which included under its command 77 Sqn Royal Australian Air Force (RAAF) and 2 Sqn South African Air Force (SAAF) .By means of skilful concealment and unremitting digging, the Chinese mitigated the effects of rear-area bombing to a considerable extent. This was apt to give the impression that this type of air action was ineffective in Korea, a natural but wrong impression. The bombing of the Chinese rear areas, with its consequent dislocation of communications and diversion of effort in repairs, digging and concealment, was a major factor in balancing the mass armies of the enemy against those of the much weaker UN. Mention must be made of the 1903rd Independent Air OP Flight, under command of Maj JMH Hailes, which performed a fine service on the Div Front. On November 2nd, Mr Erasmus, the South African Minister of Defence, visited Comm Div and witnessed an air strike by aircraft of 2 Sqn SAAF. On the same day, 1 RAR relieved 1 RCR in the line, thus completing the relief of 25 Canadian Bde by 28 Comm Bde. On the 3rd, 3 Btn PPCLI relieved 1 Btn RCR, which then returned to Canada.

Action on 'The Hook'

On November 4th, a standing patrol of 1 Btn Black Watch, in front of what was known as 'The Hook' position, on the left of the Div front, was rushed by some forty of the enemy. The patrol lost one officer and five ORs killed, six ORs wounded and two missing. Only three men escaped. Another patrol, sent out later, was able to collect the dead and wounded. The Hook position was to play a prominent part in the fighting until the end of hostilities. (See Sketch Map.) On the night of the 16th, 1 Btn DWR went into the line for the first time, in relief of 3 RAR of 28 Comm Bde. On about the 16th, the enemy began to shell The Hook, held by the Black Watch, with increasing tempo and, on the night of the 18th, made a determined assault on the position. The action started at 1900 hours, when a Black Watch patrol of one officer and ten men found itself surrounded by Chinese on a spur running northeast from The Hook. 'A' Coy was attacked in Company strength from three different directions at about 2100 hrs, the enemy advancing with, or even in front of, his own artillery and mortar fire. From this time onwards, the Div Artillery, plus that of the American 1 Marine Div on the left, fired almost continuously throughout the night in support of the defenders of The Hook. As was common practice, some US Artillery units were operating with the Div Artillery on this occasion, greatly increasing the firepower. The American gunners were always very highly trained and they and Commonwealth artillerymen worked together in complete harmony.

At about 2150 hrs, the Platoon on the western end of the feature went to ground and 'called down defensive fire' on its own positions. By 2250 hrs, 3 Btn PPCLI had been alerted and 'B' Coy of the Battalion had relieved 'B' Coy of the Black Watch, which was preparing to counter-attack. The Hook was reported clear of enemy by 2200 hrs but, soon afterwards, heavy shelling began again. The enemy attacked again at 0030 hrs and succeeded in getting a footing on the position. A deliberate counter-attack, supported by a heavy artillery bombardment and one tank, was launched at 0130 hrs, but the tank was soon put out of action by an enemy rocket launcher. The counter-attack made good progress however and, after a pause, another was launched which got farther forward. The rest of the night was occupied with hard and confused fighting, but the Black Watch held firm. They were engaged in 'mopping up' by 0430 hrs, with a few remaining enemy parties left on the position but, by 0630 hrs, the enemy had withdrawn. 'C' Coy PPCLI relieved 'A' Coy Black Watch at about 0615 hrs and, by this time, all casualties had been evacuated. It was estimated that the enemy had employed one battalion in this action and more than a hundred of his dead were actually counted. The Black Watch casualties were; five officers wounded and one missing; twelve ORs killed, sixty-seven wounded and twenty missing. Supporting units, between them, suffered one man killed, five wounded and another four missing.

Only minor clashes occurred during the remainder of the month. The Royal Fusiliers made a night raid on Pt 133 and killed fifteen of the enemy, with a loss of thirteen wounded and three missing. On the night of November 25th, two small raids were put in, 'Pimlico' by the Royal Fusiliers and 'Beat up' by 1 RAR, but neither raid was very successful. The Fusiliers were ambushed soon after leaving their own lines and had heavy casualties, fourteen killed, twenty wounded and eight missing, while the Aussies had four wounded. During these raids, the enemy put down very heavy defensive fire.

On the morning of the 26th, the Div Cdr attended a ceremony at the gun positions of the 16 NZ Fld Regt, when it fired its 500,000[th] round against the enemy in Korea. Maj Gen West fired the gun, which was directed on a target selected by Brig TJ Daly, Commander of 28 Comm Bde.

A new Divisional layout

On November 29th, the re-deployment of the Division on a new 'layout' began. It was now proposed to have all three Brigades up, each with two Battalions in the front line and one (two in 28 Bde) in reserve. It was considered that this gave better control by Bde Cdrs, with their own reserve for counter-attack. Reliefs could be carried out at their own convenience and each Brigade had a complete sector in depth, instead of only a front line.

This re-deployment was completed on the night of December 1st, with:
    Left: 25 Canadian Bde
    Centre: 29 British Bde
    Right: 28 Comm Bde

On December 1st, Brig DA Kendrew CBE DSO relieved Brig AHG Ricketts CBE DSO, in command of 29 Bde. *(N.B. In WWII, Brig Kendrew was awarded the DSO in Africa and two bars in Italy. Later, he earned the unusual distinction of a third bar for services in Korea.)* By this time, winter had set in, it was extremely cold and the first heavy snow was falling. On December 4th, Gen Eisenhower, then President-elect of the USA, visited the Division, accompanied by Gen Omar Bradley. The veteran General was received by a guard of honour, composed of the men of all Commonwealth countries represented in the Division, and later he met Component Commanders. He stayed for about forty-five minutes.

RAOC Stores Section Vehicles.

On the 11th, 'Operation Fauna' was carried out by one Company, less one Platoon, of the 1 RAR. Several enemy trenches were destroyed and between ten and twenty Chinese killed. But the price of success was heavy, with one officer and one OR killed, eighteen men wounded and two missing in action. This was also a day of great air activity, as seventy-nine UN aircraft attacked Chinese supply areas opposite the Divisional front. The two weeks before Christmas was a quiet period but, as Christmas Day approached, the Chinese engaged in intensive propaganda by means of broadcasts, banners, leaflets and 'Christmas presents'. Except for three minor patrol clashes, Christmas Day was quiet and, as far as circumstances permitted, Commonwealth troops spent it in the traditional manner with the best of fare. During that December, 1 RTR relieved 5 RIDG. The New Year period that followed was also quiet, although in the second week in January there was a noticeable increase in enemy shelling and mortaring. The early days of January were to prove also unusually fine and warm for the time of the year.

During the early morning of December 14th, a patrol of 3 RAR had a sharp encounter with an unknown number of the enemy on the northern slope of Pt 227. Later, under cover of artillery fire and smoke, another patrol went out to recover some of the wounded Australians. The enemy reacted strongly to this and fired some 700 mortar bombs on to Pt 355. Australian casualties were one killed, five wounded and a further two missing.

On the 16th, orders were received that Comm Div would be relieved in the line at the end of the month, by the American 2 Div, and go into 1 Corps reserve some ten to twelve miles to the south. Preparations for this relief began at once. On the 23rd, a patrol of 3 RAR, moving north-west from Pt 355, engaged a party of Chinese, killing two and wounding one, without casualties to themselves. On the same night, a party of 1 RCR entered an enemy-held position and blew up some caves. On the 24th, a party of two officers and fifteen men of the DWR, after very careful planning and rehearsal, carried out a raid against an enemy held feature known as 'Anthony'. The approach began under cover of artillery, mortar and tank fire at 0800 hrs and, as had been hoped, with the rising sun dazzling the enemy's vision. This movement, which included a carefully thought out deception plan, took the enemy by surprise and his reactions were slow and confused. Several of the enemy were killed and one body brought back for identification purposes. An enemy tunnel was also blown up. This was a very successful enterprise and the patrol did not have any casualties.

On the night of January 24th 1953, 'A' Coy, 3 Btn RAR, carried out operations to the northwest of Pt 355, which led to very desperate fighting. The object was to 'snatch' a prisoner by guile and, for this purpose, the raiders were split up into three parties, a 'snatch' group of one Sergeant and four men, and two protective groups each thirteen strong. The enterprise was not successful in capturing a prisoner, as the alarm was given and the snatch party was forced to kill two sentries who might otherwise have been captured. The Chinese then started to attack one of the protective groups in strength. During the course of the action, a party of Australians ambushed twenty Chinese at very close range and killed them all. The whole party was eventually extricated, due mainly to the aggressive attitude of the Aussies, who charged and routed parties of the enemy on several occasions. The action demonstrated the importance of meticulous rehearsal and briefing, and the manner in which a desperate situation can be restored by well-judged offensive action. The Aussies suffered about thirteen casualties, while it was estimated that at least ninety of the enemy were killed. On the 27th, various adjustments in the Div layout began, with the object of facilitating the impending relief by American troops. The relief itself began on the 29th and was completed by the 31st. And so Comm Div (less its Artillery, still supporting ROK troops) withdrew from contact with the enemy for the first time since its formation, almost exactly eighteen months before. It was to enjoy two months' rest and a welcome period in training.

Patrols and ambushes

It is as well at this stage to depart from the narrative to consider two matters of a general character. It will have been apparent that the main activity during the past few months had been patrolling and ambushes, with the main aim of dominating 'No Man's Land', but also with the object of securing prisoners. It is the measure of the difficulties that our troops faced that, in spite of their undoubtedly high standard and the number of patrols sent out, not a single wounded prisoner had been captured during the three months since October 1952. The price of these activities was also heavy. As an example, the following casualty figures, for the period June 1st to November 12th 1952, are given: Officers: Killed thirteen, wounded forty-five, missing three. Other ranks: Killed 178, wounded 758, missing thirty-six. A high proportion of these casualties occurred on patrol. This was a heavy price to pay but, by dominating 'No Man's Land', Commonwealth troops avoided being surprised and, in the long run, this policy undoubtedly saved lives. A very satisfactory aspect of the casualty figures was the small proportion classified as missing.

It is necessary to emphasise that, as a general rule in describing patrol activities, only those patrols that made contact with the enemy have been mentioned. By the fortunes of war, some

Accomodation not quite of the Hilton standard!

units made contact more frequently than others. It would be quite wrong, however, to think that those units who were not engaged, and are in consequence not mentioned in the narrative, were less active than others. All infantry units patrolled very actively, whenever the circumstances were made available.

The 'Katcoms' are introduced

Earlier in this narrative, the proposal had been made to attach SKA soldiers to the Division in a fighting role, as distinct from those that had been employed for some time in merely a labouring capacity. This policy was finally implemented during the early winter of 1952 - 53, when 1,000 'Katcoms' (Koreans attached Comm Div) arrived. Gen West records that, upon inspecting them, he was very impressed by their smart appearance. The policy was that the Koreans should be integrated in sub-units of the Division, the usual practice being to include two 'Katcoms' in a section, where they lived, fought, paraded and fed with Commonwealth members of that section. As a British infantry soldier is reputed to have said, *"Our section is commanded by Sgt Smith, who has under him, Jones, Robinson, 'Daisy' Bell, Brown, Ferguson, Wu and Wong"*. Not perhaps an entirely accurate quotation, but it gives the idea! This system, that was in nature of an experiment, proved very successful. Katcoms were clothed, equipped and armed (on loan) by the Commonwealth countries to whose units they were attached. All other expenses, including pay, were the responsibility of the Government of the ROK.

On February 9th 1953, Gen Van Fleet visited the Division to say good-bye and to introduce his successor in command of Eighth Army, Gen Maxwell Taylor. During the second week in March, 74 (Battleaxe Coy) Medium Bty RA (under Maj AJ Batten DCM) joined the Div from Hong Kong and moved up to join the rest in support of 2 American Div. At this late stage in the Campaign, the reintroduction of the 155mm artillery gave EME branch a problem. The author uses the term 'reintroduction' advisedly, as he was reliably informed that this calibre of gun was used in very early days in Korea, but then withdrawn because the roads were just not wide enough to carry it. As the weapon was withdrawn, after a while, the Workshop that serviced it also back-loaded its tools and spares. This in itself was a minor problem, but the ammunition that came initially with the guns to Korea, was 'Super'. In a nutshell, this meant that either the gun was put well forward and fired almost vertically, or brought back to the 'B' echelon areas and fired a long distance indirectly. Either way, the strain put on the recoil system with this type of ammunition was causing excessive damage to the recuperator glands, for which no spares were immediately available. Let it be said that the 'usual ingenuity' prevailed and the guns were kept in the field.

On March 21st, 2 Btn RAR relieved 1 Btn RAR and, on the 25th, 3 Btn RCR relieved 1 Btn of the same Regiment. On the 26th, Brig TJ Daly DSO OBE relinquished command of 28 Comm Bde and was succeeded by Brig JGN Wilton DSO OBE (Australian Army). Heavy rain fell during the last ten days of March, being much heavier than was normal for the time of year. This caused road conditions to become very bad and training was considerably curtailed.

Comm Div was due to return early in April, to the same sector of the front that it had previously held and, by the end of March, preparations were afoot to relieve the American 2 Div. During the period in reserve, Commanders and Staffs had, of course, kept in close touch with operational matters. The most important development since January had been a change of attack method by the Chinese. Previously they had relied on a great weight of artillery and mortar support but, recently, they had put in several silent attacks, mostly by night, with the object of avoiding the defenders' defensive fire.

Chapter 34

The last phase

Spring and summer April to July 1953

The period from April 1st to 5th was devoted to preparations for 'Operation Cotswold', the relief of the American 2 Div in the line by Comm Div. The preliminary moves began on the 6th in fine weather. On April 8th at 0800 hrs, HQ Comm Div assumed control of the sector and, by the night of the 8th, the relief had been completed. Comm Div was now disposed on its old front as follows:
    Left: 29 British Bde
    Centre: 25 Canadian Bde
    Right: 28 Comm Bde

Meanwhile, the 'Cease-fire' talks that had been going on since July 1951, after repeated vicissitudes, had reached a stage where one of the main disagreements was about the conditions for the release of prisoners. However, by the middle of April, arrangements for the repatriation of some sick and wounded prisoners had been made. On April 20th, Maj Gen West went to Munsan-Ni, where the prisoners were to be handed over, to see the first arrivals. One officer, a South African, and thirty-nine ORs of Commonwealth Forces were handed over between April 20th and 25th.

The period up to the end of the month was a quiet one, but on the night of April 23rd, the Black Watch captured a prisoner, the first since October 1952. On the same night, two patrols of 3 PPCLI became involved with the enemy. Four Chinese were killed, the Canadian losses being two men wounded and one missing. April 25th was 'ANZAC Day'. Between April 26th and May 2nd, there was an increase in enemy shelling and some patrol activity. On the 26th, a patrol of the DLI fought its way out of an ambush in front of Pt 355. Nine enemy dead were counted, against a loss of one killed and three wounded. On the night of 29th, the Royal Fusiliers had a sharp patrol action north of Pt 159. Enemy casualties were not known, but the patrol had one officer and one OR killed, three ORs wounded and two missing.

On the night of May 2nd, the enemy raided part of the position held by 3 RCR. The action began at 2230 hrs, when a party of Chinese just outside their position engaged a Canadian patrol of one officer and fourteen men. The patrol suffered heavy casualties and withdrew, but soon after sent out a second patrol. At midnight, heavy enemy shelling and mortaring began on the position held by the right forward Company and, at 0500 hrs, a strong enemy party rushed and overran the forward Platoon. The Platoon commander, and a few others who remained hidden in bunkers, reported the situation by wireless and, at 0015 hrs, called for artillery fire to be directed onto the position. This proved very effective and at 0130 hrs the enemy withdrew, spending the rest of the night attempting to recover his dead and wounded. There were good reasons for believing that the heavy defensive fire prevented a similar raid against the Royal Fusiliers on a feature just to the northeast. The Canadian casualties were heavy, sixteen killed, thirty-two wounded and sixteen missing. In addition, two Katcoms were wounded and four went missing. Enemy artillery and mortar fire was estimated at 2,000 rounds and, in reply, the Div Artillery fired about 8,000 rounds.

The period May 4th to 7th was quieter but, on the night of the 4th, the DLI engaged an enemy patrol in front of Pt 355. They had seven of their own men wounded, but killed at least a dozen of the enemy. On the same night, 2 RAR went into the line for the first time, in relief of the Royal Fusiliers in the Pt 159 area. At about 0600 hrs on May 7th, an *Auster* aircraft of No.1913 Light

The Forgotten Punch in the Army's Fist — Korea 1950-1953

Liaison Flight was shot down over enemy-held territory northeast of The Hook position. The pilot, Sgt Cameron, and his observer escaped by parachute and were captured. This observer was Cfn W Duffy REME, who had just left 10 Inf Wksp on posting. On that same night, the enemy, in Company strength, probed The Hook position, being held by a Company of the Black Watch. The enemy were first seen at 0150 hrs and, at 0300 hrs, a party of about twenty attacked, but were driven back. At 0350 hrs, the Black Watch sent out a patrol at Platoon strength. They soon encountered the enemy and a sharp firefight ensued. When, on orders, the patrol withdrew, it brought back three wounded prisoners. Two other patrols sent out sighted parties of Chinese, but no action resulted. The Highlanders' casualties were two officers and three ORs killed, with one officer, eight ORs and one wounded, from the Katcoms.

The Turkish Bde was now on the left of the Div and, on the night of May 15th, was heavily attacked. The Div Artillery and the mortars of the DWR were able to give the Turks considerable support and the attack was repulsed. In the middle of that month, a lot of enemy vehicle movement was seen some 6,000 to 7,000 yards north of The Hook, and was engaged by the Div Artillery. At about the same time, this was reinforced by the movement into the area of an American Battery, with two guns of 240mm. 'Howitzers, Atomic Cannons' was the description the *"Stars and Stripes"* gave to them. During the period May 18th to 29th, it became apparent that the enemy was building up his strength in front of 29 Bde and an enemy deserter, who surrendered on the 18th, stated that an early attack on The Hook was planned. Several probing attacks, with increasing artillery and mortar fire, were directed against this feature. Counter-measures to meet an attack in this area were taken, which included harassing fire by the RA, including 1 Corps Artillery, which fired 5,000 rounds in one night and twenty-four air strikes on 102 sorties – dropping a total of 129 tons of bombs. The Black Watch were also moved to The Hook area to strengthen the defences, while the Royal Fusiliers moved to the reserve position vacated by the Black Watch.

Syngman Rhee, president of Korea from its declaration in 1948 until student riots caused his downfall in 1960. Rhee had lived in the United States and was championed by them to lead South Korea when it became clear the north would remain in communist hands. Rhee has the unique distinction of being disliked by almost everyone. The Americans considered more than once removing him, while for many Koreans today he presided over a backward and subsverient country.

On May 21st, President of the ROK, Syngman Rhee, visited the Division and presented Maj Gen West with the flag of his country. On the 25th, 1 King's carried out a raid, which was intended to be a diversion for activities in The Hook area. The raiders had several men killed and wounded by a mine *en-route,* but reached the objective, where they killed some Chinese and blew up several bunkers. The next day, 2 RAR had a sharp clash with the enemy about Pt 159. The enemy fired over 500 mortar bombs into the left Company position. Casualties were four killed, fifteen wounded and two missing.

By the 27th, there were signs that the expected attack on The Hook was imminent and that it would be on a bigger scale than any which had taken place for some time. Further measures were taken to strengthen the position, including an additional Battalion in the front line. When these measures were completed, 1 Btn DWR was on the left, holding The Hook itself, and 1 Btn King's Regt held the right sector of the area. *(N.B. It should be noted that The Hook was only a small feature in the general area of the engagement.)*

Shelling and mortaring increased in tempo until, at 1953 hrs on May 28th, it became intense; some eyewitnesses consider it to have been the heaviest enemy bombardment in the Korean War. The first wave of Chinese infantry advanced soon after against 'D' Coy, throwing grenades and 'satchel' charges into the positions. Gradually the defenders were forced to withdraw into their tunnels. By this time, the Divisional and Corps Artillery were bringing down the full weight of their fire on prearranged targets. There is little doubt that this decimated the second and third attacking waves. At 2045 hrs, a second attack was launched against the right Platoon of the forward Company on The Hook. This attack, although badly mauled, succeeded in getting into the position; but the situation was restored when men from another Platoon reinforced them.

At about 2200 hrs, two enemy Companies formed up to assault the left Company (B), but they were caught by artillery fire and the attack, when put in, was very half-hearted. An hour later, enemy shelling increased on Pt 146, which was being held by a Company of 1 King's. In the glare of searchlights, large numbers of Chinese were seen forming up to attack, but were dispersed by artillery fire. Later it was discovered that this attack was in Battalion strength and that the enemy had suffered very heavy casualties. The final attack against The Hook came at 0030 hrs and was beaten off. By 0430 hrs, The Hook position – and all other Commonwealth positions in the vicinity – were reported clear of the enemy. An engineer reconnaissance carried out at once disclosed that all main bunkers had been damaged and many trenches, some eight feet deep, had been 'levelled'.

This attack, by two enemy Brigades, had been prepared over a long period and ended in failure. Over 100 enemy dead were counted on or near The Hook, while another seventy were seen in enemy-held territory. It was estimated that the enemy had lost 250 men killed and 800 wounded. Commonwealth casualties were:

    Officers … …   Three killed and two wounded
    Other Ranks …   Twenty killed, 103 wounded and twenty missing

Of this total of 148 casualties, 126 were suffered by The DWR, who fought with the greatest tenacity throughout the night. Incoming shells and mortar bombs were estimated at 1,000 by day on May 28th and 10,000 over the following night. The Comm Div Artillery fired over 32,000 and 1 Corps Artillery nearly 6,000 rounds.

Thus ended the battle of The Hook, the last sizeable engagement fought by Comm Div in the Korea war. Nevertheless, the next two months saw bitter fighting along the whole UN front, which increased in severity as the date for Armistice approached. On the afternoon of May 29th, the Royal Fusiliers relieved the Duke's on The Hook position. Enemy mortaring on the following day considerably hindered repair work on the defences, making it difficult to establish some of the standing patrols. On May 31st, twenty-six air strikes dropped 297.5 tons of bombs behind the front of the enemy facing Comm Div, which was a record for one day's air operations. The day of Her Majesty's Coronation, June 2nd 1953, was celebrated in fitting style. *(On this day, the author also had a little celebration, as it was the day he landed in Kure, Japan, en-route for the UK at the end of his 18 months in Korea.)* Div Artillery fired concentrations of red, white and blue smoke and, at 1000 hrs, the front line tanks fired one round each.

During the first week of June, many air strikes were carried out behind the enemy facing The Hook. On the 5th, a raiding party of 1 King's blew up some enemy caves, but unfortunately ran into a minefield and had two men killed and fifteen wounded. The rest of June was an exceptionally quiet period, there being no activities other than some light shelling and mortaring and a few minor patrol clashes. On July 1st, 25 Canadian Bde celebrated 'Canada Day'.

On the 9th, 'Operation Emperor' began, with the object of re-deploying the Division as follows:

	Left:	28 Comm Bde
	Centre:	29 British Bde
	Right:	25 Canadian Bde

On the same day, 1 Btn Black Watch left for Kenya and were relieved in 29 Bde by 1 Btn Royal Scots. 'Operation Emperor' was completed on July 12th. On that day, as a temporary measure, two Companies of 3 Btn 22' Regt took over two positions from 1 ROK Div on the right, in order to assist them to meet expected attack on their outpost.

The night of July 14th was one of heavy rain. A lot of damage was done to the roads, while the low-level bridge over the Imjin was submerged when the river rose rapidly and the vehicle ferry was put out of action. On the night of July 18th, a patrol of 3 RCR was surrounded and wiped out by a strong Chinese patrol. The American 1 Marine Div, which had now returned to the front line on the left, was attacked in strength on the night of July 24th. The area of assault included Pt 111 on the immediate flank of 28 Bde. Div Artillery fired 13,000 rounds in support of the Marines. 2 Btn RAR, along with some tanks, was also engaged. Over 4,000 enemy mortar bombs fell in the Div area that night, mostly on The Hook. The attacks on the Marines were repeated on July 26th and again tanks, artillery and the Aussies gave support. This, the last engagement of the war, was also one of the most desperate.

The long awaited cease-fire

Following a very quiet night, the truce was finally signed at Panmunjon at 1000 hrs on July 27th 1953 and hostilities ceased at 2200 hrs. The casualties in the Division since it had returned to the line early in April were as follows:

	Killed	Wounded	Missing	Totals
Officers	10	42	5	57
Other Ranks	130	671	74	875
Katcom	10	84	9	103
Total				1,035

And so the fighting in Korea ended, a full three years and one month after hostilities began. It had been two years and eleven months from the time that the first Commonwealth Troops had landed at Pusan and two years, all but a day, after the formation of the First Commonwealth Division.

Chapter 35

5 Medium Workshop REME in early 1951

(N.B. This chapter has been purposely left until near the end, as the Workshop in question, although on arrival in theatre went into Korea, had been a Base Workshop for most of its time. Its original establishment would have qualified for the British Korean Medal as well as the first issued UN medal but, once it left the shores of Korea, it qualified for the UN medal alone. Capt Victor Moore had come to Korea with 5 Med Wksp REME, but it was found that a Workshop of that size was not practical in a war zone with a fast moving front line. So early in 1951 it was withdrawn to Kure in Japan. John Sutton's knowledge of this Workshop amounts to two visits only, he was never on their strength, so he leaves the tale to a person that did. At the end of Chapter 30, Joe Adey had elected for rotation to Japan, changing with his opposite number there. As most personnel who rotated took this route, let us start as they did - in their unit lines.)

Joe Adey in Japan

Joe had to travel down to Pusan by train to catch the ship to Kure, Japan. Most of the troops on the train were American, with a small number of Commonwealth lads in one compartment. Apparently there were still a small number of North Koreans operating as guerrillas in the hills between Seoul and Pusan, so all the American troops carried arms. In the space at the end of each carriage was a box of ammunition for use in the event of attack but, as the Americans used a different size of ammunition, Joe guessed it was thought pointless for us to carry arms!

At Pusan, the Workshop boarded a grotty little troopship and set off on the overnight trip to Kure. While on board, they heard a rumour that there was some sort of a hunt going on for drugs. At that time, there was quite a lot of drug smuggling going on between Japan and Korea, mainly by and for the American Negro troops. It was said that the authorities knew that drugs had been put on board when the ship left Japan and that they had not gone ashore in Pusan. Consequently, when they tied up at Kure, it took hours to disembark, as the powers-that-be wanted to prevent the drugs from being taken ashore again. Every man had to pass through a large customs shed, where dozens of Japanese customs officers were paired off with MPs. They had to show every item that they were carrying and the police went through these with a fine toothcomb, even squeezing out toothpaste and tasting any pain-killing tablets that were being carried.

5 Med Wksp was located in a suburb of Kure called Hiro and not far from the JRBD. The Workshop NCOs shared a Mess with an Australian Ordnance unit and most of the Aussies had already been in Japan for about six years. The Mess accommodation was very plush but the best thing of all was the running hot water! That first evening, Joe sank a few beers with a big Aussie while he was filled in on the local situation. Then he went upstairs to his room, undressed and went into the showers. He turned on the hot water, sat on the floor and went to sleep for three hours. Joe says he can still feel that lovely hot water pouring over him to this day. He shared a room with an Aussie SSgt who was rarely ever there, as he lived out with his Japanese girl friend.

The bulk of work carried out at Hiro was the repair of Centurion tanks and other vehicles sent back from Korea. A lot of local Japanese labour was employed, but it was Joe's job to repair the tank guns and set up their sighting systems. A couple of other NCOs from 16 Inf Wksp had been posted back to Kure, so he was not among total strangers. Kure seemed to be based around one long street, the 'Nakadori', which started down by the docks and ended up at the top end in a park that contained a very old Bonsai Garden. Some of the Bonsai trees were hundreds of years old and were wonderfully shaped. Beyond the park was Ju San Chomi (13th Street), which was the Yoshiwara - or regulated brothel - area. This was very pretty looking, especially at night. It was composed of wooden bungalows with long front verandas and each with a small lawn in front. At night, the verandas would be decorated with coloured paper lanterns and the girls with their pretty kimonos. It was a pleasant evening out, just to walk round the area in the evening and to sit and talk to the girls while enjoying a cool beer. The police and medical authorities tightly controlled the area and strongly advised the Commonwealth troops to use these facilities, rather than become involved with bar hostesses from the beer-halls on the Nakadori.

There was a REME Occupation Workshop down at the edge of the harbour opposite the docks and, soon after Joe's arrival at Hiro, it was decided to amalgamate the RAEME Wksp with 5 Med Wksp and form an Advanced Base Wksp. In the re-organisation, Joe moved down to the harbour-side location, where they were given space to set up a Gun Shop. A Canadian WO2 (Guns) was posted in as his boss, together with a young REME L/Cpl. from the UK. They had about twelve Japanese who were supposed to be fitters, as well as four labourers. As soon as they had 'set up shop', they received twelve NZ 25- pdrs that had recently been condemned in Korea and set about a complete re-build of them.

The situation between the British, Aussies and Canadians inclined to be rather strained at times. The Aussies had mostly been in Japan for six years and almost all of them, including the officers, had permanent girl friends and, in many cases, children. They all 'lived out' in the town and came into work every morning, just like the Japanese civilians. The Aussie idea of discipline was much more easy going than either the British or Canadian and the idea of officers and men all living out with the Japanese really upset some of the Canadians. The British tended to shrug and take things as they came and some even tried the living out bit for themselves. But most found that being tied down to what was virtually 'married life' was not for them. In one corner of the Mess was a small store that opened only on pay day, for the sale of western type foods, such as butter, sugar and bacon. The Aussies used to fill their bags with goods each week and take it *"home to the missus"*.

Of course the British and Canadians tended to look at things only in the short term, as they were all on 18-month tours. The other thing that rankled a bit was the discrepancy in pay between the two Commonwealth forces and the British. Joe Adey had an Aussie Corporal working for him who was paid almost exactly double the amount that he (Joe) was getting as a SSgt. They had only a couple of Canadians, one of whom was his boss, working in the Comm Wksp, the rest were either Australian or British, plus several hundred Japanese. The Workshop accommodation consisted of two-storey barrack blocks, some of which were divided up into two-man rooms or bunks. Joe shared a room with an Aussie SSgt, who was in charge of all the civilian labour employed in the Workshops. He originated from Yorkshire and had immigrated to Australia before WWII. Each room had a house-girl to do the cleaning and laundry and theirs was a widow of about thirty-two years of age, although she looked much older. She had a pretty easy time, as Joe's forty-year-old roommate 'lived out' with a twenty-one-year-old Japanese girl, so they did not see much of him. Joe learned quite a lot of Japanese language from their house-girl during the lunch hours, when she would sit cross-legged on the Aussie's bed, sewing or darning socks.

The Sergeants' Mess employed about a dozen Japanese girls as waitresses and they were a nice bunch. At this stage of his life, Joe could still be made to blush easily, so the girls named him 'Tomato-San'. He had a lot of good fun with them and one evening they decided to take him to the Japanese theatre in town. The Nakadori was about a half mile of beer halls, on both sides of

5 Medium Workshop REME in early 1951

the street, except for the old buildings like the theatre and Joe had become curious about the form Japanese theatre took. Three of the girls met him one evening and took him along to the show. They paid his entrance fee of a few Yen and went upstairs to a small balcony with a bare wooden floor, where they sat cross-legged on the boards for the whole show. Most of the show seemed to consist of the enactment of ancient fables, with a sexual connotation, plus the odd interlude where a 'dolly-bird' would whirl tassels around from her breasts! The girls had fun and indulged in a lot of giggling as they explained what was going on.

Over the winter months, they had a little snow and the men were glad when the warmer weather arrived and they could play tennis and go swimming. They had two tennis courts right outside the Mess, fitted with floodlights, so in the very hot weather they could play late in the evenings, helped along with a couple of cool pints of *Asahi* beer. The Mess owned a couple of forty-foot motor launches and, on some Sundays, a bunch of them would load up the boat with food and beer for a day out on the inland sea. They would cruise among the small islands and stop off at a beach for a few hours or belt along at a tidy few knots, taking it in turns to leap into the sea. To Joe, it was a strange feeling bobbing about in the water like a cork with so much water under him, waiting to be picked up again.

Most of the Aussies owned ex-army Jeeps or motorcycles and they often used to go out with a big ginger-haired fellow named 'Bluey' Phillips, who owned a Jeep and a motorbike. Although he lived out, he would sometimes take three or four of them to Hiroshima for a weekend. Hiroshima was eighteen miles away along the coast and was beginning to recover from the devastation of the atomic bomb attack that ended WWII. They were officially only allowed into Hiroshima if they had a weekend pass to stay at the official leave centre, but the Aussies took no notice of the rules. The only MPs in Hiroshima were American and Aussie and they did not ask questions as long as the troops were behaving themselves. The Workshop lads used to stay at the same place each time they went to Hiroshima, Joe cannot recall the name of the place but it was a hotel-cum-nightclub with some very nice hostesses!

In the late spring of 1952, large drafts of replacement REME personnel arrived in the Workshops, most of whom worked up at what was now the 'Hiro Detachment'. Some of these replacements, together with some of the recent arrivals in the JRBD, were picked up by the multi-national police patrols in Kure for various offences. These patrols were made up of MPs, one each of British, Canadian, Australian and a Japanese civil policeman, riding around in Jeeps. As a result of the problems in the town, all troops were put under a curfew whereby they all had to be in camp by midnight. Joe's buddy at the time was an Australian, an ASM Instruments, by the name of Jim Wylie. Jim was a very little chap who spent his time half with his girlfriend and half living in camp and whooping it up with the lads. During the period when the curfew was imposed, Jim would sometimes take Joe out just for the hell of it. After drinking in the Mess for a couple of hours, they would go across to their barrack block to get their belts and berets. Joe's room was on the ground floor and Jim's was on the first floor. Jim owned a pretty little chromium-plated *Colt* .32 Automatic, which he liked to carry if he was going out late at night. Joe used to wait for him at the bottom of the stairs, take the gun from him and hide it in the fuse box behind the main door, where it remained until they got back from their jaunt.

They would slip out of the main gate just before midnight and slip in through the rear gate at 6am, when it was opened to admit the civilian workers. With Jim's knowledge of the back alleys of Kure, they could dodge the police patrols all night. Once in the rear gate, it was a mad dash to their rooms to slip on pyjama trousers, slippers and a greatcoat and then fall in on the square for the 0630 hrs roll call. The curfew became such a farce that it was dropped after only a couple of months.

The Commonwealth forces had a Battle Indoctrination training area at a place called Hura Mura, up in the hills about fifteen miles from Kure. Joe was once ordered to go up there to examine the gun of a Cromwell tank and, in particular, the sighting system. Apparently a live round from this tank had landed on a Japanese village just outside the training area and an investigation was going on. That was the first and last time that Joe saw 'Field Punishment' being carried out. There was only one prisoner and his accommodation was a camp bed inside a small barbed-wire cage, about 20 x 20 feet. A wooden shed with, only two sides and a roof over the bed, was the only cover. The cage was located out in open ground on the training area and, on the day that Joe was there, it was a cold wet day in March. Outside the cage was a small patch of green grass, roughly a yard square, surrounded by mud. The green patch was where the prison NCO stood to drill the prisoner and the muddy area belonged to the prisoner - when he was not digging holes and filling them in again, that is!

Before he left Hura Mura, Joe was told that a typhoon warning had been put out and, by the time he had got down out of the mountains, the rain was pouring down, with really strong winds. The rivers suddenly flooded and, of the five bridges that they could have used to get back to Kure, four of them were already washed out, while the one they actually used was looking decidedly dodgy. When he got into camp, he found everything outside of the buildings, such as vehicles, had been anchored to the ground with ropes and steel pegs. Fortunately the eye of the storm passed to the south of them and they sustained very little damage.

Mia Jima

On one Sunday, Joe accompanied Jack Drennon on a trip to the island of Mia Jima, which was just off the coast from Hiroshima. Jack was an ex-'D' Coy lad from Arborfield, soon to return to the UK to be commissioned. Mia Jima was one of the islands that had been used by the Japanese Kamikaze pilots for their last few days before their final mission and was regarded as one of the seven beauty spots of Japan. Only a few people lived on the island, although there was a large Shinto temple and some sort of shrine. The temple faced the sea and there was a large 'Tori', a sort of solid wooden arch, standing out in the water in line with the centre of the altar. To get to Mia Jima, they had to go by train to the far side of Hiroshima and then catch a small boat over to the island.

On their return, they waited an hour for the train, which was delayed for some reason and then decided to catch a bus into Hiroshima. At the same time, a Japanese man in his late fifties or early sixties, accompanied by a very pretty young girl, decided that they would do the same. While he waited for the bus, Joe could see that the man was trying to get the girl to speak to them, which she eventually did, in perfect English. She explained that the man was her uncle and that, although he could not speak English, he wanted to converse through her, because he had been to England before the war and was interested to know what London was like now. He was a big well-dressed fellow, who apparently owned two factories that

The locals digging for clams on Mia Jima beach

produced what were known as 'Elephant Coils'. These were like incense sticks wound round into a coil, which, when the end was lit, gave off a vapour which would keep the mosquitoes away. He had one factory in Hiroshima and one in Tokyo and the name Elephant Coils came about because his trademark was an elephant.

Joe and Jack were invited to visit him at his factory in Hiroshima and asked them to write to his niece to make the arrangements. She wrote her name and address on a piece of paper and, shortly afterwards, they said goodbye and left the bus. Jack Drennon returned to the UK a couple of weeks later and, several weeks after that, Joe was feeling at a loose end and decided to write to the young lady and arrange a visit to her uncle. A date was fixed for the visit on a Saturday and she arranged to meet him off the bus in Hiroshima and take him to her uncle's place. When Joe stepped off the bus, the young girl, whose name was Saori Kanda, was being chaperoned by her mother, who accompanied them on another bus to the factory. On arrival at the factory, he was introduced to a business acquaintance of the Uncle and to another of his nieces, who was about eight years old.

After a few minutes, Saori Kanda's mother left them and returned to her home while he was taken on a short tour of the factory. They then all went up to a room over the main office where they sat cross-legged on the floor round a long low table, for lunch 'Japanese style'. Joe cannot remember what they ate but he knew that he managed to avoid the raw fish. 'Uncle' and his business acquaintance drank sake, but Joe proudly produced a bottle of *Canadian Club* whisky.

Ground Zero

It appeared that Saori Kanda was eighteen years of age and that her father, who had been a railway official, had died in the A-bomb blast. Saori had been eleven years old at the time and had had a lucky escape. I those days, children over a certain age went to school for half-days only, and did war work for the other part of the day. On June 6th 1945, she was suffering from toothache and stayed at home, which was on the outskirts of the city and only suffered blast damage.

Hiroshima Station is upper far-right and Nagarekawa Church in the foreground.

After lunch, they all climbed into an old *Dodge* car, which had been kept in excellent condition, and Uncle took them for a drive in the city. The thing that Joe really remembers about the car was the tiny rear window, which made it look like a gangster car from the 1920's. They showed Joe the spot that had been designated as 'Ground Zero' of the atom burst and he also saw the scorched outlines of people that had been left on the ground. They walked in the gardens around the lake where thousands of people had crowded into the water to try and get away from the heat in the aftermath of the explosion. Joe also learned that Saori spoke good English because she was one of the first children to attend the American School that was set up in Hiroshima by the Americans, after the war. It was a most enjoyable interlude during his stay in Japan and he still has the letter that Saori wrote to him, when they were making the arrangements for his visit.

Time was rolling on for him, as it was for most of the Aussies who had been in Japan for up to seven years. The end of the occupation was in sight and the Australian government hired the British troopship *'Devonshire'* to take their boys home. The quayside at Kure was just like New York when the Yanks were sailing for Blighty, with the sides of the ship covered in coloured paper streamers and the quay packed with weeping women! A couple of them went down to see Jim Wylie off and they passed him up a bottle of whisky on the end of a line that they had thrown to him. Little did Joe know that he would be whooping it up with Jim in London and Germany, very soon after waving him farewell!

It was around then that the Australian government policy of 'whites only' immigration came to an end. The lads who were leaving unofficial wives and children behind in Japan had been promised that, once they were home, they would be able to bring their girls to Australia and marry them. As Joe waved to Jim Wylie, he realised that it would soon be his turn to get on to a boat for home. He had been in the Far East for two years and been stationed in three countries, Hong Kong, Korea and Japan, with ten days in Singapore. He had enjoyed the tour immensely, even if it had been a bit hectic at times, but he was now ready to go home.

Joe had been most surprised by what he found in Japan; by the fact that there was practically no crime; by the respect shown to the elders of every family; by the impeccable behaviour of the children and by the fact that he never even saw a child slapped. Although the majority of houses were made mainly of wood, with interior walls of bamboo and rice paper, they were kept spotlessly clean. People always removed their wooden shoes at the door of the house before entering and the wooden floors were covered with straw mats called 'Tatami' made not of rice straw as many people might think but from the stems of a soft rush (juncus effusus) that grows in wetland areas. On December 12th 1952, Joe boarded a fairly small troopship called the *'Halladale'* and sailed out of Kure harbour just as a very old friend called Dougie Cresswell was sailing in on a large troopship called the *'Fowey'*. Dougie was to do an eighteen-month tour in Korea, followed by eighteen months in West Africa.

Chapter 36

REME Inspections

prior to the withdrawal of the 1 Commonwealth Division

A short article has recently come to light, the contents of which relate events that took place two to three years after the end of hostilities in Korea. But it is felt that it will ring bells with many of those who saw action during the Korean campaign from 1950 to 1953, or who supported that action from Japan. What follows are the personal views of a young naïve twenty-year-old, ex-apprentice regular soldier from Arborfield.

Reflections from Nick Webber

Having trained as a Tels Mechanic in REME, Nick now found himself "cut free", as he says, of so many UK restrictions. He was now in a weird world of "women and sex" at night but, during the daylight hours, seeing places and things that simply 'blew' his mind. These events all drastically changed him but he was glad that they happened. In late 1955, the Base Wksp REME in Kure, Japan, was called upon to form a REME Inspection Team, which was to travel to Korea, to inspect and categorise 1 Comm Div's military hardware, prior to their withdrawal. Cpl Nick Webber had been with 5 AA Command in the UK prior to this posting. As a Tels Mechanic, there was very little work for him and he was in fact employed as a senior clerk in a scaling section for vehicle parts. This meant that very soon he would be out of work, following the demise of the Division.

The night before he was due to sail from Japan for Korea, being a somewhat innocent lad amongst friends of a similar persuasion, they all decided to go for a few drinks and to see a 'sexy house'. So, it was up the 'Dichomi' to a house with a red light and all that goes with it, where Nick "spent the night", to be awakened by the Mama-san in time to get back to camp to board their ship for Korea. Having made it on time, and then formed up with his colleagues on parade, something happened that made him have a great respect for the human race. As they all stood in formation on parade, with an Aussie officer in charge, a taxi roared up and out stepped an old lady in a working kimono, who he suddenly recognised as the Mama-san where he had spent the night. Nick's heart sank as she ignored the officer and came straight up to him, bowed and took out from her kimono what looked like simple pieces of paper. On

A naive 20-year-old ex-boy and regular soldier Cpl Nick Webber.

Page 221

looking at them properly, he realised to his horror they were all his Army ID cards, which to lose was a criminal offence - especially in a brothel! Mama-san bowed again, re-entered her taxi and left the scene. The officer also looked at the items, then at Nick, and exclaimed, *"Corporal, you must be more careful"* and that closed the incident. Lucky for Nick it wasn't a UK officer!

The boat was the *'Wosang'*, rather small, but it had carried thousands of troops backwards and forwards to Korea over the past five years. It arrived at Inchon late afternoon and, on disembarking, Nick was unsure what to expect. This was soon corrected, as they travelled across the land, through treeless areas, to Seoul. This town at least seemed civilised, but they did not stop long enough to find out. Moving beyond Seoul, the areas got even bleaker until eventually they got to the Comm Div Wksp, located on a small area of high ground amid a Korean cemetery. It was a few hundred yards from the Turkish Zone and some few miles from the famous Gloucester Valley and 38th Parallel. The old accommodation in tents was now on its way out, the inspection team was allocated a 'Quonset hut'. This was a building constructed of corrugated metal that formed a full curve, with no straight sides at all. They had this for a few weeks, before they managed to burn it down, when trying to make the space heater give off more heat by increasing the size of the fuel drip hole.

There was nothing here to compare with a 'Japanese night out', they had to take over what others had left behind for them - straw and mud 'huchi', just outside the camp gates, run by a man called 'O', and four girls with one young baby. There was all the 'hospitality' one could expect - local food, a drink called 'Macaly', Yun Yung and sex, it had it all, it seemed so normal. They even supplied *'Asahi'* beer and chocolate. The lads went out most nights, but it must be borne in mind that they were 'Out of Bounds', with MP raids a constant danger.

The days moved on and it was soon March 1956. The weather was typically Korean – a blizzard snowed up the Div Wksp so severely that the point was reached when they had to stop work. The final parade of 1 Comm Div took place at Kohima Camp that March. As an Inspection Team, they were not involved on the parade, so they went merely as spectators, to see the proud Aussies, Kiwis, Canadian Field Medical and the British contingent, together with 48 Fld Regt RA, who never left the firing line from 1950 to 1953.

The Wosan

The Cameronians Pipe Band, with its Pipe Major in full dress, led the parade, while the salute was taken by the British *charge d'affaires* from the Seoul Embassy. As usual, the parade ground was just mud and water.

Despite the complete changes that had taken place in their country, to the local inhabitants little Korean villages were still the centres of their social life. There was the story of one girl who carried her bed from up-country for her man! There was a kind of unwritten control as the American's kept away from the villages, coming only on invitation. The reason behind this was VD control, which was very important, as the two Armies had different rules about this. Nick was still pretty naïve but, despite everything, he had a lady called Judy, in the little village of Song Do. She was married, but her husband was in the ROK Army in Pusan, in the south. Nick gave her £5 a week to look after him - his wage was then only about £11 a week, he called it *his "insurance"*. He is pleased to relate that one night, when on Orderly Sergeant duties, one of the lads tried to get over the sea wall. Nick was waiting for him and, on seeing him, the lad said that he had been in Song Do and had tried to go with Judy. But she had said *"No"*, she was *"Nick-san's girl"*. This 'faithfulness' was quite amazing when one considers the sheer poverty in the village.

What remained of the Comm Div was now known as the Commonwealth Contingent Korea (CCK) and located by the sea at Inchon, where it was rather cold. At first, they were in tents, the only improvement being that there were now more of them, which made for a better social life. After a while they started to take down the tents and metal Quonsets appeared in their place. But from this point, all the old camaraderie seemed to go and, to Nick, it seemed more like a UK camp.

By October 1956, Nick's substantive rank of Sergeant had come through. This was the last step in the requirements for his 'Tiffy' course, so he had to move to the Senior Ranks' lines, away from all the people that had shared his time whilst up-country. His room was at the very end of a group overlooking the rest of the camp; he was now on the beginning of another ladder in his Army career. Later in the year, he flew out from an American Air Base in a *Valletta* of the RAF, stopping off at Tachikawa Base in Japan. Then it was a stopover at Clark Field in the Philippines before arriving at Kai Tak Airport, Hong Kong to continue his Far East tour.

Comrades

Index

10 Inf Wksp 12, 13, 16, 21, 31, 43, 112, 121, 130, 141, 183
11 (Sphinx) Light AA Bty RA 16, 138
11 Inf Wksp 11, 12, 13, 38, 99, 102, 103, 129
14 Fld Regt RA 94, 95, 171
16 Fld Regt Royal NZ Artillery 103, 106, 138
16 Inf Wksp 129, 141
170 Independent Mortar Battery 16
170 Light Bty RA 138
18 Command Workshop 12
191 Inf Wksp RCEME 141
1 Btn Argyll and Sutherland Highlanders 98. 103, 119, 126
1 Btn Black Watch 205, 206, 214
1 Btn Gloucestershire Regt 16, 138
1 Btn King's Liverpool Regt 194, 204
1 Btn King's Own Scottish Borderers 126
1 Btn King's Shropshire Light Infantry 127
1 Btn KSLI 138, 172, 204
1 Btn Middlesex Regt 103
1 Btn Royal Northumberland Fusiliers 16, 43, 111, 138, 170
1 Btn RUR 16, 43, 111, 138, 148, 150
1 Btn the Welch Regt 171, 172
23 Heavy Recovery Company 17, 63
25 Canadian Bde 127, 128, 137, 141, 149, 169, 172, 177, 178, 202, 205, 206, 207, 211, 214
25 Canadian Fld Ambulance RCAMC 138
25 Canadian Inf Bde 126, 138, 142, 143, 144, 148
26 Fld Ambulance RAMC 16, 138
27 Inf Bde 4, 5, 6, 7, 10, 11
27 Cmd Wksp 17, 18
27 OFP RAOC 103
28 Comm Bde 120, 126, 127, 128, 129, 143, 144, 148, 149, 170, 177, 178, 202, 203, 204, 206, 207, 210, 211, 214
28 Fld Engineer Regt RE 138
29 British Bde 98, 106, 111, 128, 177, 178, 202, 204, 207, 211, 214
29 Support Troops LAD 78, 137
2 Btn PPCLI 103, 108, 119, 120, 126, 138, 149
2 Btn Royal Canadian Regt 126, 138
2 Fld Regt 126
2 Mortar Btn 109
2 Regt RCHA 137
38th Parallel 3, 5, 23, 37, 38, 55, 95, 97, 98, 106, 113, 126, 127, 142, 174, 222
3 Btn RAR 38, 39, 107, 119, 120, 138, 172, 174, 177, 201, 202, 205, 208
3 RAR 38, 98, 103, 143, 145, 148, 178, 202, 203, 204, 206, 208

41 Royal Marines Independent Commando 40
45 Fld Regt RA 16, 43, 70, 74, 75, 83, 87, 137, 138, 171, 191
4 Fld Park Sqn RE 138
55 Field Squadron 16
57 Company RASC Workshop 20
57 Coy RASC 20, 21, 22, 103, 140
57 Independent Fld Sqn Royal Canadian Engineers 126, 138
5 Cavalry Regt 109, 111
5 Medium Wksp 17
5 Royal Inniskilling Dragoon Guards 174
60 Indian Fld Ambulance 16, 98, 103, 151, 165, 203
72 Heavy Tank Btn 120
74 (Battleaxe Coy) Medium Bty RA 210
88 Outfit 34, 42
8 Hussars 12, 45, 50, 100, 111, 117, 132, 141, 154, 174
8 KRIH 16, 18, 22, 25, 26, 27, 28, 43, 78, 138

A

Acanthus 17, 18
ADEME 121, 125, 159
Aden 19
Adey, SSgt Joe 160, 166, 215
Adler, Larry 203
Alexander, WOII Alec 161
Al Jolson Bridge 98
Anderton, Col G 138
Arborfield 5, 12, 13, 34, 44, 52, 69, 90, 95, 161, 164, 179, 218, 221
Armstrong, Capt 188
Army Technical School 22
ARV 22, 24, 25, 26, 27, 28, 29
Asahi 32, 33, 47, 56, 74, 91, 161, 217, 222
ASM 50, 69, 76, 124, 136, 184, 185, 217
Astley-Cooper, Captain 100
Atkinson, Lt Col AL 138
Atlee, Clement 3
Attwood, SSgt 166

B

BAFs 95
Bailey, Lt Col AJB 137
Barlow, Lt Col VW 177
Barry 18
Battle of Chong Song 44
Beale, Cfn 57
Bechelli, Bill 55
Bedford 15-cwt 7, 47, 74, 77, 78, 85, 86, 89, 93
Bedford QL 51, 63, 71, 72, 79, 86, 87, 93, 94, 132, 161, 163, 183

Bed Check Charlie 91, 135, 167
Beech, Maj Hugh 64, 134
Belgian Btn 113, 114, 116, 117, 127, 139, 143
BEME 34, 129, 153, 188
Binnie, Cpl R 166
Bishop, SSgt Fred 185
Blackwell, L/Cpl 166
Blake, Cfn Sid 54
BLR 50, 158, 159, 165
Bluebell 27, 28
Boswell, Eve 203
Bovington 12
Bradley, Gen Omar 208
Brandon, Lt Ian 17
Bren-gun Carriers 5, 62
Bridgeford, Lt Gen W 174
Britannia Camp 94
Britannia Club 181
Brodie, Brig 42, 118
Brotherhood, Les 13
Brown, Paddy 23
Buck, Cpl R 167
Bug Out 65, 71, 197
Burke, Brig 119

C

Cameron, Sgt 212
Carne, Lt Col 118
Carr, Carole 203
Carrington, ASM 124
Cassels, Maj Gen AJH 128, 137, 138, 174, 195
Ceylon, HMS 5
Chariwon 20
Chipyong-Ni 108, 109
Choksong 111, 113, 114, 128
Chonan 4, 76, 78, 101, 121, 130
Chongan-Ni 107
Chongchon River. 39
Chongju 39, 40, 105
Chorwon 113, 114, 127
Christie-Smith, Maj 137, 152
Christmas Day 32
Churchill ARV 22, 25, 29
Clark, Gen Mark 109
Clark Field 223
Coad, Brig 108
Coles Crane 12
Collier Quay 19
Collins, Jimmy 146
Colombo 95, 181
Conway, Sgt Brian 22
Cooper, AQMS Ted 190
Corps Museum 34
Cowgill, Maj 22

Crater City 19
CREME 32, 33
Cribb, Lt 55, 145, 131, 152
Cromwell Recovery Tank 57
Crosby, Lt Col MGM 138

D

Dakota 54, 122, 136, 157, 160
Daly, Brig TJ 210
Danby, Lt Col ED 138
Dangerfield, Cpl 166
Darby, Jim 22
Degnan, Lt Col 22
DEME 121, 125
Dennis, Capt 17, 66
Desert Rat 48
Devonshire, HMTS 93, 157, 168, 219
Die Hards 127
Dix, Captain MC 136, 152
Dixon, AQMS Sam 56
Doig, SSgt Johnny 160, 166
Drennon, Jack 218
Duffy, Cfn W 212
Dutton, SSgt John 57, 150, 179, 183, 188, 189, 191, 192, 193, 199

E

East Wretham 12
ECE 188, 200
Empire Fowey 18, 22
Empire Pride 13, 43, 54, 95
Empire Windrush 43
Empress of Australia 20, 69
ENSA 57, 132
Erasmus, Minister of Defence 206
Ewing, Capt Gordon 17, 64, 131, 132, 137, 152

F

Fagurland, Lt Keith 21
FAMTO 72
FARELF 121, 125
Farrar-Hockley, Gen Sir Anthony 43
Faulkner, Col 125
Fillis, Cpl Stan 56
Finlayson, Cfn 196
Fordyce, Cfn Ted 56
Fowey, HMTS 220
Freeman, Capt 22

G

Gadsby, Maj 17
Gadsby, Maj Desmond 65
General Patrick 126
Georgic MV 15, 174, 179, 180, 183, 185

Germain, Maj 129, 137, 166
Gibbings, SSgt 198
Gibraltar 18
Globemaster 160
Gloucesters 43, 45, 46, 47, 48, 49, 54, 57, 71, 88, 94, 100, 111, 113, 114, 116, 117, 118, 119, 127, 143, 164, 165, 189
Gloucestershire Regt 16
Gloucester Hill 117, 118, 135
Good, Lt Col 121, 125, 137, 138, 165, 195
Graham, Mick 164
Graham, SSgt 166
Gray, ASM Tom 69, 76
Gray, Dolly 57
Grist, Lt Col D B 127

H

Hailes, Maj JMH 206
Hantan River 111, 113, 127
Han River 20, 27, 28
Happy Valley 26
hardtack 47
Harper, WOII N 166
Harvey, Capt M G 119
Harvey, Cpl 56
Hauser, Capt 154
Hawkins, Steve 24
Heath, Brig 121, 125
Hedworth-Young, Capt CH 164
Hesketh, Capt 'Chuck' 17, 65
Hetherington, 2/Lt SJ 164
Hill, Capt GR 160
Hillier, Sgt 166
Hills, Peter 189
Hind, Capt RK 41, 102
Hiroshima 123, 217, 218, 219
Howard, Frankie 203
Howe, Maj 76
Hura Mura 218
Husband, Capt 12, 54, 131
Husband, Capt J S 55
Hutchins, Lt Col GEP 170
Hyon-Ni 109

I

Imray, Jock 184
Iron Triangle 127

J

Jackson, Sgt W 166
Joslin, Maj Gen 13

K

Kabuki Imperial Theatre 85
Kaeson 20
Kaesong 1, 38, 51, 55, 56, 70, 71, 72, 73, 82, 99, 101, 105, 134, 151
Kai Tak 223
Katcoms 169, 210, 211, 212
Kelly, Capt J D 129
Kendrew, Brig DA 207
Kepple Harbour 19
Kimpo 1, 38, 51, 88, 90, 93, 119, 127, 129, 160, 161
Kinshott, AQMS Mike 20
Kiwis 58, 106, 122, 125, 165, 222
KOSB 94, 119, 127, 129, 138, 144, 148, 149, 150, 165, 170, 172, 178, 202
Koyang 99
Kumnyangjang-Ni 127
Kure 15, 17, 22, 54, 105, 122, 123, 140, 157, 158, 168, 182, 183, 200, 214, 215, 217, 218, 219, 220, 221

L

LADs 17, 62, 134, 135, 143, 147, 151
Lamont, SSgt Jock 183, 185
Leicestershire Regt 94
Lewis, Maj 137
Lister 162, 163, 187
Littlewood, Charlie 56
Liverpool Docks 13
Lord Strathcona's Horse 126, 138, 203
Lowther, Lt Col Sir Guy 22
Luger, SSgt Cyril 188, 200
Lupson, Ssgt Chippy 195

M

Maala 19
MacArthur, General Douglas 3, 37, 51, 82, 113
Macdonald, Lt Col JFM 170
MacLean, Lt Col MF 138
Main, SSgt Ian (Jock) 161, 166
Malta 18
Manchuria 1, 40, 96, 174
Mann, Col 121
Maplehill, SS 13
Marine Adder 126
Marshall, Jimmy 29
Marsoguri 15
MASH 15
Masogu 112
Meadows, Cfn Jim 56
Meteor 158
Michaelis, Lt Col John 27
Middlesex Btn 6, 7, 8, 9, 97
Middlesex Hill 35
MIG 97
Milburn, Lt Gen 98

Mitchell, L/Cpl R 166
Mobile Inspection Team 145, 147
Moore, Capt Victor S 17, 121, 130, 131, 132, 215
Morgan, 2Lt 152
Morris 15-cwt 77, 85, 93
Mount Fujiyama 85
MSR 44, 47, 56, 63, 64, 65, 67, 68, 70, 71, 73, 82, 85, 86, 89, 91, 99, 130, 131, 133, 134, 135, 152, 153, 161, 193, 197, 198, 199
Mullhern, CSM Jock 57, 184
Munsan 41, 82, 102, 153, 211
Murphy, Gerald (Spud) 24
Mustangs 52, 83, 94
Myers, Col ECW 138

N

NAAFI 15, 32, 57, 61, 89, 103, 112, 147
Naktong River 4, 5, 10, 34, 64, 68, 70
Newman, Captain RA 41
Nicel, Capt J 55
Nicholson, Nick 131
Norman, Brian 146

O

O'Daniel, Lt Gen JW 139, 174
OCTU 33
Okinawa 129, 160
Operation Claymore 143
Operation Fauna 208
Operation Pepper-pot 169
Operation Snare 177
OP 35 194
Oxford Carriers 62, 77, 151

P

Pakchon 39, 40, 97
Palmer, Lt Col PG 22
Parke, Cfn Len 56
Parker, AQMS 20
Patterson, Maj 22
Peace Camp 156
Peking 45, 151
Petrie, SSgt 166
Pettingell, Maj Jack 22
Philippines 29, 129, 223
Pike, Brig WGH 138
Pirnie, Cpl 166
Plexiglas 57
Plum Pudding Hill 35
Pogmore, Maj 137
Poperinghe Barracks 69, 179
Port Said 19
President Jackson 126
Princess Patricia's 7, 94, 126

Prior, Capt Neil 17
Pt 227 171, 172, 173, 174, 177, 201, 208
Pt 235 117
Pt 282 35, 36
Pt 325 35
Pt 355 148, 149, 150, 151, 172, 173, 193, 204, 208, 209, 211
Pt 388 35, 36
Puckeridge 13
Pukhan River 112, 118, 119, 123, 124, 125, 129
Purple Heart 7, 54
Pusan 1, 4, 5, 10, 11, 14, 15, 17, 18, 19, 20, 22, 23, 24, 34, 41, 42, 44, 45, 47, 53, 54, 56, 58, 59, 61, 66, 67, 68, 69, 70, 71, 72, 73, 93, 95, 105, 121, 122, 123, 128, 130, 136, 137, 139, 140, 141, 150, 168, 174, 182, 183, 189, 200, 214, 215, 223
PX 15
Pyongtaek 4, 50, 51, 56, 65, 100, 106, 111, 121, 130
Pyongyang 1, 7, 12, 20, 38, 39, 44, 45, 46, 55, 70, 71, 73, 75, 97, 98, 99, 101, 102, 113

R

radio sets 43
RAEME 105, 163, 216
Raffles Hotel 19
Rainer, 'Jumbo' 164
RAOC, Capt CW Nicholson 152
RAP 53, 202, 203
Rawlings, AQMS Phil 185
Rawlins, Phil 200
Ray, Ted 203
Red Sea 19
Reece, Brian 89
Reservists 13
Rest and Recuperation 30
Reynolds,, Ray 154
Rhee, President Syngman 20, 34, 182, 212, 213
Ricketts, Brig 178, 207
Ridgeway, Gen Mathew B 26, 82, 98, 113, 151
Robertson, Douglas 12
Robertson, Lt Gen Sir Horace 128, 139, 174
Robertson, SSgt Robbie 48, 57
Rogers, Maj 137, 152, 191
Rose, Lt 136, 152
Royal Northumberland Fusiliers 16
Royal Tank Regt 16
RUR 16, 22, 26

S

Sabres 83, 87, 94
Samichon River 144, 178, 202, 204
Sasebo 11, 15, 136
Saunders, AQMS Bill 57, 184

Scammell 12, 15, 56, 57, 61, 62, 66, 67, 69, 70, 73, 76, 78, 90, 92, 131, 133, 155, 158, 163, 166, 188, 198
Seoul 1, 4, 6, 9, 14, 15, 20, 25, 26, 27, 28, 34, 37, 38, 40, 41, 47, 51, 52, 57, 63, 65, 70, 73, 75, 81, 82, 83, 86, 87, 88, 94, 95, 98, 99, 101, 103, 106, 111, 112, 113, 117, 119, 126, 127, 129, 130, 133, 134, 135, 136, 137, 139, 140, 141, 142, 147, 150, 152, 159, 160, 161, 164, 168, 189, 190, 195, 199, 215, 222, 223
Simmonds, Sgt Peter 5, 6, 7, 8, 9, 10
Sinton, ASM Jack 136, 184
Sinton, Capt J 136, 160, 166
Sitrep 44
Skymaster 83, 85
Smith, Maj 131
Smith, Maj J Christie 55
Snow, Capt 25
Snow, Lt Col 22
Snow, Lt M C 55
Speakman, Bill 94 , 165, 170
Spittle, Lt R 55, 152
Stand To 44, 47, 53
Stanford 12, 13
Star, John 43
Starfighters 147
Steamer Point 19
Stevens, Lt Col GR 202
Stevens, SSgt Ron 69
Stokes, Sgt Howard 69
Stone, Ken 72
Suez Canal 19
Sutton Veney 17
Swift, Capt R 160, 166

T
T34 25
T54 25
Tachikawa 83, 85, 93, 223
Taegu 1, 4, 10, 14, 20, 34, 38, 56, 58, 59, 61, 63, 64, 65, 66, 68, 105, 130
Taejon 20
Tail-end Charlie 50
Taylor, Brig G 111
Taylor, Gen Maxwell 210
Teal Bridge 135, 155, 156
Tels Wksp 141, 145, 146, 164, 167
Thorneycroft 14
Tinkham, Capt F C D 55, 131, 132
Tokchon 32, 57, 83, 88, 91, 97, 134, 135, 152, 153, 196, 197, 198, 199, 200
Tokyo 51, 83, 84, 93, 107, 123, 136, 152, 154, 157, 203, 218
Toombs, Capt Jake 145

Truman, President Harry 3, 113
Turkish Bde 127
Turp, Maj 122

U
Uijongbu 15, 51, 57, 86, 88, 95, 98, 117, 119, 127, 129, 134, 136, 137, 159, 160, 161, 163
Unicorn, HMS 5
Universal Carrier 151

V
Valletta 223
Van Fleet, Lt Gen James A 113, 174, 210
VC 36, 94, 98, 165, 170
Vernon, WOII H 166
Vickers, Lt Col AWNL 128, 138
Victoria Cross 36

W
Waegwan 34, 37, 40
Wallace, Capt M J P 55
Ward, RSM 76
Ward, Sgt Jack 25
Warminster 17, 18
Warner, Jack 160
Watson, Capt Jack 17
Way, Capt HWG 164
Webb, Lt KL 31
Webber, Nick 221
West, Maj Gen 203, 207
Westbrook, Sgt Bob 173
West Tofts 12
Williams, Ted 136
Willy's Jeep 47, 132
Wilson, Lt G 159
Wilton, Brig JGN 210
Windler, Peter 91
Wonju 106
Woodward, Sgt 22, 154
Worthington, Brian 43
Wosang 183, 222
WOSB 13

X
X Corps 37, 40, 97, 106, 107, 109, 111, 113, 127

Y
Yalu River 1, 37, 42, 44
Yoju 106, 107, 108, 109
Yokohama 65
Yongdongpo 119, 133
Yongyu 39

Z
Z wagons 145

Lightning Source UK Ltd.
Milton Keynes UK
UKHW012017070921
390207UK00007B/340/J